Regions AND Resources

Silver Burdett Ginn
Parsippany, NJ • Needham, MA
Atlanta, GA   Deerfield, IL   Irving, TX   Santa Clara, CA

PROGRAM AUTHORS

Juan R. García
Associate Professor of History and Associate Dean
  of the College of Social and Behavioral Sciences
University of Arizona
Tucson, AZ

Daniel J. Gelo
Associate Professor of Anthropology, Division of
  Behavioral and Cultural Sciences
University of Texas at San Antonio
San Antonio, TX

Linda L. Greenow
Associate Professor and Acting Chair
  Department of Geography
S.U.N.Y. at New Paltz
New Paltz, NY

James B. Kracht
Professor of Geography and Educational
  Curriculum and Instruction
Texas A&M University
College Station, TX

Deborah Gray White
Professor of History
Rutgers University
New Brunswick, NJ

Silver Burdett Ginn
A Division of Simon & Schuster
299 Jefferson Road, P.O. Box 480
Parsippany, NJ 07054-0480

ISBN 0-382-32686-5   5 6 7 8 9 10 RRD 05 04 03 02 01 00 99 98

CONTENTS

UNIT 3 — IN SEARCH OF OPEN SPACES

REFERENCE

MAPS

*Found in Summing Up Geography and You

ATLAS MAPS

MAP ADVENTURES

TIME LINES

GRAPHS, TABLES, CHARTS, AND DIAGRAMS

SKILLS

LITERATURE

The following books are recommended for optional reading and research.

Map Handbook
CONTENTS

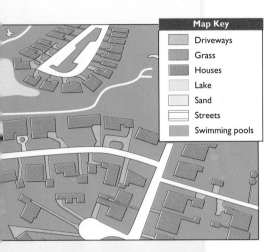

Map Key
- Driveways
- Grass
- Houses
- Lake
- Sand
- Streets
- Swimming pools

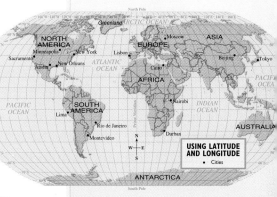

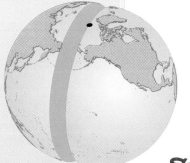

How Do You Make a MAP From a PHOTO?

Would it be hard to take a long car trip without a road map? How many words would it take to tell where your state is located if you couldn't show it on a map? With the right map, you can quickly find the information you need to take a trip or describe a location.

A map shows what a place would look like if you were looking down from a hot-air balloon. The higher you went, the more you would see. But as you went higher, the features of the land would get smaller.

Look for the details.

- ◆ Study the photograph.
- ◆ Make a list of the things that you see.

Here is how a mapmaker shows the same scene as the photograph. The mapmaker picks out the most important features of the photograph. The map has **symbols**, or signs, that stand for these features. Sometimes the symbols are colors. The symbols are explained in the **map key**.

Use the symbols in the key.

Find the lake in the photograph.

◆ What color on the map stands for the lake? Find the lake on the map.

◆ Now find the main streets, the houses, and the swimming pools. Does the map show these in the same spots as the photograph?

Now Try This!

Think of a place you know well, such as a room in your home or school. Then draw a map that shows how the place would look if seen from above. Make up symbols for important features on the map. Explain your symbols in a map key.

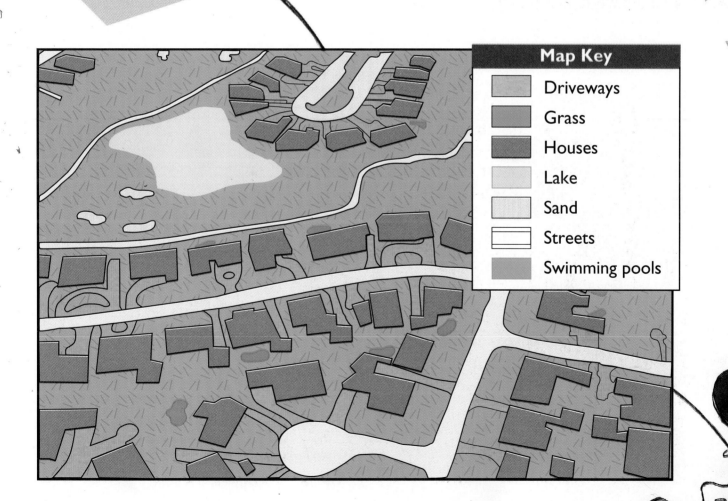

Map Key

	Driveways
	Grass
	Houses
	Lake
	Sand
	Streets
	Swimming pools

How Much Can You Learn About

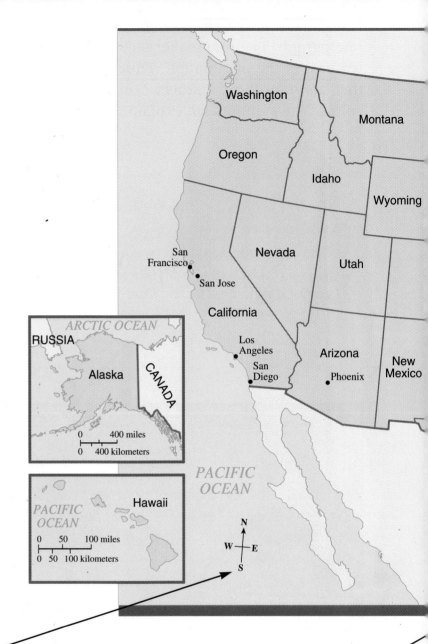

L̲earning about our country would be a lot harder if we didn't have maps to help us. Maps are our most important tools for finding out where a place is and how to get there.

Look at the map of the United States on these pages. When you read a map like this to find information, you use its title, symbols, compass rose, scale, and other features. Read on to find out how these special features can help you to understand maps.

The Compass Rose

The compass rose is a drawing that shows where north, south, east, and west are on a map.

◆ Look at the map of the United States. Is San Francisco north or south of San Diego?

The Title

In this book you will find a map title at the top of the key. The title tells what kind of information is on the map.

◆ What is the title of this map?

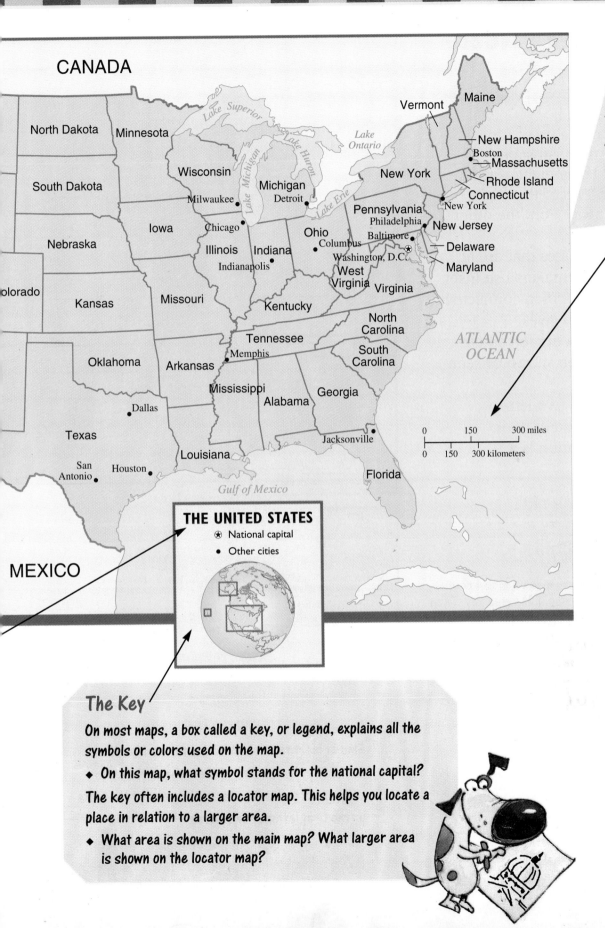

CANADA

North Dakota
Minnesota
South Dakota

Lake Superior
Lake Michigan
Lake Huron
Lake Erie
Lake Ontario

Vermont
Maine
New Hampshire
Boston
Massachusetts
Rhode Island
Connecticut
New York

Wisconsin
Michigan
Detroit
Milwaukee

New York

Iowa
Chicago
Illinois
Indiana
Indianapolis

Ohio
Columbus

Pennsylvania
Philadelphia
Baltimore
Washington, D.C.
West Virginia

New Jersey
Delaware
Maryland

Nebraska
Colorado
Kansas
Missouri
Kentucky
Virginia

Oklahoma
Arkansas
Tennessee
Memphis

North Carolina
South Carolina

ATLANTIC OCEAN

Dallas
Texas
Mississippi
Alabama
Georgia

Louisiana
San Antonio
Houston
Jacksonville

Florida

Gulf of Mexico

MEXICO

| 0 | 150 | 300 miles |
| 0 | 150 | 300 kilometers |

THE UNITED STATES
- ✪ National capital
- • Other cities

The Scale

The scale helps you to find the actual distances between places.

◆ About how many miles does one inch stand for on this scale?

Now Try This!

Draw a map of your neighborhood or town.

◆ Draw in the major streets, and put in the most important or interesting places. Be sure to include your house and your friends' houses!

◆ What title will you give to your map?

Save this map. You'll use it later on!

The Key

On most maps, a box called a key, or legend, explains all the symbols or colors used on the map.

◆ On this map, what symbol stands for the national capital?

The key often includes a locator map. This helps you locate a place in relation to a larger area.

◆ What area is shown on the main map? What larger area is shown on the locator map?

Why Do We Need INSET MAPS?

The United States is made up of fifty states. These fifty American states stretch over a huge area. Forty-eight of the states touch one another. Two of the states, however, are located far away from the other 48. Which two states are they?

In order to show the two states that are far away from the other 48, mapmakers use **inset maps**. An inset map is a small map connected to a larger one. The inset map gives information about places that are too small, too large, or too far away to be shown or seen clearly on the larger map.

Mapmakers sometimes use two-letter **abbreviations** for states instead of their complete names. An abbreviation is a shortened form of a word.

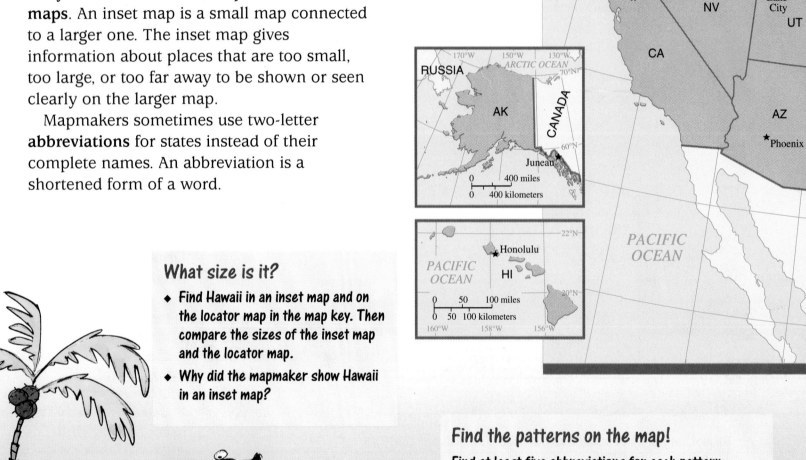

What size is it?

- Find Hawaii in an inset map and on the locator map in the map key. Then compare the sizes of the inset map and the locator map.
- Why did the mapmaker show Hawaii in an inset map?

Find the patterns on the map!

Find at least five abbreviations for each pattern.

- the first two letters of the name of the state
- the first and last letter of the name of the state
- the first letter of two words

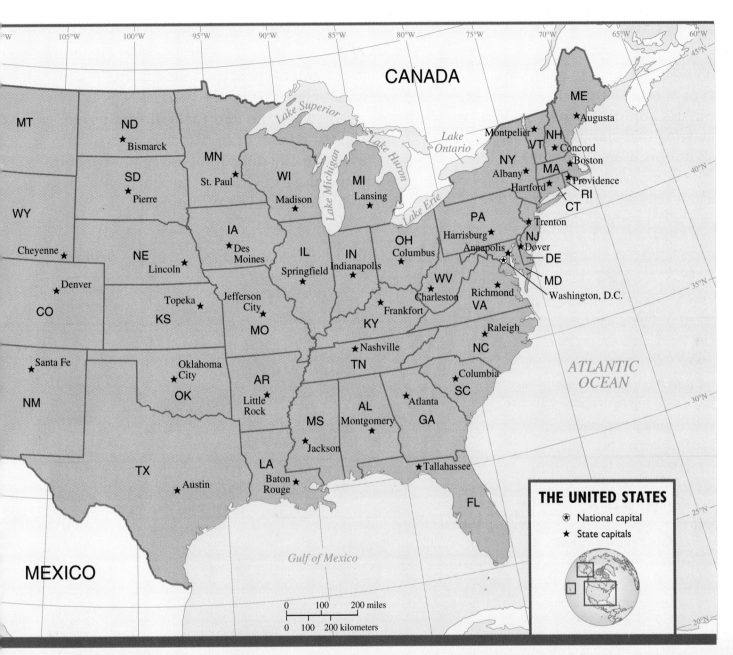

CANADA

MEXICO

MT

ND
★ Bismarck

MN
St. Paul ★

WI
Madison ★

MI
Lansing ★

SD
Pierre ★

WY

Cheyenne ★

NE
Lincoln ★

IA
★ Des Moines

IL
Springfield ★

IN
Indianapolis ★

OH
Columbus ★

Denver ★

CO

KS
Topeka ★

MO
Jefferson City ★

KY
Frankfort ★

Santa Fe ★

NM

OK
Oklahoma City ★

AR
Little Rock ★

TN
★ Nashville

WV
Charleston ★

VA
Richmond ★

NC
Raleigh ★

TX

Austin ★

LA
Baton Rouge ★

MS
Jackson ★

AL
Montgomery ★

GA
Atlanta ★

SC
Columbia ★

FL
★ Tallahassee

Lake Superior
Lake Michigan
Lake Huron
Lake Ontario
Lake Erie

ME
★ Augusta

Montpelier ★
VT
NH
★ Concord
★ Boston
MA
Providence ★
RI
CT

NY
Albany ★
Hartford ★

PA
Harrisburg ★

Trenton ★
NJ
Dover ★
DE

Annapolis ★
MD

Washington, D.C.

ATLANTIC OCEAN

Gulf of Mexico

THE UNITED STATES

✪ National capital
★ State capitals

0   100   200 miles

0 100 200 kilometers

45°N

40°N

35°N

30°N

25°N

20°N

110°W 105°W 100°W 95°W 90°W 85°W 80°W 75°W 70°W 65°W 60°W

Now Try This!

Draw a map of your state that could be used as an inset map for the United States map on these pages. Make a drawing or tracing of your state that is at least twice as large as it is on the U.S. map. Then add some important features, such as cities and rivers, to your inset map.

What Can a COMPASS ROSE Do for Me?

How do we use a map to get from one place to another? A good way to start is to use the map's **compass rose**. The compass rose is a drawing that shows where north, south, east, and west are on the map.

Look at the compass rose on the map of Georgia below. On this compass rose the longest pointers show the four **cardinal**, or main, directions. They are marked N, S, E, and W. Between the four main directions are four **intermediate**, or in-between, directions. For example, the direction between north and east is northeast. NE stands for northeast. What do NW, SE, and SW stand for?

On the Road

- Find Georgia's capital city and start a road trip from there.
- In what cardinal direction should you set out to go to Sweetwater Creek State Park?
- From Sweetwater Creek State Park, what intermediate direction should you take to travel to Indian Springs State Park?

Now Try This!

Plan a trip to several interesting places in your state. Start from the state capital or from your community. Describe the cardinal and intermediate directions you take to travel from one place to the next.

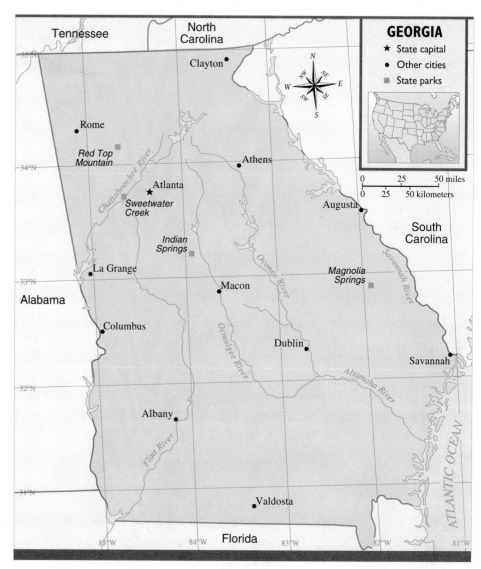

What Doors Does a MAP KEY Open?

All maps have their own language. You need to "read" that language to understand the map. The "words" of this map language are the symbols on the map. A mapmaker gathers all the symbols together in one place on the map, called the **key**. Another term for the key is the **legend**.

The map on this page is a **precipitation map**. It shows how much rain, snow, sleet, and hail fall in the Pacific West region of the United States in an average year.

Umbrella Alert!

Look at the colors in the map key that show precipitation.

- Which color shows the most precipitation?
- Which color shows the least precipitation?

Wetter or Drier?

- Is it wetter in eastern or western Washington?
- Which state receives over 64 inches of precipitation only in its southern part?
- How many inches of precipitation fall in the southeast corner of Oregon?

Now Try This!

Find a map in this book that has a key with at least three symbols. Write a paragraph that tells what every symbol or color in the map key stands for.

AVERAGE ANNUAL PRECIPITATION IN THE PACIFIC WEST REGION

Inches	Centimeters
Above 96	Above 244
65-96	164-244
33-64	82-163
17-32	42-81
0-16	0-41

RUSSIA
ARCTIC OCEAN
Alaska
CANADA
0 150 300 miles
0 300 kilometers

PACIFIC OCEAN
Hawaii
0 50 100 miles
0 50 100 kilometers

0 150 300 miles
0 150 300 kilometers

CANADA
Washington
MT
Oregon
ID
NV
UT
California
AZ
PACIFIC OCEAN
MEXICO

Why Use a SCALE That Can't Weigh Anything?

How far is it from your home to your school? How big is a soccer field? How far is it from Chicago to Cleveland? With a map, a piece of paper, and knowledge of the **distance scale**, you can find all these distances.

Distances on maps are always smaller than the real distances on Earth. The distance scale tells us how much smaller. A certain number of inches on a map stand for a certain number of feet, yards, or miles on Earth. Distance scales may also use centimeters to stand for meters or kilometers. On the distance scale below, 1/4 inch stands for five yards. How much does one inch stand for?

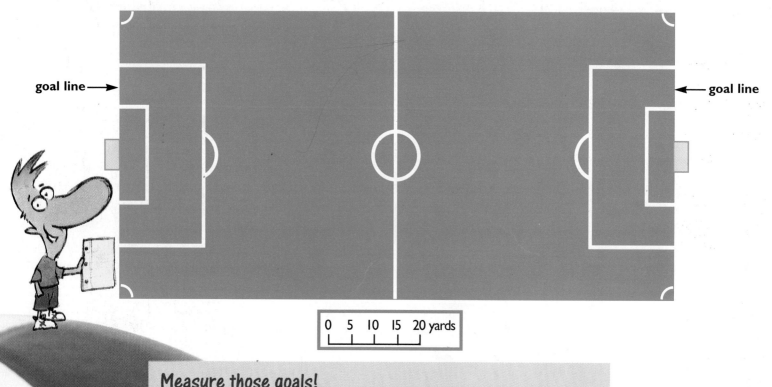

goal line →   ← goal line

0 5 10 15 20 yards

Measure those goals!

How far apart are the goals on a soccer field? To find out, use a piece of paper with a straight edge.

- Place the top left corner of the paper at the beginning of the scale.
- Mark the point where the scale ends.
- Mark as many scale divisions as will fit on the paper.
- Then put the paper so that the straight edge connects the two goal lines.
- Count the number of marks between them. How far apart are they?

MADE IN U.S

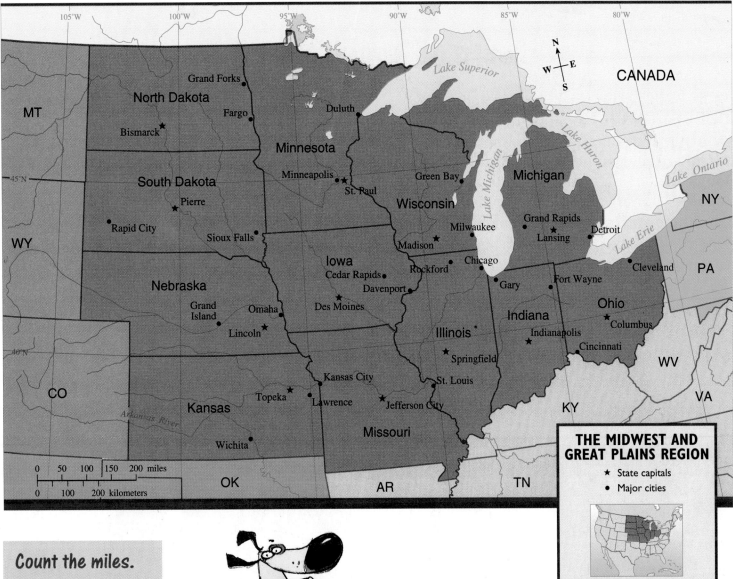

THE MIDWEST AND GREAT PLAINS REGION

★ State capitals
● Major cities

Count the miles.

Use a ruler to find out about how many miles one inch stands for on the map.

- How many inches are there in a straight line from Bismarck, North Dakota, to St. Paul, Minnesota? About how far apart are these cities?

Tour the capitals.

- Starting at Pierre, travel to Lincoln, then finish your tour in Jefferson City. About how many miles did you travel?

Now Try This!

Draw a map of your bedroom. Begin by measuring the length of each wall in feet. Round off lengths to the nearest foot. Then create a scale that uses an inch to show a certain number of feet. For example, you may decide to let one inch stand for two feet. Show the scale on your map.

M11

LATITUDE and LONGITUDE
Learn All About Them!

Every place on Earth has an "address." This allows us to pinpoint every city, town, or village in the world. In order to locate a place you need its **latitude** and its **longitude**. Latitude and longitude provide the "address" for any place you want to locate.

Latitude and longitude are part of a special kind of grid system for Earth. This system uses two sets of lines that crisscross. All the lines that run across the map from west to east are latitude lines. The latitude line that circles Earth around its middle is called the **equator**. It is numbered 0°. (You say this as "zero degrees.")

Lines of latitude measure distance north and south of the equator. These lines never meet. Because they run parallel around Earth, another name for them is **parallels**.

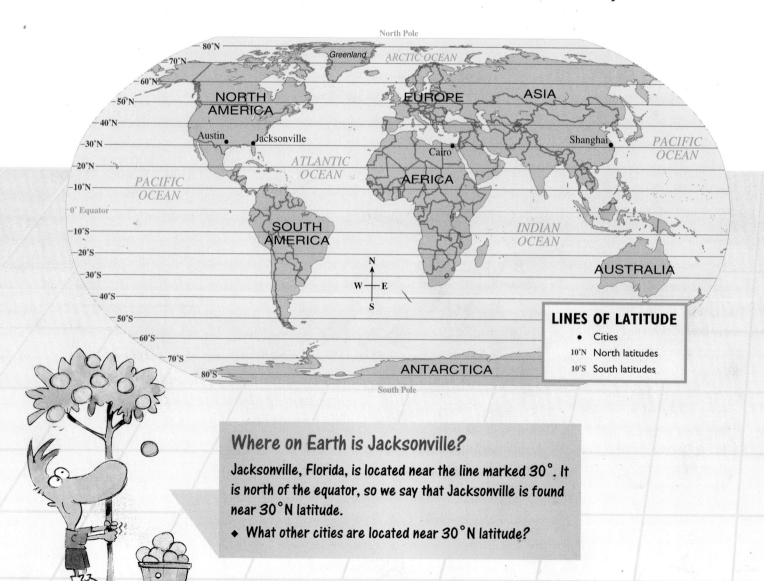

LINES OF LATITUDE
- • Cities
- 10°N North latitudes
- 10°S South latitudes

Where on Earth is Jacksonville?

Jacksonville, Florida, is located near the line marked 30°. It is north of the equator, so we say that Jacksonville is found near 30°N latitude.

◆ What other cities are located near 30°N latitude?

Mapmakers also use another set of lines, called lines of **longitude**. Longitude lines run north and south on maps. The most important line of longitude is the **prime meridian**. It is numbered 0° longitude. (Say "zero degrees.")

All other lines of longitude measure distance east or west of the prime meridian. Any line located east of the prime meridian is called east longitude. It is marked 15°E, 30°E, and so on. Lines west of the prime meridian are called west longitude. Lines of longitude are not parallel. They meet at the North Pole and the South Pole.

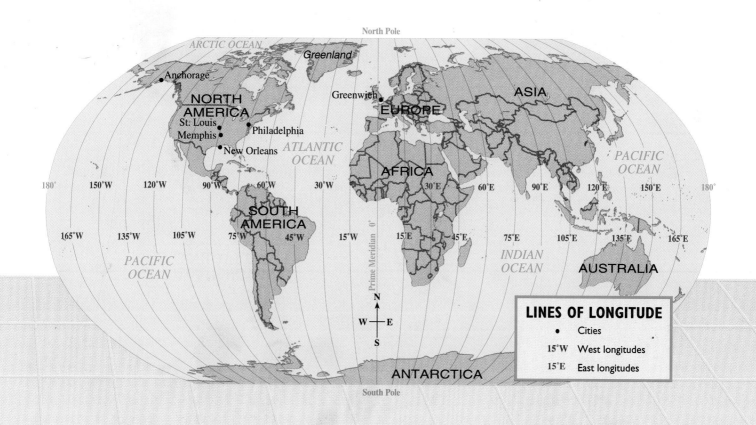

Where on Earth is Memphis?

Memphis, Tennessee, lies near the 90° meridian west of the prime meridian. We call its longitude 90°W.

◆ What other cities lie near the 90°W meridian?

Latitude and longitude make it possible to find places on a map quickly. Use the map on this page to find Minneapolis, Minnesota. Minneapolis does not fall exactly on a line of latitude or longitude shown on the map. The latitude of Minneapolis is 45° north. This is written as 45°N. The longitude of Minneapolis is 93° west. This is written as 93°W. So, Minneapolis is located at 45°N latitude, 93°W longitude. No other place on Earth has that location.

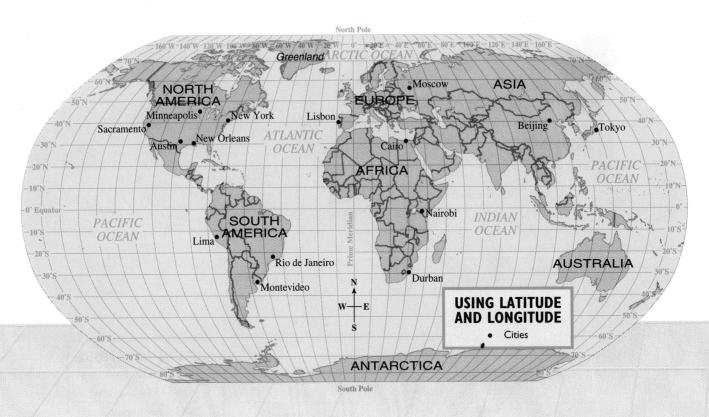

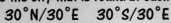

Where on Earth are these cities?

◆ Give their locations in degrees of latitude and longitude.
   Rio de Janeiro, Brazil
   Beijing, China
   Sacramento, California

◆ Name the city that is found at each location.
   30°N/30°E   30°S/30°E

The equator divides Earth into **hemispheres**, or two equal halves. Any place north of the equator is in the **Northern Hemisphere**. Any place south of the equator is in the **Southern Hemisphere**. Do you live in the Northern Hemisphere or in the Southern Hemisphere?

The map on page M13 shows that the prime meridian runs through Greenwich, England. Any place located east of the prime meridian is in the **Eastern Hemisphere**. Any place west of the prime meridian is in the **Western Hemisphere**. Do you live in the Eastern Hemisphere or in the Western Hemisphere?

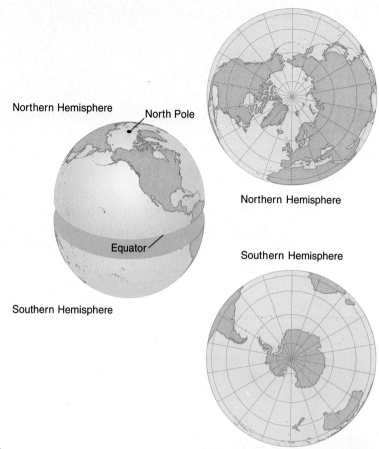

Northern Hemisphere

North Pole

Equator

Southern Hemisphere

Northern Hemisphere

Southern Hemisphere

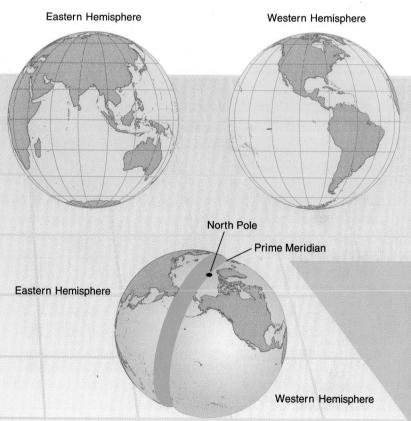

Eastern Hemisphere

Western Hemisphere

North Pole

Prime Meridian

Eastern Hemisphere

Western Hemisphere

Now Try This!

A message crawled across the bottom of the TV screen.

WARNING: A tornado watch is out for people living in the area of 40°N/100°W. The warning zone extends east to 40°N/80°W.

Should you prepare to take cover, or should you watch another comedy rerun? To find out, look up the locations on pages 402–403. Make a list of some of the communities that might be affected.

What's So Special About SPECIAL-PURPOSE Maps?

Maps can show many things besides where places are and how far apart one place is from another. Maps can tell about the climate in a place. They can also tell about the history of a place. They can show what kind of work people do in a place. Maps that are drawn to give us information like this are called **special-purpose maps**.

The map below is a **population density map**. The map uses color to show which places have more people and which places have fewer people. Population density is figured out by measuring the number of people who live in a square mile—a square area with sides that are one mile long.

The color is the code.

◆ What does each color in the map key stand for?

Who's counting?

◆ How many people per square mile live in the area around Philadelphia, Pennsylvania?

◆ In what parts of Pennsylvania do the fewest people live?

◆ In general, do more people live in the middle or eastern parts of the Middle Atlantic region?

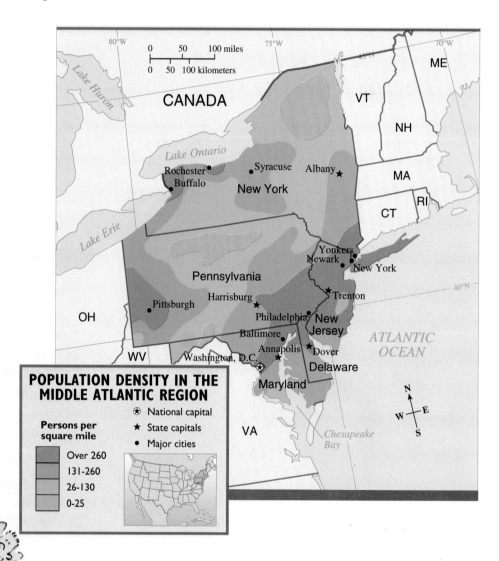

POPULATION DENSITY IN THE MIDDLE ATLANTIC REGION

✹ National capital
★ State capitals
● Major cities

Persons per square mile

- Over 260
- 131-260
- 26-130
- 0-25

Some special-purpose maps, called **product maps**, tell about where foods and other crops are grown. The map below shows where corn is grown in the Southeast region of the United States.

They're all ears!

◆ Is more corn grown in the northern part or in the southern part of Georgia?

◆ Which states along the Gulf of Mexico grow corn?

Now Try This!

Make a tracing-paper copy of the map you drew for page M5. Use symbols or colors to turn the copy into a special-purpose map. For example, you could

◆ show the stores and restaurants in your neighborhood or town

◆ show the largest buildings

◆ show the apartment houses and the private homes.

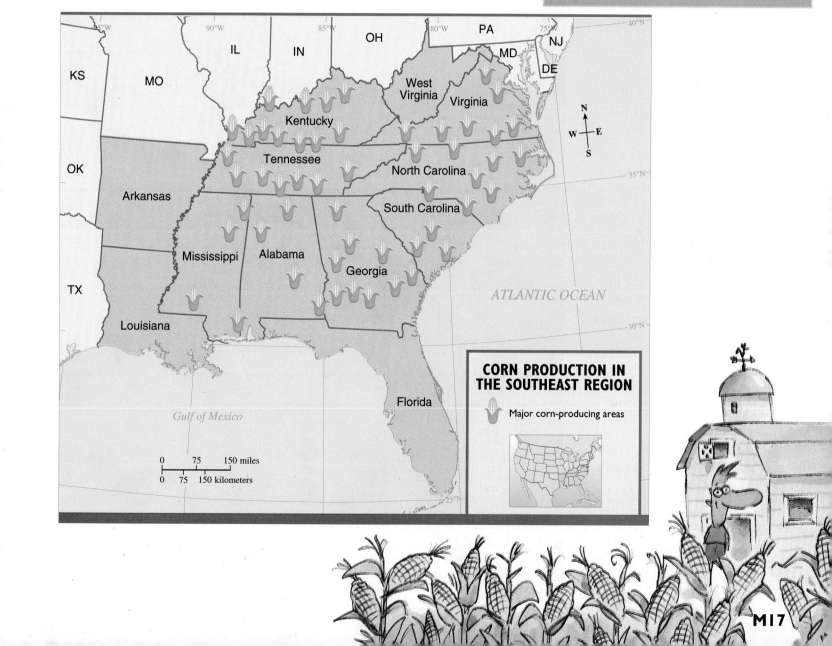

CORN PRODUCTION IN THE SOUTHEAST REGION

🌽 Major corn-producing areas

Which GEOGRAPHIC TERMS
Should You Know?

The diagram on these pages shows important forms of land and water. All of these are natural forms that are found on Earth's surface. To see what a form looks like, check the number next to its description. Then find the form on the diagram.

1 **bay** A bay is a part of an ocean or lake that is partly enclosed by land.

2 **canyon** A canyon is a deep, narrow valley with steep sides.

3 **coast** Coast is land that borders on the sea or ocean.

4 **gulf** A gulf is a part of an ocean or sea that reaches into land. It is larger than a bay.

5 **harbor** A harbor is a sheltered area of water where ships can anchor safely.

6 **island** An island is an area of land that is surrounded by water.

7 **lake** A lake is a body of water that is almost completely surrounded by land.

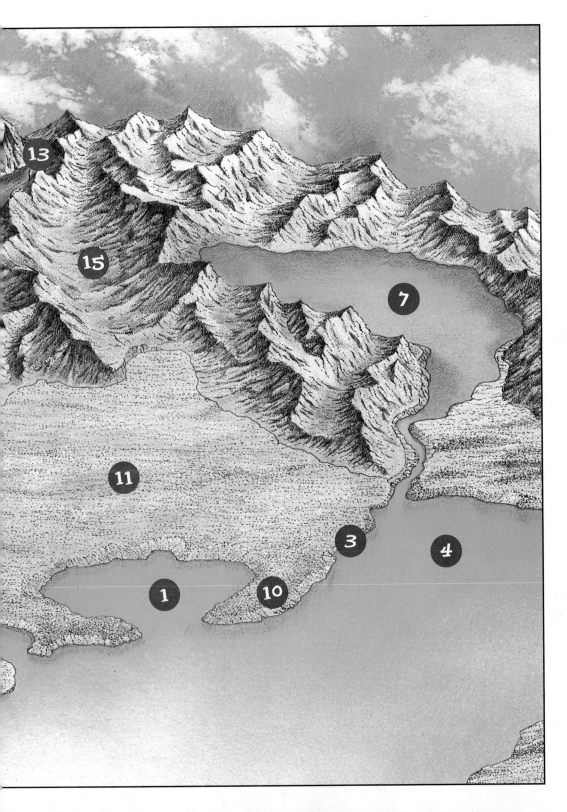

8 **marsh** A marsh is low land that is wet and soft.

9 **mountain range** A mountain range is a group of connected mountains, or steep, high land areas.

10 **peninsula** A peninsula is a piece of land that is almost surrounded by water. It is connected to a larger body of land.

11 **plain** A plain is a broad stretch of level or nearly level land.

12 **plateau** A plateau is a large level area of high land.

13 **source of a river** A river source is the place where a river begins.

14 **tributary** A tributary is a stream or river that flows into a larger river.

15 **valley** A valley is a long, low area of land, usually between mountains or hills.

THE World Around Us

Where Is Our Place in the World?

Let's explore the physical world we all share. Along the way we'll learn about the geography of our country and about seven land regions of the United States.

U.S. GEOGRAPHY

REGIONS & STATES

Rivers

Boundaries

Landforms

1

Where in the World

The world often seems like a place too big to know. By looking at maps and globes, you can put your finger on the world's continents, oceans, mountains, and rivers. You can find your place on Earth and begin to learn about the world around you.

CONTENTS

Expand your knowledge of your world. On page 7 you will find out how globes and maps can help you.

Is the United States?

These books can help you map your way around the world. Read one that interests you and fill out a book-review form.

READ AND RESEARCH

Amelia Earhart Flies Around the World by Kath Davies
(Silver Burdett Press, 1994)
Learn all about the life of Amelia Earhart— from her childhood dreams to her last flight across the Pacific Ocean. *(nonfiction)*

Amazon Boy by Ted Lewin (Simon and Schuster, 1993)
A trip to a big city is always exciting for a child who lives on a river, whether the Mississippi or the Amazon. When Paulo visits the harbor and market at the mouth of the Amazon, he learns an important lesson. *(fiction)*

Rand McNally Children's Atlas of the World
(Rand McNally & Co., 1994)
After practicing five map skills, you will enjoy learning about the land, animals, people, and countries of each continent. *(reference)*

Territories and Possessions: Guam, American Samoa, Puerto Rico, U.S. Virgin Islands, Wake, Midway and Other Islands, Micronesia by Thomas G. Aylesworth and Virginia L. Aylesworth (Chelsea House Publishers, 1996)
Explore the people, places, and history of U.S. territories and possessions. Use the photographs and maps and compare these places with the state you call home. *(nonfiction)*

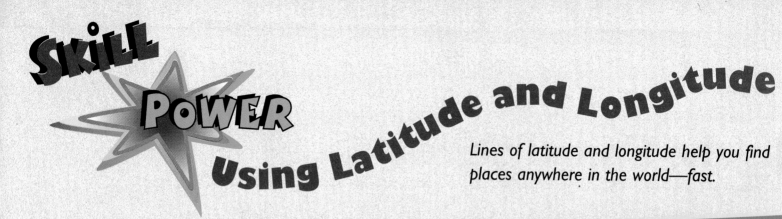

Using Latitude and Longitude

Lines of latitude and longitude help you find places anywhere in the world—fast.

UNDERSTAND IT

Suppose someone asked you to find the city of Algiers on a world map. It would take a long time if you had to look at all the cities in the world! But what if there were lines and numbers on the map?

Map makers draw lines and numbers on maps and globes. Lines of latitude run from east to west all the way around the globe. The equator, which is numbered 0° (zero degrees), is the line of latitude exactly halfway between the North Pole and the South Pole.

Lines of longitude run north to south around the globe. These lines measure distances from the prime meridian, which is the line of longitude numbered 0°. Lines of both latitude and longitude help you find places on a map or globe.

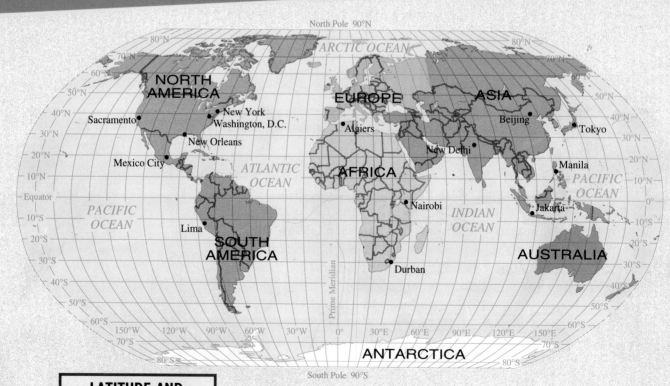

LATITUDE AND LONGITUDE
- Cities

EXPLORE IT

Using the map on the opposite page, put one finger on the 0° line of latitude. Follow it until you reach the 0° line of longitude. Then move your finger up to 30°N latitude. Find Algiers, which is between 30°N latitude and 40°N latitude.

Try to find the city that's at 30°N latitude and 90°W longitude. Put your finger on the 0° line of latitude in the middle of the map. Then move your finger north to the 30°N latitude line. Now move your finger west until you locate the 90°W longitude line. Where are you?

TRY IT

Choose three cities on the map at the left. Write the name of each city on a separate piece of paper. Fold each paper in half. On the outside, write the numbers and letters of the lines of latitude and longitude that are closest to the city. For example, you would write 20°N latitude and 100°W longitude for Mexico City, Mexico.

Trade your three papers with a partner. Use the map to find your partner's places.

WHERE AM I ?

▲ Find the cities of Tokyo and New York on the map on page 4. What are their locations given in latitude and longitude?

SKILL

POWER SEARCH Look through the chapter and study the maps. How many of them have lines of latitude and longitude?

Setting the Scene

★ **KEY TERMS**

continent
landform
natural resource
rain forest
climate

The World Around Us

FOCUS *Where in the world are you? Find out where you fit in the global community from your special place in the United States.*

Finding Your Place

An earthquake strikes Japan. The bark from a tree in Peru is used to help cure a rare disease. A humpback whale gets stuck in shallow water. Events like these happen every day all over the world. But how do these events affect you in your small corner of the world? How do you fit in?

The town or city where you live is a good place to start. It's also helpful to see where your community is located compared with other places in the world. But how would you do this?

One way to find out might be to ride in a hot-air balloon over your community. From way up high, you'd see not only the whole community but also parks, highways, and bridges nearby. You might also find out whether your community is located on a river or is surrounded by mountains.

But even up this high, you wouldn't be able to see the location

▼ A ride in a hot-air balloon gives you a bird's-eye view of your community.

of your town compared with the rest of the United States. To get that kind of view, you would have to go deep into space, like a satellite.

A satellite can be equipped with a camera. The camera takes pictures of Earth and sends them back for us to look at. But even from deep in space, a satellite camera can take a picture of only one part of the globe at a time.

Using Maps and Globes

The only way to get a total view of the world and to find out where you fit is to use maps and globes. By looking at maps and globes, we can also divide up our world in many different ways.

One of the ways the world can be divided on a map or globe is by the equator. The equator is a line of latitude that is drawn on maps and globes of Earth. It divides the globe into the northern half, or the Northern Hemisphere, and the southern half, or the Southern Hemisphere.

In the same way, you can look at a map or a globe to see that the prime meridian divides Earth into the Eastern Hemisphere and the Western Hemisphere. The prime meridian is a line of longitude.

As you learn more about the hemispheres and how they help you locate your town or city, you can continue the journey of finding your place on Earth.

A World of Continents

An easy and direct way to find out where you fit in the world is to look at Earth's **continents**, or large landmasses. By looking at a map or globe, you can see that the United States is located on the continent of North America.

But North America is not the only continent on Earth. The six other continents on Earth are Africa, Asia, Australia, Europe, South America, and Antarctica.

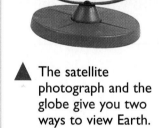

▲ The satellite photograph and the globe give you two ways to view Earth.

continent   One of the seven large land areas on Earth

Not all the continents are the same size. Asia is the largest of the seven continents. Australia is the smallest continent. Most continents contain more than one country. For example, the continent of North America is shared by the United States, Canada, and Mexico. Central America, which contains several countries, is also part of North America. Australia is the only continent that does not have more than one country.

What Do Continents Share?

So what do continents and the countries in them have in common? All continents have many different kinds of **landforms**. Some of these landforms are mountains and hills. Other kinds of landforms are valleys and islands.

For example, the United States is a large country, so it has many different kinds of landforms. We have many high mountains, such as the Rocky Mountains in the western part of the country. Mount McKinley, part of the Alaska Range, is our highest mountain peak. It reaches an elevation of 20,320 feet. Mount McKinley is so high that many mountain climbers can't resist trying to climb it.

CONTINENTS AND OCEANS OF THE WORLD

But Mount McKinley is not the highest mountain in the world. Most of the world's highest mountains are located in Asia, in the Himalaya Mountains. Mount Everest, the highest mountain in the world, is 29,028 feet high. That means that Mount Everest reaches up over 5 miles into the sky!

landform A feature of the earth's surface created by nature

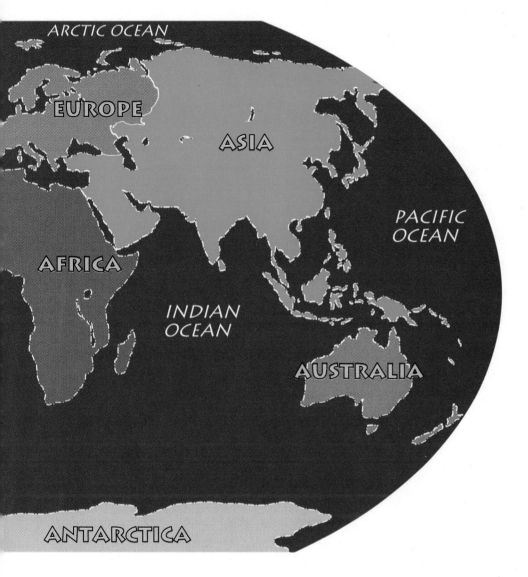

Rivers of the World

The United States has a very long and important river, the Mississippi River. This river is 2,348 miles long. Other rivers and streams from many miles around it flow into the Mississippi River. They help make it powerful. However, an even longer river than the Mississippi exists in Africa. It is the Nile River.

The Nile flows 4,145 miles through the northern part of Africa before it empties into the Mediterranean Sea. Like rivers throughout the world, the Nile and the Mississippi are very important to the survival of people living near them.

More Natural Resources

Some of the other natural resources that continents have are minerals, animals, and forests. But not all continents have exactly the same kinds of natural resources. For example, the trees that make up a **rain forest** in South America are natural resources on the South American continent. But that doesn't mean that the same varieties of trees would be found on the continent of North America.

To find out the kinds of natural resources that continents might

A World of Water

What other things do continents have? The answer is **natural resources**. One of Earth's most important natural resources is water. Large bodies of water, such as oceans and seas, surround most of the continents. Continents also have smaller bodies of water, including rivers, lakes, and streams.

 natural resource Something that is provided by nature and is useful to people

 rain forest A tropical forest with a thick growth of trees and a heavy rainfall

 Water is one of our most important natural resources. The Amazon River is a water resource that people use for leisure activities and for earning a living.

have, you would need to look at the **climate**, the location, and the types of landforms of each continent. But even by doing all this, you'd see that not all the countries on a continent have the same natural resources. Each country on a continent might contain very different natural resources.

Climate

The climate of a continent differs from country to country. But did you also know that the climate within one country can differ, too? Let's look at the United States to see how climates vary.

With such a large land area, the United States has a great variety of climates. You can travel to snowy icecaps in northern Alaska or Colorado. You can visit a hot, dry desert in Arizona. Or you can even walk through a tropical rain forest in Hawaii. All these climates exist in the United States!

Of course, other continents have a variety of climates, too. Some countries on a continent might have hot, dry climates most of the year, and other countries might have cold, wet climates. But there are very few countries in the world that have as many different climates as the United States.

climate The kind of weather a place has over a long period of time

10

The mountains of Colorado offer many kinds of resources and chances for recreation. ▶

People Are Resources, Too

No matter where you live on Earth, no matter which country or continent you might visit or choose to study, remember that there is one very important resource that all continents share. That resource is people! People are the world's most valuable resource.

Even if a country has rich land and plenty of minerals and forests, it still needs people to determine how to use those resources wisely. More and more we are learning just how important natural resources are for all of us. Through ideas, plans, and hard work people are seeking the best possible ways to use these resources.

So where in the world are you? The answer is right in your community in the United States, part of the North American continent, and a part of the world. Welcome to your global home, the home for all of us. Its name is Earth!

SHOW WHAT YOU KNOW!

REFOCUS
COMPREHENSION

1. What is the only way to get a total view of the world?

2. What are some kinds of landforms that continents have in common?

THINK ABOUT IT
CRITICAL THINKING

How might the resources found in a country affect the kinds of work and leisure activities of people in that country?

STATE CHECK
ACTIVITY

What rivers are in your state? Start a scrapbook about rivers. Paste in drawings or photos of rivers, name the rivers, and write how people use them.

Ducks Overboard

FOCUS *Scientists are using toys spilled from a cargo ship to study ocean currents. These spilled toys remind us that an ocean is like a highway. This highway connects continents and moves things along from place to place.*

ASIA

JAPAN

 Japan Current

PACIFIC OCEAN

HONG KONG

N
W—E
S

Ocean Adventure

Oceans are exciting parts of the earth, constantly moving with great force. Each ocean has **currents**, which are like powerful rivers moving through the ocean. Scientists are using toys to learn more about currents. In January 1992 a cargo ship loaded with plastic toys left Hong Kong for Tacoma, Washington. As the ship crossed the Pacific Ocean, storm winds knocked the containers overboard. About ten months later, these toys started washing up on beaches along the western **coast** of North America. The toys had floated nearly 3,000 miles, along currents in the Pacific, before reaching North America.

current A stream that flows in the ocean
coast The land along the edge of an ocean or a sea

12

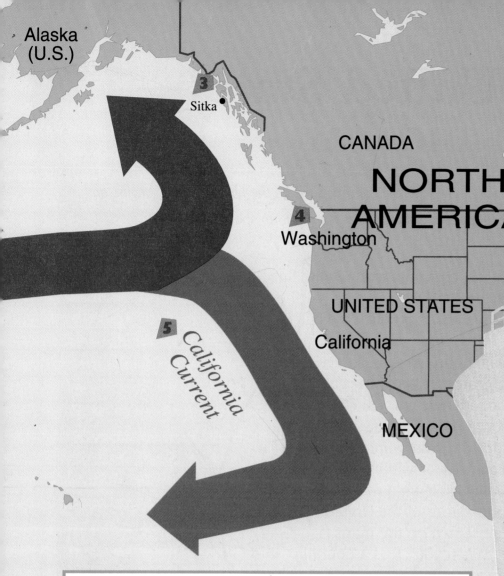

Alaska
(U.S.)

3 Sitka •

CANADA

NORTH AMERICA

Washington 4

UNITED STATES

California

5 *California Current*

MEXICO

Map Key

1 **Hong Kong** The ship began its journey in Hong Kong.

2 **Japan Current** The red arrow on the map shows you where this ocean current is located.

3 **Sitka** Some of the toys first washed up in North America at the city of Sitka in 1992.

4 **Washington** About two years later, in 1994, more toys washed up in this location.

5 **California Current** The blue arrow on the map shows you where this ocean current is located.

MAP IT

1. On which continent is Hong Kong located?

2. On the map, trace with your finger the movement of the ocean current at number 2. Start at Hong Kong and follow the arrow. If a ship followed this current after leaving Hong Kong, which Asian country would it pass on its route?

3. In which state is Sitka located?

4. Where in the United States did the toys begin to wash up in 1994?

5. Trace the ocean current at number 5 on the map. If the toys continue to follow this ocean current, where might they wash up next?

EXPLORE IT

If some of the toys continued north from Sitka, where might they end up? How?

Citizenship

KEY TERMS
boundary
law
population
commonwealth
territory

The United States— Near and Far

FOCUS *How do you know where a country, such as the United States, begins and where it ends? Boundaries are the answer. They help to shape our world.*

of a soccer field is the white line. It defines the playing area, as shown at the left. If you kick the ball out of bounds, play stops and someone has to throw the ball back in.

States and countries also have boundaries, but you can't see or touch most of these boundaries. Most boundary lines between countries or within countries are only visible on a map. Find the boundaries of the United States that are shown on the maps.

When you cross a boundary into another country, you usually have to stop, check in with an official to identify yourself, and explain how long you plan to visit. This is because you are not a citizen of the country you are visiting.

What's a Boundary?

An athletic field has **boundaries**, and the rules of games played on that field apply within those boundaries. If you have ever played soccer, you know that the boundary

Being a Citizen

Being a citizen of a country means that you must obey its **laws**. You also must obey the laws of any other country that you visit. As a citizen of the United States, you

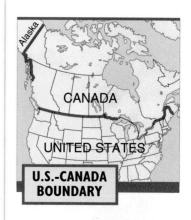

U.S.-CANADA BOUNDARY

U.S.-MEXICO BOUNDARY

★ **boundary** A line that separates one place from another

★ **law** A rule made by the government for all the people in a town, state, or country

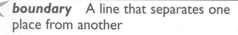

have many rights, such as freedom of speech. Adult citizens also have an important right—the right to vote in elections. Citizens of the United States must obey our country's laws. Because you are a citizen of the United States, you would not have the same rights and privileges in another country that you have in your home country.

United States Boundaries

The United States has thousands of miles of boundary lines. Some boundaries are natural, such as rivers and coastlines. Other boundaries are special lines that appear only on maps or globes.

The boundary that separates the lower 48 United States and Canada is 3,987 miles long. Alaska also borders Canada. That boundary is 1,538 miles long.

Between the United States and Mexico, the Rio Grande serves as a boundary. West of this river, the boundary follows a line that was set when the United States bought land from Mexico in 1853.

Have you ever wondered just how long the entire coastline of the United States really is? Including the coastlines of Alaska and Hawaii, the United States has 12,383 miles of shoreline.

Puerto Rico

Although each of the 50 states of our country has separate state laws, all Americans are citizens of one country—the United States. But did you know that the United States also stretches beyond these 50 states? What are these places,

▼ A United States post office in Puerto Rico issues United States postage stamps.

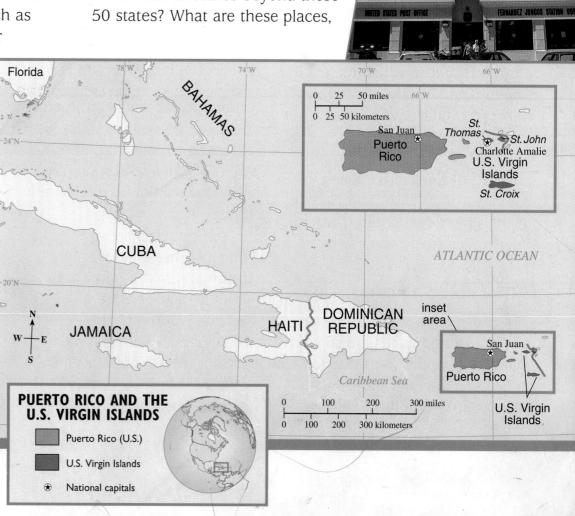

PUERTO RICO AND THE
U.S. VIRGIN ISLANDS

■ Puerto Rico (U.S.)

■ U.S. Virgin Islands

✪ National capitals

and how do they affect the boundaries of our country?

Puerto Rico is one of these lands. It is an island in the Caribbean Sea, 1,000 miles southeast of Florida. It is located on a map at about 18°N latitude and between 65° and 68°W longitude. Puerto Rico became a part of the United States in 1898 at the end of the Spanish-American War. Until then, Puerto Rico belonged to Spain, and Spanish remains the main language of the island.

Puerto Rico has a **population** of nearly 4 million. It is a **commonwealth**, which means that Puerto Ricans enjoy most of the rights of United States citizens but cannot vote in presidential elections. Puerto Ricans can visit any part of the United States whenever they wish, and citizens of the United States can travel to Puerto Rico freely, too.

A Possible Change

The ties between Puerto Rico and the United States are so close that some people want Puerto Rico to become our 51st state. Other citizens of Puerto Rico want the island to remain a commonwealth, while others would like it to become an independent country.

The United States Virgin Islands

The United States Virgin Islands are also located in the Caribbean Sea. They are only about 50 miles east of Puerto Rico. Three large islands—St. Croix (saynt KROI), St. Thomas, and St. John—and more than 50 tiny ones make up the United States Virgin Islands.

The United States bought these islands from Denmark in 1917. The islands then became a **territory** of the United States. People of the Virgin Islands are United States citizens, but they cannot vote in presidential elections.

---

population The number of people in a given area
commonwealth A political unit similar to a state

territory Land ruled by a nation or state

GUAM

- Rainfall measures about 90 inches a year.
- Important agricultural products include coconuts and sweet potatoes.

UNITED STATES VIRGIN ISLANDS

- Some places in the Virgin Islands receive only 40 inches of rain in a year.
- Farmers produce agricultural products, such as eggs, cucumbers, peppers, and tomatoes.

Guam and American Samoa

Guam is an island that lies in the western Pacific Ocean. The United States won Guam from Spain during the Spanish-American War in 1898. Since that time the island has become an important air and naval base for the United States military.

Guam is a United States territory. People of Guam too are United States citizens, but they cannot vote in presidential elections.

The people of the seven islands in the Pacific Ocean that make up American Samoa are not United States citizens. Instead they are United States nationals. United States nationals are people who can travel freely between their country and the United States but who do not have all the rights of United States citizens.

American Samoa is a territory of the United States. It holds elections and has its own government, but the United States is responsible for defending the territory.

Many lands are linked to the United States. Some are near the boundaries of the 50 states and some are very far away. Whether they are near or far, our country's boundaries stretch well beyond the 50 states.

AMERICAN SAMOA

- The yearly rainfall averages over 200 inches.
- Rich soil in the valleys is used to grow coconuts and bananas.

SHOW WHAT YOU KNOW!

REFOCUS
COMPREHENSION

1. Explain the relationships the United States has with Puerto Rico.

2. Describe the location of the United States Virgin Islands.

THINK ABOUT IT
CRITICAL THINKING

Explain the difference between natural boundaries and other boundaries.

STATE CHECK
ACTIVITY

Look in the States Almanac on pages 340–397 for information about Guam. Make a poster, inviting someone to visit Guam.

Passport to the World

FOCUS *Communication, the movement of products, and the use of services all help to connect people around the world.*

Many Kinds of Passports

For years, most countries have issued passports to their citizens. A passport is an important **document** that identifies a person as a citizen of a country. You might think of a passport as proof of who you are and where you live.

Passports are important for traveling from one country to another. Sometimes when you go to a country outside of your own, your passport gets stamped.

The word *passport* has come to mean "anything that helps you be accepted or admitted to a place." If you think about passports in this way, there are many different kinds of passports. For example, you can think of education as a passport that increases your opportunities for success. Communication is also

a kind of passport. Communication allows people in one area of the world to connect with people in other parts of the world.

Travel Then and Now

A hundred years ago, most people had to travel from one place to another to visit and communicate with each other. Travel was slow and often difficult.

In 1873, Jules Verne wrote a story in which a man named Phileas Fogg claimed that he could travel around the world in 80 days. Rushing by ship, train, and even horseback, Fogg did succeed in circling the globe in 80 days. Now people fly on airplanes from New York City to London, England, in about six hours.

▲ This passport stamp is from the Republic of China, which is also called Taiwan.

 document A written or printed statement that gives proof and information

Your Communication Passport

Today, you can communicate with people around the world without even leaving home. You can pick up a telephone and talk with residents of countries on the other side of the globe. Linked by computers, people send and receive information in seconds. Facsimile (fak SIHM uh lee) machines allow us to send printed messages to each other over telephone lines. Satellites beam live television broadcasts from one continent to another. All of these **inventions** have made it easy to cross the boundaries of countries around the world.

⭐ *invention*   Something that is created for the first time

More Ways to Communicate

The more traditional ways of connecting with other people and with the past are valuable, too. Each day, newspapers present many kinds of information from around the world. And books contain wisdom collected over hundreds of years. By reading a book you can find out more about yourself, your family, and your world.

Exchanging stories is another way people connect with each other. Grandparents and other relatives may be able to tell you things about your family that no one else could. Family photographs can also help you connect with the past.

▼ Through communication you can receive information and share it with people all around the world.

SNEAKER STEPS AROUND THE WORLD

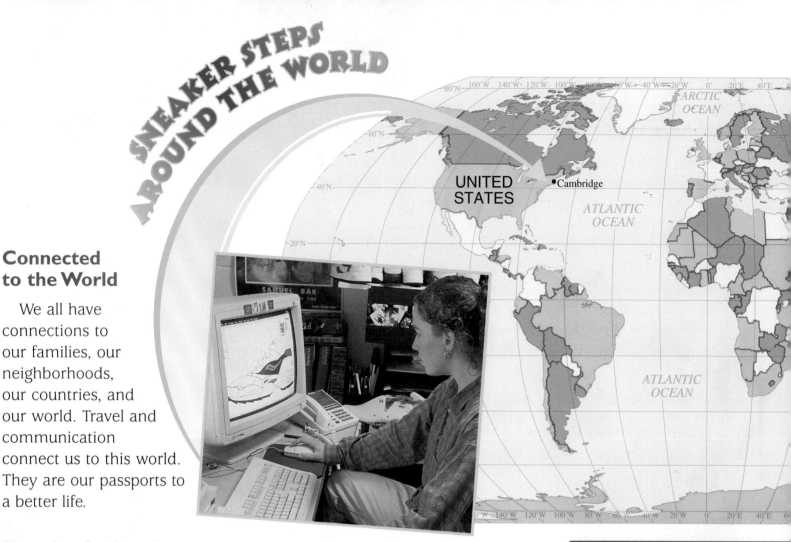

UNITED STATES
•Cambridge

ARCTIC OCEAN

ATLANTIC OCEAN

ATLANTIC OCEAN

Connected to the World

We all have connections to our families, our neighborhoods, our countries, and our world. Travel and communication connect us to this world. They are our passports to a better life.

Travels of a Sneaker

The movement of products and the use of **services** around the world also connect people and countries. For example, when you walk into a store and buy a pair of sneakers, you benefit from the resources of many countries and the talents of many people. Sneakers represent the work of many people throughout the world.

First, people who work in companies that produce sneakers study the needs and wants of sneaker buyers. They also study

▲ A worker in Cambridge, Massachusetts, U.S., designs a sneaker.

how to produce sneakers in the most **economical** way. Many shoe designers create sneakers by using computers, as shown on this page.

Now that you know how your sneaker began, take a closer look at it. It has three main parts: the upper, the sole, and the heel.

The upper, which covers your foot, may be made of leather that came from Taiwan, Australia, Japan; from countries in South America

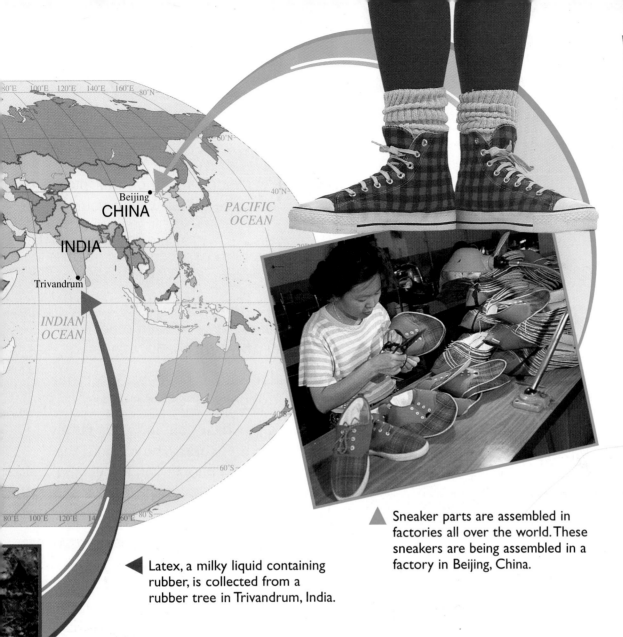

Latex, a milky liquid containing rubber, is collected from a rubber tree in Trivandrum, India.

Sneaker parts are assembled in factories all over the world. These sneakers are being assembled in a factory in Beijing, China.

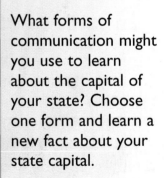

REFOCUS
COMPREHENSION

1. Name two kinds of passports that can connect you to the world.

2. Describe how sneakers represent the work of many people.

THINK ABOUT IT
CRITICAL THINKING

At about what latitude and longitude is Beijing, China?

STATE CHECK
ACTIVITY

What forms of communication might you use to learn about the capital of your state? Choose one form and learn a new fact about your state capital.

and Europe; or from the United States. The upper might also be made of cotton or other materials.

The sole is the bottom part of your sneaker. It may be made from natural rubber tapped from trees in the forests of Malaysia, India, or Indonesia. Or it may be made from artificial rubber produced in the United States. The same is true for the rear part of the sole—the heel.

Pieces of any sneaker may come from many parts of the globe. These pieces are then shipped to a factory where workers assemble the shoes. Many sneakers are made in factories in China, Taiwan, Indonesia, India, and Thailand. Once the shoes are completed, they are shipped all over the world. The finished product—a simple pair of sneakers—is not really simple at all.

SUMMING UP

1 DO YOU REMEMBER . . .
COMPREHENSION

1. How are the equator and the prime meridian alike? How are they different?

2. What are the seven continents that make up Earth?

3. How might a plastic toy dropped into the sea near Asia wash up on North America?

4. What are some natural boundaries of the United States?

5. What is the purpose of a passport?

3 WHAT DO YOU THINK?
CRITICAL THINKING

1. Tell about a new idea or invention that puts resources to work in a better way in your community.

2. Explain how sailors in past centuries might have taken advantage of ocean currents.

3. Americans and Canadians do not need passports to travel between each other's countries. Why might this be?

4. Why is education said to be a "passport that increases your opportunities for success"?

5. List three ways in which you and your family are connected to the world. Think about the products you use, the people you know, and the ways you communicate.

2 SKILL POWER
USING LATITUDE AND LONGITUDE

Play "geography bingo" with a group of your classmates. Using a map, one student begins by giving the latitude and longitude of a city somewhere in the world. Members of the group all try to find the city. The first student to call out the correct name of the city chooses the next city and announces its latitude and longitude.

4 SAY IT, WRITE IT, USE IT
VOCABULARY

Suppose you could travel around the world in a hot-air balloon. Describe what you would see. Use as many words from the key terms as possible in your description.

boundary	invention
climate	landform
coast	law
commonwealth	natural resource
continent	population
current	rain forest
document	service
economical	territory

5 GEOGRAPHY AND YOU
MAP STUDY

Use the map below to answer these questions.

1. Which oceans form boundaries of North America?

2. What other bodies of water form boundaries of North America?

3. Which three large countries make up North America?

4. Which is the largest island in North America?

NORTH AMERICA

6 TAKE ACTION
CITIZENSHIP

American citizens have many rights. But with these rights come responsibilities, or duties. With your classmates, make a chart like this one. First list some rights that Americans have. Then name responsibilities that come with these rights.

RIGHTS	RESPONSIBILITIES
voting	to learn about candidates and to vote
trial by jury	to serve on juries
freedom of speech	

7 GET CREATIVE
SCIENCE CONNECTION

With a group of classmates, brainstorm ideas for possible new inventions. The goal of your inventions should be to put natural resources to work in the best ways possible. Choose the one invention that you think has the most possibilities. Draw a picture or make a model of your invention and tell how it would work.

LOOKING AHEAD Find out in the next chapter that there are many different kinds of land and natural resources in the United States.

Regions and States

In what region of the United States do you live? In this chapter, you'll discover what a region is and learn about different regions of our country. You'll also discover how the states came to be part of the United States.

CONTENTS

This harmless corn snake lives in the same region as a copperhead snake. Turn to page 32 to learn what this region is.

These books give you lots of information about the regions of the United States. Read one that interests you and fill out a book-review form.

READ AND RESEARCH

The Young People's Atlas of the United States
by James Harrison and Eleanor Van Zandt (Kingfisher Books, 1992)
This atlas will show you how our country is divided into regions. Colorful photographs and drawings will take you to each state to learn about its history, land, and people, plus many interesting facts. *(nonfiction)*

Scholastic Environmental Atlas of the United States
by Mark Mattson (Scholastic, 1993)
Find out how the states in each region you are studying are handling the problems of our environment. The photos, maps, charts, and graphs will provide you with the facts you need to become more aware of the needs of each region. *(nonfiction)*

Be Your Own Map Expert **by Barbara Taylor**
(Sterling Publishing Co., 1994)
Did you ever wonder how a map is made? This book will help you become a cartographer, or mapmaker. It gives you ideas for making a map to show the way to your home. You'll learn to make a map to hunt treasure, one to recall an event in history, and many more. *(nonfiction)*

The Great Midwest Flood **by Carole G. Vogel**
(Little, Brown, and Co., 1995)
Use the maps and photographs in this book to follow the Midwest flood of 1993. Read how so many people came together to try to hold back the flood waters and to help one another. *(nonfiction)*

SKILL POWER
Using Special-Purpose Maps

Knowing how to use special-purpose maps helps you learn interesting facts about places.

UNDERSTAND IT

Did you ever wonder how the food stores in your town get oranges in February? Long ago, people grew almost all of their own food. If you lived in New Hampshire in 1750, you probably did not eat many oranges because they did not grow in that region.

Today, you can find almost any kind of food in a supermarket or food store. All kinds of food gets shipped in from all over the country. A special-purpose map can help you see where the foods you eat might come from.

EXPLORE IT

You can use a special-purpose map to find out which food crops grow in your region and which ones have to be shipped in. The first thing you need to do when you look at a special-purpose map is to read the title to see what the map shows. What is the title of the map on the next page?

The next thing to check is the map key. It tells what the symbols on the map mean. Use the map on the next page to answer the following questions.

1. What are the names of three states that grow apples?

2. What is one crop that grows in both Maine and Alaska?

3. What is a crop that grows in Ohio, Indiana, Illinois, Iowa, Nebraska, and Minnesota?

4. Do apples, potatoes, and corn grow in your state?

Grocery stores like this one sell foods that are grown or produced in different parts of the country.

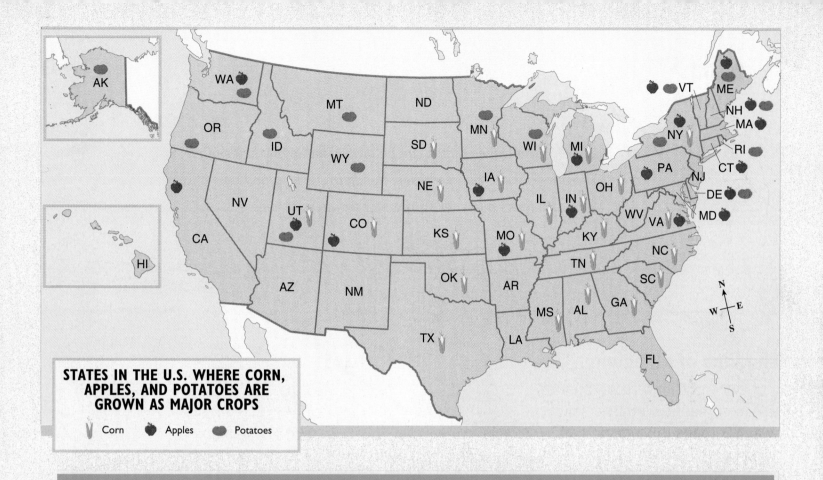

STATES IN THE U.S. WHERE CORN, APPLES, AND POTATOES ARE GROWN AS MAJOR CROPS

🌽 Corn 🍎 Apples 🥔 Potatoes

TRY IT

Work with a group of your classmates to make a special-purpose map. Think of something you are curious about or are interested in. You might think about where professional sports are played in the United States. These sports would include baseball, football, hockey, and basketball.

Choose the sports you want to include on your map. Then find the information you need. For your sports map, you would find out the cities and states that have professional sports teams.

Next, decide on symbols to use on the map. For professional sports, you could use miniature footballs, basketballs, baseballs, and hockey pucks as symbols. Then make your map by placing the symbols where they should go. Share what you have done with the class.

SKILL POWER SEARCH *Look through this chapter. What special-purpose maps can you find?*

KEY TERMS

region
temperature
precipitation
desert
plain
geography

What's in a Region?

FOCUS *The United States can be divided into many kinds of regions. Three regions are climate regions, landform regions, and animal regions. Special-purpose maps tell us more about these regions.*

The Idea of a Region

Have you ever written a letter to someone who lives far away? Perhaps this person has never seen your home. How would you describe where you live?

You might break up your town or city into smaller parts called **regions**. A region is an area that has something special that is common to the area.

Read the letter on this page to see how someone your own age describes the regions of her community. Then look at the map showing where these regions are located.

If you wrote a letter like this, what would you describe in your community? You might include the downtown region, the area where your home is located, and your favorite parks and stores.

region An area of land whose parts have one or more common characteristics

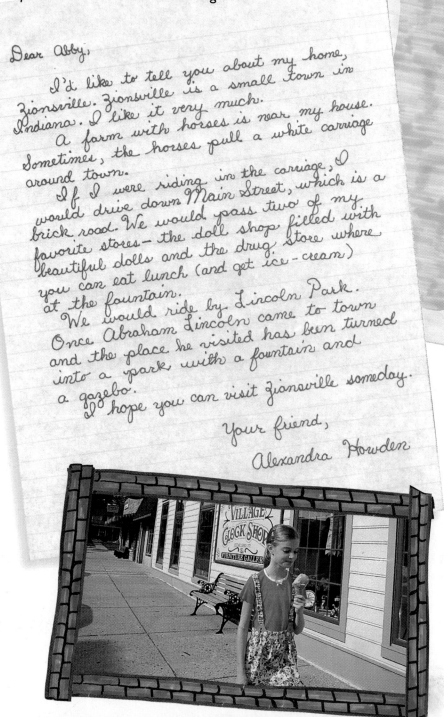

Dear Abby,

I'd like to tell you about my home, Zionsville. Zionsville is a small town in Indiana. I like it very much.

A farm with horses is near my house. Sometimes, the horses pull a white carriage around town.

If I were riding in the carriage, I would drive down Main Street, which is a brick road. We would pass two of my favorite stores — the doll shop filled with beautiful dolls and the drug store where you can eat lunch (and get ice-cream) at the fountain.

We would ride by Lincoln Park. Once Abraham Lincoln came to town and the place he visited has been turned into a park with a fountain and a gazebo.

I hope you can visit Zionsville someday.

Your friend,
Alexandra Howden

The park and the downtown area might be two regions of a community. Find two more regions on the map below.

My house

Park

Stores

Main Street

Breaking a large area of land into regions helps you study a large country such as the United States. You can divide a country into different kinds of regions, based on what you want to study.

You might want to study coal mining in the United States. First you would find out what parts of the country have mines that produce the most coal. Then you'd use this information to show coal mining regions on a map.

Climate Regions

Where would you look for a warm place to go on vacation? You might look first at a map of the United States that gives you information about climate regions.

A climate map shows **temperature** and **precipitation**. Temperature tells us how hot or cold the air is. Water that falls to the earth in the form of rain, snow, sleet, or hail is called precipitation. You have probably heard the word *precipitation* in a weather report.

The southern part of the United States has a climate that is warmer than that of the northern part of the country.

temperature The degree of heat or coldness
precipitation The falling of water in the form of rain, sleet, hail, or snow

29

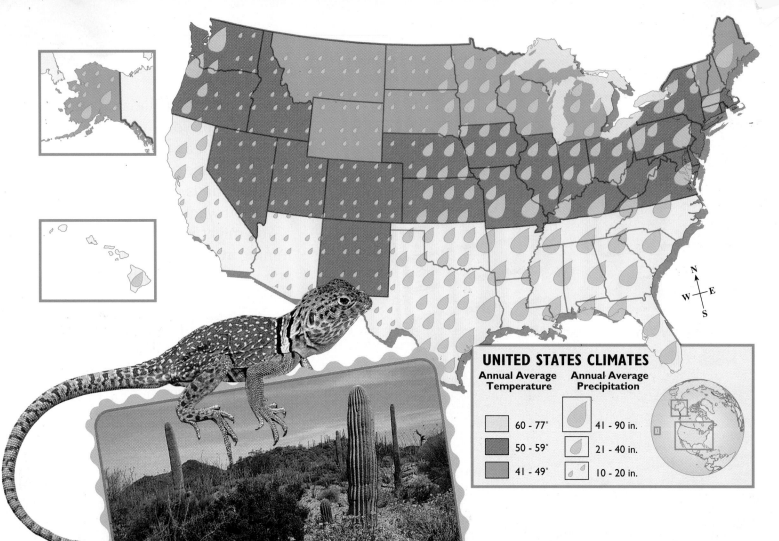

UNITED STATES CLIMATES

Annual Average Temperature	Annual Average Precipitation
60 - 77°	41 - 90 in.
50 - 59°	21 - 40 in.
41 - 49°	10 - 20 in.

growing in interesting shapes and sizes. In the spring a small amount of rain falls. The cactuses produce colorful flowers for a short period of time.

▲ The Southwest region is home to a variety of animals and plant life, such as the collared lizard and saguaro (suh GWAHR oh) cactus, both shown above.

The western part of the United States has a drier climate than the eastern part of the country. More rain falls in the eastern and central parts of the United States.

Some people of the United States live in extremely dry places, called **deserts**. Here you can see cactuses

Landform Regions

We can also divide the United States into regions of similar landforms. You learned that different continents and countries have different landforms. Let's look at some landforms that we find in the United States.

 desert A place with very little rainfall and few plants

30

The Rocky Mountains are in the western part of the United States. They form our largest mountain region. These mountains begin at our boundary with Mexico and stretch all the way to Alaska. The highest mountains are in Alaska.

The Appalachian Mountains are in the eastern part of the United States. They begin in Canada and extend south to the state of Alabama. Both the Rocky Mountains and the Appalachian Mountains provide us with minerals and lumber.

The central part of the United States, between the Appalachian Mountains and the Rocky Mountains, is a large **plains** region. We call this region the Great Plains. Can you see why by looking at the map below? The region along the Atlantic Ocean and the Gulf of Mexico is called the coastal plain.

Where the land is flat, you will usually find many farms that provide plenty of food to feed people. Large factories also are found in the plains regions of the country.

⭐ **plain**   A wide area of flat or gently rolling land that is often treeless

▽ You can divide the United States into different kinds of landform regions, such as mountains and plains.

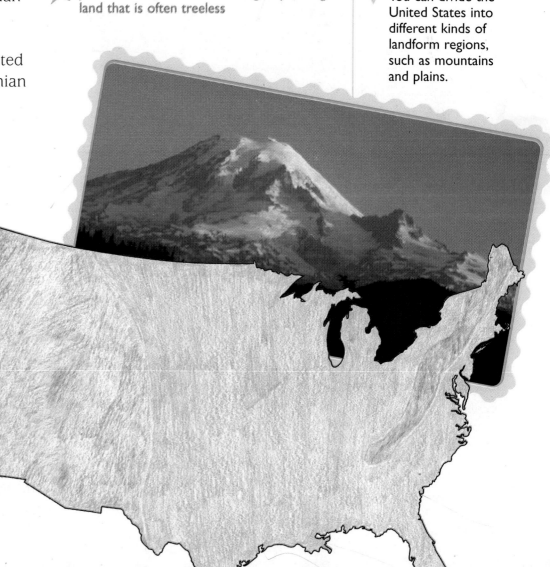

MOUNTAINS AND PLAINS

▨ Plains

▨ Mountains

CANADA

Caribou

Wolf

Puffins

Cougar

Indiana Bat

Copperhead Snake

Prairie Dog

Sea Lion

Coral Snake

Armadillo

Crocodile

Flamingo

Polar Bear

ALASKA

Hawaiian Honeycatcher

HAWAII

Animal Regions

Suppose you had a school project about the kinds of animals that are found in the United States. You could make a map like the one on this page. It shows where some kinds of animals are found.

Some animals are found only in certain parts of the United States. Large animals, such as caribou, need lots of space in order to find enough food. They are found in the northwestern part of the country, in the Rocky Mountains. How is the caribou animal region shown on the map on this page?

▲ This map shows regions of the country in which particular kinds of animals are found in large numbers.

32

Crocodiles need warm weather to survive. They are found in a region with a year-round warm climate. Where is the crocodile region on the map of the United States?

People and Regions

Now that you've learned about some different kinds of regions, you can see how regions help us study an area better. You saw that regions can be different parts of a community. Dividing a community into regions helps us to understand what the community is all about.

You also learned that a large country, such as the United States, can be divided into climate regions, landform regions, and even animal regions. Each kind of region tells us something important about our country.

When you look closely at a region, you are studying its **geography**—its land, water, animals, plants, and climate. But geography is more than that. People, too, are part of a region. In fact, people make up a very special part of a region.

Geography, then, is the study of Earth and how people use it. Geography helps us to understand how and why people live and work the way they do in different regions of the United States and the world.

---

geography   The study of Earth and how people use it

▼ Navajo sheepherder and flock in the desert region of the Southwest

SHOW WHAT YOU KNOW!

REFOCUS
COMPREHENSION

1. What is a region?

2. What are some different kinds of regions?

THINK ABOUT IT
CRITICAL THINKING

Review the different ways of showing regions that you saw on the maps in this lesson. Which map had the most unusual way of showing a region?

STATE CHECK
ACTIVITY

Find out what the major crops are in your state. Make a map to show regions where these crops are grown.

Regions of the United States

FOCUS *You will be studying seven regions of the United States. The states in each region share many things—geography, climate, and natural resources.*

UNITED STATES REGIONS

- New England
- Middle Atlantic
- Midwest and Great Plains
- Southeast
- Southwest
- Mountain West
- Pacific West

Studying Regions

This book divides the United States into seven land regions. Each state in a region has many things in common with the other states in that region. By studying these seven regions, you will begin to piece together the geography of the whole country. You can also learn about the history of these regions and about the people who live in them. The names of the seven regions are New England, Middle Atlantic, Southeast, Midwest and Great Plains, Southwest, Mountain West, and Pacific West. In which region do you live? Find your region on the map above. Name each region that is a boundary of your region.

MIDWEST and GREAT PLAINS

The Midwest and Great Plains region has some of the best farmland in the world. Missouri farms grow soybeans, vegetables, and fruit. Iowa farms produce 20 percent of our country's corn.

Wisconsin's pastures grow food for cows that produce 40 percent of the country's cheese products. Minnesota also has many large dairy farms. In the northern part of the state there are pine forests and hundreds of lakes.

To the west stretch the drier **prairies** of the central United States. Long ago the prairies were covered with a sea of grass over 6 feet tall. Today, the fields of North Dakota, South Dakota, Nebraska, and Kansas produce huge crops of corn and wheat.

The cities of Detroit, Chicago, Milwaukee, Cleveland, and St. Louis produce cars and steel. The states of Michigan, Ohio, Indiana, Illinois, and Wisconsin have port cities on the Great Lakes. Ships carry grain and other goods from these ports to the world.

NEW ENGLAND

The Appalachian Mountains and a rich history make the six New England states a region. The story of our country's birth is part of the rich **heritage** of this region.

The shores of Maine are famous for lobster fishing. Forests cover more than 80 percent of New Hampshire. It is also the most mountainous of the New England states. Mills produce lumber and paper in both of these states.

Nearly 75 percent of the people of Vermont live on farms or in small towns. Mountains are found in the northern and western parts of Massachusetts. **Industries** are found throughout the state. The smallest state, Rhode Island, has no mountains, but it has over 400 miles of coastline. The Connecticut coast attracts many tourists and vacationers.

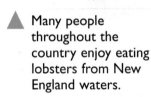

▲ Many people throughout the country enjoy eating lobsters from New England waters.

---

 prairie   Flat or rolling land

 heritage   What is handed down from past generations, such as beliefs and customs
industry   The making and selling of a product or service

35

SOUTHWEST

The Southwest is home to the Grand Canyon, one of the natural wonders of the world. Texas includes lakes, forests, and broad grasslands. Ranches and oil rigs surround Houston, the largest city in Texas and the Southwest region.

The states of New Mexico and Arizona also have the growing cities of Santa Fe and Phoenix. Albuquerque is a key transportation center in the region.

MIDDLE ATLANTIC

The Middle Atlantic is a region of mountains, which include the Allegheny, Adirondack, and Catskill mountain ranges. The state of Pennsylvania has nearly 4,500 streams and several large rivers.

The Middle Atlantic is also a region of cities. New York City is one of the world's most important centers for business and the arts. Philadelphia has been a major trade center since our country's early history. Baltimore, Maryland, is a busy port on Chesapeake Bay.

▲ This piece of Native American pottery was made in New Mexico.

The bay is famous for its crabs and oysters.

In New Jersey, most people live in cities, but half of the state is woods and farmland. Delaware is also a state of farms south of the city of Wilmington.

MOUNTAIN WEST

The Mountain West region has a small population and few large cities. The peaks and deep **canyons** of the Rocky Mountains make up much of this land. Gold mining and ranching in Colorado are part of the history of the state. Montana mountain passes allowed settlers to travel west. Determined pioneers settled in the rugged land of Utah, and cattle ranchers made their homes in the wilds of Wyoming.

Idaho is famous for its potato farming, and Nevada, for its vacation spots. Yellowstone and Grand Teton are two popular national parks that attract tourists and campers to the Mountain West region.

⭐ *canyon* A deep valley with high, steep sides

In Alaska, grizzly bears stand 8 feet tall and weigh 800 pounds on average. ▶

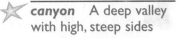

SOUTHEAST

The 12 states of the Southeast region are bound together by their location and climate. The Appalachian Mountains stretch from Virginia and West Virginia in the northern part of the region through Kentucky, Tennessee, North Carolina, and South Carolina, and into Alabama and Georgia.

West of these mountains lie forests. East of the mountains stretch **foothills** that slope down to the Atlantic coast.

To the south is the coastal plain on the Gulf of Mexico. Rich soil deposits on the west side of the Mississippi River support fields of rice and soybeans in Louisiana and Arkansas.

Georgia is famous for its peaches and peanuts. Mississippi industries produce clothing, electronics, and furniture.

Florida is the flattest and most southern state in the region. Its coastline is 1,350 miles long. Florida is famous for fruit growing and for being a vacation state.

PACIFIC WEST

Blue waters of the Pacific Ocean touch each of the five states in the Pacific West. You'll find mountains in each state. Washington, Oregon, and California are on the western coast of the United States. These states have rugged coastal areas and forested foothills.

California has one of the major deserts in the country. Yet parts of California are famous for growing grapes and oranges.

Alaska is a huge land area with many mountains. It makes up 20 percent of the land area of the entire United States. Yet Alaska has only as many roads as the smaller state of Vermont. The Aleutian Islands with their 40 volcanoes sweep west from the mainland of Alaska into the Pacific Ocean.

Hawaii became the 50th state in 1959. Its mountains are volcanoes that rise from the ocean floor. Hawaii is a popular vacation state because of its warm climate year-round.

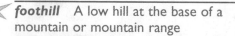

⭐ **foothill**   A low hill at the base of a mountain or mountain range

SHOW WHAT YOU KNOW!

REFOCUS
COMPREHENSION

1. Name the seven regions you will be studying.

2. List at least three things you remember reading about the region in which you live.

THINK ABOUT IT
CRITICAL THINKING

Some of the largest populations of people are found in the smallest regions—New England and the Middle Atlantic. Why, do you think, is this so?

STATE CHECK
ACTIVITY

Look in the States Almanac on pages 340–397 for clues about the geography of your state. Start a scrapbook about the state's geography.

37

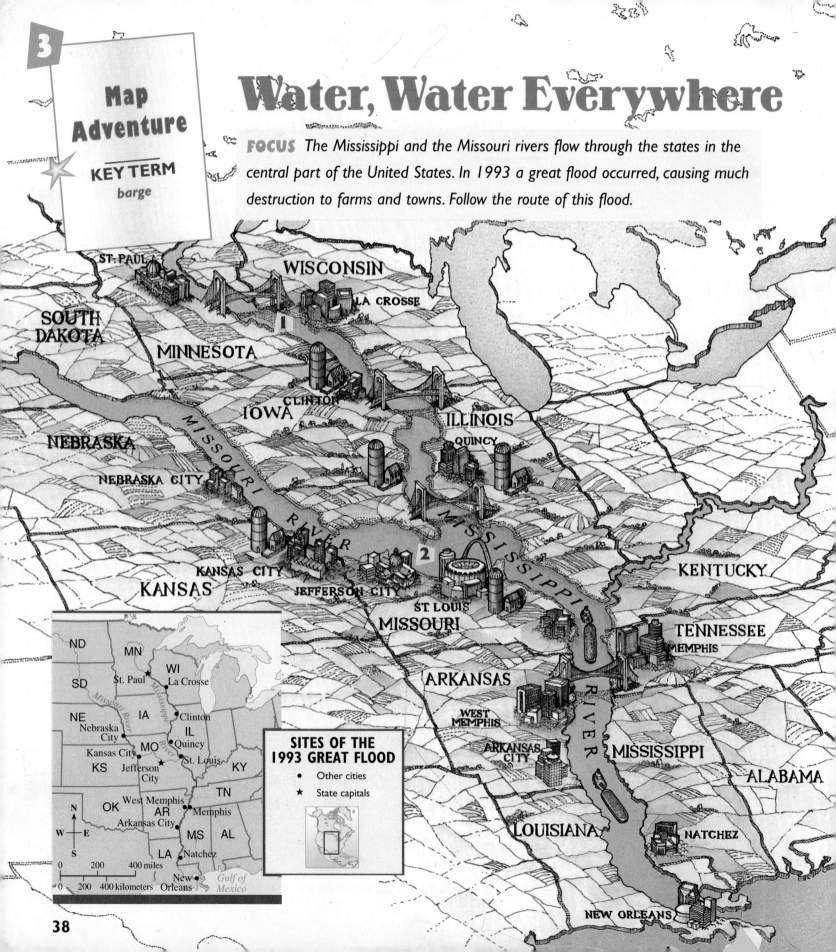

Map Adventure

★

KEY TERM

barge

Water, Water Everywhere

FOCUS The Mississippi and the Missouri rivers flow through the states in the central part of the United States. In 1993 a great flood occurred, causing much destruction to farms and towns. Follow the route of this flood.

ST. PAUL

WISCONSIN

LA CROSSE

SOUTH DAKOTA

MINNESOTA

CLINTON

IOWA

ILLINOIS

QUINCY

NEBRASKA

MISSOURI RIVER

NEBRASKA CITY

MISSISSIPPI

KANSAS CITY

KENTUCKY

KANSAS

JEFFERSON CITY

ST. LOUIS

MISSOURI

TENNESSEE

MEMPHIS

ARKANSAS

WEST MEMPHIS

ARKANSAS CITY

RIVER

MISSISSIPPI

ALABAMA

LOUISIANA

NATCHEZ

NEW ORLEANS

ND

MN

SD

WI

St. Paul

La Crosse

NE

IA

Missouri River

Clinton

Nebraska City

IL

Quincy

MO

Mississippi River

Kansas City

St. Louis

KS

Jefferson City

KY

TN

OK

West Memphis

AR

Memphis

Arkansas City

MS

AL

LA

Natchez

SITES OF THE 1993 GREAT FLOOD

• Other cities

★ State capitals

N
W   E
S

0   200   400 miles

0 200 400 kilometers

New Orleans

Gulf of Mexico

The Great Flood

News Bulletin—June, 1993. Weeks of heavy rain are causing the Mississippi and other rivers to rise. Water is flowing over riverbanks onto farmlands and into river towns. Thousands of people are fleeing their homes to escape the raging water. People are helping each other survive by building sandbag walls to try to keep back the water.

Map Key

1 Mississippi River The river begins in the state of Minnesota and flows south for 2,348 miles into the Gulf of Mexico.

2 Missouri River This river begins in Montana and goes through six states. It flows into the Mississippi River near St. Louis, Missouri.

Farms The rivers of this region are bordered by many farms. Flooding destroys crops because fields are under water and mud for weeks at a time.

Bridges There are many bridges that cross the Mississippi and Missouri rivers. Bridges are closed when serious floods cover the roads to the bridges.

Ships and barges Many ships and barges travel along the Mississippi River. During the flood of 1993, the river was closed to shipping north of St. Louis for two months.

barge A flat-bottomed boat used on inland waters to transport goods

MAP IT

1. You are a television news reporter. Your assignment is to report on how people are helping each other survive the flood. On June 26 you arrive in flooded St. Paul, Minnesota. Look at the map. What is the name of the river that runs through St. Paul?

2. The Mississippi River is rising. You know that floodwaters will continue downstream. Use your finger to trace the route of the river from St. Paul to the city of Clinton. In what state is Clinton?

3. It is July 5, and the Mississippi River overflows at Clinton. Farmland becomes flooded. You travel south to Illinois and the site of more flooded farms. What city are you near in Illinois?

4. You next go to Nebraska City, where the Missouri River is rising. Use your finger to trace the route of the Missouri River as it flows downstream. What other cities will you need to visit to report on the flood before you reach the state of Arkansas?

EXPLORE IT

Put your finger on New Orleans and travel north on the Mississippi. Name the cities and states affected by the flood. How do you think this flood affected the lives of people?

How States Were Made

FOCUS *The 13 colonies became the first 13 states. As time went on, the United States grew larger as more states were added. Our states have many things in common.*

The First 13 States

The United States is made up of 50 states. Each state has a story to tell about how and why it became a state and about the people who helped shape its history.

When people from Europe first began coming to this land in the 1600s and 1700s, they settled on the eastern coast. The areas where they settled were called **colonies**. In all, there were 13 colonies. The names of the colonies are in red type on the time line on page 41.

These colonies belonged to Great Britain. People in the colonies did not make laws for themselves. Instead they followed Great Britain's laws.

Many colonists wanted to have the right to make their own laws. They banded together and fought Great Britain in a war called the **American Revolution**. The colonists won the war and began to plan the first government of our country.

Leaders in the colonies agreed on how the government of the new country should be set up. They wrote a document

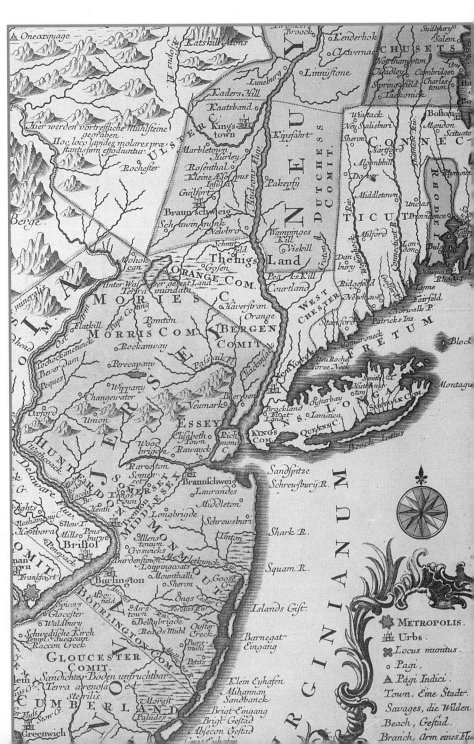

colony   A territory settled by people from a distant land but under the control of that land
American Revolution   The war between Great Britain and its 13 colonies from 1775 to 1783

These dates show when the states became part of the United States. States in red type are the original 13 colonies.

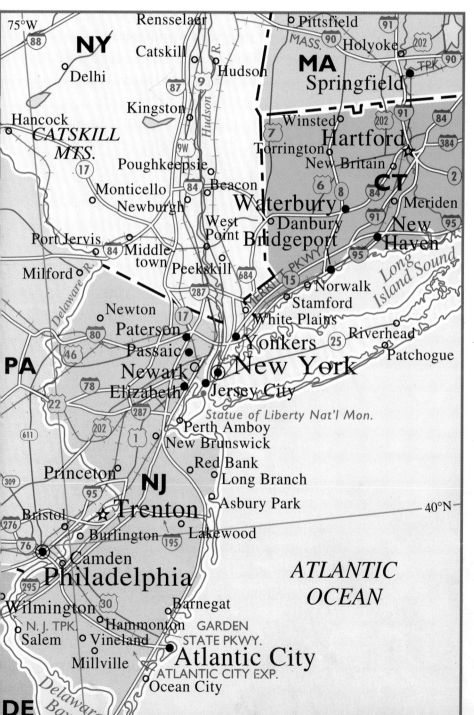

called the **Constitution of the United States**. It explained the new government and the rights of the people. The Constitution also called the colonies by a new name—states.

Some people from each of the 13 colonies signed the Constitution and made it into law. The original colonies now became the first states.

State Boundaries

All states have boundaries. Some of these are natural boundaries, such as rivers, coastlines, or mountains. Other boundaries are lines drawn on maps.

The Delaware River forms the western boundary of New Jersey. The Atlantic Ocean is the eastern boundary. Delaware Bay is its southern boundary. The northern boundary is a line on a map that separates New Jersey and New York.

Sometimes, boundaries change on a map. You can see examples of this kind of change when you look at old maps. Many early maps had boundaries that no longer exist today. Look at the 200-year-old map on page 40. Then compare it with the modern map on this page. How have the boundaries of some states changed? What other changes can you see?

 Constitution of the United States   The document that contains the basic laws of the United States

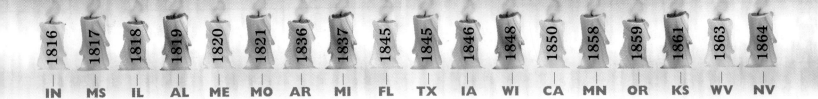

| 1816 | 1817 | 1818 | 1819 | 1820 | 1821 | 1836 | 1837 | 1845 | 1845 | 1846 | 1848 | 1850 | 1858 | 1859 | 1861 | 1863 | 1864 |
| IN | MS | IL | AL | ME | MO | AR | MI | FL | TX | IA | WI | CA | MN | OR | KS | WV | NV |

Territories

Becoming a state grew more complicated as time went on. People started living beyond the area of the first 13 states. When people settled a new section of land, this land was called a territory. When a territory had at least 60,000 people, it could become a new state.

People in a territory first had to agree on the rules for governing themselves. The rules were written into a state constitution. Then the territory asked to become a state. The United States government then voted to make the territory into a new state.

Surveying New Land

By 1785, more and more settlers were moving west and living outside the original 13 states. Thomas Jefferson, our third President, came up with a plan to mark off the land in squares. He made a map with lines running north to

A surveyor's compass ▶

Map:
115°W · 110°W · CANADA · 105°W
49°N
N / W-E / S
Montana
Idaho
45°N

IDAHO AND MONTANA BOUNDARY LINES
— International boundary
— Idaho - Montana boundary
— Other state boundaries

south and east to west. This divided the land into townships. Each township was in the shape of a square. Each side of the square was 6 miles long.

People who marked off the land were called surveyors. By 1803, surveyors were dividing up the land around the Mississippi River. As settlers moved west, a map of the United States began to look like a checkerboard!

Drawing Boundaries

Many state boundaries had to be drawn on maps. They sometimes followed lines of latitude and longitude. This is why some states in the central and western parts of the country are rectangular in shape.

Look at the map of Montana and Idaho on this page. These states share boundaries with the country of Canada. On a map, these boundaries are set at a line of latitude called the 49th parallel. This makes the northern boundaries of these states a straight line.

1867	1876	1889	1889	1889	1889	1890	1890	1896	1907	1912	1912	1959	1959
NE	CO	ND	SD	MT	WA	ID	WY	UT	OK	NM	AZ	AK	HI

State Government

Each state in our country differs in its geography and history. But the states also have many things in common.

Each state has a **governor** elected by the people of the state. Each state also has its own government. Different parts of state government do different jobs, such as making laws and deciding how money collected from **taxes** will be spent.

Most states are divided into counties. In Louisiana the counties are called parishes, and in Alaska they are called boroughs.

⭐ **governor** The top elected official of a state or other political unit

tax Money that people must pay to support the government

The citizens of each state live by the laws of their state. They pay taxes to the state government, and the people vote for elected officials in their state. People of a state benefit from the education, parks, and other things that the state has to offer.

HOW TO MAKE A STATE

Ingredients: land, people, work, pride

Directions: Open one large territory and divide it into sections. Add a hard-working population that cares about the land. Sift in rules and rights for all people. Simmer slowly and stir frequently. Season well with a pinch of pride. Remove from heat and serve on the Fourth of July.

SHOW WHAT YOU KNOW!

REFOCUS
COMPREHENSION

1. What is a boundary? What are two types of boundaries?

2. What are some things that states have in common?

THINK ABOUT IT
CRITICAL THINKING

Why do you think rules were needed before a territory could become a state?

STATE CHECK
ACTIVITY

In what year did your state become a state? Look up the story of how your state became one of the 50 states.

SUMMING UP

1 DO YOU REMEMBER...
COMPREHENSION

1. What are some landform regions in the United States?

2. Which states are found in the Middle Atlantic region? Which states are in the New England region?

3. What caused the great Mississippi flood of 1993?

4. Why do some states in the Midwest and West have rectangular shapes?

5. What are some things that all our states have in common?

2 SKILL POWER
USING SPECIAL-PURPOSE MAPS

What is a special-purpose map? Give two examples of information that you can show on a special-purpose map. Why is it helpful to display information in this way?

3 WHAT DO YOU THINK?
CRITICAL THINKING

1. Create a region of the country that you think would be an ideal place to live. Describe its climate, landforms, and natural resources.

2. Choose two regions of the country as they are described on pages 35 to 37. Read the descriptions of the landforms in the two regions. How is the geography of the regions similar? How is it different?

3. During the great flood of 1993, barges were not able to travel north of St. Louis. What effects do you think this might have had on rail and highway transportation?

4. Why, do you think, did settlers in the 1600s and 1700s live mainly along the eastern coast of this country?

5. Why was it necessary for surveyors to mark off the land in the territories of the United States?

4 SAY IT, WRITE IT, USE IT
VOCABULARY

Suppose that you were one of the first people to explore and survey a region of the United States. Write about your experience. Use as many of the key terms as possible in your writing.

American Revolution	desert	plain
barge	foothill	prairie
canyon	geography	precipitation
colony	governor	region
Constitution of the United States	heritage	tax
	industry	temperature

CHAPTER 2

Vote on Election Day

5 GEOGRAPHY AND YOU
MAP STUDY

Use the map below to answer the following questions.

1. Name each of the seven regions as they are numbered on the map.

2. Which region has the Pacific Ocean as a natural boundary?

3. Which regions have the Atlantic Ocean as a natural boundary?

4. How many regions have Canada as all or part of their northern boundaries?

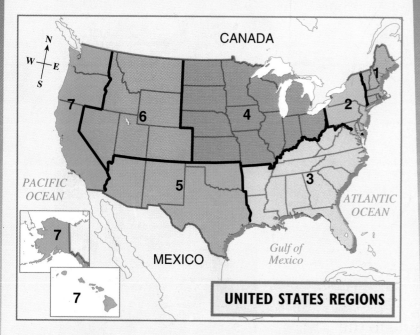

UNITED STATES REGIONS

6 TAKE ACTION
CITIZENSHIP

On page 43 you read that each state has its own government. The people of the state elect who should run the government and make the laws for their state.

Investigate the requirements for voting in your state. Then work with a group of classmates to prepare posters or other displays to encourage people to vote. Display your posters in a public place before the November election.

7 GET CREATIVE
LANGUAGE ARTS CONNECTION

Create a brochure that will attract tourists to your region of the country. List the main features of your region that visitors might enjoy. Illustrate your brochure with images that capture your region in a special way.

LOOKING AHEAD

Explore in the next chapter the first of seven regions that you will study—New England.

Doorway TO THE Eastern Regions

What Three Regions Are in the Eastern United States?

Travel from the northern boundary of Maine to the southern tip of Florida to discover the states that make up the regions of the eastern United States. Learn about the geography, people, and events that have shaped each region.

New England

New England is a region rich in history, natural resources, and places to visit. Learn about this region—its past and present—in this chapter.

CONTENTS

◀ Do you know what this girl is doing? Find out when you read page 67.

These books tell about some of the people, places, and events that are special to the New England region. Read one that interests you and fill out a book-review form.

READ AND RESEARCH

A New England Scrapbook: A Journey Through Poetry, Prose, and Pictures by Loretta Krupinski
(HarperCollins Publishers, 1994)
Discover the beauty of New England by taking a journey through the pages of this book. *(poetry)*
•*You can read a selection from this book on page 60.*

Return of the Sun: Native American Tales From the Northeast Woodlands by Joseph Bruchac, illustrated by Gary Carpenter (The Crossing Press, 1990)
You will read stories from many different Native American groups, including the Penobscot and Abenaki. *(folk tale)*

N. C. Wyeth's Pilgrims by Robert San Souci
(Chronicle Books, 1991)
Read about the Pilgrims who came to Plymouth, Massachussetts, in search of religious freedom. *(nonfiction)*

The Farm Summer, 1942 by Donald Hall, pictures by Barry Moser (Dial Books, 1994)
Peter travels from San Francisco to New Hampshire over 50 years ago to spend the summer on his grandparents' farm. *(fiction)*

Skill POWER

Using Primary Sources

Using primary sources helps you learn important information about the past.

UNDERSTAND IT

There are many ways to find out about the past, but the best source you can use is a primary source. Primary sources are original sources of information. They can be written records, such as letters and newspaper articles, or objects, such as photographs and tools.

Has anyone in your family saved any old letters? A letter might say how long it took to make a certain trip years ago. A letter might also tell you what people did for fun or how they dressed long ago.

EXPLORE IT

E. B. White is the author of *Charlotte's Web*, a children's book written in 1952. You can see a picture of E. B. White's farmhouse on this page. You can also see part of a letter he wrote to a group of students. The photograph and letter are primary sources that give us information about E. B. White's life.

Study the photograph and the letter. What can you learn about E. B. White from these primary sources?

26 December 1952

Dear Pupils of 5-B:

I was delighted to get your letters telling me what you thought about "Charlotte's Web."

...It is true that I have a farm.... My barn is big and old, and I have ten sheep, eighteen hens, a goose, a gander, a bull calf, a rat, a chipmunk, and many spiders.... I didn't like spiders at first, but then I began watching one of them, and soon saw what a wonderful creature she was and what a skillful weaver. I named her Charlotte, and now I like spiders along with everything else in nature.

I'm glad you enjoyed the book, and I thank you for the interesting letters.

Sincerely,
E. B. White

TRY IT

With a group of your classmates, go on a search for primary sources. Find old photographs in books in your library and make photocopies of them. Write the dates of the photos on the photocopies. Look for different kinds of photos, such as city streets, country scenes, family portraits, and news photos.

When you have finished, exchange primary sources with another group in your class. Carefully study this group of photographs. Then make a list of the things your group has learned from the photographs. If you want to make a primary source streamer, tape all the lists of the class together.

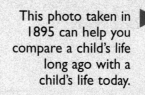

◀ Many families keep photo albums to remember the past. Photos are good examples of primary sources.

This photo taken in 1895 can help you compare a child's life long ago with a child's life today. ▶

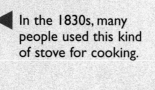

◀ In the 1830s, many people used this kind of stove for cooking.

SKILL POWER SEARCH *Look through this chapter. What primary sources can you identify?*

1

Setting the Scene

⭐ **KEY TERMS**

Native American
ancestor
elevation
economy
manufacture

What Is New England?

FOCUS *The New England region is in the northeastern part of the United States. Beginning with the first settlers here, people have made good use of the region's natural resources.*

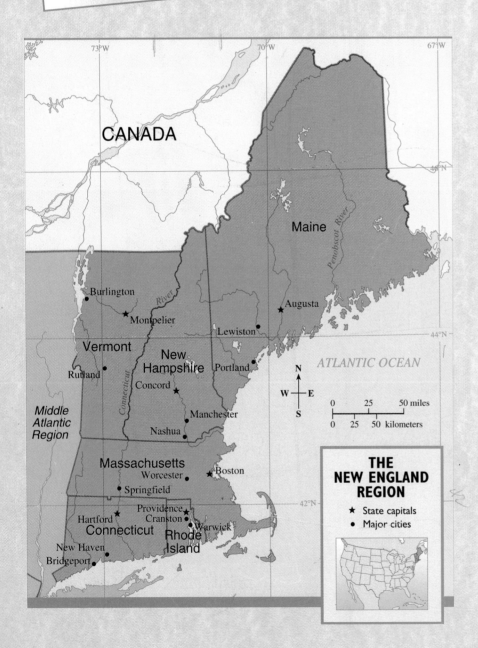

THE
NEW ENGLAND
REGION

★ State capitals
• Major cities

Where Is New England?

You can begin to explore the New England region without even leaving your chair if you use your imagination and the map on this page. For example, you can see that New England includes the states of Connecticut, Rhode Island, Massachusetts, New Hampshire, Vermont, and Maine.

The map also shows that the Atlantic Ocean is a boundary to all of the New England states except one—Vermont. Even New Hampshire has a short coastline on the Atlantic Ocean.

Canada is located to the north of New England. So the northern boundaries of Maine, New Hampshire, and Vermont form part of the boundary between the United States and Canada.

The eastern tip of Maine is the farthest east you can travel without leaving the United States.

Handmade tools of stone and wood helped Native Americans hunt, fish, and farm.

The First Americans

New England has a harsh climate, with long, cold winters. Thousands of years ago, **Native Americans**, who were living in the land now called New England, learned how to fish, hunt, and farm. They survived the New England winters by building strong houses and by burning wood for cooking and heating. They preserved, or dried, their food so that it lasted for many months.

In some areas of New England, Native Americans built long houses in which eight to ten families lived.

Most Native Americans lived in the river valleys or along the coast where the land was flat. They grew vegetables such as squash, corn, and beans. There were plenty of fish in nearby waters. Small animals were another source of food.

Native American Groups

As their numbers grew, Native Americans in New England formed into many different groups. The Wampanoag group lived in the area now called Massachusetts. In Rhode Island there were Narragansett Indians. Members of both groups still live in these areas today.

Each group had its own language, beliefs, and ways of doing things. But the different groups all came from common **ancestors** called the Algonquians (al GAHNG kee unz). They all were successful at using the land around them—to hunt, trap, fish, and farm—for survival.

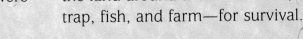

Native American A member of the first group of people who settled and lived in North America

ancestor A person or group of people from whom someone is descended

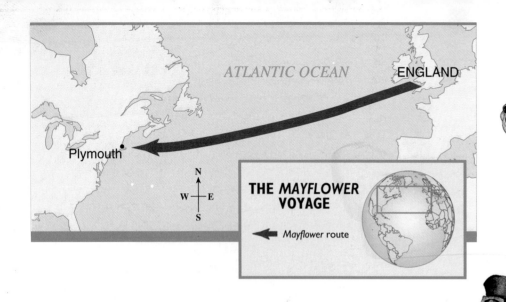

ATLANTIC OCEAN

ENGLAND

Plymouth

N
W — E
S

THE MAYFLOWER VOYAGE

← Mayflower route

The Pilgrims' trunks contained needed items and other things that made them feel comfortable in their new home.

Pilgrim Settlers

Suppose you left your home to live in a faraway land. You traveled on a ship crowded with people and animals. All your belongings were packed into one trunk. The journey was long and hard.

This was just how the first people from Europe came to New England. On the map above find the route of the *Mayflower*, a ship from England that landed on the coast of today's Massachusetts in 1620.

Most of the passengers on board were known as Pilgrims. They had left England to be free to have their own religion in North America. The place where they settled became known as Plymouth.

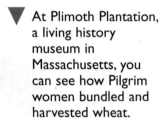

At Plimoth Plantation, a living history museum in Massachusetts, you can see how Pilgrim women bundled and harvested wheat.

Puritans

In 1629, another group of English settlers came to New England. They were Puritans. The Puritans came because they wanted to change the way they had been required to practice their religion in England.

The Puritans settled in the area of Massachusetts Bay. Once they arrived in the new land, they built houses and started small businesses and farms. Over time their settlement grew into a large colony called the Massachusetts Bay Colony. Today, the city of Boston is located near their settlement of long ago.

Farming in New England

Many of the early New England settlers farmed along the Atlantic Coastal Plain. The Atlantic Coastal Plain is a flat area along the Atlantic Ocean. In the New England region, the Atlantic Coastal Plain is very narrow. And so, there were no large farms along the coast.

Some settlers took up farming in valleys such as the Connecticut River valley where the soil was rich. The rest of the region was rocky, but supported small farms. Find the Green Mountains of Vermont and the White Mountains of New Hampshire on the map.

These mountains were high and had steep slopes. The height of a place above sea level is known as its **elevation**. You will learn more about elevation in Chapter 4.

⭐ **elevation**   The height of something, often in relation to sea level

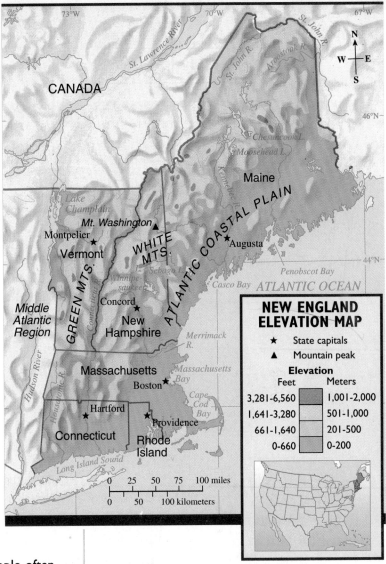

NEW ENGLAND ELEVATION MAP

★ State capitals
▲ Mountain peak

Elevation

Feet	Meters
3,281-6,560	1,001-2,000
1,641-3,280	501-1,000
661-1,640	201-500
0-660	0-200

▼ Young people often worked 12-hour days in New England mills.

Lumber and Cloth Mills

As time went on, New Englanders learned to use other natural resources around them in many ways. They cut down trees and sawed them into logs. The logs were carried to mills and made into lumber to build ships, houses, furniture, wagons, and other items.

Later, New Englanders worked in mills that produced cloth. During the 1800s there were many mills like the one shown on this page.

Greetings from New England

From cranberry growing to mountain climbing, New England resources are used by people throughout the country.

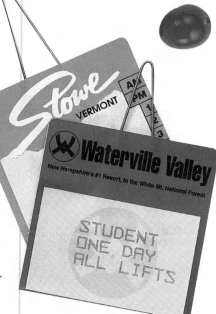

For hundreds of years, many New Englanders have looked to the sea to make their living. People of New England still use the natural resources of the ocean in many ways. Fishing and lobstering are important to the **economy** of this region.

People also use the ocean for relaxation and fun. Whale-watching off the New England coast is a popular event. Sailing is another popular form of recreation. Can you name something you like about the ocean?

New England has many clean, clear lakes and miles of sandy beaches. While you're on the coast, you might try some tasty seafood, such as Maine lobster or New England clam chowder.

New England's Economy

You could have a lot of fun planning a trip to New England because there is something here for everyone. Tourism in the summer and winter is big business in this region of the country.

The mountains of Maine, New Hampshire, and Vermont are both beautiful and peaceful. In the summer, camping and hiking are popular mountain activities.

New England mountains are also busy in the winter, when thousands of skiers flock to these snowy slopes to have fun.

New England's cold winter climate and snow-covered mountains make skiing a popular sport.

 economy The production and distribution of goods and services

NEW ENGLAND

From Syrup to Cranberries

Some people can't wait to get to Vermont to try some pure maple syrup. In the early spring, you might see people in the woods tapping maple trees to get sap for making syrup. Cranberries grow well in the state of Massachusetts. In fact, more cranberries are grown each year in Massachusetts than in any other state in the country.

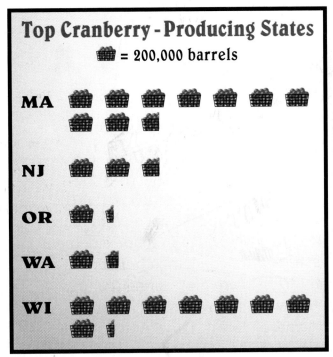

Top Cranberry - Producing States

🧺 = 200,000 barrels

MA	🧺	🧺	🧺	🧺	🧺	🧺	🧺
	🧺	🧺	🧺				
NJ	🧺	🧺					
OR	🧺						
WA	🧺						
WI	🧺	🧺	🧺	🧺	🧺	🧺	🧺
	🧺						

From Mills to Factories

The English settlers who came to New England were called Yankees. They were known for their hard work and clever inventions. For example, the invention of a machine that spun cotton into thread helped to make New England a leading region for making products. Today, New England is still a **manufacturing** region.

Along many New England rivers are old mills that used water power to grind grain into flour. In other mills, water power was used to run machines that wove cloth or cut lumber. If you visit the mills in Lowell in the state of Massachusetts, you can see how mill workers lived and worked in the 1800s.

The mills of early New England have been replaced by modern factories. From shoes to clocks, New England's factories produce goods that people all over the United States use.

manufacture To make or process something by using machinery

REFOCUS
COMPREHENSION

1. What natural resources did Native Americans in the New England region use to survive?

2. Why is tourism big business in the New England region?

THINK ABOUT IT
CRITICAL THINKING

What were some of the hardships the Puritans and Pilgrims faced when they came to a new land?

STATE CHECK
ACTIVITY

Find out about the first group of people to live in your state. In your state scrapbook draw a map of your state and show where these first people lived.

March of Time

1617 TO 1773

LITERATURE
A New England Scrapbook

New England Long Ago

FOCUS *Follow some important events in the early history of this region.*

NATIVE AMERICANS

In the year 1600 about 20 groups of Native Americans lived in what is now the New England region. In the summer they fished and raised corn and other vegetables. When fall arrived, they moved their villages close to places where they could hunt through the winter.

The Massachusett people numbered about 3,000, scattered in 20 coastal villages. They used birch bark to make canoes and cone-shaped dwellings.

In 1617 a deadly disease spread rapidly through the region. It wiped out most of the Massachusett group.

LIFE AT PLYMOUTH

In 1620 the ship *Mayflower* found its way to Plymouth Rock in Massachusetts. The new settlers agreed to make a new life in their settlement called Plymouth. But many of them died during the first hard winter at Plymouth.

Two Native Americans in the area, Squanto and Samoset, helped the Pilgrims build homes and plant crops. When the fall of 1621 arrived, the Pilgrims, and the Native Americans who had helped them, celebrated the first harvest of the Plymouth settlement. Each year the United States remembers that celebration in the national holiday Thanksgiving.

MASSACHUSETTS BAY COLONY

Five English ships crowded with Puritans sailed into Massachusetts Bay in 1629. Like the Pilgrims of Plymouth, the Puritans wished to escape their hard life in England and build a better future.

The Puritans were hard-working and expected much from each other. Each person also had to attend church every Sunday. There were many rules to follow.

| 1617 | 1621 | 1629 | 1773 | 1773 |
| Disease strikes Native Americans | The first Thanksgiving is celebrated | Puritans settle in Massachusetts | Colonists protest tea tax | Phillis Wheatley's poems are published |

| 1600 | 1620 | 1640 | 1660 | 1680 | 1700 | 1720 | 1740 | 1760 | 1780 |

BOSTON TEA PARTY

Sixty colonists dressed as Indians silently climbed aboard three British ships docked at Boston Harbor. They dumped the ships' cargoes overboard. It was December 16, 1773. The colonists were angry because of the new tax on tea. All tea brought into the colonies had to be carried on the ships of a single British company. The tea was now even more expensive because of the British tax.

England had already made settlers pay a tax on stamps. Both of these new taxes had made the colonists angry. What gave England the right to rule the settlers of faraway New England?

To show their anger, the men of Boston dumped 90,000 pounds of tea into the water. To punish them, England passed even stricter laws and closed Boston Harbor. That made the colonists more determined than ever to break away from England.

PHILLIS WHEATLEY

In 1761, an African girl was bought from a slave ship to become part of the family of Boston merchant John Wheatley. Phillis wrote her first poem when she was just a teenager. When she became ill, the Wheatleys sent her to England, hoping for a cure. Phillis Wheatley became the first black woman poet in the colonies when her only book, *Poems on Various Subjects*, was published in 1773.

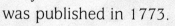

A New England Scrapbook

A Journey Through Poetry, Prose, and Pictures

by Loretta Krupinski

When the Pilgrims arrived in Plymouth in December of 1620, the land appeared bleak and empty to them. A year later, the first harvest was a time for a special celebration.

The First Thanksgiving

For a long time
all we knew was the hiss
and heave of the sea
the empty shore.

Our little ship
has such a springtime name—
MAYFLOWER—like an armful
of bright blooms
from the garden!

But rocking there last fall
in the cold harbor
we wondered if a single
flower
ever grew in this hard land.

We sat chained
to the long dark days
until a warm wind
twisted sunlight through our hair
beat down on the new
rooftops.

It filled the woods with
mayflowers
and pulled green leaves
of corn
up from the earth.

Now summer has come
and gone, and we have
survived.

We give thanks.
The wind and the sea
are cold again
but fire blazes on the hearth
and the harvest is golden
in our hands.

—Barbara Juster Esbensen

Do you want to discover what makes New England special today? You can read about its remarkable sights by checking the book out of your school or public library.

SHOW WHAT YOU KNOW!

REFOCUS
COMPREHENSION

1. How did the tradition of Thanksgiving begin?

2. What were the colonists' reasons for dumping tea into Boston Harbor?

THINK ABOUT IT
CRITICAL THINKING

What effects did the seasons have on the people in the poem?

STATE CHECK
ACTIVITY

Find out about the first Native Americans in your state. In your state scrapbook write about their homes, food, clothing, and ways of life.

Citizenship

KEY TERMS

cove
mammal
extinct
port
pollution
overfishing

To Fish or Not to Fish?

FOCUS *Fishing and shipbuilding have been important to New England's economy for a long time. But what is the future of these two businesses?*

Early Fishing

Food from the sea helped the earliest settlers in New England survive. As the population grew, colonists began to count on the sea as a way to earn money as well as to provide food. Fishing grew into an industry. New England **coves** and harbors sheltered fishing boats that caught oysters, lobsters, and clams as well as fish. In addition to fishing boats, the colonists built fast sailing ships to carry their cargoes.

Dried and salted fish from New England was shipped long distances. The preserved fish was a source of protein for many people.

Whaling

The sailors of New England also hunted whales, which are among the largest **mammals** in the sea. During the 1800s more than 300 whaling ships sailed out from Nantucket and New Bedford in Massachusetts. They brought back millions of dollars' worth of cargo year after year.

People of Connecticut too earned income from whaling. Whale fat supplied oil for lamps, and whalebones were used in clothing and for carving.

▲ Whale oil was used in lamps, like this one, to light homes.

▼ Today, whaling is against the law in the U.S. Saving the whale is saving an important resource of Earth.

WHALE FACTS

In the early 1800s, American fishers used parts of the whale in various ways.

WHALE PART	PRODUCT
blubber	candles
intestines	perfume
mouth plates	fishing rods
	umbrellas

cove A small sheltered body of water
mammal An animal that is warmblooded and has a backbone

By the early 1900s, hunters had caught so many whales that there were few left in the ocean. Even by the late 1800s, some kinds of whales were almost **extinct**.

Protecting Whales

People finally began to worry about the future of the world's whales. They established an organization called the International Whaling Commission to limit how many whales could be caught each year by each country.

The oceans will never again contain the wealth of whales that helped the New England colonies to grow. In fact, some whales may become extinct if the fishers of today hunt too many of them.

New England Shipping

Shipbuilding developed along with the fishing industry. Fishers needed sturdy boats to master rough weather. To make money, colonists needed ships to get their catch to markets outside of the New England region.

▲ Shipbuilding in the 1800s required a variety of resources, including workers with special skills.

Soon the people of New England began shipping other goods from market to market. Seamen sailed to China and other places around the world. They took with them goods from New England and returned with spices and other goods to sell.

The **port** of Boston became a major trade center. Boston Harbor was home to ships that circled the world. Ships delivered cotton, rice, and tobacco from southern farms to Boston. And they left the harbor loaded with New England goods to deliver around the world.

Building Ships

The town of Mystic, Connecticut, became one of the most important centers for shipbuilding during the mid-1800s. More than 300 ships

---

 extinct Having no more living members; having died out

 port A place on a river, lake, or ocean where ships can safely unload and load supplies

were constructed in the shipyards of Mystic and launched to sail the world. Many of them were graceful clipper ships, whose sails made them among the fastest ships on the ocean.

The shipbuilding industry lives on in Connecticut, but the kind of ship that is built there has changed. Submarine building is now a major industry. The town of Groton (GRAHT un) is known as the Submarine Capital of the World.

Fishing Slows Down

In the 1960s, fishing slowed in New England—there just weren't as many fish in the sea as there used to be. By the late 1980s, some areas that had become known for having huge numbers of fish had hardly any fish left.

Modern inventions have made it possible to catch more fish than before— perhaps too many.

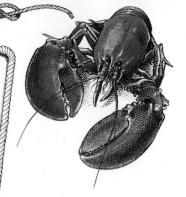

MAINE MENU

MAJOR FISH CAUGHT PER YEAR IN NEW ENGLAND WATERS

Rank	Fish	Millions of pounds
1	Sea Herring	115
2	Cod	61
3	Flounder	53
4	Lobster	52
5	Squid	46

Electronic machines locate and track whole schools of fish so that a ship can catch thousands of fish at one time. **Pollution** from cities also adds to the problem of less fish in the sea. Pollution drains into the world's oceans and harms fish and other sea life.

The Future

As the numbers of fish in the New England waters and in the ocean waters around the world continue to fall, people must deal with the problem in responsible ways. Should modern machines be used for fishing? What should be done about ocean pollution? There is no one correct answer. But to get an idea of the problems faced by today's fishers, read the tough situations on the next page.

pollution Something that makes the air, soil, or water dirty or harmful

Modern fishing boats, such as this trawler, use the latest technology to catch fish in New England waters.

GO FISH!

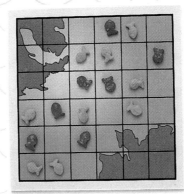

PLAY THE FISHING GAME ... *Make your own decisions about fishing when you play the game of "go fish," described below.*

Suppose you are asked to help solve the problem of **overfishing** in New England. What new laws are needed to make sure there are enough fish for future fishers? But new laws must not cause fishers to lose their jobs.

Work with a partner to make a fishing board like the one shown above. Place 10 game markers, representing fish, on the blue squares of the board. Your goal is to add more fish to the sea so that you have 25 game markers on the board at the end of the game. Take turns reading the numbered statements and following the instructions.

> ⭐ **overfish** To fish so as to use up the supply of fish in certain waters

1. You help make a law that limits the amount of herring each fisher can catch in one day. Add five markers to the board.

2. To keep their jobs, fishers need to catch more cod. Cod are plentiful so you allow them to catch 20 more pounds of cod per day. Take away three markers.

3. You close off a large fishing area so that the number of squid can double. Add seven markers.

4. A fishing area that had been closed is now opened to fishers. Take away two markers.

5. You get local fishers to agree not to use electronic tracking machines for three months in an area where they are allowed to use them. Add six markers.

How will you add your last two pieces to the board? What makes the problem of overfishing hard to solve?

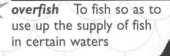

SHOW WHAT YOU KNOW!

REFOCUS
COMPREHENSION

1. What goods did New Englanders ship from Boston Harbor?

2. What problems occur when fishers overfish?

THINK ABOUT IT
CRITICAL THINKING

How might a state that has a big fishing industry be different from other states?

STATE CHECK
ACTIVITY

Look at the map of your state in the States Almanac. In your state scrapbook, list the products that are important to your state's economy.

Welcome to Old Sturbridge Village

FOCUS *Can you guess what life might have been like in the early 1800s? Find out on a trip to Old Sturbridge Village in Massachusetts.*

Welcome to Sturbridge

Yesterday my class rode the school bus to Old Sturbridge Village, not far from Boston, Massachusetts. It is an outdoor museum village that shows you what life was like in the early 1800s. There are houses, water-powered mills, stores, and a farm with cows, sheep, and chickens. When we arrived, the workers at the village were dressed in costumes of that time. They were harvesting crops and making shoes, buckets, and pots. We began our visit at the Pliny Freeman farm, since we would have lived on a farm back then. As we visited the school and other buildings, I began to think about what my life would have been like in 1830.

▲ This recent photograph shows how a store in Sturbridge might have looked in the early 1800s.

Back in Time

It is dark and cold as I run downstairs to put on my pants, stockings, and shoes in front of the kitchen fire. My mother was up early, heating water in kettles to wash clothing. My sisters begin to make breakfast while my father, brothers, and I feed the animals and clean out the barn. Two hours later, we gather in the kitchen for breakfast. The table is piled with beef, cheese, pies, bread, and beans.

▼ Old Sturbridge Village is filled with primary sources. What primary source is shown here?

We younger children walk about a mile to the one-room school. From schoolbooks we bring from home, we learn arithmetic, spelling, and reading. We also use goose **quills** and ink to write lessons in our copybooks. I never miss a day of school because I get to go only three months in the winter.

Home Life

At home, after school, I see all the work that's been done. Clean clothes are drying on the line, and straw has been braided to sell to the storekeeper to make into hats. Corn and potatoes have been gathered and taken to the barn.

We sit near the fire to eat our evening supper of bread and milk. Father says it will soon be cold enough to kill our hog. We will then salt and smoke the meat to preserve it so that it doesn't spoil. Mother will begin making candles from **tallow**. She dips a candle a total of 40 times before it is finished.

Off to the Village

We always look forward to going to the village. Some days, Father takes our extra butter, cheese, and straw to sell at Mr. Knight's store. Father might even purchase some cotton cloth, made at the nearby factory. Next, he might go to the tin shop to have our coffee pot repaired or to the blacksmith to purchase a new bread toaster.

Return to the Present

Just as I begin to think about games I enjoy playing, like one that uses a hoop and stick, I hear the school bus honking its horn. I sure enjoyed learning how people lived long ago, but I'm also glad to get back to my own life again.

◀ A bread toaster and other handmade items from the 1800s can be seen today at Old Sturbridge Village.

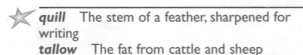

quill The stem of a feather, sharpened for writing
tallow The fat from cattle and sheep

Hartford: A Capital Place to Be

FOCUS *Hartford, Connecticut, is a modern and interesting city and the center of the state's government.*

CONNECTICUT
★ State capital

Dutch and English

The golden dome of the capitol announces that Hartford is the center of government for the state of Connecticut. This city, located on the Connecticut River, has a long history. **Dutch** people built a fort on the site and traded furs with Native Americans. A few years later, in 1635, about 50 English colonists from the Massachusetts Bay Colony moved to the river valley and started a settlement.

Dutch Of or relating to the Netherlands, its people, or its language
suburb An area with homes next to or near a city

A New Look

Today, with a population of about 140,000, Hartford is one of the largest cities in Connecticut. After 1945, many people moved out of the city to live in **suburbs**. The center of the city became run-down. In recent years new buildings have replaced many of the old, worn-out buildings. Hartford is proud of its efforts. One of the first and most successful projects was Constitution Plaza. It is a shining group of two office buildings,

▼ The golden dome of Connecticut's capitol rises above the city of Hartford.

MARK TWAIN'S HOUSE
While Mark Twain lived in this house, he wrote his best-known stories.

OLD STATE HOUSE
Built in 1796, the Old State House was the center of Connecticut's government for nearly 100 years.

CONSTITUTION PLAZA
The buildings in Constitution Plaza are an important part of Hartford's economy.

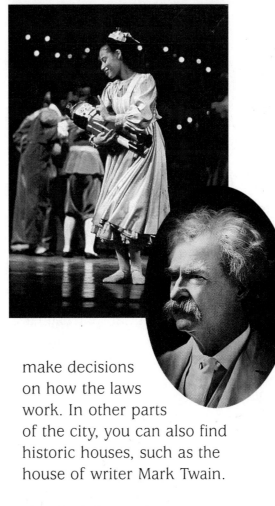

Hartford's many resources include its artists—such as this ballet dancer and the famous American writer Mark Twain.

a hotel, a research center, a garage, and a shopping mall, all spread out across 11 acres.

Hartford's Economy

The economy of Hartford is a balance between business and industry. Many insurance companies have **headquarters** in the city. Factories produce everything from jet engines to makeup. Thousands of people **commute** from nearby towns to work here.

A Center for Government

Like any state capital, Hartford is the center of government. It is the place where decisions are made that affect the entire population. In the marble capitol, people in the government make laws about speed limits, voting, and public education. The Supreme Court building is where judges make decisions on how the laws work. In other parts of the city, you can also find historic houses, such as the house of writer Mark Twain.

Capital Locations

Hartford is located near the center of Connecticut, as the map on page 68 shows. Not all state capitals are near the centers of their states. Over time, some capitals were moved to central locations in their states to make them more convenient to all their citizens. Today, state capitals connect the people of their states in many ways—through government, business, and history.

---

headquarters A center of operations or business

commute To travel back and forth on a regular basis

SHOW WHAT YOU KNOW!

REFOCUS
COMPREHENSION

1. Who were the first settlers of Hartford?

2. What activities take place in a state capital?

THINK ABOUT IT
CRITICAL THINKING

How does life in a state's capital compare with life in another city in the state?

STATE CHECK
ACTIVITY

Find out the capital and the governor of your state. Write a letter to your governor, telling him or her things that you like about your state.

SUMMING UP

1 DO YOU REMEMBER ...
COMPREHENSION

1. Why was farming difficult for the first New England settlers?

2. Why did the Boston Tea Party take place?

3. Why did fishing become an important industry in New England?

4. Why did people build Old Sturbridge Village?

5. Why is Hartford an important city in Connecticut?

2 SKILL POWER
USING PRIMARY SOURCES

Primary sources, such as written records and photos, helped you learn about New England. Create a scrapbook of primary sources that tell about your own region of the country. Collect originals and photocopies of letters, photographs, and other primary sources that reveal something about your region.

3 WHAT DO YOU THINK?
CRITICAL THINKING

1. How did the New England environment influence the ways settlers in New England supported themselves?

2. What opportunities did early settlers have in New England but not in England?

3. Do you think it's important for people to do whatever they can to prevent animals from becoming extinct? Why?

4. Can places like Old Sturbridge Village help people today learn lessons they can use in their everyday lives? Explain.

5. After 1945, many people left cities like Hartford, Connecticut, and moved to the suburbs. What are the advantages of the suburbs? What are the advantages of the cities?

4 SAY IT, WRITE IT, USE IT
VOCABULARY

Suppose that a Puritan child from New England in the 1600s returned to that region today. What change might he or she find most amazing? Write a paragraph in which the child compares "the two New Englands." In your paragraph use as many of the key terms as possible.

ancestor	manufacture
commute	Native American
cove	overfishing
Dutch	pollution
economy	port
elevation	quill
extinct	suburb
headquarters	tallow
mammal	

5 GEOGRAPHY AND YOU
MAP STUDY

Use the map below to answer these questions.

1. Which states make up the New England region?

2. Which states in the New England region have a boundary with Canada?

3. Which capital city in this region is closest to the Atlantic Ocean?

4. Find the approximate latitude and longitude of Augusta, Maine.

THE NEW ENGLAND REGION
★ State capitals
● Major cities

0   25   50 miles
0   25   50 kilometers

6 TAKE ACTION
CITIZENSHIP

Good citizens help protect the land and wildlife of their regions for future generations to enjoy. That's why New Englanders are working to limit fishing and whaling. Find out about animals, plants, and natural areas in your region that are threatened. Make posters that show what the dangers are. With your classmates, discuss how the land and wildlife might be protected.

7 GET CREATIVE
LANGUAGE ARTS CONNECTION

In "The First Thanksgiving" on pages 60–61, Barbara Juster Esbensen expresses her feelings about New England. With your classmates, find poems about your region of the United States. Or try writing your own poem, sharing how you feel about the land and people and history of your region. At a group poetry reading, read aloud the poems you found or wrote.

LOOKING AHEAD Find out in the next chapter how the New England region is connected to other parts of the world.

CHAPTER 4

New England

This chapter will take you from New England to other parts of the world. You'll see how this region is linked to Canada, our neighbor to the north. You'll compare New England with Switzerland.

CONTENTS

Wooden marionettes are fun to play with. Find out about the country that makes such marionettes on pages 82 and 83.

Links Near and Far

The following books will give you information about how New England is connected to the world. Read one that interests you and fill out a book-review form.

READ AND RESEARCH

Planet Earth edited by Jill Bailey and Catherine Thompson
(Oxford University Press, 1993)
From climate to physical features, you will discover exciting facts about the world. Compare the features of the regions you are studying to features of regions around the world. Open your eyes to the similarities and differences of the many places that make up our "planet Earth." *(nonfiction)*

Boston by Ingrid Monke (Silver Burdett Press, 1988)
Have you ever visited the city of Boston? With this book's beautiful photographs, you will be able to explore it all! From history to entertainment and sights, find out why so many people visit this port city every year. *(nonfiction)*

Journey Through Japan by Richard Tames
(Troll Associates, 1991)
Learn about the important seaport city of Tokyo and travel through other parts of Japan in this book that contains colorful photographs. *(nonfiction)*

The Alps and Their People by Susan Bullen
(Thomson Learning, 1994)
Read about the highest mountains in central Europe. Find out why so many people from around the world love to go skiing in the Swiss Alps. *(nonfiction)*

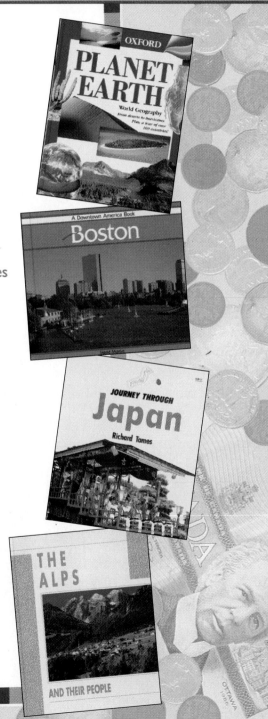

SKILL POWER

Reading an Elevation Map

Knowing how to read an elevation map will help you understand Earth's different landforms and their heights.

UNDERSTAND IT

You know that the surface of the earth is low in some places and a little higher in others. And then there are the great mountain peaks that are the highest places on Earth.

To show the different heights of land, mapmakers create elevation maps. The starting point for measuring and showing the heights of different land areas is at *sea level* because the sea is a level, or flat, place. The height, or *elevation*, of a land area is the land's distance above sea level.

Different heights of land are shown on an elevation map through use of several colors or in shades of one color. A key, or legend, on the map tells the range of feet or meters that each color stands for.

Look at the map key on page 75. You can see that the elevations are shown in feet and meters. Start reading the key at the base, or sea level. Read the range in feet or meters that each color stands for. It's as easy as that!

▲ You can see different elevations in this photograph of Hawaii. Is the elevation of the cliff higher, or lower, than that of the land along the sea?

EXPLORE IT

Now that you know about elevations, you can read an elevation map! The map on this page is of the state of Maine. Remember, as with any map that has a key, you need to read the key first to know what the symbols and colors stand for. Then you can look at the different symbols and colors on the map itself and be able to understand them.

Look at the map key again. What does each of the colors on the key stand for? Now look at the map. What is the elevation of land along the coast of Maine? Where are the highest elevations of land? Where are the lowest?

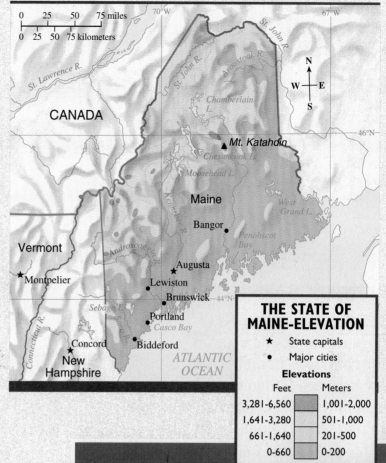

THE STATE OF MAINE-ELEVATION

★ State capitals
● Major cities

Elevations

Feet	Meters
3,281–6,560	1,001–2,000
1,641–3,280	501–1,000
661–1,640	201–500
0–660	0–200

TRY IT

On a sheet of paper, write three questions that can be answered by reading the elevation map. Use the questions asked in Understand It and Explore It as models.

Trade your paper with a partner. Use the elevation map to answer your partner's questions.

SKILL POWER SEARCH

Look through the chapter for another elevation map. What landforms and heights are shown on the map? Be sure to study the map key first.

Setting the Scene

Ties to Other Regions

FOCUS *Canada and the United States are separate countries with a common boundary. The people of both countries share many interests that tie them together.*

Our Northern Boundary

New England shares an **international** boundary with the southern part of Canada. The boundary between Canada and the New England region runs along the northern parts of Vermont, New Hampshire, and Maine, and down the northeastern edge of Maine. Use your finger to trace this boundary on the map on this page.

In some parts of the world, the boundary between two countries is difficult to cross. Mountains and rivers make crossing a boundary more difficult.

People of certain countries are not allowed to cross into other countries. But the boundary between the United States and Canada is a friendly boundary. Even though the United States and Canada are separate countries, people of each country are allowed to cross into the other country.

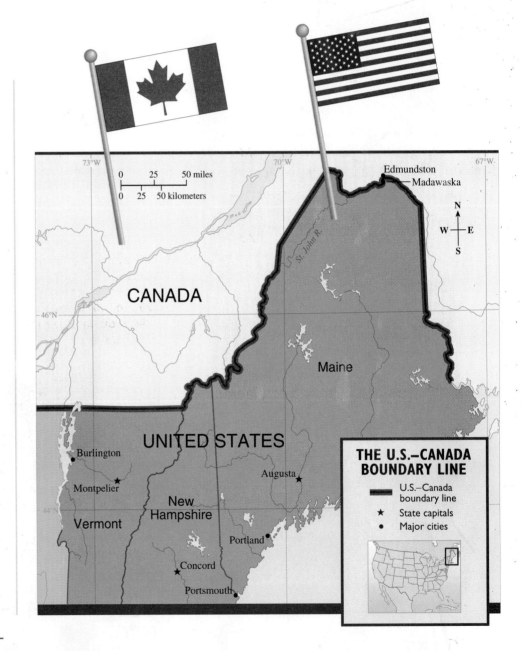

THE U.S.–CANADA
BOUNDARY LINE

— U.S.–Canada boundary line
★ State capitals
● Major cities

---

international Involving two or more countries

If you enter Canada from the United States, you are actually going to a **foreign** country. But you would experience many of the same sights and sounds as in the United States. English and French are Canada's official languages. Many Canadians speak both.

Canadians enjoy many of the same foods that Americans eat. Canadian **currency** uses the same kinds of coins as U.S. currency—quarters, dimes, and pennies. How are the coins on this page alike? How are they different?

An International Family

There are places along the United States–Canada boundary where one city is on the American side and another city lies directly across the boundary line in Canada. People cross the boundary daily. What is life like for people who live so close to a foreign country?

Linda and Claude Beaulieu (boh-LYOO) and their 13-year-old daughter, Michelle, live in Madawaska, Maine. This is a small town of about 4,800 people. Across the international boundary line is

Canada has a two-dollar bill as its smallest paper currency.

Michelle Beaulieu stands on the American side and her parents stand on the Canadian side of the international boundary line.

Edmundston, Canada, a city of about 11,000 people. Find Madawaska and Edmundston on the map on page 76.

The St. John River, shown below, is the natural boundary that separates the United States and Canada here. Mr. Beaulieu works in a paper mill on the St. John River. People from Canada cross over the river daily to work in parts of the mill on the American side.

The ancestors of the Beaulieu family came from France and settled in Canada. Some of these French Canadians later moved to New England towns to get jobs. They decided to stay in New England and in time became American citizens.

---

foreign   Outside a person's own country
currency   The money in use for buying and selling goods

Claude, Linda, and Michelle Beaulieu speak French as well as English. In her school, Michelle studies French as one of her regular subjects. The family is proud of its ancestry.

Daily Life

People cross the bridge from Madawaska to Edmundston to go to work and attend concerts. They enjoy seeing the city's botanical garden and using its bike path. Michelle Beaulieu takes dance lessons in Canada, and the family enjoys going there for horse shows.

Edmundston is a much bigger city than Madawaska. It has a large shopping mall, which the Beaulieu family uses. But many families from Edmundston, Canada, have their favorite shops in Madawaska, too.

American and Canadian sports fans follow their favorite teams in Canada and the United States.

Common Sports

Young people in Madawaska and Edmundston have their own ice-hockey teams. The teams play in the same league, even though they are in different countries.

Because of the cold winter climate, people in both countries have learned to enjoy ice-skating and skiing. Canada and the United States are known for being tough competitors in both of these sports on the professional level.

For years, most professional hockey players were Canadian and most championships were won by Canadian teams. In recent years American teams have done much better. Americans have developed an interest in watching and playing ice hockey.

Among Canadians, a similar interest has developed about baseball. Today, Canada has two professional baseball teams—the Montreal Expos and the Toronto Blue Jays. These common interests in sports bring together the people of the United States and Canada.

◀ Acid rain is destroying this New England forest and harming its wildlife.

The Acid Rain Problem

The governments of Canada and the United States often cooperate to solve problems that affect the people of both countries. One project they are working on together is the problem of acid rain.

Acid rain is regular rain that has combined with air pollution from cars and smokestacks. When acid rain falls on land areas, it eventually kills the trees and plants. The acid rain also harms animals. When it falls on lakes, it can cause damage to the fish. All this destruction has happened over time in the eastern parts of both Canada and the United States.

The problem of acid rain may start in one region of a country. Sooner or later it can affect people in other regions. The pollution in the air comes from places where there are many factories and cars. In the United States some factories produce a lot of this kind of air pollution. Winds carry this polluted air to the east, where it falls on the forests and cities of New England and the eastern part of Canada.

Working Together

Canadian and American officials are acting together to try to solve the acid rain problem. Both countries have new laws to decrease air pollution. People in both countries realize that they are responsible for protecting the environment. They know they have to work together to keep the air clean and healthful.

SHOW WHAT YOU KNOW!

REFOCUS
COMPREHENSION

1. Which New England states share a boundary with Canada?

2. Name two ways the United States and Canada are alike and two ways the countries are different.

THINK ABOUT IT
CRITICAL THINKING

What might you learn by living near the boundary of two countries?

STATE CHECK
ACTIVITY

Find Toronto on a map of Canada. Then on a map of the United States plan a trip to Toronto from your state. In your state scrapbook, describe the route you would take.

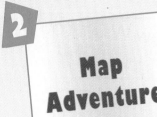

Two Seaport Cities

FOCUS *Seaport cities, such as Boston and Tokyo, are important centers of world trade. These two cities have many similar features.*

Boston and Tokyo

Some of today's busy seaports began as villages on protected **bays**, where boats could dock safely. Colonists settled Boston in the 1600s. The location helped Boston become the biggest city in New England, with about 600,000 people today. Tokyo also developed around a bay. In 1868, Tokyo became the capital of the country of Japan. Today, it has about 9 million people.

Map Key

1 Bays Massachusetts Bay and Tokyo Bay are natural harbors that allow ships to dock safely.

2 Railroads Railroad lines transport people and goods in and out of the cities.

3 Expressways Expressways are large roads on which cars and trucks move around city areas.

4 Airports Each city has a major airport. Logan International Airport serves the Boston area. Haneda Tokyo International Airport serves the Tokyo area.

5 Universities Both cities are educational centers with universities. Boston University and Northeastern University are in the Boston area, and Tokyo University is in Tokyo.

6 Rivers The Charles River runs through Boston, and the Sumida River runs through Tokyo.

⭐ **bay** A part of a lake or an ocean that extends into the shoreline
university A school of the highest level

MAP IT

1. What features do Boston and Tokyo have that help them to be major seaports?
2. What transportation systems link Tokyo and Boston with areas outside those cities?
3. Find Tokyo University on the map. To get to Haneda Tokyo International Airport, how would you travel—by expressway or railroad?
4. Find Northeastern University in Boston. In which direction is Boston University from Northeastern University?

EXPLORE IT

What kinds of jobs do you think might be available in seaport cities, such as Boston and Tokyo?

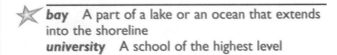

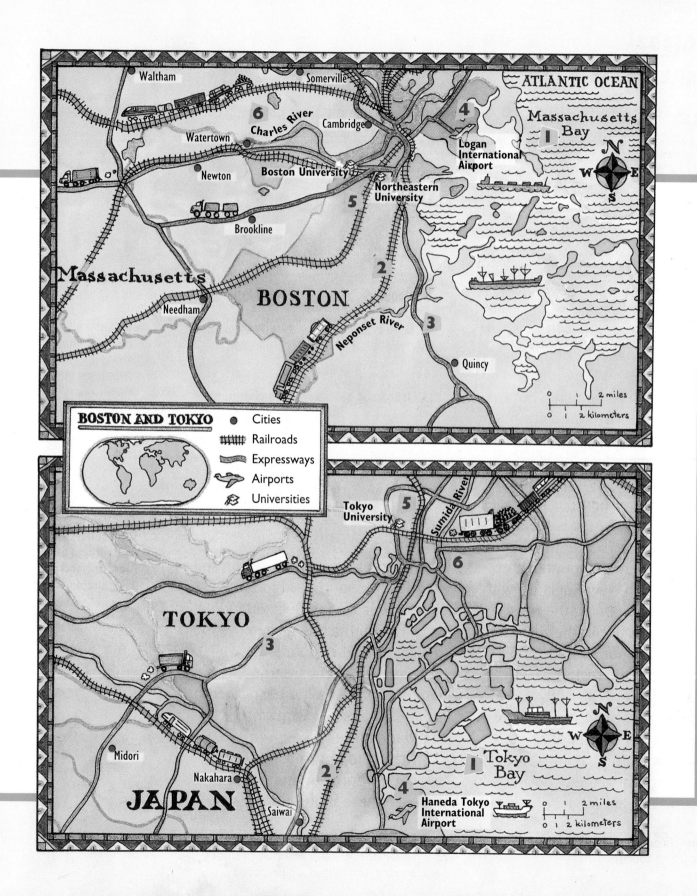

Waltham

Somerville

6

Charles River

Cambridge

Watertown

Boston University

Newton

Northeastern University

5

Brookline

Massachusetts

2

BOSTON

Needham

Neponset River

3

Quincy

ATLANTIC OCEAN

Massachusetts Bay

4

Logan International Airport

1

N W E S

0 1 2 miles
0 1 2 kilometers

BOSTON AND TOKYO

● Cities
░░░ Railroads
〰 Expressways
✈ Airports
⚑ Universities

Tokyo University

5

Sumida River

6

TOKYO

3

Midori

Nakahara

Saiwai

JAPAN

2

4

Haneda Tokyo International Airport

1

Tokyo Bay

N W E S

0 1 2 miles
0 1 2 kilometers

Global Connections

Alike but Different

FOCUS *All places are alike in some ways and different in others. See how the New England region compares with Switzerland, a country in Europe.*

Alike in Many Ways

Thousands of miles separate New England from Switzerland, a country in central Europe. Yet the two areas are alike in many ways.

Switzerland and New England both have high mountains. But the mountains in Switzerland are much higher than those in New England. Called the Swiss Alps, they are part of a mountain region that extends through much of Europe. The tallest peak in the Swiss Alps is Mount Rosa. It reaches 15,203 feet high.

The Appalachian Mountains extend through New England, with New Hampshire being the most mountainous state in the region. Mount Washington, located in New Hampshire, is the region's highest peak at 6,288 feet high.

Both places attract people who enjoy mountain sports, such as skiing, mountain climbing, and hiking. **Tourism** is a key business in both New England and Switzerland.

SWITZERLAND

- Is a country
- Is famous for Swiss cheese
- Manufactures watches and clocks

ALIKE

- Have tall mountains
- Dairy products are important
- Make handmade wooden items

NEW ENGLAND

- Is a region
- Is famous for cheddar cheese
- Produces electronic instruments

▲ This Venn diagram shows ways that Switzerland and New England are alike and different.

Using the Land

In most of New England, the soil is rocky, thin, and hard to farm. The same is true in Switzerland. People in both areas **graze** cows on the slopes of the mountains. Milk and dairy products are important to both economies. Who hasn't heard of Swiss cheese or Vermont cheddar cheese?

Switzerland and most of New England import **raw materials** and then use these materials to make

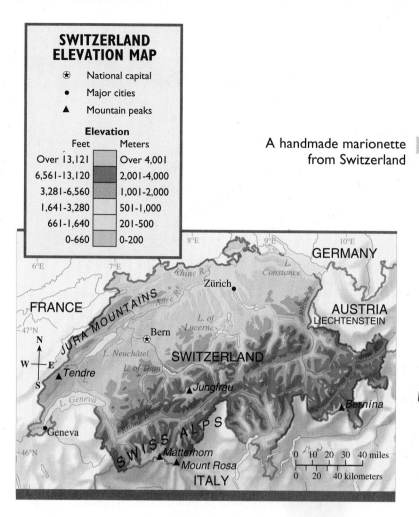

SWITZERLAND ELEVATION MAP

⊛ National capital
• Major cities
▲ Mountain peaks

Elevation

Feet	Meters
Over 13,121	Over 4,001
6,561–13,120	2,001–4,000
3,281–6,560	1,001–2,000
1,641–3,280	501–1,000
661–1,640	201–500
0–660	0–200

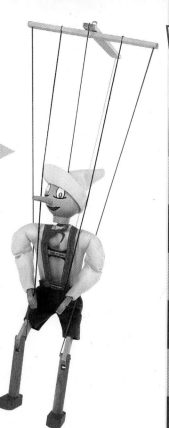

A handmade marionette from Switzerland

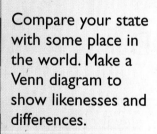

SHOW WHAT YOU KNOW!

REFOCUS
COMPREHENSION

1. In what similar ways do people in New England and Switzerland use their land?

2. What are the large mountain systems in New England and Switzerland?

THINK ABOUT IT
CRITICAL THINKING

Using the elevation map, explain why people enjoy the Swiss countryside.

STATE CHECK
ACTIVITY

Compare your state with some place in the world. Make a Venn diagram to show likenesses and differences.

finished products. Switzerland is famous for its watches and clocks. New England produces electronic instruments and other goods. Both areas are also famous for handmade wooden items.

Seeing the Differences

While New England and Switzerland are alike in many ways, the two areas are also very different. One of the biggest differences is that New England is a region of the United States. It is made up of six different states. Switzerland is one entire country.

But there are some other differences, too, such as language. Switzerland has four national languages—French, German, Italian, and Romansch (roh MAHNSH). People in Switzerland speak one or more of these languages, depending on where they live in the country. In New England, many languages might also be spoken— but English is the one main language of our country.

SUMMING UP

1 DO YOU REMEMBER . . .
COMPREHENSION

1. In what way is the boundary between Canada and the United States a friendly boundary?

2. What are two ways that Canada and the United States are similar?

3. What is acid rain? Why is acid rain a problem?

4. What geographical feature helped Boston and Tokyo become major cities for trade?

5. What landform is found in both Switzerland and New England?

3 WHAT DO YOU THINK?
CRITICAL THINKING

1. Why might people in some countries not be allowed to cross the boundaries into other countries?

2. What are some of the advantages of two countries working together on a problem such as acid rain?

3. Compare a large city in your region with Boston. What do the two cities have in common? How are they different?

4. What might be some reasons that people prefer to live in a port city instead of somewhere else?

5. Switzerland and New England produce watches, electronic equipment, and scientific instruments. What special resources do you think are needed to make these products?

2 SKILL POWER
READING AN ELEVATION MAP

In this chapter, you practiced reading an elevation map of the state of Maine. Now choose a state in the United States that you would like to compare with Maine. Find the two states on the elevation map of the United States in the Atlas at the back of this book. Use a Venn diagram to compare the two states. Be sure to include the elevation of each state in your comparison.

4 SAY IT, WRITE IT, USE IT
VOCABULARY

Write a short paragraph that summarizes what you learned about New England's links to other places in the world. Try to include as many key terms as possible.

bay	international
currency	raw material
foreign	tourism
graze	university

5 GEOGRAPHY AND YOU
MAP STUDY

Use the map below to answer the following questions.

1. What New England states share a boundary with Canada?

2. What New England state has the longest boundary line with Canada?

3. Which community in Vermont is closer to the boundary with Canada—Norton or Montpelier?

4. What city is located at about 44°N latitude and 70°W longitude?

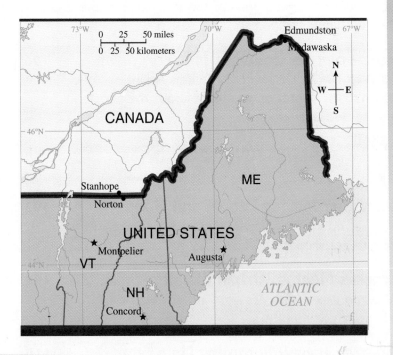

6 TAKE ACTION
CITIZENSHIP

Find out how your region is linked to other countries around the world. Have people from another country settled in your area? Do tourists from other countries visit your region? Are there stores with products from other countries? Now show these links on a large world map.

7 GET CREATIVE
SCIENCE CONNECTION

In this chapter, you learned that acid rain kills plants and fish. Find out more about acid rain or about some other form of air, water, or land pollution. Draw a diagram that shows how the pollution occurs. Show or list the effects of the pollution. Work with a group to brainstorm a list of ways to limit this type of pollution.

LOOKING AHEAD
Find out in the next chapter about exciting things to do and see in the Middle Atlantic region.

Middle Atlantic

Majestic mountains and rich farmland, large cities and rural communities—all are a part of the Middle Atlantic region. In this chapter, discover other features that make this region special.

CONTENTS

What form of transportation does this girl represent? Find out when you read page 105.

Region

These books tell about some people, events, and challenges that relate to the Middle Atlantic region. Read one that interests you and fill out a book-review form.

READ AND RESEARCH

George Washington's Socks by Elvira Woodruff
(Scholastic, 1991)
Join Matt and his friends in a mysterious old rowboat as they adventure back in time to the American Revolution. *(fiction)*
• *You can read a selection from this story on page 98.*

Transportation: Automobiles to Zeppelins
by June English (Scholastic, 1995)
Explore the history of forms of transportation that are found in the Middle Atlantic region and throughout the United States. *(nonfiction)*

The Amazing Impossible Erie Canal by Cheryl Harness
(Simon & Schuster Books for Young Readers, 1995)
Find out why the Erie Canal was so important for America. Let maps transport you from the Hudson River to the Great Lakes. *(nonfiction)*

Trouble at Marsh Harbor by Susan Sharpe
(Penguin Books USA, 1991)
When Ben discovers that someone is dumping oil into Chesapeake Bay, he realizes that the crabs are in trouble. Find out how Ben deals with the situation. *(fiction)*

SKILL POWER Using Time Lines

Using a time line helps you remember when events happened and in what order they occurred.

UNDERSTAND IT

Did you learn to tie your shoelaces before you learned to count, or after? Did you start school the year your brother was born, or the year after?

Sometimes it's hard to keep track of when events happened. A time line is a tool to help you remember. It shows you when and in what order events occurred. If you made a time line of all the places you've visited, you'd have an easy way to see and remember all the places you've gone to.

A time line is divided into equal periods of years, called a scale. The time line on this page is divided into time periods of 20 years each.

EXPLORE IT

The time line below shows you some of the main events in the early history of Maryland. To read the time line, first look at the earliest event shown on the left. Then continue to read the events and dates from left to right. What is the earliest event on the time line? What happened in 1691? What is the most recent event on the time line?

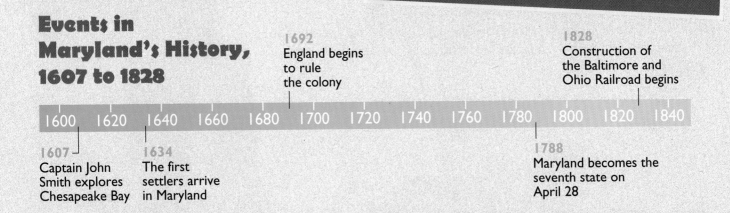

Events in Maryland's History, 1607 to 1828

1692 England begins to rule the colony

1828 Construction of the Baltimore and Ohio Railroad begins

1600 1620 1640 1660 1680 1700 1720 1740 1760 1780 1800 1820 1840

1607 Captain John Smith explores Chesapeake Bay

1634 The first settlers arrive in Maryland

1788 Maryland becomes the seventh state on April 28

Sometimes a time line covers a long period of time. Sometimes it can cover a shorter period. First, make a time line similar to the one on this page. Start with the year you were born and end with the present year. Then make a list of seven or eight events in your life and the years they happened. Place these events on the time line. Have fun decorating your time line with photographs, drawings, or other things that illustrate the events you've listed.

When you're finished, share your time line with a partner. Have you chosen similar important events? Why are these events important to your lives?

I start 4th grade

Tina's Life 1986 to Present

| | | | | August 2 Tina's brother is born | | | | | | September 7 Tina starts 4th grade |

| 1986 | 1987 | 1988 | 1989 | 1990 | 1991 | 1992 | 1993 | 1994 | 1995 | 1996 |

October 19 Tina is born

October 19 Tina's first birthday

September 18 Tina starts preschool

September 9 Tina starts kindergarten

June 6 Tina's first dance recital

My first birthday

SKILL

POWER SEARCH *As you read the chapter, find other groups of events that you can make into a time line.*

89

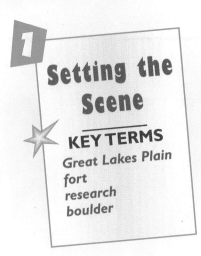

Setting the Scene

KEY TERMS

Great Lakes Plain
fort
research
boulder

An Important Location

FOCUS *The Middle Atlantic region includes five states—Delaware, Maryland, New Jersey, New York, and Pennsylvania—and the city of Washington, D.C., our nation's capital. Their locations and shared history tie them together into one region.*

Between Two Regions

The Middle Atlantic region is not really in the middle of the United States. But the region is located near the middle of the Atlantic coastline. To the north is the colder New England. To the south is the warmer Southeast region. The Atlantic Ocean forms the boundary to the east, as the map on this page shows. And to the west are the rich lands of the Midwest and the Great Plains.

Because of its location, the Middle Atlantic region has been important since colonial times. Early European colonists settled along the coastline, where deep-water harbors sheltered ships. The region also offered early farmers the rich soil of the Atlantic Coastal Plain. This is the flat lowland strip between the mountains of the region and the ocean.

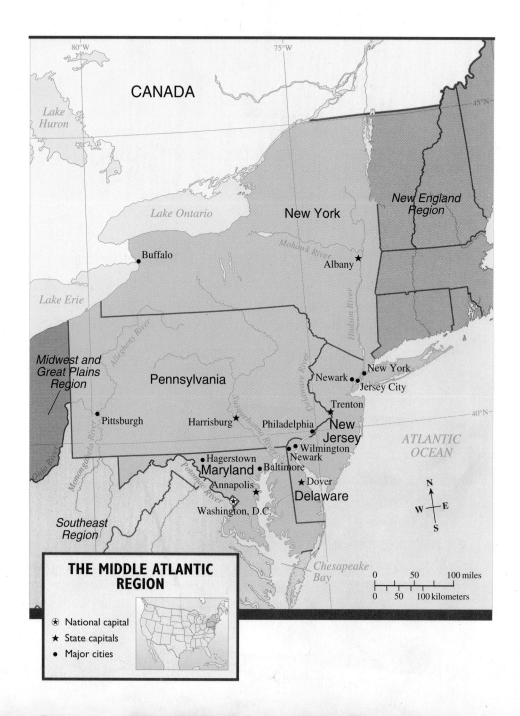

THE MIDDLE ATLANTIC REGION

⊛ National capital
★ State capitals
• Major cities

Mountains and Plains

Except for the Atlantic Coastal Plain and the **Great Lakes Plain**, the region is mostly mountains. Most of these mountains are part of the Appalachian Mountains. In New York there are the Catskill and Adirondack Mountains, and Pennyslvania has its Allegheny Mountains. Find these mountains on the map on this page. In New Jersey, the Kittatinny Mountains are part of the Appalachians.

Early settlers found it very hard work to farm the ridges of the Appalachian Mountains. Yet the mountains offered another kind of living. Their forest-covered slopes offered trees for lumber. And where there was lumber, mills were soon built.

★ **Great Lakes Plain**   Low land that stretches along Lake Erie and Lake Ontario

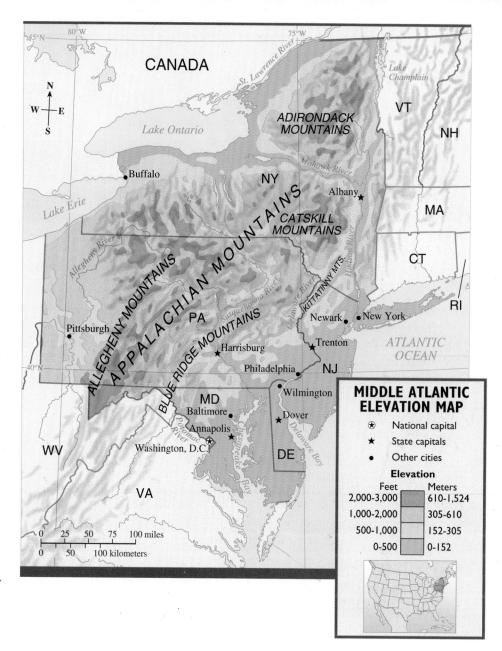

MIDDLE ATLANTIC ELEVATION MAP

⊛ National capital
★ State capitals
• Other cities

Elevation

Feet	Meters
2,000–3,000	610–1,524
1,000–2,000	305–610
500–1,000	152–305
0–500	0–152

Four Middle Atlantic Mountain Facts

Slide Mountain, the highest point in the Catskills, is 4,180 feet high.

Catskill

Spruce Knob, the tallest peak in the Alleghenies, is 4,861 feet tall.

Allegheny

The Kittatinny Mountains contain High Point, which reaches an elevation of 1,803 feet.

Kittatinny

Mount Marcy, the highest peak in the Adirondack Mountains, rises 5,344 feet.

Adirondack

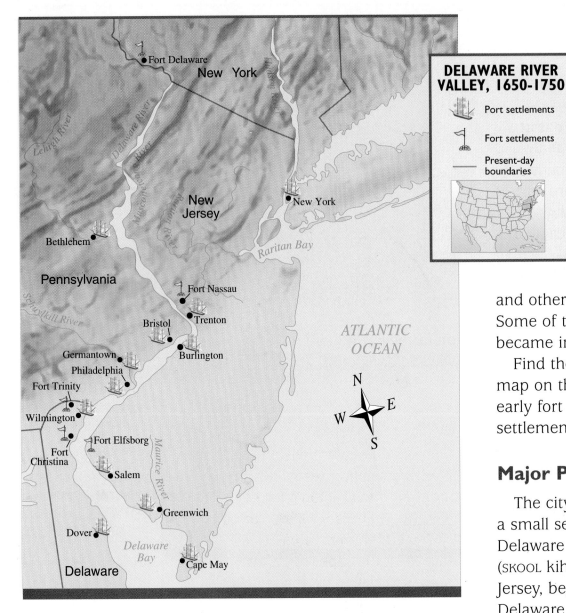

Fort Delaware

New York

New Jersey

Bethlehem

Pennsylvania

Fort Nassau

Bristol
Trenton

Germantown
Burlington

Philadelphia

Fort Trinity

Wilmington

Fort Christina

Fort Elfsborg

Salem

Greenwich

Dover

Delaware

New York

Raritan Bay

ATLANTIC OCEAN

Delaware Bay

Cape May

N
W E
S

DELAWARE RIVER VALLEY, 1650-1750

Port settlements

Fort settlements

Present-day boundaries

River Valley Settlements

Many early settlers chose to live along the waterways in the Middle Atlantic region. Rivers offered a steady source of food as well as a way to travel. River valleys also had rich soil for farming.

Many of the early settlers built **forts** along the Delaware, Hudson, and other rivers in the region. Some of the fort settlements became important ports.

Find the Delaware River on the map on this page. Locate some early fort settlements and settlements that were also ports.

Major Port Cities

The city of Philadelphia began as a small settlement where the Delaware River meets the Schuylkill (SKOOL kihl) River. Trenton, New Jersey, began as a port on the Delaware River. New York City started where the Hudson River meets the Atlantic Ocean. In Maryland, the city of Baltimore was built on Chesapeake Bay. And Washington, D.C., was built on the banks of the Potomac River. The locations of these port cities helped them grow into centers for trade and industry.

 fort A strong building or enclosed area that can be defended against an enemy

Farm Products

The Middle Atlantic region produces a great variety of farm products. Milk is a top dairy product in three states in the region, as the table below shows.

One reason dairy farming is successful in the region is that certain kinds of grasses that dairy cattle eat grow well there. Nearby big cities provide markets for fresh dairy products, such as milk and ice cream.

Delaware and Maryland are big producers of poultry and poultry products. In fact, poultry is the most important source of income for many Delaware farmers.

Fruits and vegetables are also top farm products in the region. New Jersey's rich soil has given this state its nickname—the Garden State. The state is also known for farm **research**. People at universities and

Dairy cows are an important source of farm income in the Middle Atlantic region.

on farms in the state look for new ways to grow crops and to produce even better crops.

From Coal to Crabs

The Middle Atlantic is a region filled with natural resources. In addition to the region's forests and rich soil, there is coal. It is mined in western Pennsylvania. In Maryland, Chesapeake Bay is famous for its crabs, the state's number-one product.

---

research   A careful study or investigation to find facts about a subject

MAJOR FARM PRODUCTS OF THE REGION

STATE	MEAT AND DAIRY	FRUIT	VEGETABLE
Delaware	Broiler Chickens	Apples	Soybeans
Maryland	Broiler Chickens	Apples	Tomatoes
New Jersey	Milk	Cranberries	Tomatoes
New York	Milk	Apples	Sweet Corn
Pennsylvania	Milk	Apples	Sweet Corn

Tall buildings form part of the skyline of New York City, the largest city in the region.

See Our Cities

The Middle Atlantic is a region of many cities—all within a day's car ride of one another. In Philadelphia, visit the Liberty Bell. This bell rang out when the Declaration of Independence was read in Philadelphia in July 1776. In New York City visit the Empire State Building or take a tour through the Wall Street business district.

In Baltimore, you'll find a restored harbor area filled with shops. At the National Aquarium in Baltimore, you'll see thousands of fish, reptiles, and birds. And in Washington, D.C., you can visit famous monuments, tour the White House, or visit the national zoo.

Visit Great Sites

If you were to visit all the sites in this region, you could spend every vacation for years and years and never see the same place twice. Some sites are natural wonders, such as Niagara Falls on the New York State–Canada boundary. These falls occur where the Niagara River plunges more than 150 feet over a wall of rocks and **boulders**.

Or you may decide to visit one of the region's planned sites, such as Hershey Park. This park is located in Hershey, Pennsylvania, the chocolate capital of the country. Here you can visit an amusement park with rides, stroll through downtown streets with names such as Cocoa Avenue, or tour the visitors' center of the Hershey Food Corporation.

 boulder A large rock rounded or worn by the action of water or weather

94

Middle Atlantic

Learn Our History

If you're interested in history, then the Middle Atlantic region is the place to visit. Start at Fort Christina Monument, located in Delaware. This is where the first Swedish settlers built log cabins hundreds of years ago.

During the American Revolution, George Washington and his army spent many months in the region. Visit Morristown, New Jersey, or Valley Forge, Pennsylvania, to get an idea of what life was like during these hard years.

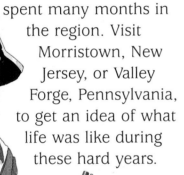

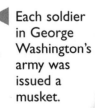

◀ Each soldier in George Washington's army was issued a musket.

Climb New Heights

If you like the outdoors, a perfect vacation spot for you might be the Allegheny National Forest in Pennsylvania. Within its 500,000 acres of forest land, you can fish, boat, or hike.

If you prefer vacationing near the ocean, you might head to New Jersey. Here, over 100 miles of shoreline are sprinkled with beaches that invite you to enjoy the sun and sea.

Or you might climb the stairs to the top of one of the region's many lighthouses, such as the Cape Henlopen Lighthouse, shown below, in Delaware Bay. Lighthouses were built along the region's coastline to keep ships from wandering too close to shore. At the top of one of these lighthouses, enjoy a breathtaking view of the ocean and the Atlantic Coastal Plain.

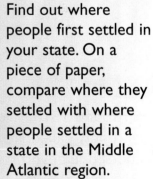

March of Time

1570 TO 1892

LITERATURE

George Washington's Socks

Gone but Not Forgotten

FOCUS *From the first Americans to new Americans arriving as immigrants, the people and events of this region have given the area a rich history.*

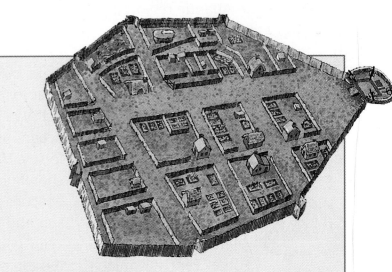

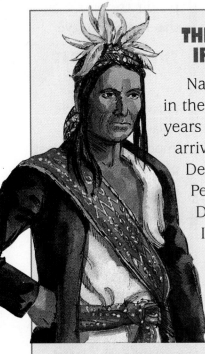

THE LEAGUE OF THE IROQUOIS

Native Americans lived in the region for many years before Europeans arrived. There were the Delaware of New Jersey, Pennsylvania, and Delaware, and the Iroquois of New York. The Delaware and Iroquois were made up of many small groups, sometimes called tribes.

Around 1570, five tribes living in the land now called New York banded together under one government. They formed the League of the Five Nations, or the League of the Iroquois. Uthawah was the chief in the League of the Iroquois.

FORT ORANGE

In 1609, explorer Henry Hudson claimed much of the region's land for the Netherlands, a country in Europe. In 1624, eighteen Dutch families left the Netherlands to journey up the Hudson River. They settled Fort Orange. This was one of the first European settlements in the area. When the English took the region from the Dutch, they renamed the settlement Albany. Today, Albany is New York's capital.

DECLARATION OF INDEPENDENCE

On July 4, 1776, representatives from the 13 colonies met in Philadelphia's Old State House to sign the Declaration of Independence. This document informed England that the colonies were declaring their freedom from British rule. It also stated that the colonies were one country—the United States of America.

1570	1624	1776	1778	1778	1892
League of the Iroquois is formed	Dutch settle Fort Orange	Declaration of Independence	Battle of Monmouth	Hamilton visits Paterson	Ellis Island opens

1550   1600   1650   1700   1750   1800   1850   1900

THE AMERICAN REVOLUTION

On June 28, 1778, Mary Hays and her husband left home to fight the British at Monmouth, New Jersey, during the American Revolution. While her husband directed cannon fire at the enemy, Mary took pitchers of water to the thirsty soldiers. Soldiers would call out to her, asking for water. "Molly! Pitcher!" they cried. That's how Mary Hays got her nickname—Molly Pitcher.

When her husband collapsed from the heat, Mary took his place firing the cannon.

IMMIGRATION

The United States is often called a nation of immigrants. Immigrants are people who enter a country to settle there and start a new life.

Starting around 1830, large groups of immigrants came to this country from all over Europe. Many settled in the Middle Atlantic region. By 1890, New York's immigration center had become too small to handle the daily arrival of immigrants. A new center opened on Ellis Island in New York Harbor in 1892.

INDUSTRY FOR A NEW COUNTRY

In 1778, Alexander Hamilton visited the waterfalls of the Passaic River in New Jersey. He believed that the new country should produce its own goods instead of importing them from Europe. The Great Falls of the Passaic River, he felt, could power machines in factories to be built there.

Paterson, New Jersey, became the new country's industrial center. Its many factories produced everything from locomotives to silk cloth.

George Washington's Socks

by Elvira Woodruff

Matt, his little sister, and three of his friends meet General George Washington as they become involved in the American Revolution.

"Help! Help!" Tony and Hooter cried out in unison. They could hear voices getting closer.

"We're coming, Katie," Matt yelled as loudly as he could. But their cries were met with a sudden silence.

Then out of the darkness a deep voice commanded, "Halt, in the name of the Continental Army!"

"Halt?" Tony whispered. "Is he kidding?"

"The Continental Army? Did he say the Continental Army?" Q asked, wiping the sleet off his glasses. Everyone in the boat was peering in the direction of the voice, when Matt suddenly sat back in his seat. He had just gotten a glimpse of the long wooden boat as it nudged its way between the ice floes.

Huddled in the craft were a group of men in tattered clothes. Some were wearing tricornered hats, and others had rags wrapped around their heads. Their faces were raw and weathered, and they were each clutching long guns in their rag-covered fingers.

Matt breathed a sigh of relief as he watched a tall man in a dark cape reach over the boat's side and pull Katie from the ice floe. He quickly wrapped her in his thick cape and handed her to one of the men beside him. Matt was so overcome with relief that he was unable to talk, even though he had wanted to call Katie and let her know that he was there.

As he stood staring from the old rowboat, Matt couldn't take his eyes off the man who had rescued her. He was a tall imposing figure in a blue and buff uniform. Matt had the strange feeling that he knew the man, for his figure was unmistakable, with his white hair rolled on the sides, and tied in the back with a ribbon. His face was strong and proud. It was the face of a leader, the face of a determined man. His eyes stared straight into Matt's, as if one commander had recognized another. It took all of Matt's courage to speak.

"My . . . sister. Is she all right?"

"The child is alive. No harm will come to her."

"Who . . . who are you?" Matt stammered.

"General George Washington, leader of the Continental Troops," came the firm reply.

"This is some kind of joke, right?" Matt mumbled. The general was not smiling, however, as the wind lashed the freezing rain and snow all about them.

"You had better explain what business brings you out on the river this night and whether you be friend or foe to the Revolution," the general called above the roar of the river.

He doesn't seem like a crazy man, Matt thought as he observed the fierce determination on the general's face. Matt looked at the faces of the other soldiers in the boat. They didn't seem crazy either. They looked serious, dead serious, as they held their muskets at Matt and the other members of the club.

"Are we on television?" Hooter started to smile. "Is this Totally Hidden Video?"

"They speak queerly, sir. And their dress is foreign." An officer in the general's boat spoke up. "They could be spies."

The general nodded. "Where do you make your homes?" he asked.

"Rumson," Matt called back. "Rumson, Nebraska."

"Nebraska? Where is this place, Nebraska?" The general and his men looked perplexed, but the state of their confusion was nowhere near that of Matt and his friends.

"I never met anyone who didn't know where Nebraska was," Hooter mumbled through chattering teeth.

"Where . . . where do you think they're from?" Tony stammered.

"I don't know," Matt whispered, staring at the soldiers and their muskets. "But I have this strange feeling, like . . . like . . ."

"Like we've seen them someplace before," Q concluded.

"Where?" Hooter wanted to know. "Where have we seen them?"

"In our history book," Q whispered. "We've gone back in time!"

"You mean before TV and stuff?" Hooter asked, looking at the old-fashioned muskets that were pointed at them.

How do General George Washington's socks become a part of this adventure? You can find out by checking this book out of your school or public library.

SHOW WHAT YOU KNOW!

REFOCUS
COMPREHENSION

1. What was the purpose of the Declaration of Independence?

2. What was Alexander Hamilton's idea for the city of Paterson?

THINK ABOUT IT
CRITICAL THINKING

 Why was Matt confused when General George Washington introduced himself?

STATE CHECK
ACTIVITY

Find out about an important industry in your state. Describe how the natural resources of your state have helped the industry to grow.

3

Spotlight

KEY TERMS

canal
toll
freight
mass-produced

Moving People and Goods

FOCUS *Many people and goods move into, out of, and around the Middle Atlantic region daily. New forms of transportation have helped the region develop.*

Steamboat Travel
With the invention of the world's first steamboat in 1807, people and goods could be carried up and down rivers.

Wagon Travel
In the early 1700s, wagons carried heavy loads over unpaved roads and paths.

More Roads Needed!
By the 1800s, roads paved with tar began to replace dirt roads.

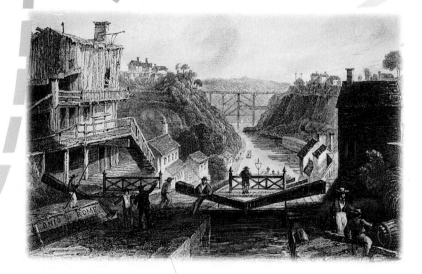

Travel by Canal
The Erie Canal cut through the Appalachian Mountains in northern New York. With its completion in 1825, other canals began to be built in the Middle Atlantic region.

Railroad Travel
By 1850, railroads had become the major form of transportation in the United States. Today, railroads link the major cities in the Middle Atlantic region.

Airplane Travel
By the late 1950s, millions of people began to depend on airplanes for swift transportation.

Automobile Travel
In the 1950s, many families owned cars. As a result, miles and miles of new roads were constructed.

Early Water Travel

The Middle Atlantic was, and still is, a region to be crossed. But the region's forests and mountains made land travel difficult in colonial times. So for the early settlers, travel was easiest by water. Canoes, wide boats, or crude rafts ferried people and goods along the region's rivers.

Steamboats

One drawback to early water travel was the difficulty in going against a river's current. Then, in 1807, Robert Fulton sent his boat, the *Clermont*, up the Hudson River from New York City to Albany.

How could this boat go 150 miles upriver—against the current? The answer is that Fulton's boat was powered by a steam engine that turned its paddle wheels around to fight the current. Soon, steamboats were a common sight traveling the Hudson River.

▲ By the 1930s, large barges traveled the Erie Canal, carrying coal, lumber, and other bulky materials.

Canals

With the invention of the steamboat engine, goods could be transported by water fairly easily. However, that did not solve the problem of land travel. The key was to find a way to move goods and people over both land and water. The answer was the **canal**.

The Erie Canal

On July 4, 1817, work began on a canal that would connect the Hudson River and Lake Erie. When it was finished eight years later, the Erie Canal cut the time of a trip from Buffalo to New York City from almost a month to just seven days! And the cost of moving a ton of grain, lumber, or coal dropped from $100.00 to $10.00!

The Erie Canal was a huge success. By collecting **tolls** as boats used the canal, this project paid for itself within ten years. Its success also meant that New York became a very important port city. That's because goods could now be

canal A waterway dug across land and used for boats and ships to travel through
toll A fee paid for the right to do or use something

104

moved by canal to and from New York Harbor to the western parts of the country. Soon, thousands of miles of canals moved people and goods across the region.

Railroads

In 1830, Peter Cooper, a New York manufacturer, conducted a race between a little locomotive named the *Tom Thumb* and a horse-drawn railroad car. The horse won the race. That same year, the *Tom Thumb*, with 36 passengers, chugged from Baltimore to Ellicott's Mills (13 miles away) and back again in just over two hours. This was something no team of horses could match. Railroads were here to stay.

By 1840, there were as many miles of railroad track as there were of canals. Railroads competed with canals for passenger and **freight** traffic.

Sometimes, railroads and canals worked together. Beginning in the 1830s, a combination of canals and rails was used to transport freight and passengers from Philadelphia to Pittsburgh, Pennsylvania.

Pittsburgh became an important location for trade. From Pittsburgh,

Today, many people in the region rely on trains to transport them to and from work.

railroads moved products from the East to western markets. Pittsburgh grew in other ways, too. The city provided iron and steel for making railroad cars and tracks. The area's coal deposits fueled the trains' steam engines.

Today's Rails

Railroads are still important to this region. Ports depend on trains to help transport goods that arrive by ship. And passenger trains help people to travel around the region. But the railroad business is not as busy as it once was. Much of the traffic has moved off the rails and onto the roads.

On a train, a conductor collects fares and watches out for the safety of the passengers.

freight Goods transported by train, ship, truck, or other vehicle

Highways connect the large cities and hundreds of smaller cities in the Middle Atlantic region.

The First Roads

For early settlers, travel overland usually meant walking along paths made by Native Americans. Settlers widened these paths to allow horse travel. Then the paths were widened again for horse-drawn carriages and wagons. Soon, new roads were made, connecting the Middle Atlantic's major cities.

By 1750, you could travel between Philadelphia and New York in just three days! But you did not travel on the paved roads we have today. You traveled on crudely cut dirt roads, filled with tree stumps and rocks.

By the 1800s, even more roads were built. Most of the roads connected cities in the Middle Atlantic and New England regions. Some of these roads, called turnpikes, were hard-surfaced roads built by private companies. The companies charged travelers money for the use of these roads.

Automobiles

With the invention of the automobile, road-building became more important. In the early 1900s, autos began to be **mass-produced**. This method of making autos made them affordable to more people. And the many new car owners demanded better roads.

Today, the Middle Atlantic region is a maze of roads and highways, connecting many towns and cities. Roads and cars have become important parts of our lives.

 mass-produced Made in large quantities, usually by machinery

1903 Crestmobile

1936 Pontiac

1956 Chevrolet

electric car

Air Travel

With the invention of the airplane in 1903, Americans were soon to have another way to get around. By 1950, airports were rapidly being built to serve the major cities in the region. New York City opened an airport in the 1940s. The Friendship International Airport opened near Baltimore. And Washington's National Airport began flights to and from the nation's capital.

Airport Locations

Some of the busiest airports in the country are in the Middle Atlantic region. All three of the airports that serve the New York City area rank in the nation's top 20 for passenger traffic. Every year, over 25 million people depart from and arrive at John F. Kennedy International Airport. Almost as many passengers use New York's La Guardia Airport and New Jersey's Newark International Airport.

▸ For much of the twentieth century, people have depended more and more on cars for transportation.

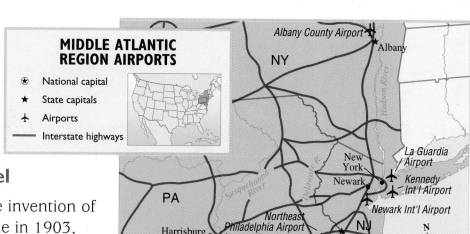

MIDDLE ATLANTIC REGION AIRPORTS

✪ National capital
★ State capitals
✈ Airports
— Interstate highways

Most airports are located near major highways. And since most of the region's airports are located far from the cities they serve, highways are important connections for air travel. For example, the Philadelphia International Airport has its own exit on Interstate 95.

Sometimes, two or more cities share one airport. This is true of Baltimore and Washington, D.C. In 1972, the name of Friendship International Airport was changed to Baltimore-Washington International Airport. This new name shows that the airport serves residents of both cities.

SHOW WHAT YOU KNOW!

REFOCUS
COMPREHENSION

1. How did steamboats change river travel?

2. How did railroads change Pittsburgh?

THINK ABOUT IT
CRITICAL THINKING

What form of transportation might not have developed if bulky goods were still shipped on canals?

STATE CHECK
ACTIVITY

Find out what forms of transportation connect your state with other regions. Make a chart to show some of the connections.

KEY TERMS

urban planner
marina

Meet an Urban Planner

FOCUS *The government of a city or town helps local businesses and makes the community a better place to live in. Often, urban planners help communities accomplish these goals.*

Urban Planners

Some of the Middle Atlantic's early cities, such as Philadelphia and Washington, D.C., were planned. Others just grew over time, without much planning at all.

Today, cities and other communities realize the importance of planning for the future. Many places hire **urban planners**. These are people who think about how a community will develop over time. They plan for growth and try to improve community life.

Camden, New Jersey

Charles Lyons, Jr., is an urban planner for the city of Camden. He plans for the city's future.

To learn how to plan something as big and complicated as a city, Mr. Lyons, like most urban planners, had to go to college.

Mr. Lyons's day-to-day job is to improve a specific area of Camden. To do this, Mr. Lyons must think about where people live, work, go to school, shop, and play. He also attends community meetings and asks residents to describe the needs of their neighborhoods. He considers these things as he makes plans for Camden.

▲ Charles Lyons, Jr., as an urban planner, looks for ways to improve community life in Camden.

---

 urban planner   A person whose job is to plan the development of a community

Aerial View of the Garden & Visitor Center
January 31, 1995

City officials hope that a children's garden and a marina will give Camden its own special personality.

SHOW WHAT YOU KNOW!

REFOCUS
COMPREHENSION

1. What is the job of an urban planner?

2. What must an urban planner think about?

THINK ABOUT IT
CRITICAL THINKING

What kinds of things are important for a community to have?

STATE CHECK
ACTIVITY

Suppose you are an urban planner. Make a map of the area around your school. On a piece of paper, write down what you would change in that area.

A Master Plan

There is another part to Mr. Lyons's job. He is responsible for making a five-year master plan for the whole city. This plan tells how city land should be used for the next five years.

The master plan might include replacing rundown buildings or improving old playgrounds or shopping malls. He then presents his ideas to the mayor and the city council. These government leaders will make the final decisions on which improvements to make.

Mr. Lyons also makes suggestions that will help keep businesses in Camden from moving away. One way Camden can keep present businesses and attract new ones is to have something that makes the city special. Mr. Lyons believes that "every city needs its own personality." As

Children have their own plots of land to plant in a city garden.

examples, New York is a banking center, and Baltimore is known for its hospitals and universities.

Camden's Future

With state help, Camden is trying to find a personality of its own. Not long ago, an aquarium and an arts center opened in Camden. Plans are also underway for a **marina** and even a children's garden. Officials hope these changes will bring new life to an old city.

---

marina A docking area where supplies are available for small boats

109

SUMMING UP

1 DO YOU REMEMBER...
COMPREHENSION

1. What states make up the Middle Atlantic region?

2. Why did Philadelphia, New York City, and Baltimore grow into large centers for trade and industry?

3. Why was Mary Hays nicknamed Molly Pitcher?

4. What effect did the Erie Canal have on the cost of moving freight?

5. Describe the job of an urban planner.

2 SKILL POWER
USING TIME LINES

The time line in Skill Power, page 88, shows the main events in the early history of Maryland. With a partner, choose another state in the Middle Atlantic region. Make a time line about its history. Use events from this book and from an encyclopedia or almanac. You may want to illustrate your time line with drawings. When you have finished, display your time line in the classroom.

3 WHAT DO YOU THINK?
CRITICAL THINKING

1. How did the land in the Middle Atlantic region change as the early settlers moved west? How did settlers have to change their way of living?

2. Why is keeping the water clean in Chesapeake Bay especially important to people who live in Maryland?

3. Was Alexander Hamilton right in his belief that the newly born United States should produce its own goods? Explain your answer.

4. What new form of transportation, if any, will be needed in the Middle Atlantic region in the coming century?

5. Suppose that you are a mayor about to hire an urban planner for your city. What skills will you look for in the candidates for the job?

4 SAY IT, WRITE IT, USE IT
VOCABULARY

If you have an Australian pen pal who enjoys hearing all about the United States, what would you write about the Middle Atlantic region? Use as many of the key terms as you can in your letter.

boulder	marina
canal	mass-produced
fort	research
freight	toll
Great Lakes Plain	urban planner

CHAPTER 5

5 GEOGRAPHY AND YOU
MAP STUDY

Use the map below to answer these questions.

1. Which mountains are located in the northern part of New York?

2. In which state are the Allegheny Mountains— New Jersey or Pennsylvania?

3. What bodies of water form parts of the boundary of New York?

4. Which state capitals are located on bodies of water?

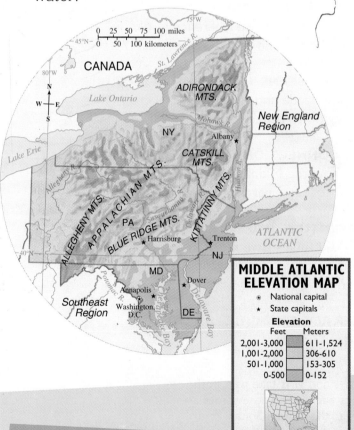

6 TAKE ACTION
CITIZENSHIP

Every community, whether large or small, needs to face challenges that exist today as well as to plan for its future. Is there enough housing for people? Will there be enough schools for future citizens? Together with your classmates, make a chart, listing some of the present-day challenges to your community and possible future challenges. Then, beside each challenge write a possible solution.

7 GET CREATIVE
ART CONNECTION

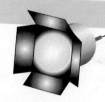

Choose one event in the history of the Middle Atlantic region that interests you. Then design a diorama that shows the event, the people who were involved, and the date of the event. Use a shoebox for the stage and create details out of cardboard, clay, or paper. Give your diorama a title before you put it on display.

LOOKING AHEAD Explore in the next chapter some of the ways that the Middle Atlantic region is linked to other regions.

CHAPTER 6

Middle Atlantic

In this chapter, you'll investigate how trade and technology link the Middle Atlantic region to the rest of the world. You'll compare Washington, D.C., our national capital, with Paris, the national capital of France.

CONTENTS

◀ Hundreds of boys and girls take part in the Special Olympics each year. These games are broadcast all over the United States. Find out how on pages 118 and 119.

Links Near and Far

The following books give you information about how the Middle Atlantic region is connected to the world. Read one that interests you and fill out a book-review form.

READ AND RESEARCH

Washington, D.C. by Catherine Reef (Dillon Press, 1990)
Have you ever visited Washington, D.C.? Take a walk through the city and learn about its historic places, famous sights, and present-day neighborhoods. *(nonfiction)*

Special Olympics by Fern G. Brown (Franklin Watts, 1992)
This book tells you about the beginning days of the Special Olympics and how the organization works. You'll see that it is really about the people—athletes and volunteers—who make the Special Olympics games happen. *(nonfiction)*

. . . If Your Name Was Changed at Ellis Island
by Ellen Levine, illustrated by Wayne Parmenter (Scholastic, 1993)
When immigrants came to the United States, many wondered if there would be a place for them in the new land. In this book of questions and answers, you will discover what happened when people arrived at Ellis Island in search of their own American dreams. *(nonfiction)*

My Name Is María Isabel by Alma Flor Ada, illustrated by K. Dyble Thompson (Simon & Schuster Children's Publishing, 1993)
María Isabel was born in Puerto Rico and is now living on the mainland. She is nervous about being the newest child in her class. Find out how she really becomes a part of her class. *(nonfiction)*

SKILL POWER   Finding Information

Knowing how to find information can help you get facts quickly and easily.

UNDERSTAND IT

The library is one of the best places to find information. The facts you need are right there in the library's books, videocassettes, and computer discs.

Libraries have many books that give facts on special topics. There are books about the geography of your state. There are stories about people's lives, called biographies.

Other books are called reference books. They contain many facts on different subjects. Encyclopedias are reference books with articles about people, places, and things. If you want to know the meaning of a word, you would use a dictionary. For a map of your state, you would use a book of maps, called an atlas. An almanac, published yearly, is a book of facts on many subjects.

▶ Many libraries have encyclopedias and other reference books on computer.

EXPLORE IT

Suppose you want to learn about famous people who were born in your state. With so much library material to choose from, how would you find the needed information? One of the best ways is to use a card catalog. This is a list of all the books and materials that are in the library. This list is made up of cards that are kept in drawers. Each item is listed in alphabetical order in three ways—by subject, by title, and by the author's last name. Some libraries keep these lists on a computer.

UNITED STATES - CONSTITUTIONAL HISTORY.

973   Silver Burdett.
          The Constitutional Convention. --
       Morristown, NJ : Silver Burdett Company,
       1985.
          63p. : ill. -- (Turning Points in
       American History)

          1. United States – Constitutional
       history. I. Title II. Series

HL
SS
1893   Philips, George Morris.
          Elements of civil government in the
       Commonwealth of Pennsylvania : with a
       brief outline of the political history of
       the state / by George Morris Philips. --
       New York : Silver, Burdett & Company,
       1893.
          108p. : ill.

          I. Title

▲ The cards in a card catalog at a library list each book by its title, author, and subject.

114

What facts can you discover in the library about Niagara Falls?

TRY IT

Select a place in the Middle Atlantic region that you would like to know more about. For example, you might want to find out about Niagara Falls, on the United States–Canada boundary. Or perhaps you want to learn more about the giant dinosaur exhibit at the American Museum of Natural History in New York City. Use the library's reference books to find some interesting facts about the place you have chosen. Investigate what your library's computer has to offer.

Find classmates who have selected places to visit that are similar to the one you have chosen. Work with a group to prepare a travel brochure that highlights the places in the Middle Atlantic region which you have studied.

▲ You can use your school library to find out about dinosaurs and about museums with dinosaur exhibits.

SKILL

★ **POWER SEARCH** *Select five facts presented in this chapter. Use materials in the library to look up each fact and check whether it is correct.*

1

Setting the Scene

⭐ **KEY TERMS**
trade
broadcasting
federal
democracy

Ties to Other Regions

FOCUS *The Middle Atlantic region is linked to other regions in the United States through trade and modern technology. It is also linked to all the regions in the United States through Washington, D.C., our nation's capital.*

Trade Links

No region of the United States can produce everything it needs. Each region is linked to other regions by the exchange of natural resources, products, and services. This exchange, usually involving money, is called **trade**.

Trade in the Middle Atlantic region began with the early settlers who set up trading posts along the rivers of the region. People traded for food, cloth, and tools.

Later, towns and cities replaced the trading posts. After the American Revolution, the present-day city of Pittsburgh, Pennsylvania, for example, became a starting point for settlers traveling west. The city grew as a center of trade. As time went on, these same settlers ordered horseshoes, plows, and other goods made by Pittsburgh blacksmiths using Pennsylvania iron.

⭐ **trade** The exchange of one product or service for another product or service

▼ The Middle Atlantic region produces many products that are transported to other regions in the United States.

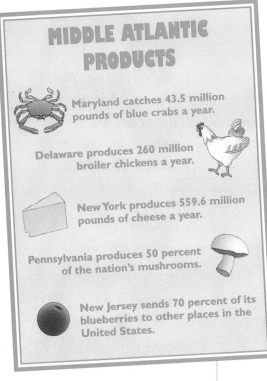

MIDDLE ATLANTIC PRODUCTS

Maryland catches 43.5 million pounds of blue crabs a year.

Delaware produces 260 million broiler chickens a year.

New York produces 559.6 million pounds of cheese a year.

Pennsylvania produces 50 percent of the nation's mushrooms.

New Jersey sends 70 percent of its blueberries to other places in the United States.

Food Products

Today, the states of the Middle Atlantic region produce many farm products that are in demand in other parts of the country. Some of these products are shown on the map below.

Located in the Appalachian Mountains in Pennsylvania there are many dark, damp caves. The caves have just the right conditions for growing large and delicious mushrooms. These mushrooms are sent to places where mushrooms cannot be grown.

Maryland ships tons of clams, crabs, oysters, and fish to various parts of the country. These products are transported by truck, train, and plane. In fact restaurants far away from the Middle Atlantic region advertise "Maryland crabs, flown in fresh daily."

People Links

Planes and trains transport more than products from one region to another. They transport many of the people who come into the Middle Atlantic region each year.

Some people come to see family and friends who live in the region. Some come to visit cities in the region, to see historic sites, or to enjoy the region's beaches.

Other people come to the Middle Atlantic region for business reasons. The world headquarters of many large companies are located in the Middle Atlantic region.

Travel helps people become familiar with places outside their own regions. It helps to link the people of the United States together.

How Broadcasting Works

The video-camera operator takes live pictures of sports events.

Satellite Broadcasting

One major industry in the Middle Atlantic region is radio and television **broadcasting**. Many of the television programs you watch are made or recorded in New York City.

Early television signals could not be sent very far from TV stations. To reach a much wider area and more customers, television stations today send their signals through a system of satellites.

A satellite is a complex electronic machine and computer in space above Earth. There are over 100 communications satellites. Every day, streams of television signals, as well as radio and phone signals, are directed toward these satellites. The satellites then send these signals to other television stations all over the country. In fact satellites can broadcast signals all over the world.

Special Olympics Broadcasting

Look at the photographs on these pages to trace the steps involved in broadcasting the 1995 Special Olympics from New Haven, Connecticut. First, the video-camera operator used a camera to follow the events to be televised. The communications truck at the site sent the video-camera pictures to a satellite in space.

Next, the satellite beamed the signals to a large antenna atop a building in New York City. Then the people in a television studio made the Special Olympics pictures part of the evening news broadcast.

The studio beamed the news program to the communications satellite in space. Then local television stations received the signal and sent it to home television sets. People were able to see "live" pictures of the sports events on their TV screens.

The communications truck sends these live pictures to a satellite in space.

⭐ *broadcasting* Making something public by means of radio or television

Communications Links

Being able to watch the Special Olympics on television is just one way that broadcasting brings many people throughout our country together. Many televised events can unite people. For example, the broadcast of a natural disaster, such as an earthquake in California or a hurricane in Florida, brings people together in a special way. People become concerned for the people in the stricken area and look for ways to help.

In addition, radio and television programs can teach much about the geography and features of different regions in the United States. Even commercials on radio and television link people by encouraging them to buy certain products. The broadcast industry helps to unite people in all the regions in our country.

After receiving the TV signals by air or by cable, people watch the Special Olympics "live" on their TV sets.

The large antenna at the TV studio receives the picture signals from the satellite.

The TV studio sends the news program to the communications satellite.

The local TV station receives the satellite signals and broadcasts them to home TV sets.

119

▲ This building is the Capitol, in Washington, D.C. Laws for the entire country are made here.

Capital Links

Another link that unites the people of a country is government. The government of the United States met in various cities after the Declaration of Independence was signed in 1776. Two capitals included Philadelphia and New York City.

The growing country soon realized that it needed a capital located on land that didn't belong to any one state. The land would become a **federal**, or national, city.

After some debate, the final decision on where to build this federal city was made by George Washington, our first President. He chose a site along the Potomac River, about midway between the northern and southern states.

The Potomac River provided a transportation route for the new city. Boats carried passengers as well as supplies and goods to and from the new capital.

The city of Washington was named after George Washington, and was first officially known by that name in 1791. The letters *D.C.* stand for "District of Columbia," which was named after Christopher Columbus. The city of Washington and the District of Columbia are names for the same area.

Washington, D.C., is recognized the world over as a center of **democracy**. In a democracy like ours, freely elected officials represent all the people of our country. The officials make laws and plans for our country that protect our freedom.

 federal Having to do with the national government of the United States

 democracy A form of government in which the people elect representatives to make the laws and run the country

Show What You KNOW!

REFOCUS
COMPREHENSION

1. How did Pittsburgh help settlers who were headed west?

2. How have satellites changed radio and television broadcasts?

THINK ABOUT IT
CRITICAL THINKING

How is Washington, D.C., different from other cities in our country?

STATE CHECK
ACTIVITY

List the ways in which your state is connected to the Middle Atlantic region.

Global Connections

⭐ __KEY TERMS__

export
import

The World Right Here

__FOCUS__ *The United States is connected to the rest of the world through trade. The country is also linked to the world through the people who have come from other lands and who now call the United States home.*

__Leading Trade Partners of the U.S. in 1994__

CANADA
JAPAN
MEXICO
GREAT BRITAIN
GERMANY

The Product Link

The early colonists who settled the Middle Atlantic region in the 1700s raised crops on farmlands near the port cities of Philadelphia, New York, and Baltimore. Families at first grew only what they needed. But gradually, colonists raised enough to **export**, or send, their products to other countries.

The ports of New York and Philadelphia exported wheat and large amounts of beef and pork from farms farther west. Baltimore became a major exporter of tobacco from Maryland farms.

Today, the people of the Middle Atlantic region continue to export farm crops and other products. Look at the crate of products on this page. These products are just some of the items that are sent from the Middle Atlantic ports.

⭐ **export** To send goods to another country for sale or use
import To bring in goods from another country for sale or use

Port Newark

The ports of the Middle Atlantic region today also **import**, or bring in, goods and materials from other countries to be sold in the United States. Port Newark in New Jersey is one of the main ports for the import and export trade.

Today, most of the goods coming into or going out of the country are packed in large steel or wood containers before being delivered to the port. These containers are usually 8 feet deep, 8 feet wide, and from 20 to 40 feet long.

▼ The Middle Atlantic region ships chemicals, electronics, and food products all over the world.

This building on Ellis Island in New York Harbor is where millions of immigrants first entered the United States.

Because of the weight and size of these containers, ships must use ports that have special cranes for loading and unloading them.

New Jersey's Port Newark is the largest port in the United States for container ships. Over 100 shipping companies use Port Newark. About 240 trucking companies and many railroads distribute the imported goods across the region.

The People Link

The people who settled the Middle Atlantic region came from different countries in Europe. Like the Puritans in New England, they sought a better opportunity in life.

Over time, many thousands of immigrants came from countries such as Germany, Ireland, and Italy. Most entered the United States through Ellis Island in New York Harbor. Look at the picture of the immigration station on Ellis Island on this page. The building is now a museum. The museum captures some of the history of immigrants who came to the United States between 1892 and 1954.

Newcomers Today

Today, people who seek to make their homes in the United States come from more than 100 different countries. Since the 1970s, some of the largest groups of newcomers have arrived from Mexico, the Philippines, South Korea, and Vietnam. Recent immigrants have also come from Jamaica, Haiti, Cuba, and the Dominican Republic.

These children, from 12 different countries, pose for a picture at Ellis Island in 1912.

PUERTO RICO TO THE MIDDLE ATLANTIC REGION

← Puerto Rico to New York, NY and surrounding area
• Cities

ATLANTIC OCEAN

PUERTO RICO (U.S.)

San Juan

0   200   400 miles
0   200   400 kilometers

Puerto Rico

During the 1950s many people who lived in Puerto Rico began to move to the United States mainland. They followed a pattern that had been set by other new groups of people. Most settled in New York City and the surrounding area as the map on this page shows.

These new arrivals informed their families in Puerto Rico about job and housing opportunities. They encouraged others in Puerto Rico to come to the United States. They even saved their own money to pay for others' trips to the United States.

When newcomers, such as Puerto Ricans, come to this country, they bring with them new ideas as well as their homeland traditions. These traditions and ideas are then shared with other Americans to make our lives better.

▼ Puerto Ricans are proud of their heritage. Here they take part in a Puerto Rican Day Parade.

SHOW WHAT YOU KNOW!

REFOCUS
COMPREHENSION

1. What does it mean to export goods? What does it mean to import goods?

2. From which European countries did many immigrants come in the late 1800s and early 1900s?

THINK ABOUT IT
CRITICAL THINKING

Why is it important for a country to have links with other countries?

STATE CHECK
ACTIVITY

Suppose you are an immigrant who is seeing, for the first time, the state in which you will live. Write down some unusual things that you find.

Two National Capitals

FOCUS *Washington, D.C., and Paris, France, are both national capitals. As cities, they also share many other things.*

A Plan for D.C.

George Washington hired Pierre L'Enfant (pee AIR lahn FAHN) to design a new capital city for the United States. This French-born **engineer** and designer knew how important the city of Washington, D.C., would be to the people of this new country.

L'Enfant's design for the new capital included parks and space for large government buildings. It was for a city in which people could live and work.

The Contribution of Paris

L'Enfant planned for the new capital to be like Paris. He had been born and educated there. He believed that Washington should be the great city of the United States, as Paris was the great city of France.

★ **engineer** A person who is trained to plan and build structures such as roads, canals, bridges, and buildings

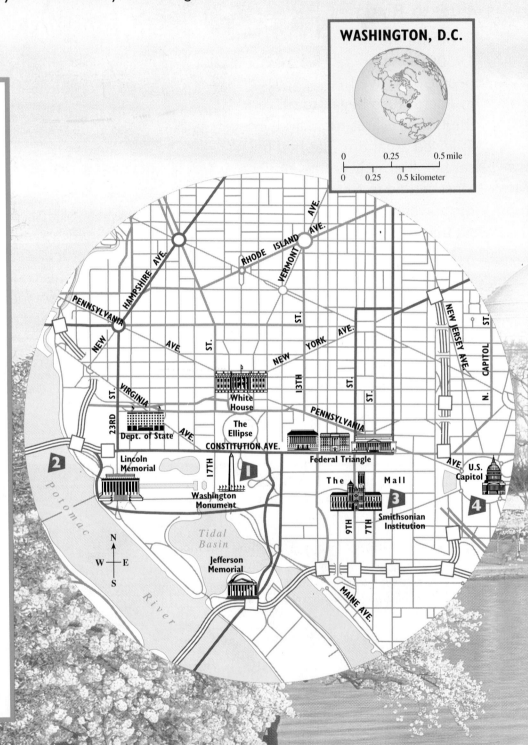

WASHINGTON, D.C.

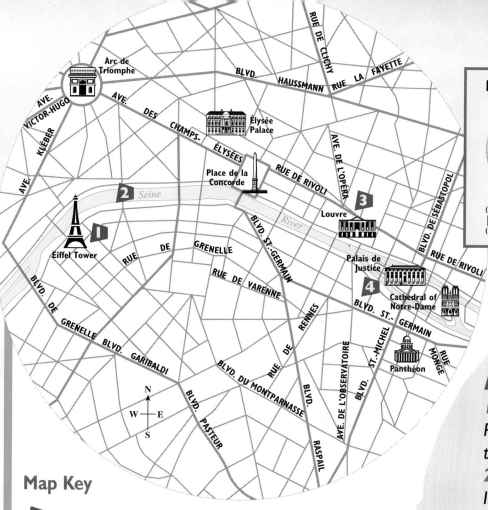

PARIS, FRANCE

| 0 | 0.25 | 0.5 mile |
| 0 | 0.25 | 0.5 kilometer |

Map Key

1 Monuments The Eiffel Tower in Paris is an iron framework 984 feet high. It was built in 1889. The Washington Monument is a 555-foot-high marble-faced **obelisk**, or pillar, built in 1884.

2 Rivers Paris lies on the banks of the Seine River. Washington is on the Potomac River.

3 Museums Washington has many museums. One of the most popular is the Air and Space Museum, a part of the Smithsonian Institution. Paris has the Louvre, with its eight miles of **galleries**.

4 Government Buildings Elected officials meet to make laws in the Capitol in Washington. The higher courts of France are in the Palais de Justice in the city of Paris.

⭐ **obelisk** A tall stone pillar that has a pyramid-shaped top
gallery A room where paintings and statues are shown

MAP IT

1. Find the Eiffel Tower on the map of Paris. What river do you have to cross to get to the Arc de Triomphe?
2. Find the Palais de Justice in Paris. In which direction would you have to travel to reach the Arc de Triomphe?
3. Find the Potomac River on the map of Washington. Which is closer to the Potomac River—the White House or the Jefferson Memorial?
4. Find the Smithsonian Institution on the map of Washington. Which is closer to the Smithsonian Institution—the Capitol or the Lincoln Memorial?
5. Compare the two maps. What do Paris and Washington have in common?

EXPLORE IT

With a partner, prepare guidebooks to Paris and Washington that might be used by visitors to these cities.

SUMMING UP

1 DO YOU REMEMBER...
COMPREHENSION

1. Name three food products that people in the Middle Atlantic region send to other parts of the country.

2. Why was the present site of Washington, D.C., chosen as the federal capital?

3. Why is Ellis Island a famous place in American history?

4. Name two products that are exported from the Middle Atlantic region to other parts of the world.

5. Who was Pierre L'Enfant, and why is he remembered?

2 SKILL POWER
FINDING INFORMATION

Here is a list of famous people from the Middle Atlantic region. Choose one person and then go to the library to find information about the person. Present a report to the class. Try to include pictures of the person in your report.

Marian Anderson   Francis Scott Key
Benjamin Banneker   Samuel Morse
Guion Bluford, Jr.   Eleanor Roosevelt
Annie Jump Cannon   Harriet Tubman

3 WHAT DO YOU THINK?
CRITICAL THINKING

1. Why do many large companies locate their world headquarters in the Middle Atlantic region?

2. Why do most national news broadcasts come from the Middle Atlantic region? Hint: The East Coast is three hours ahead of the West Coast.

3. Where would you have advised President Washington to build the nation's capital? Explain your reasoning.

4. How is Washington, D.C., similar to other capitals around the world?

5. Immigrants to this country bring their traditions and ideas to share with other Americans. How does this help the country?

4 SAY IT, WRITE IT, USE IT
VOCABULARY

Match each of the meanings with a key term. Then use each term in a sentence.

1. making a television program public
2. a room for paintings or statues
3. one type of monument
4. to send goods out of a country
5. someone who is trained to plan and build structures
6. a form of government
7. having to do with the national government
8. to bring goods into a country
9. the exchange of one product or service for another product or service

broadcasting   export   import
democracy   federal   obelisk
engineer   gallery   trade

5 GEOGRAPHY AND YOU
MAP STUDY

Use the map below to answer the following questions.

1. What city in Puerto Rico is shown on the map?

2. What large body of water is between Puerto Rico and mainland United States?

3. In which direction would you travel to get from San Juan to New York City?

4. Use the scale bar on the map to find the distance between San Juan and New York City.

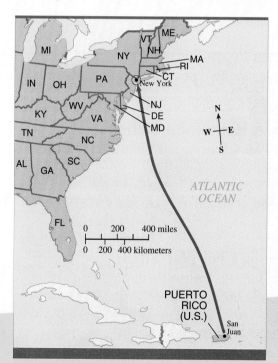

6 TAKE ACTION
CITIZENSHIP

Have you ever watched a television program that you thought was too violent? Have you seen one that was unfair to a group of people? You can do something! Write a letter to the television station, telling why the broadcast bothered you. Send a copy to the Federal Communications Commission (FCC) in Washington D.C. The addresses of television stations and the FCC can be found in the library.

7 GET CREATIVE
MUSIC CONNECTION

Do you know the melody for "America"? Use the melody to write a song for one of the Middle Atlantic states. First, check the facts about the states in the States Almanac on pages 342–397. What information can you use to write a song for a state? Then work with a group of classmates to put new words to the old melody. Perform your song for the whole class.

LOOKING AHEAD
Travel in the next chapter to the Southeast region and learn about its land and people.

Southeast Region

The first settlers in the Southeast region farmed the land. In this chapter, you will learn about ways in which the region has changed through the years.

CONTENTS

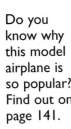

Do you know why this model airplane is so popular? Find out on page 141.

These books tell about people, events, and places that are important to the Southeast region. Read one that interests you and fill out a book-review form.

READ AND RESEARCH

The Trail on Which They Wept: The Story of a Cherokee Girl **by Dorothy and Thomas Hoobler, pictures by S.S. Burrus** (Silver Burdett Press, 1992)
Sarah Rogers and her Cherokee family are forced to leave their home in Georgia. Find out about Sarah's journey to a new land. *(historical fiction)*
• *You can read a selection from this story on page 142.*

Marjory Stoneman Douglas: Voice of the Everglades **by Jennifer Bryant, illustrated by Larry Raymond** (Twenty-first Century Books, 1992)
Even as a young girl, Marjory Stoneman Douglas knew about the beauty and mystery of nature. Read about how she led the fight to save the Florida Everglades. *(biography)*

Misty of Chincoteague **by Marguerite Henry** (Rand McNally & Co., 1947)
Paul and Maureen live on Chincoteague Island, off the coast of Virginia, taking care of the horses on their grandparents' ranch. Find out what happens when they get a pony of their own. *(fiction)*

The U.S. Space Camp Book of Rockets **by Anne Baird, photographs by David Graham** (William Morrow & Co., 1994)
Girls and boys from all over the country visit the U.S. Space Camp in Huntsville, Alabama. Here, teams of children learn the history of rocketry and participate in their own space adventure in a mock shuttle. *(nonfiction)*

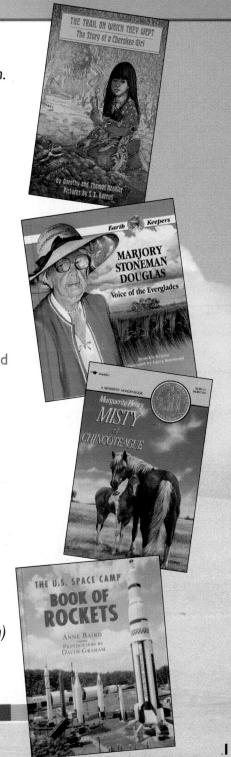

SKILL POWER Using a Grid Map

Knowing how to use the grid on a map makes it easier to locate places.

UNDERSTAND IT

If you have ever played the game of bingo at home, you have used a grid. When the bingo caller gives a number, he or she begins with one of the letters in the word *bingo*. So the number G46 means you have to look in the G column to see if you have the number 46. This makes the game easy to play. You only need to look at the five numbers in the column to find out if you have the number 46, instead of looking at all 25 boxes on the card.

The game of bingo becomes easier and more enjoyable when the players use the grid system on the bingo cards.

EXPLORE IT

A cartographer (kahr TAHG-ruh fur) is a person who makes maps. He or she can make a map easier to read by adding a grid. A grid is a system of crossing lines that form boxes.

Suppose you want to attend the Watermelon Festival in Mize, Mississippi, but you are not sure where Mize is. You can find Mize on the map on page 131 by first finding Mize in the Index below the map. According to the Index, Mize is located at D-3. This means that Mize is in grid box D-3.

Now put your finger on the letter D at the left side of the map. Then put a finger of your other hand on the number 3 at the bottom. Move both fingers until they meet. You have found Mize. Now you are ready for watermelon!

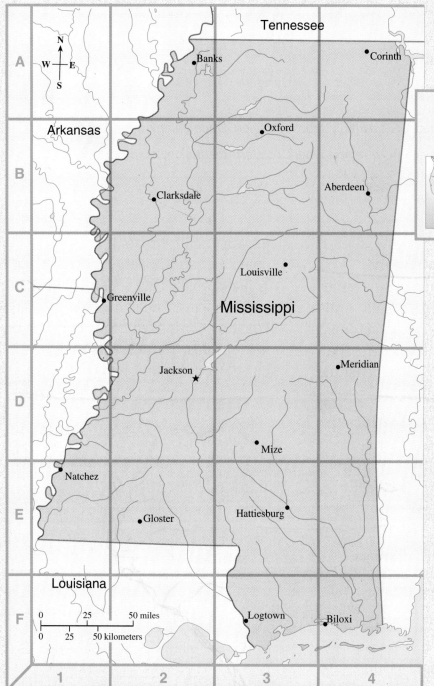

Tennessee

A

| Banks | Corinth |

MISSISSIPPI

★ State capital
● Cities or towns

Arkansas

B

Oxford

Clarksdale   Aberdeen

C

Louisville

Greenville   Mississippi

D

Jackson ★   Meridian

Mize

E

Natchez

Gloster   Hattiesburg

Louisiana

F

Logtown   Biloxi

N
W · E
S

0   25   50 miles
0   25   50 kilometers

1   2   3   4

TRY IT

With a group of your classmates, make up a game that uses a map with a grid. Find or draw a map of your town or state, a place you would like to visit, or even an imaginary place. Add grid lines to the map, and label them with numbers across the top and letters along one side. Then think of things you might need for your game, such as clue cards, a timer, game markers, a spinner, and rules. Be creative! Play the game with your group.

SKILL POWER SEARCH

There is a large map with a grid in this chapter. How will the grid help you use that map?

131

Setting the Scene

KEY TERMS

environment
plantation
textile
high-tech industry

A Growing Region

FOCUS *The Southeast is a rapidly growing region. Once chiefly a land of farms, the Southeast has become a region where modern technology is important.*

An Ideal Location

More people live in the Southeast than in any other region of the United States. And the population of the Southeast keeps on growing! Several reasons that people settle in the Southeast are its warm climate, its miles of coastline, and its large cities.

Jacksonville, the region's largest city, is located near the Atlantic coast of Florida. Another large city is Memphis, Tennessee. Find both cities on the map below.

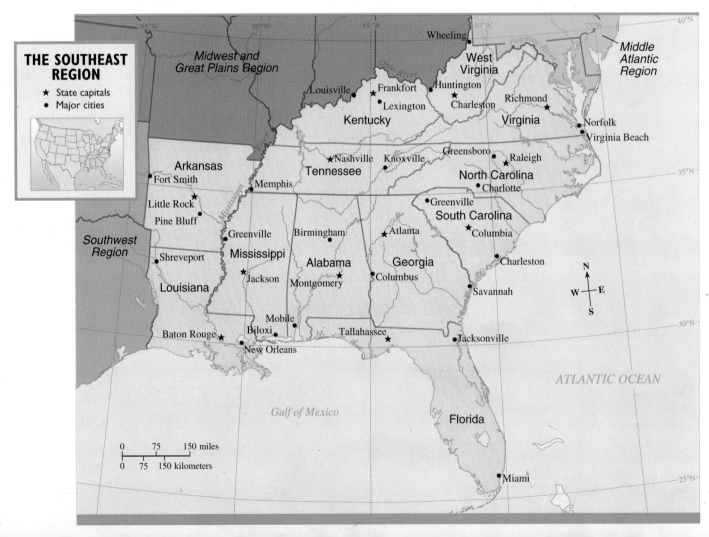

THE SOUTHEAST REGION

★ State capitals
● Major cities

The First People Here

The Southeast region was not always the busy place it is today. Long ago, several nations of Native Americans, including Cherokees, Creeks, and Seminoles, made their homes in the Southeast. They were the first people in the region.

These people grew corn, squash, beans, and tobacco on the land they farmed. They hunted in the forests and fished in the rivers.

Today, there are not nearly as many Native Americans in the Southeast region as there once were. Some descendants of the Cherokees live in communities of the Cherokee Reservation in western North Carolina. Some Native Americans produce pottery, beaded jewelry, baskets, and other crafts. Many others work in industries, such as manufacturing and lumbering, in the region.

European Settlers

People from Spain were the first Europeans to explore the Southeast region. They came in the 1500s to search for gold and other treasures.

In 1607, people from England arrived in the Southeast. They set up a settlement along a river that empties into Chesapeake Bay. They named their settlement Jamestown, in honor of their king, James I. Their community became the first permanent English settlement in North America.

People from countries other than England came to the Southeast, too. For example, French settlers moved onto the rich farmland along the Mississippi River. They called their colony Louisiana, in honor of King Louis of France.

Farming

At first, life was hard for the settlers. They had to learn how to live in a new **environment**. But geography was on their side. The coastal plains offered plenty of low, level land with good soil. The region also had a mild climate and enough rain each year.

Most of the people in the Southeast were farmers. They usually had small family farms near the coasts or in the valleys that ran

▲ This Seminole basket was made of threads and sea grass, a plant that grows in South Carolina and Georgia.

The Four Most Populated Southeast States in 1830

VIRGINIA	1,044,000
NORTH CAROLINA	738,000
KENTUCKY	688,000
TENNESSEE	682,000

 environment The surroundings in which a person, animal, or plant lives

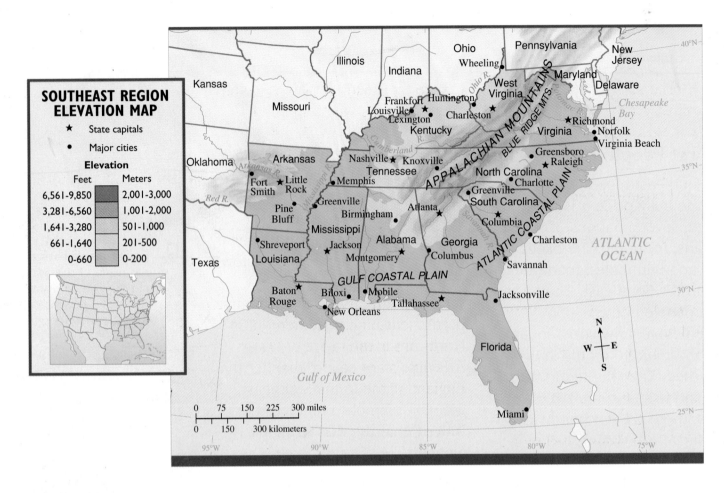

SOUTHEAST REGION ELEVATION MAP

★ State capitals
● Major cities

Elevation

Feet	Meters
6,561–9,850	2,001–3,000
3,281–6,560	1,001–2,000
1,641–3,280	501–1,000
661–1,640	201–500
0–660	0–200

between the mountains in the region. You can see on the map above that land between the coasts and the mountains does not have a high elevation. These farmers raised corn, sweet potatoes, poultry, and vegetables, mostly for their own families to eat.

In time, some people began to own very large farms called **plantations**. Some plantations were bigger than 100 small farms put together. The plantation owners often depended on just one main crop, such as cotton, rice, or tobacco. Plantation owners sold the crops they planted to merchants, who sold the crops in Europe.

Many workers were needed to raise and harvest crops on plantations. A large plantation might need 50 to 100 workers, or even more. The one thing planters lacked for making a profit was workers.

Plantation Workers

In the 1600s many shipowners sailed to Africa to find workers. They captured people

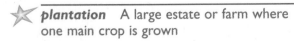

★ *plantation*   A large estate or farm where one main crop is grown

134

there, often separating them from their families, and sold them to planters in the Southeast to use as enslaved workers. Some worked in the plantation fields, and others worked as household servants or as artisans, making barrels and wagons or repairing machines.

King Cotton

The plantation system was very successful for the planters. It became even more successful after 1793. That was when Eli Whitney invented the cotton gin, a machine that removed cotton seeds from the cotton plants. Whitney's machine cleaned fifty times more cotton than a person could clean in a day. Much of this cotton was sold to

textile industries in New England. Many planters who had been growing other crops changed to cotton. Cotton became the king of crops in the Southeast.

Not all cotton grown on the plantations was shipped north for manufacturing. Businessmen built factories for processing cotton and producing textiles in the Piedmont (PEED mahnt) of the Appalachian Mountains. The Piedmont is the range of lower foothills to the east of the highest Appalachian peaks.

The Country Divides

The success of the plantation system depended more and more on having many enslaved people to work on the plantations. Many people in the United States, including some people in the Southeast, believed that no person should be enslaved. The plantation owners argued that they had a right to own enslaved workers.

Disagreement grew between plantation owners and people who wanted freedom for everyone. This became one cause of a terrible war known as the Civil War, or the War Between the States. You will read more about the Civil War on pages 144 and 145.

▶ Plantations were often located on rivers, so that crops could easily be loaded onto ships for export.

▲ Eli Whitney's cotton gin increased cotton production from 500,000 pounds in 1793 to 18 million pounds by 1800.

 textile Having to do with weaving fabrics; fabric made by weaving

Industries Today and Tomorrow

Think of all the everyday things a textile factory might produce: thread and fabrics for socks and coats, for bedsheets and curtains, for towels and upholstery. Many people have been employed over the years in textile factories in the Southeast. Even today, textiles are important in Georgia, Virginia, North Carolina, and South Carolina.

Recently, some companies have moved their textile factories to other countries where workers receive less pay than workers in the Southeast. As those companies have left, other companies have been moving into the Southeast. Many are **high-tech industries**.

Research in the Triangle

North Carolina's research triangle is a center of high-tech industries in the Southeast. The cities of Raleigh, Durham, and Chapel Hill, shown on the map, form the triangle's three points. These cities have many of the facilities, such as universities, needed for scientific research. This is why dozens of large corporations have moved here.

NORTH CAROLINA RESEARCH TRIANGLE
★ State capital
● Major cities

But research centers are not really useful without people to work in them. This area has an enjoyable climate and pleasant surroundings, with cities not too large or too small. Corporations that move into the research triangle attract talented workers from all over the United States.

Today, computers are used in textile factories to produce high-quality goods.

---

high-tech industry Manufacturing that uses the latest engineering methods

SOUTHEAST

A City That Links the Southeast

In 1996, Atlanta, Georgia, became the focus of worldwide attention when it hosted the 1996 Summer Olympic Games. The city welcomed thousands of the world's athletes who participated in the Games. Atlanta also hosted millions of visitors.

Atlanta, Georgia, was not always a busy city. The first people to live in the area that is now Atlanta were the Creek and Cherokee Indians. People from England settled in and around present-day Atlanta in the 1700s. In 1813 a fort and trading post were built. The trading post kept growing, especially after railroad routes came through here on their way around the Appalachian Mountains. This was how the city of Atlanta got its start in business and transportation.

Atlanta's transportation facilities are still growing. Today, its airport is one of the busiest in the world. Its railroads and highways make Atlanta an excellent location for large companies.

There are many interesting places to visit in Atlanta. One of them is the Martin Luther King, Jr., National Historic Site. Dr. Martin Luther King, Jr., was a great civil rights leader who worked to help African Americans get rights equal to those of white Americans. He was born in Atlanta.

Atlanta is also the home of a famous art museum and concert hall, many parks, and universities. Its sports facilities include the Olympic stadium.

Atlanta, Georgia, is the center of one of the fastest-growing regions in the U.S. Through its systems of air, rail, and road transportation, it links many cities in the region.

REFOCUS
COMPREHENSION

1. Why has the Southeast region been a good place for farming?

2. How did cotton become the king of crops in the Southeast region?

THINK ABOUT IT
CRITICAL THINKING

How has the development of technology changed the Southeast?

STATE CHECK
ACTIVITY

Suppose you are visiting a city in the Southeast. In your state scrapbook, write a letter to a friend back home, describing the city you are visiting.

How It Works

⭐ **KEY TERM**

growing season

Products From Peanuts

Peanut Punch

CANDY BAR

Peanut Butter

Peanut Power

FOCUS *Peanuts are an important crop in the Southeast region. George Washington Carver helped farmers understand the value of growing peanuts.*

Where Peanuts Grow

Peanuts are grown in many countries of the world. China, India, and the United States are the leading peanut-growing countries.

Nearly all the peanuts grown in the United States are grown on the coastal plains of the southeastern states. The light, well-drained, sandy soil in the region and the long **growing seasons** produce good peanut crops.

Georgia produces more peanuts each year than any other state—more than 800,000 tons. That is nearly half of our nation's annual crop. Alabama, North Carolina, and Virginia also grow large amounts of our country's peanuts.

Modern farming methods have helped farmers grow even more peanuts. An acre of peanut

farmland in Georgia today produces five times as many peanuts a year as it produced in the 1930s. Peanuts have helped the economy of the Southeast region grow.

The Popular Peanut

Can you picture life without peanut butter and jelly sandwiches? But do you know that peanuts were not always a popular food? Until the early 1900s, few farmers in the Southeast planted peanuts. Peanuts were used mainly as food for hogs.

Cotton was the crop that brought farmers the most income. So year after year farmers planted cotton in the same fields. Gradually the soil became worn out. As a result, cotton production fell.

⭐ **growing season** The length of time between the last frost in spring and the first frost of fall

Paper

SHAVE

Coffee

GLUE

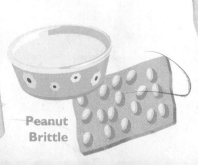

Peanut Brittle

After peanuts are harvested, they are crushed and processed in large vats to be made into peanut butter.

George Washington Carver

About 1914, a scientist named George Washington Carver tried to find a plant that could bring farmers as much money as cotton had brought. He began to study peanuts. Carver discovered more than 300 uses for peanuts. Shampoo, paint, shaving cream, and metal polish are only a few of the peanut-based products he developed. Later, Carver traveled around the country to help people become more aware of the value of peanuts and their many uses.

George Washington Carver at work in his laboratory

SHOW WHAT YOU KNOW!

REFOCUS
COMPREHENSION

1. Where are peanuts grown in the United States?

2. What did George Washington Carver discover about peanuts?

THINK ABOUT IT
CRITICAL THINKING

How did George Washington Carver's discoveries help Americans?

STATE CHECK
ACTIVITY

Find out the chief crop in your state. In your state scrapbook, make a list of different uses for that crop.

March of Time

1565 TO 1955

LITERATURE

The Trail on Which They Wept

Remember When

FOCUS *Discover how some events and some people have helped to shape the history of the Southeast.*

ST. AUGUSTINE

In 1565 a Spanish explorer named Pedro Menéndez de Avilés anchored his ship off the Atlantic coast of present-day Florida. Here he established the settlement of St. Augustine.

Jamestown, Virginia, the first permanent English settlement, was not founded until 1607.

St. Augustine is the oldest permanent European settlement on the continent of North America.

THE ARRIVAL OF AFRICANS

The first Africans brought to Jamestown arrived in 1619. These people had been captured in their homeland by traders and were sold to Jamestown colonists. They worked as servants for a number of years and then were set free. Many years later, more Africans were brought to Virginia as slaves.

THE TRAIL OF TEARS

In the winter of 1838, about 15,000 Cherokees were forced to leave their homes in parts of North Carolina, Georgia, Tennessee, and Alabama. They were moved to the Indian Territory that later became the state of Oklahoma. The Cherokees had lived on land that settlers wanted. The Cherokees' terrible journey from their homelands became known as the Trail of Tears.

1565	1619			1838	1861	1903	1955
Founding of St. Augustine	First Africans in Jamestown			The Trail of Tears	The Civil War starts	Wright brothers fly at Kitty Hawk	Rosa Parks seeks equal rights

1560 1590 1620 1650 1680 1710 1740 1770 1800 1830 1860 1890 1920 1950 1980

THE CIVIL WAR

On April 12, 1861, Southern troops in South Carolina opened fire on Fort Sumter, held by the U.S. Army. Northern and Southern states had disagreed over important issues for years. The shelling of Fort Sumter marked the beginning of the American Civil War, or the War Between the States. In 1865, General Robert E. Lee, leader of all the Southern states' armies, surrendered. The North won, but more than half a million people lost their lives.

FLIGHT AT KITTY HAWK

On a sandy beach at Kitty Hawk, North Carolina, Wilbur and Orville Wright made a dream come true in December of 1903. They became the first people to successfully fly a motor-driven aircraft. Orville flew first, traveling 120 feet in 12 seconds. By the end of the day, Wilbur had flown 852 feet in 59 seconds. The Wright brothers proved that people could fly.

ROSA PARKS AND CIVIL RIGHTS

In 1955, Rosa Parks was riding in the middle of a bus in Montgomery, Alabama. The bus driver told her to move to the back. At that time in the South, black Americans did not have the same rights as white Americans. When Parks did not move, she was arrested and fined.

Rosa Parks became part of the civil rights movement, in which African Americans worked to obtain rights equal to those of white Americans. In 1964, Congress passed the Civil Rights Act, which protected the rights of all Americans.

The Trail on Which They Wept

The Story of a Cherokee Girl

by Dorothy and Thomas Hoobler

THE TRAIL ON WHICH THEY WEPT
The Story of a Cherokee Girl

by Dorothy and Thomas Hoobler
Pictures by S.S. Burrus

You read something about the Trail of Tears on page 140. What was it like for the Cherokees just before they were ordered to leave their land, you may wonder. A Cherokee girl about your age can help you understand as she faces the possibility of being forced to leave her home.

It was harvest time in the land of the Cherokees. At dawn, from the front porch of her family's house, Sarah Tsaluh Rogers watched blue mist rise above the floor of the valley. She stepped onto the grass, feeling the dew tickle her bare feet. The rising sun gradually lit up the hills in the distance. Every tree was ablaze with gold and crimson leaves.

It was a wonderful sight, but in the back of Sarah's mind was the thought: Will this be the last harvest?

The year had been a good one on the Rogers plantation. The workers had filled wagon after wagon with corn, taking it to the mill to be ground into meal. The corn plants had been gathered into sheaves and left to dry.

The hard work of picking the cotton was finally finished. The plantation had produced nearly a thousand bales, and Sarah's family had sold them for a high price. When the trees lost the last of their leaves and winter came, the big plantation house would be warm, and there would be more than enough food for everyone.

But then the sun went behind a cloud. A chilly breeze blew down from the hills. Sarah wrapped her arms around her body, thinking again of the shadow that hung over her people.

The state government of Georgia wanted the Cherokees to leave their land. For years the Cherokees had fought Georgia in the courts. Finally the Supreme Court of the United States had ruled in favor of the Cherokees.

But President Andrew Jackson would not enforce the Supreme Court's order. He wanted the Cherokees to move hundreds of miles west, across the Mississippi River. He said they would be happier there. Of course everyone knew that wasn't true. The Cherokees were happy right here in the land where they had always lived.

It's our land! Sarah thought angrily. We won't leave it!

Will Sarah have to leave her Cherokee land? You can find out what happens to Sarah and her family by checking the book out of your school or public library.

SHOW WHAT YOU KNOW!

REFOCUS
COMPREHENSION

1. Why were Africans first brought to North America?

2. What was the outcome of the Civil War?

THINK ABOUT IT
CRITICAL THINKING

Why was Sarah so determined to remain in her homeland?

STATE CHECK
ACTIVITY

Find five important events in your state's history. In your state scrapbook, make a time line of these events.

Map Adventure

KEY TERMS
Confederate States of America
Union

Civil War Sites

FOCUS The Civil War is an important part of the history of the Southeast region. Journey to some Civil War sites in the Southeast region. Remember the people who were part of this terrible war.

= CIVIL WAR BATTLE SITES

The Civil War

In the 1850s the United States had a serious issue to deal with. That issue was slavery. Some southerners owned enslaved people, but many more favored slavery. Most northerners were against slavery. In 1861 eleven Southern states formed a separate country called the **Confederate States of America**. As a result, a war broke out. It was called the Civil War, or the War Between the States, which was fought from 1861 to 1865.

In 1865 the **Union** army defeated the Confederate forces. The United States was united again. Use what you know about a grid map to tour some of the battle sites of the Civil War.

Map Key

1 Fort Sumter, South Carolina: April 12, 1861
The Confederate army fires cannons on Fort Sumter. The Civil War begins.

2 Manassas Junction, Virginia: July 21, 1861
Union and Confederate troops clash just 25 miles from Washington, D.C., in the battle of Bull Run.

3 Pittsburg Landing, Tennessee: April 6–7, 1862 Over 24,000 Union and Confederate soldiers die at the battle of Shiloh.

4 Vicksburg, Mississippi: May–July 1863
Union troops try to capture the Confederate city of Vicksburg, on the bluffs above the Mississippi River.

5 Chickamauga, Georgia: September 19–20, 1863 Confederate troops force the Union army to retreat to Chattanooga, Tennessee.

6 Appomattox, Virginia: April 9, 1865
Confederate general Robert E. Lee surrenders his army to General Ulysses S. Grant, the Union army commander. The Civil War ends.

Confederate States of America The nation formed by the Southern states that withdrew from the Union
Union The Northern states during the Civil War

MAP IT

1. Let's begin our journey at D-6. What happened in that area in 1861?
2. Next, put a finger on site 2 on the map. Which grid box are you in? What happened here during the Civil War?
3. Travel to site 3 on the map. In which state are you? What battle took place here?
4. Find D-2 on the grid map. What city is in that grid box? What happened here in 1863?

EXPLORE IT

Using the map on page 144 as a model, make your own map of Civil War sites. You might include such battle sites as Richmond, Virginia; Fort Donelson, Tennessee; and Mobile Bay, Alabama.

Citizenship

KEY TERM

irrigate

The Everglades

FOCUS *The Everglades region in Florida is a major source of fresh water for millions of people. But the Everglades is drying up. Join the debate and decide what to do.*

About the Everglades

The Everglades region in the southern part of the state of Florida looks like a grassy swamp. Actually, it is a sheet of slow-moving water, like a river 50 miles wide and 6 inches deep. Some water seeps down into a spongy layer of rock called limestone. Later, the water is pumped out for use in homes and on farms.

The Everglades is home to thousands of birds and reptiles. Many of these animals have been dying. Some animals that live there, including the crocodile and the manatee, are on the national list of endangered animals.

What has caused this change? On the edges of the Everglades, people have built farms, ranches, and homes. They have needed fresh water for drinking, cooking, and **irrigating** their farm crops. People have used water from streams that flow into the Everglades. As a result, less water is available in the underground water supply of the Everglades.

The population of South Florida continues to grow. On the map find the populated area on the edge of the Everglades. As people continue to build near the Everglades, more and more fresh water is needed for daily living and for irrigating farms. Which is more important—preserving the Everglades or taking care of the needs of people?

0   50   100 miles
0   50   100 kilometers

ATLANTIC OCEAN

Gulf of Mexico

N
W—E
S

Florida

THE FLORIDA EVERGLADES

- National Park/ Wildlife area
- Everglades region
- Populated area surrounding Miami

Miami

Visitors travel through the shallow waters of the Everglades in a special flat-bottomed boat moved by a giant fan.

irrigate   To supply land with water through ditches or sprinklers

Steven

The Everglades is no big deal. I've been there, and it looks like an old swamp. It's hot, it's damp, and it's full of bugs. Who cares if it dries up? The land is what's important. We need it so people can build new houses and stores!

Janelle

Wait! The Everglades is a swamp, but it's home to lots of animals, like manatees and crocodiles. The Everglades is a very special place. Even if it means trying to use less water and cutting back on new homes and jobs, we should try to protect the Everglades.

Katie

Trying to keep the animals in the Everglades safe might cost my dad his job. We've got a farm near the Everglades. We may have to sell it if we can't use water for irrigation. We might have to move if Dad loses his job.

Greg

Maybe your dad could get together with other farmers and grow crops that need less irrigation water. Maybe people shouldn't build any more houses or farms on land near the Everglades.

YOU DECIDE...

Should Florida cut back on development and try to use less fresh water? Why?

How might the people who lose their jobs be helped?

Do you think people should sell their land and move in order to protect wildlife in the Everglades?

What suggestions do you have for protecting the Everglades?

SHOW WHAT YOU KNOW!

REFOCUS
COMPREHENSION

1. How does the Everglades help the people in Florida?

2. Why is the Everglades drying up?

THINK ABOUT IT
CRITICAL THINKING

What might happen if the Everglades dries up completely?

STATE CHECK
ACTIVITY

Find out if there are any swamps, parks, or wildlife centers in your state. Make a special-purpose map of your state that shows these features.

SUMMING UP

1 DO YOU REMEMBER . . .
COMPREHENSION

1. What were the first crops grown in the Southeast and who grew them?

2. Why is the Southeast well-suited to peanut production?

3. Why are the Wright brothers remembered?

4. What happened at Appomattox, Virginia, on April 9, 1865?

5. How has the Everglades changed in the last hundred years?

2 SKILL POWER
USING A GRID MAP

Make a grid map of the Southeast region. Here's how.

Draw or trace the map on page 132 of this book. Using a ruler, add horizontal lines that are 1 inch apart and vertical lines that are 1 inch apart. Label the boxes formed by the lines with numbers across the top and letters along the right side. Then, on a piece of paper, list the capital of each southeastern state. Next to the name of each capital, write its grid letter and number.

3 WHAT DO YOU THINK?
CRITICAL THINKING

1. How does the land elevation in the Southeast region make it a good place for farming?

2. What might have happened in the Southeast region if George Washington Carver had not studied the peanut?

3. Which of the historical events in this chapter do you think did the most to change the Southeast region?

4. What might the United States be like today if the Confederate States of America had won the Civil War?

5. In the next hundred years, will the population of South Florida be able to continue to grow as it has? Explain your thinking.

4 SAY IT, WRITE IT, USE IT
VOCABULARY

Write and illustrate a travel brochure about the Southeast region. Be sure to include historical sites and information about the region's agriculture and industries. Include as many of the key terms as you can. Share your brochure with your classmates.

Confederate States of America	irrigate
environment	plantation
growing season	textile
high-tech industry	Union

5 GEOGRAPHY AND YOU
MAP STUDY

Use the map below to answer these questions.

1. In which states was rice grown?

2. In which state was more cotton grown—Florida or Alabama?

3. In which states was only tobacco grown?

4. In which state was more tobacco grown—Virginia or Arkansas?

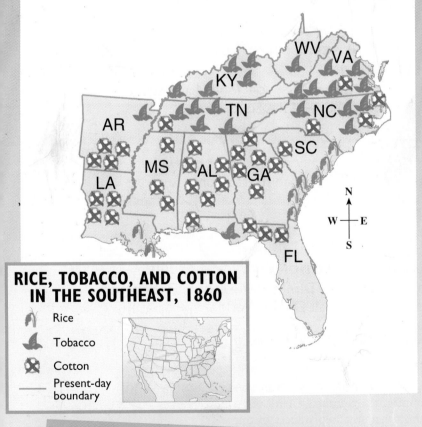

RICE, TOBACCO, AND COTTON IN THE SOUTHEAST, 1860

🌾 Rice

🍂 Tobacco

✖ Cotton

— Present-day boundary

6 TAKE ACTION
CITIZENSHIP

Look in your local newspaper for stories about an environmental problem in your area. With a classmate, discuss both sides of the problem. Choose one side of the issue and have your classmate choose the other side. Come up with a solution to the problem. Explain it in a letter to the editor of the local newspaper. You just might find your ideas in print!

7 GET CREATIVE
HEALTH CONNECTION

In Thailand, a country in Asia, peanut butter is used in dressings for salads and noodles. In parts of Africa, it is baked in breads. What are some new ways that you might eat peanut butter? You might start by spreading some peanut butter on carrot sticks or on apple wedges or between slices of cucumber. Create a special treat that combines peanut butter and a healthful food. Share your treat with a friend or a family member.

LOOKING AHEAD Find out in the next chapter some of the ways that the Southeast region is linked to the world.

Southeastern Links

The Southeast region is linked to the world in many ways—through its specialty crops, foods, busy cities, and special kinds of music known as country and jazz.

CONTENTS

◄ The Appalachian dulcimer is a traditional instrument of the Southeast. Find out more about handmade products of this region on page 159.

Near and Far

The following books give you information about how the Southeast region is connected to other regions and the world. Read one that interests you and fill out a book-review form.

READ AND RESEARCH

The Story of Walt Disney, Maker of Magical Worlds
by Bernice Selden (Dell Publishing, 1989)
Read how Walt Disney became known throughout the world for his cartoons, movies, and theme parks, especially Walt Disney World in Florida. *(biography)*

Pocahontas: Princess of the River Tribes by Elaine Raphael and Don Bolognese (Scholastic, 1993)
When the sailors from England came to the New World, they were helped by Pocahontas, daughter of the Chief of the River People. Use the drawing tips at the end of the book to sketch Pocahontas and her people. *(historical fiction)*

Melting Pots: Family Stories & Recipes by Judith Eichler Weber, illustrated by Scott Gubala (Silver Moon Press, 1994)
Many families in America celebrate their special days with recipes passed down from generation to generation. One of the stories tells how children in an African American family in Louisiana prepare a creole meal for their grandmother's birthday. *(nonfiction)*

Nashville by Amy Lynch (Silver Burdett Press, 1991)
Because of its location, Nashville is an important southeastern city. Find out why people from all over the world visit Nashville, which has become known as Music City, USA. *(nonfiction)*

SKILL POWER Organizing Information

When you organize information, you put it in a form that makes it easier to understand.

UNDERSTAND IT

Sometimes you have a lot of information that you want to show to other people. To make the information easier to understand, you can organize facts and figures into graphs and tables. Look at the table on this page, showing the national seashore parks in the United States. The name, state location, year established, and size of each park are shown in columns. You read a column by starting at the top and reading down to the last line on the table.

Tables also have rows. You read a row from left to right, the same way you read a book. Each row on the national seashore parks table contains information about one park.

NATIONAL SEASHORE PARKS

Name	State	Year Established	Size in Acres
Assateague Island	MD-VA	1965	39,631
Canaveral	FL	1975	57,662
Cape Cod	MA	1961	43,571
Cape Hatteras	NC	1937	30,319
Cape Lookout	NC	1966	28,415
Cumberland Island	GA	1972	36,415
Fire Island	NY	1964	19,579
Gulf Islands	FL-MS	1971	135,625
Padre Island	TX	1968	130,434
Point Reyes	CA	1972	71,049

Look at the columns and rows in the table about national seashore parks on page 152. Use the table to answer these questions.

1. How many national seashore parks are listed?

2. Which seashore parks are in more than one state?

3. Which national seashore park is larger in size—Canaveral in Florida or Point Reyes in California?

4. Which national seashore park was established first—Cape Cod in Massachusetts or Padre Island in Texas?

The national seashore parks in this table are arranged in the order of the alphabet. How else could you organize the information?

TRY IT

Think of other information that can be organized in a table. If you collect baseball cards, you could make a table showing which ones you have, the year you purchased each card, and how much each card is worth. If you are helping to organize a school event, you could make a table showing the jobs to be done, who will do each, and when they need to be finished. Look at the table on this page, showing the rehearsal schedule for a school play.

Work by yourself or with a small group of classmates to develop a useful table. Don't forget to give your table a name. Share your table with the class.

4th-Grade Play
Pocahontas

Name	Part	Rehearsal Times
Reiko	Pocahontas	3:30–4:30
Juan	Captain John Smith	3:30–4:30
Michael	Powhatan	3:30–4:30
Karl	Kocoum	3:30–4:30
Sami	John Rolfe	4:30–5:30
Sean	Sir Thomas Dale	4:30–5:30
Chris	Sir Samuel Argall	4:30–5:30
Marc	Opechancanough	4:30–5:30

SKILL POWER SEARCH Look in this chapter to find at least three ways in which information is organized.

From Cotton to Country Music

FOCUS *The Southeast region is known for special farm products, its unique style of cooking, and important industries.*

Louisiana supplies the country with 90 percent of all crayfish eaten—18 million pounds per year.

Farming in the Southeast

Farming today is big business in the United States. Farm work done for a profit is called **agriculture**. One way that farmers can make a profit and be successful is to grow crops that farmers in other places can't grow.

The Southeast region has large farms that grow crops which need a warm, moist climate. Peanuts, rice, cotton, and sugar cane are among the chief crops grown in the Southeast. Farmers of the Southeast region have grown these crops for many years.

There are about 73 million orange trees in Florida's **orange groves**. Large farms also produce lemons, limes, grapefruits, and other citrus fruits. Many citrus fruits are shipped from the Southeast region to the northern regions of the United States where citrus fruits do not grow.

Georgia is a leading peach-growing state. Peaches are shipped throughout the country. On the map on page 155, find many of the foods that are grown in the Southeast region.

Harvesting Fish

Along the coastlines of the Southeast states, shallow **marshes** and deeper ocean waters provide wonderful living places and food for many kinds of fish. Shrimp and crabs are found along the Gulf Coast, especially in Louisiana and Mississippi.

Some southeasterners have adopted a very old kind of farming called fish farming. A fish farm has large tanks or ponds for raising fish. The farmer controls everything

---

agriculture The science and business of growing crops and raising livestock
orange grove A field of orange trees planted in straight rows

marsh An area of soft, wet land

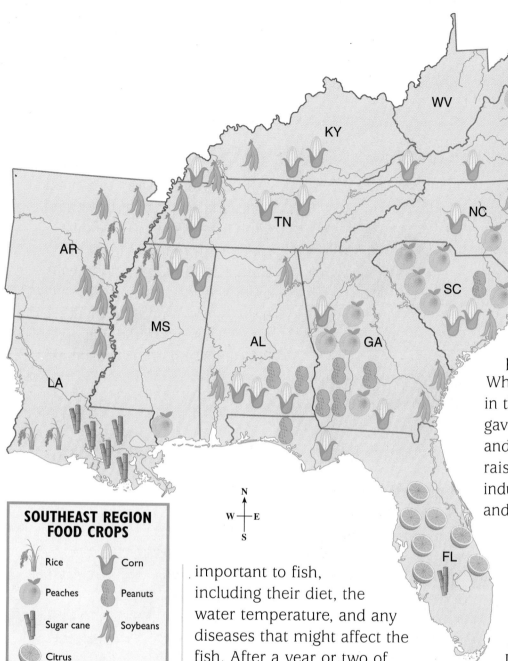

SOUTHEAST REGION FOOD CROPS

Rice
Corn
Peaches
Peanuts
Sugar cane
Soybeans
Citrus

Cattle Farms

Farmers sometimes decide to change what they grow if a different food product is in greater demand. When eating beef became popular in the United States, many farmers gave up growing tobacco or cotton and began to raise cattle. Cattle raising is now an important industry in Virginia, West Virginia, and Tennessee.

Cattle can graze on land that is too poor to use for growing crops. But cattle need more than grass for food, so many farmers in the Southeast now grow soybeans for their cattle. Look at the map on this page to see where soybeans are grown in the Southeast region.

Not all the soybean crops are set aside for cattle food. Some are used in making pet food, some kinds of candy, and industrial products such as paint and adhesive tape. Soybeans are also shipped to other countries throughout the world.

important to fish, including their diet, the water temperature, and any diseases that might affect the fish. After a year or two of growth, the fish are ready for harvesting. They are cleaned, packaged, and sent to stores and supermarkets.

Catfish and crayfish are important products of fish farms. Southeasterners have developed ways to cook these fish that are popular throughout the country.

Mouth-watering foods of the Southeast

Rice

Pecan Pie

Traditional Foods of the Southeast

If you were invited to a picnic in Louisiana, you might be served jambalaya. This is a rice dish made with many ingredients. Ham and tomatoes, along with onions, celery, shrimp, sausage, or oysters, are simmered together in a pot. This is a traditional dish of Louisiana and other coastal areas.

Jambalaya

Fried Chicken

Corn Bread

Orange Juice

Corn on the Cob

Mashed Sweet Potatoes

Crayfish stew, called étouffée (ay too FAY), is another popular food in the Southeast region. That's because crayfish are plentiful in the Gulf Coast waters. Sweet potato casserole, corn bread, and peach pie are also well-known foods of this region.

At the picnic you might also have the chance to taste gumbo. Gumbo is a thick soup that may contain chicken, sausage, shrimp, and rice as well as okra or other vegetables. Okra is a plant that was brought to North America from Africa.

People of the Southeast region developed special dishes because of the foods that were available to them. It was natural to use the fish, fruits, vegetables, and other products of the region.

Over time, people tried different ways of combining ingredients. Some recipes became so popular that people handed them down from one generation to the next. A good example of a southeastern recipe is Southern fried chicken. Virginia ham and hickory-smoked bacon are also popular foods throughout our country. People of the Southeast region found that ham and bacon had a special flavor when cooked over wood chips from a hickory tree.

Growing Rice

Rice is an ingredient in many southeastern recipes. One reason is that more rice is grown in the Southeast than in any other region of the United States. Rice plants need long, hot summers and short, mild winters to grow well. They also need a lot of water. The plains along the Mississippi River have a mild climate, and they are wet enough for growing rice. Arkansas, Louisiana, and Mississippi are among the leading rice-growing states in the United States.

LEADING RICE-GROWING STATES

RANK	STATE	TONS
1	Arkansas	4,047,000
2	California	2,061,000
3	Louisiana	1,472,000
4	Texas	1,063,000
5	Mississippi	923,000

Peach Pie

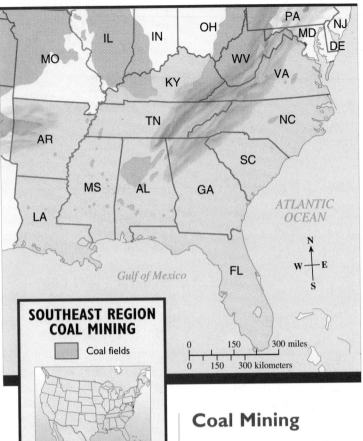

SOUTHEAST REGION
COAL MINING

Coal fields

0   150   300 miles

0   150   300 kilometers

Trains are used to carry coal from the Southeast to other regions of the country.

Coal Mining

Some of the richest coal fields in the world are found under the Appalachian Mountains of West Virginia and Kentucky. On the map above, find other coal-mining states in the Southeast region.

By the middle of the 1800s, coal was used as fuel for steam engines in trains and other machines. Many people living in the mountains of Tennessee, Virginia, Kentucky, and West Virginia turned to mining coal. They began this dangerous work in order to make a better living.

Today, most of the coal in the Southeast is shipped to other places. Some of the coal is moved across Virginia and out through the port of Norfolk to other countries. Large shipments of coal are sent by barge down the Ohio River or by railway to cities in the middle part of the United States. Factories in Cleveland, Detroit, and Chicago use the coal for fuel to run the machines that make cars, farm equipment, tools, and other goods.

Coal that is mined in Alabama is shipped to the city of Birmingham for use in making steel. Iron ore, the basic ingredient in steel, is found in abundance near that Alabama city.

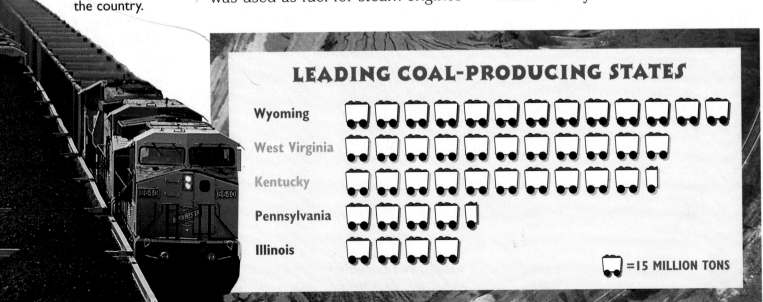

LEADING COAL-PRODUCING STATES

Wyoming

West Virginia

Kentucky

Pennsylvania

Illinois

= 15 MILLION TONS

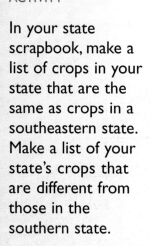

This dulcimer was made by a craftsperson from the Appalachian Mountains of Virginia.

Handmade Products

Some of the country's finest handmade products come from the Southeast region. These are objects that are designed and made with great care. Quilts in interesting designs and colors are an example of such craft work.

People of the Southeast use the available wood to produce many handmade items. They make baskets for carrying or storing things. String instruments, such as dulcimers, are also well-known products of the region.

Horses and Country Music

Kentucky and Tennessee are famous for their horse farms. If you visited these states, you would see miles of fences, pastures, and horse stables. You'd also see many beautiful prize-winning horses!

The Southeast is also well-known for its country-music industry, especially in the cities of Nashville and Memphis, Tennessee. The Southeast was the birthplace of country music. Many of the instruments, melodies, and words of early country music were similar to those used by English, Scottish, and Irish settlers in the Appalachian Mountains.

Today, visitors to the Southeast region attend music festivals that feature various forms of country music. Many people visit the Grand Ole Opry House in Nashville, a concert hall where old country fiddles share the stage with modern electric guitars.

Horse farms are found in the western part of Kentucky.

Next Stop New Orleans

FOCUS *The city of New Orleans is a busy port and a popular tourist spot. The city is famous for its music, cooking, and architecture.*

A Port City

New Orleans, Louisiana, is one of the busiest ports in the United States. Oceangoing ships travel about 100 miles up the Mississippi River to reach the port of New Orleans. More than 5,000 ships from all over the world call at the port of New Orleans every year.

Cotton, rice, corn, iron, and steel are among the major exports that leave the port of New Orleans. Sugar, bananas, coffee, cocoa beans, and chemicals are imported from countries in Central America and South America for **distribution** in the United States.

Two ports in the northern part of South America ship goods to New Orleans, especially coffee. On the map below, find Maracaibo, Venezuela. Then find the port of Barranquilla in Colombia.

★ **distribution** The process of getting goods to stores and markets

Coffee Fact

The United States imports almost 3 billion pounds of coffee each year.

IMPORTING COFFEE

→ Coffee route
• Port cities

Mississippi River

LA

New Orleans

Gulf of Mexico

Caribbean Sea

Barranquilla Maracaibo

VENEZUELA

N
W—E
S

0   250   500 miles
0 250 500 kilometers

COLOMBIA

Six Leading Ports in the United States

RANK	PORT	TONS PER YEAR
1	South Louisiana, LA	199,665,000
2	Houston, TX	137,664,000
3	New York, NY and NJ	115,311,000
4	Valdez, AK	93,737,000
5	Baton Rouge, LA	84,699,000
6	New Orleans, LA	66,441,000

A Mixture of French and Spanish

New Orleans is one of the oldest cities in the Southeast region. It was started in 1718 as a French trading post. The part of the city originally built by the French settlers is called the French Quarter, or the Old Square. A fire destroyed this section of the city in the late 1700s.

Spaniards, who ruled Louisiana at the time, rebuilt the French Quarter. They added fancy iron grillwork to the balconies of many buildings. Look at the design at the top of this page to see a detail of the Spanish grillwork.

French and Spanish influences remain strong in New Orleans today. **Descendants** of the city's early French and Spanish residents are called Creoles (KREE ohlz). Creole cooking, a spicy mix of French and Spanish dishes, is served in many restaurants in New Orleans.

⭐ **descendant** A person born of a certain family or group

Music Called Jazz

In the early 1900s, musicians in New Orleans developed a special kind of music called jazz. This lively music is a blend of African and European music. An important feature of jazz is improvisation. To improvise means "to make up on the spur of the moment." A good jazz soloist seldom plays anything the same way twice.

Today, one of New Orleans's most popular attractions is the old Preservation Hall. Visitors sit on hard wooden benches for hours and listen to musicians play jazz.

Wynton Marsalis is part of a long tradition of great jazz players. ▶

SHOW WHAT YOU KNOW!

REFOCUS
COMPREHENSION

1. Where is the port of New Orleans located?

2. Name five products that are exported from the port of New Orleans.

THINK ABOUT IT
CRITICAL THINKING

Why is New Orleans a busy port?

STATE CHECK
ACTIVITY

Read about a place in your state that you would like to visit. In your state scrapbook write down what makes that place interesting to you.

161

Global Connections

A World of Fun

FOCUS *Walt Disney looked for a perfect location before he decided to build Walt Disney World in central Florida.*

▼ Walt Disney's dream was to build a second theme park similar to Disneyland in California.

Walt Disney World

Not so long ago, alligators roamed in an area that is now home to the most popular vacation destination in the United States— Walt Disney World. This huge **theme park** is located near Orlando, Florida. It first opened in 1971 with its Magic Kingdom that included a storybook castle, amusements, rides, and restaurants.

In 1982, EPCOT Center was added to Walt Disney World. EPCOT stands for Experimental Prototype Community of Tomorrow. It is a village in which visitors are given a view of the world of the future. They can learn about new **technology** and about countries around the world.

The Perfect Location

Walt Disney chose Florida for a theme park for several reasons. He saw that many tourists visited Florida each year because they liked its mild climate. Airports and highways already existed nearby. They would make it easy for visitors to reach the new park.

Disneyland, which Walt Disney had built in Anaheim, California, in 1955, was already very popular. Disney wanted his new park to be so far away from California that people wouldn't have to choose one park over the other. Walt Disney World, in Florida, would be the park for people on the East Coast.

★ **theme park** An amusement park in which all the attractions have a central theme

★ **technology** The scientific methods and ideas used in industry, agriculture, and trade

▲ Orlando is home to Walt Disney World and is the center of the citrus industry in central Florida.

Disney wanted land he could easily change and shape. The site he chose in central Florida was mostly flat, grassy lands, **swamps**, and orange groves. Such land did not require cutting through mountains or clearing forests before building a theme park.

Growth of a City

Walt Disney's selection of central Florida brought many people to the Orlando area. Thousands of people found work building the theme parks and then running them. Businesses, such as banks and supermarkets, grew as the population increased.

★ **swamp** An area in which water and wet, soft land mix together

Today, people arrive daily in Orlando from cities all over the world. Walt Disney World attracts about 30 million visitors a year. Many other people come to do business in this fast-growing part of central Florida.

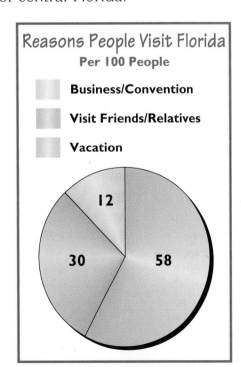

Reasons People Visit Florida
Per 100 People

- Business/Convention
- Visit Friends/Relatives
- Vacation

12
30
58

SHOW WHAT YOU KNOW!

REFOCUS
COMPREHENSION

1. Why did Walt Disney choose Florida as the location for Disney World?

2. What effect did Walt Disney World have on businesses in Orlando, Florida?

THINK ABOUT IT
CRITICAL THINKING

Which of Walt Disney's reasons for choosing Florida for the location of Walt Disney World do you think was the most important? Why?

STATE CHECK
ACTIVITY

Suppose you are designing a theme park in your state. Write down where you would build it and why you would choose that site.

SUMMING UP

1 DO YOU REMEMBER . . .
COMPREHENSION

1. Name five foods that come from farms of the Southeast region.

2. What is fish farming?

3. In which Southeast states are some of the richest coal fields in the world found?

4. What are two things for which New Orleans is famous?

5. Name three reasons why Walt Disney chose central Florida as the site for his second theme park.

2 SKILL POWER
ORGANIZING INFORMATION

With a partner, organize the following information about southeastern cities in a table.

Miami, Florida, has a yearly rainfall of 60 inches, and an annual snowfall of 0 inches. Thirty days per year are 90 degrees or more. In Charleston, South Carolina, the annual snowfall is 0.5 inches. The city averages 47 days per year over 90 degrees. The annual rainfall is 52 inches. The annual rainfall in New Orleans is 57 inches, and the yearly snowfall is 0.2 inches. It has 67 days per year in the 90s. Louisville, Kentucky, gets 17 inches of snow and 43 inches of rain a year. Only 24 days per year are over 90 degrees.

Be sure to give the table a title. Then compare your table with those of other students.

3 WHAT DO YOU THINK?
CRITICAL THINKING

1. How might farming in the Southeast change if Americans stopped eating beef?

2. Why did people in the Appalachian Mountains give up farming in the 1800s to risk their lives in coal mines?

3. Why is it important for craft making to continue in the Southeast?

4. How does the location of New Orleans make it a busy port?

5. What other place in the Southeast region would have been suitable for Walt Disney World? Explain your choice.

4 SAY IT, WRITE IT, USE IT
VOCABULARY

Suppose that you work for an advertising company in the Southeast region. Your company asks you to design a poster that will attract visitors to a state in the Southeast. For your poster, use some of the key terms from the chapter. Illustrate your poster with your own drawings or with photographs cut from magazines.

agriculture	orange grove
descendant	swamp
distribution	technology
marsh	theme park

5 GEOGRAPHY AND YOU
MAP STUDY

Use the map below to answer these questions.

1. Where are most coal fields in the Southeast region located—along the Atlantic Ocean or inland?

2. In which state are there more coal fields—West Virginia or Louisiana?

3. In which state are there more coal fields—South Carolina or Arkansas?

4. In which states of the Southeast are there no coal fields?

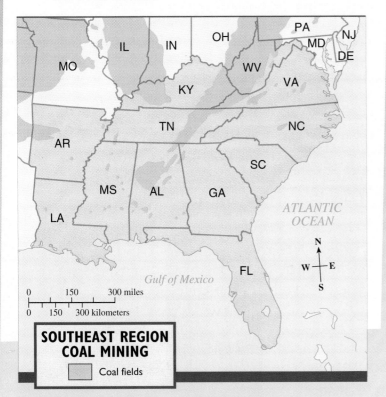

SOUTHEAST REGION COAL MINING
☐ Coal fields

6 TAKE ACTION
CITIZENSHIP

You can learn a lot about people by listening to the music they enjoy. Listen to music created by Native Americans or to music from countries in Asia, Africa, or South America. You may not understand the words of the music. But the music can tell you about the people from other lands.

7 GET CREATIVE
MATH CONNECTION

Some automobile clubs make map routes for members who are planning trips. The club marks on a road map the best roads to take.

Find a road map of a southeastern state. Using tracing paper, map the shortest route between two major cities in the state that are at least 200 miles apart. Mark down the mileages between the towns and smaller cities along the way. Then find the total number of miles a driver would travel between the two large cities.

LOOKING AHEAD Discover in the next chapter the states of the **Midwest and Great Plains region.**

IN Search OF Open Spaces

What Riches Are Found in the Central United States?

The Midwest and Great Plains region and the Southwest region form the central corridor of our nation. These regions contain some of the richest natural resources in the world—as well as land of breathtaking beauty.

THE MIDWEST AND

The Midwest and Great Plains region stretches from the Appalachian Mountains in the east to the Rocky Mountains in the west. In this chapter, find out more about this region.

This girl is dressed for school as a pioneer girl might have dressed. Find out about a pioneer school on page 185.

CONTENTS

GREAT PLAINS REGION

These books are about people and events in the Midwest and Great Plains region. Read one that interests you and fill out a book-review form.

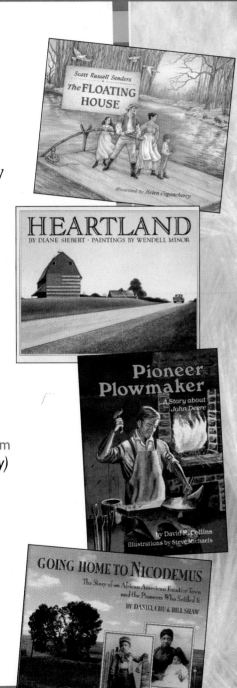

READ AND RESEARCH

The Floating House **by Scott Russell Sanders, illustrated by Helen Cogancherry** (Simon & Schuster, 1995)
Join a pioneering family as they travel down the Ohio River in search of a new homestead. *(historical fiction)*
•*You can read a selection from this story on page 180.*

Heartland **by Diane Siebert, paintings by Wendell Minor** (Harper Trophy, 1992)
Visit the central farm region of the United States through the vivid paintings and matching poetry in this book. *(nonfiction)*

Pioneer Plowmaker: A Story About John Deere **by David R. Collins, illustrated by Steve Michaels** (Carolrhoda Books, 1990)
Read about blacksmith John Deere and how his invention solved a problem faced by many farmers in the Midwest and Great Plains region. *(biography)*

Going Home to Nicodemus: The Story of an African American Frontier Town and the Pioneers Who Settled It **by Daniel Chu and Bill Shaw** (Silver Burdett Press, 1994)
In 1878, a group of African Americans set out from Kentucky for Kansas where they began a town that they named Nicodemus. Read about the settlement established by these courageous people. *(nonfiction)*

Skill POWER Using an Atlas

Knowing how to use an atlas can help you learn more about the geography of places around the world.

UNDERSTAND IT

Has anyone ever said to you "Look it up" when you asked where a place was located? You probably know how to look up words in a dictionary and how to use an encyclopedia to find information about people, places, and things. Another way to find information about places is to use an atlas. An atlas is a collection of maps.

Dictionaries, encyclopedias, and atlases are reference sources. You do not read reference sources from front to back as you would read a story. You just read the parts you need.

EXPLORE IT

Find the Atlas on pages 398–411 of this book. Take a minute now to look through it. What kinds of maps do you see? Look at the maps in the Atlas and decide which map you would use to answer each of these questions.

1. Which part of the United States has the highest elevation?

2. Where are the Great Plains located?

3. If you have a pen pal in St. Paul, does he or she live in the capital of Minnesota?

4. Which states does the Mississippi River touch?

Atlases, globes, and maps help you locate any place in the world. ▶

TRY IT

Form teams and plan an atlas quiz show. Use the Atlas in this book or one from your school library. Then, on index cards, write questions that can be answered by looking in an atlas. With the other teams, decide on rules and prizes for your quiz show. You might want to make signs and other decorations for the show.

On what river is the capital of South Dakota located?

Missouri River

Which states have a boundary with Lake Superior?

Minnesota, Wisconsin, and Michigan

◀ These students are using the geography questions they worked on for their quiz show.

SKILL POWER SEARCH

Write down two or three places mentioned in this chapter. Then use an atlas to get more information about each place.

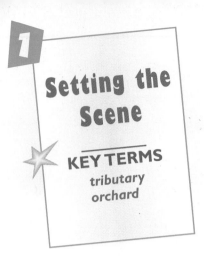

THE HEARTLAND OF THE UNITED STATES

FOCUS *The Midwest and Great Plains region is the largest region of the United States. People in the region have made it an important agricultural and manufacturing region.*

THE MIDWEST AND GREAT PLAINS REGION

★ State capitals
• Major cities

A Special Place

Many people call the Midwest and Great Plains region the Heartland of the United States. They call it the Heartland for two important reasons. The first reason is location. The Midwest and Great Plains region is located in the center, or heart, of our nation.

The map on this page shows the 12 states in the Midwest and Great Plains region. Minnesota is the largest state in the region. The state of Michigan has two sections. The smaller section to the north is separated from the rest of the state by Lake Michigan.

The second reason the Midwest and Great Plains region is called the Heartland is that it is our country's greatest farming region. The Midwest and Great Plains region sends out its many products to the entire country and to other parts of the world as well.

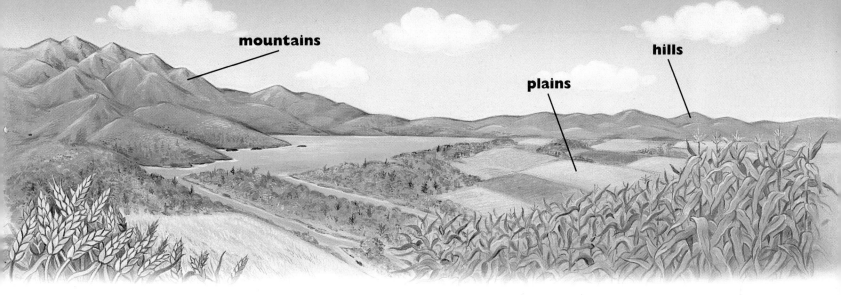

mountains

plains

hills

Breadbasket to the Nation

The Midwest and Great Plains region is our country's breadbasket. A breadbasket region is a country's most important region for producing nutritious food. It provides a country with wheat, corn, vegetables, meat, and other foods that people need for survival. Some regions give us favorite foods, such as sugar or chocolate for making candy, but we don't need those foods to survive. So those regions are not breadbaskets.

The farmers of this region are known around the world for their modern machinery. Using machines to plow and to plant and harvest crops is faster and more efficient than doing these jobs by hand. With machinery, one farmer can produce enough food to feed many thousands of people.

▲ Landforms of the Midwest and Great Plains region

▼ Mount Rushmore in the Black Hills is a memorial to Presidents Washington, Jefferson, Theodore Roosevelt, and Lincoln.

Miles of Plains

If you could run your hand over the land of the Midwest and Great Plains region, you would feel mostly smooth, level land. But you would also feel a few bumps in the land. Some of these would be the Superior Upland, which is a range of mountains in the far northern parts of Wisconsin and Minnesota. Other bumpy areas would be the Black Hills of South Dakota and the Sand Hills of Nebraska.

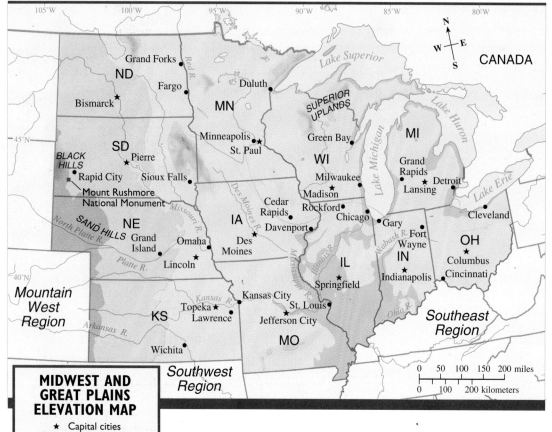

MIDWEST AND GREAT PLAINS ELEVATION MAP

★ Capital cities
• Other cities

Elevation

Feet	Meters
More than 3,281	More than 1,001
1,641-3,280	501-1,000
657-1,640	201-500
0-656	0-200

Rivers of the Region

Running through the middle of the Midwest and Great Plains region is the greatest river in the United States. This is the Mississippi River. The Missouri River joins the Mississippi River about 20 miles north of St. Louis, Missouri. And the Ohio River empties into the Mississippi River in the southwestern corner of Illinois. The Missouri and the Ohio rivers are **tributaries** of the Mississippi River. Find these three major rivers of the Midwest and Great Plains region on the map on this page.

Waterways to the Ocean

Five large lakes, the Great Lakes, are in the northeastern part of the United States. Our boundary with Canada runs through four of these lakes. Only Lake Michigan is wholly within the United States. Four of the Great Lakes are in the Midwest and Great Plains region. Find these lakes on the map at the left.

At one time, ships could not travel between the Great Lakes and the Atlantic Ocean. But new waterways have been built and old ones enlarged so that ships can reach the farthest of the Great Lakes from the Atlantic Ocean.

A Variety of Climates

Some states in the Midwest and Great Plains region reach far to the north, where the winters are very cold. The region's states that are farther south are much warmer. Summer days there can be sunny and very hot.

In Ohio, Indiana, Illinois, Iowa, and Missouri, there is plenty of rain. Farmers take advantage of the

 tributary A stream or river that flows into a larger stream or river or into a lake

174

warm summers and the rainfall to grow millions of tons of corn and soybeans. Such large crops of corn and soybeans are grown here that there are many tons left to be exported to other countries.

Wisconsin and Michigan, two northeastern states of the region, have a climate similar to that of the New England region and to that of the northern states of the Middle Atlantic region. So it's not surprising to find dairy farms and fruit trees in all these states.

Products of the Region

Wisconsin is our country's main dairy state. Summers there are cooler than those in Iowa, Indiana, and Illinois. In places with short growing seasons, grass grows better than corn. Grasses provide feed for the dairy cows that give milk to be made into cheese and butter.

Michigan is famous for its fruits, especially its cherries, apples, and plums. Such fruits grow best in **orchards** found in cool states with plentiful rainfall. Michigan also provides many of our vegetables, such as carrots, cucumbers, and asparagus.

In the southwestern corner of the region, Nebraska and Kansas are two states famous for dry-climate products, such as wheat. Wheat flour is a product that we use in many breads, breakfast cereals, spaghetti, and other foods. Like corn, wheat is exported by the United States.

⭐ **orchard** A field of fruit trees planted in straight rows

▲ These huge machines, called combines, harvest wheat and separate the husks from the grain, which will be made into flour for bread.

▼ Many varieties of apples grow in Michigan.

Welcome to the Fair

A state fair is a place to exhibit the results of hard work.

Visiting a state fair in the Midwest and Great Plains region is a great way to learn why we all depend so much on the region. And it's fun, too.

For many people, a state fair is one of the most exciting events of the year. At a state fair, visitors can see products that people have worked hard to grow or make, such as the biggest pumpkin in the state, the most delicious jelly, the best baked bread, or the sheep with the most beautiful coat of wool. Boys and girls your age often exhibit animals they have helped to raise. And the blue ribbons that the judges award are highly prized.

More cherries are grown in Michigan than in any other state.

Many people attend state fairs to examine the latest models of tractors and pickup trucks. They want to keep up with the newest farm equipment. Farm machines displayed at state fairs are products of the Midwest and Great Plains region. And the steel, aluminum, and chemicals that are used to manufacture farm products are themselves important industrial products of the Midwest and Great Plains region.

State Fair

MICHIGAN   WISCONSIN

MIDWEST/GREAT PLAINS

SHOW WHAT YOU
KNOW!

Konza Prairie

Most of the Midwest and Great Plains region was once covered by prairies, from the Rocky Mountains to the Mississippi River and from Canada to Texas. But today on most of those prairies are wheat fields, corn fields, ranches, and cities.

In Kansas, an area has already been set aside for scientists to study. The area is called Konza Prairie. The name *Konza* comes from the Kansa Indians, who once lived there.

Fields of corn are seen throughout the Midwest and Great Plains region.

More than 100 kinds of grasses grow on Konza Prairie. Just one clump of grass can have roots that are several miles long. The roots are tightly wound around themselves and make a thick layer of earth where the top layers of soil should be.

As grasses age and die, the roots break up and decay. Earthworms and tiny insects chew on the decayed materials and help make rich soil under the prairie grasses. But scientists know that rich soils cannot remain rich forever once they are made into fields for farming. The scientists are now studying ways by which farmers can help keep prairie soil fertile.

Hay is harvested as feed for cattle.

REFOCUS
COMPREHENSION

1. Why is the Midwest and Great Plains region called the Heartland?

2. Name three major rivers of the Midwest and Great Plains region.

THINK ABOUT IT
CRITICAL THINKING

Why is corn rather than wheat grown in the eastern part of the Midwest and Great Plains region?

STATE CHECK
ACTIVITY

Draw a Venn diagram, comparing products of your state with those in the Midwest and Great Plains region.

FINDING NEW WAYS

FOCUS *People came to the Midwest and Great Plains region to explore the land, to settle it, and to make their lives better. Discover who some of those people were.*

A PORT ON THE OHIO

In an area along the Ohio River where the Miami Indians once lived, settlers established a village in 1788. They called the settlement Losantiville, but it was renamed Cincinnati in 1790. Cincinnati became an important port when steamboats began to move along the Ohio River. Many people made a living there by building or repairing boats. By 1810 more than 2,500 people lived in Cincinnati.

A SEARCH FOR A RIVER

In May 1673, a mapmaker named Louis Joliet (JOH lee et) set out to find a river that Native Americans living near the Great Lakes called the Mississippi, or great river. With Joliet was Jacques Marquette (zhahk mahr KET). The two men traveled from Lake Michigan down the Mississippi to the Arkansas River and back again. They were probably the first white explorers of the Mississippi.

A JOURNEY WESTWARD

In May 1804, Meriwether Lewis and William Clark set out from a camp near the present-day city of St. Louis, Missouri, to explore the wilderness to the west. They started up the Missouri River. By autumn they had reached what is now North Dakota. There they hired a fur trapper as a guide. They allowed his young Native American wife, Sacajawea (sak uh juh WEE uh), and baby to come on the expedition, too. Sacajawea helped Lewis and Clark communicate with Native Americans they met along the way. They reached the Pacific Ocean in November 1805. Lewis and Clark returned to St. Louis in September 1806, having traveled 8,000 miles.

PACIFIC OCEAN OR BUST!

| 1673 | | | | | 1788 | | 1804 | | 1877 | | 1889 | |
| Joliet explores the Mississippi River | | | | | Village that became Cincinnati is started | | Lewis and Clark begin exploring the west | | Nicodemus, Kansas, is settled | | Jane Addams starts Hull House | |

| 1670 | 1690 | 1710 | 1730 | 1750 | 1770 | 1790 | 1810 | 1830 | 1850 | 1870 | 1890 |

AN AFRICAN AMERICAN COMMUNITY

Many African Americans who received their freedom in 1863 during the Civil War left the South to find new homes west of the Mississippi River. In 1877 a group of African American pioneers from Kentucky established a settlement in Kansas that they called Nicodemus. The settlement grew into a busy community. Then, little by little, many of its residents moved to Colorado or California.

Today, Nicodemus is a small town. It is the only remaining early African American settlement west of the Mississippi River. Each summer hundreds of African Americans from throughout the United States return to Nicodemus to take part in the annual homecoming celebration.

HELPING HANDS

In 1889, Jane Addams moved into a big house in Chicago and established a neighborhood center called Hull House. Many of the people who came to Hull House were immigrants who had just moved to Chicago. They had no homes, no friends, and no jobs. At Hull House, Addams taught young mothers how to care for their children. She provided day-care centers for children whose mothers had to work to support their families. And she helped both men and women find jobs so that they could support themselves. She offered classes in English for immigrants who did not speak or understand English.

THE FLOATING HOUSE

by Scott Russell Sanders

The McClures left their home in Pittsburgh, Pennsylvania, in search of a new homestead. Several other families traveled with them along the Ohio River.

The winter of 1815 was so cold, the Ohio River froze from shore to shore. Wayne and Birdy McClure and their two children, Mary and Jonathan, huddled in the cabin of their flatboat, wrapped in quilts, listening to the ice groan and creak like the stairs in an old house.

Their boat still rested on dry land in Pittsburgh, along with hundreds of other flatboats, keelboats, skiffs and scows, canoes and barges and rafts, even a few of the newfangled steamboats, all waiting for the spring thaw to open the river.

Then one morning after a week of sunshine, the McClures woke to a sound like thunder. They looked out to see the green ice cracked into slabs, and black water showing through.

"Look," Mary cried. "The river's yawning!"

"Sleepy old river," said Jonathan.

The current soon swept the river clear. Everybody started launching boats, one family helping another. Those looking for new land, like the McClures, were eager to reach the wild country downstream, where you could buy farms for a dollar an acre and where the dirt was so rich, people said, you could plant a stick and it would break out in leaves.

In a crowd of boats, the McClures set off.

The swifter boats pulled away, leaving the McClures to drift in company with a few other families.

Mr. McClure balanced on the cabin roof and steered with a long sweeping oar. Mrs. McClure read aloud from *The Navigator*, a book of advice for travelers on the Ohio. The horse, the cow, the mule, and the pig rode behind the cabin, munching corn, thumping the deck. The children rode up front with the wagon and plow, among barrels, bundles, and tools. Mary and Jonathan were a little afraid to feel the boat rocking, but they were also excited to be riding the great river at last. Their job was to watch for sandbars and snags, and to give a holler if they saw danger ahead.

You can find out about the adventures Mary and Jonathan and their parents experienced on their journey by checking the book out of your school or public library.

SHOW WHAT YOU KNOW!

REFOCUS
COMPREHENSION

1. For what are Joliet and Marquette remembered?

2. What helped Cincinnati grow as a port city?

THINK ABOUT IT
CRITICAL THINKING

Why did the McClure family take farm animals with them on their flatboat?

STATE CHECK
ACTIVITY

Locate a river on a map of your state. Choose one city that is on or near the river. Describe how that city is linked by the river to other cities in the region.

You Are There

★ **KEY TERMS**
Conestoga wagon
cottage industry
livestock
barter
apprentice

A VISIT TO PRAIRIETOWN

FOCUS *The 1836 Village of Prairietown near Indianapolis, Indiana, is part of Conner Prairie, a living-history museum where you can learn how people in Indiana once lived.*

Traveling Back to 1836

What if it were possible to enter a time machine that would take you and your family back to the year 1836? Suddenly everything would be different! There would be no cars, no telephones, no television, and no computers.

And suppose that, in 1836, you lived in Philadelphia, Pennsylvania, and your family decided to move to Prairietown, a community not far from Indianapolis, Indiana. Your father has heard that Indiana soil is good for farming and that he can earn a comfortable living there.

▼ Many families moving westward traveled in Conestoga wagons.

You travel to Prairietown in a **Conestoga wagon** over rough roads. You can feel every bump in a road, but at least the canvas top protects the loaded-down wagon from bad weather. The huge wheels of the wagon often sink into the mud, and you have to help push the wagon out of the deep ruts.

Stopping at an Inn

When you arrive in Prairietown late in the evening, your family decides to stop at an inn to rest. You notice a two-story white frame house. A large sign with a golden eagle hangs above the front porch.

Mrs. Martha Zimmerman, the innkeeper, greets you at the door.

★ ***Conestoga wagon*** A covered wagon drawn by horses or oxen

She is accustomed to travelers coming to her inn, the Golden Eagle. Mrs. Zimmerman tells you that she does not own the inn— Dr. Campbell does. Dr. Campbell, who lives in the community, asked Mrs. Zimmerman to manage the inn for him. He was sure that she could maintain a fine inn for travelers coming through Indiana on their way west. Mrs. Zimmerman admits that managing an inn is something unusual for a woman to do in the 1830s.

Mrs. Zimmerman shows you to your sleeping quarters upstairs. She assures you that she keeps the cleanest inn around. The payment for a room is $12\frac{1}{2}$ cents a night.

Seeing the Village

The next morning, after a hearty breakfast, you take time to look around Prairietown. As you pass a whitewashed one-room log cabin, a man named Alex Fenton introduces himself. Mr. Fenton tells you that he is the village weaver. He was raised in South Carolina, where weaving

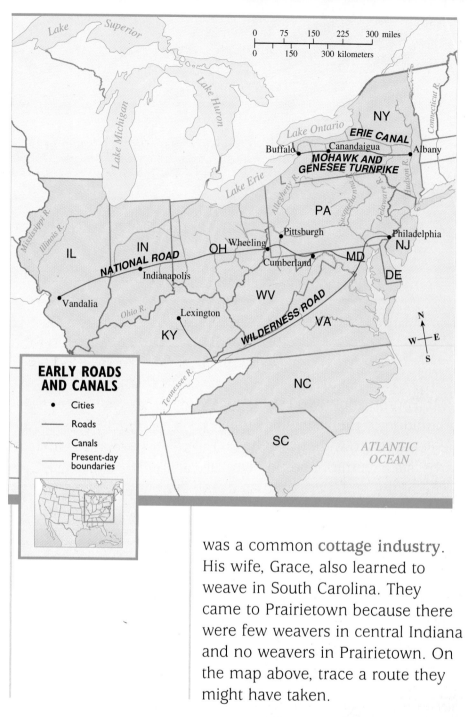

EARLY ROADS AND CANALS

- • Cities
- Roads
- Canals
- Present-day boundaries

was a common **cottage industry**. His wife, Grace, also learned to weave in South Carolina. They came to Prairietown because there were few weavers in central Indiana and no weavers in Prairietown. On the map above, trace a route they might have taken.

⭐ **cottage industry** The production, for sale, of goods at home, usually on a small scale

Farmers in Prairietown depended on horses as farmers today depend on machines.

The Blacksmith

Ben Curtis owns Prairietown's blacksmith shop. Mr. Curtis and his **apprentice** work each day repairing farming tools, making horseshoes to protect horses' feet, and supplying kitchen utensils, such as pots and pans.

Mr. Curtis and his family came to Prairietown from Canandaigua (kan un DAY gwuh), a town in western New York. They made the trip by steamboat and canalboat. People also came to Indiana by land routes, traveling by horseback or in horse-drawn wagons.

The Community Store

Prairietown has only one store. It is filled with a variety of goods, such as cotton fabric, shoes, food items, farming equipment, and imported teas and spices. Some of the items come from cities along the eastern coast of the United States. Others come from countries in Europe.

Mr. Fenton shows you his garden. In addition to the vegetables that the Fentons grow, they also have herbs, such as mint and pennyroyal. Some of the herbs are used as dyes for the wool he weaves, and some are used in cooking.

Next you come to the home of Daniel and Hannah Jane McClure and their four children. At one time Mr. McClure had a farm in Ohio, but he and his wife moved to Prairietown because he always dreamed of becoming a full-time carpenter. Mr. McClure fills orders for his customers, who usually pay him with food or **livestock** or by doing him a service. Paying for goods with other goods or services instead of money is called **barter**.

---

livestock Animals such as cattle or sheep that are raised for home use or to be sold
barter To pay for goods or services with other goods instead of with money

apprentice A person learning a trade or craft from a master craftsperson

School Days

A one-room schoolhouse is located near the store. Mr. Caleb Ashley Ferguson is the only teacher for all the students in the school. Mr. Ferguson's desk and a blackboard stand at the front of the room. The students sit on wooden benches. A large fireplace provides heat for the room. Students attend school six days a week during the winter. They learn how to read and write and how to do arithmetic. They study history and a few other subjects. Students learn by what is known as the "loud" school method. That means that all the students recite their different lessons at the same time. That makes for a noisy classroom.

The school is closed during the other seasons because the students are needed at home. They help in the fields, take care of the livestock, and tend their families' gardens.

Prairietown's Founder

Dr. Campbell is the founder of Prairietown. He moved here from Lexington, Kentucky, after he purchased land in Indiana. His wife, Harriet, grew up on a plantation in Virginia and lived in Lexington, Kentucky, until she moved north with her husband. Dr. Campbell is proud of this growing community with its general store, inn, school, and many capable craftspeople.

You and your family agree that you want to settle in Prairietown. You, too, already feel proud to call Prairietown your home.

◀ Guides in Prairietown today dress as people might have dressed in 1836.

SHOW WHAT YOU KNOW!

REFOCUS
COMPREHENSION

1. Why did some people move to Prairietown?

2. What work did the blacksmith do?

THINK ABOUT IT
CRITICAL THINKING

What might you find most interesting about living in Prairietown in 1836?

STATE CHECK
ACTIVITY

Think of yourself as a traveler to Prairietown in 1836. On a map, trace a route from your present home to Prairietown, near Indianapolis, Indiana. In your state scrapbook, describe your trip.

THE STEEL INDUSTRY

FOCUS *Making steel is an important industry in the Midwest and Great Plains region. The natural resources and transportation systems of the region make steel making possible.*

Steel in Everyday Life

If you look around your classroom, you may find more things made of wood or plastic than of steel. But outside, steel plays the leading role. Cars and trucks are made largely of steel. Railroads run on steel rails. And ships are built almost entirely of steel.

Tall buildings have skeletons made of long beams of steel over which concete is poured. The concrete is mixed in a steel mixer. And the tools that the workers use are made mostly of steel.

Steel Making

Large amounts of one of the most important minerals on Earth are found in the Midwest and Great Plains region. That mineral is **iron ore**, which is used in making steel. Coal and limestone are also needed to make steel. Look at the map on this page to find where coal, iron ore, and limestone are found in the Midwest and Great Plains region.

Steel is made by **refining** iron and mixing it with other metals. Iron is found in kinds of rocks called iron ores. A large deposit of iron

MINERAL RESOURCES OF THE MIDWEST AND GREAT PLAINS REGION
- Coal
- Iron ore
- Limestone

iron ore Rock or earth containing iron
refine To make into a pure matter

186

U.S. STEEL PRODUCTION: 1890–1990

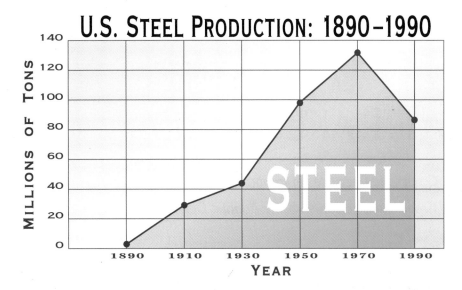

MILLIONS OF TONS

140
120
100
80
60
40
20
0

STEEL

1890   1910   1930   1950   1970   1990

YEAR

ore is found in the Mesabi Range in northern Minnesota. Only a small part of the ore contains iron.

Processing Iron Ore

Much of the iron ore is transported by train or truck to ports on Lake Superior. Duluth is the busiest port for handling iron ore. In Duluth the iron ore is loaded onto an **ore carrier**. The ship travels across Lake Superior, through a part of Lake Huron, and down Lake Michigan to Gary, Indiana.

There the iron is removed from the ore and processed into steel. The steel is molded into blocks, which are then rolled into long sheets or strips that are used to make steel products.

A Changing Industry

About two thirds of all the steel made in the United States is produced in the Midwest and Great Plains region. But as you can see on the graph above, less steel was produced in the United States in 1990 than in 1970. One reason is that products once made of steel are now produced from other materials, such as plastic.

▼ Workers in a mill in Ohio are pouring iron that will be used to make tools.

 ore carrier   A large ship built for carrying ore

187

Spotlight

★

KEY TERMS

lock
grain elevator

WHAT MAKES THE GREAT LAKES GREAT?

FOCUS *The Great Lakes provide an important transportation route that links the Midwest and Great Plains region with the Atlantic Ocean.*

THE GREAT LAKES– ST. LAWRENCE WATERWAY

— Great Lakes–St. Lawrence Waterway

• Port cities

Five Large Lakes

The map on this page shows that the Great Lakes are five large bodies of water. Four lie along the boundary between the United States and Canada. By looking at the map you can name the Great Lakes. You can also learn that all the Great Lakes are connected.

There are lakes in the world that are larger than any of the Great Lakes, but they contain salty water because they are connected to oceans. The Great Lakes are the largest freshwater lakes in the world. Freshwater lakes contain no salt.

The Great Lakes– St. Lawrence Waterway

In 1954 the United States and Canada began a project to link the Great Lakes with the Atlantic Ocean. Canada and the United States joined together in this project because the St. Lawrence River as well as four of the Great Lakes lie in both countries. The United States– Canada boundary runs through the St. Lawrence River and lakes Superior, Erie, Huron, and Ontario.

The project, called the St. Lawrence Seaway, was completed in 1959. The seaway stretches 450 miles, between Montreal, Canada, and the eastern end of Lake Erie.

The St. Lawrence Seaway is part of the Great Lakes–St. Lawrence Waterway. This waterway allows ships to travel between the Great Lakes and the Atlantic Ocean.

Building Locks

Building the waterway was a difficult task. Lake Superior is about 600 feet above sea level. To make up for the changes in water level, the waterway has a number of **locks**. A ship enters a lock when the water in that enclosure is level with the water the boat is in. Then the water in the lock is raised or lowered, and the ship floats smoothly into water that is at a different level.

The Great Lakes–St. Lawrence Waterway extends from the Gulf of St. Lawrence at the Atlantic Ocean, along the St. Lawrence River, through the Great Lakes to Duluth, on Lake Superior. It forms the greatest inland waterway in the world.

⭐ **lock** An enclosed area, with a gate on each end, used for raising and lowering ships, allowing them to go from one water level to another

▲ A ship passes through a lock at Iroquois, Ontario, Canada.

Great Lakes Ports

The shores of the Great Lakes are lined with ports. Some of the largest cities in the Midwest and Great Plains region are ports on the Great Lakes. Milwaukee, Wisconsin, and Gary, Indiana, are busy ports on Lake Michigan.

Chicago, Illinois, the third largest city in the United States, lies on the southwestern shore of Lake Michigan. Canals and rivers connect Chicago and the Mississippi River. The city is the only place in North America where the Great Lakes connect with the Mississippi River system. From Chicago, goods can move east to the Atlantic Ocean or south on river barges to the Gulf of Mexico.

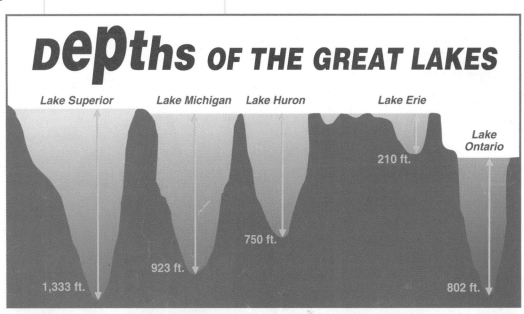

Depths OF THE GREAT LAKES

Lake Superior	Lake Michigan	Lake Huron	Lake Erie	Lake Ontario

210 ft.

750 ft.

923 ft.

1,333 ft.

802 ft.

The port area of Duluth, Minnesota, has many grain elevators and storage sheds.

Duluth to Lake Ontario

Duluth, Minnesota, is at the western end of Lake Superior. It is the busiest freshwater port in all of North America. The harbor extends 49 miles and contains more than 110 docks for transferring goods such as wheat, coal, and iron ore. Gigantic **grain elevators** store the wheat and other agricultural products before they are shipped.

⭐ **grain elevator** A large building where grain is stored before it is shipped

Cleveland, Ohio, is on Lake Erie. It handles about 13 million tons of goods every year. Toledo, Ohio, also lies on Lake Erie. Detroit, Michigan, is on the Detroit River, which flows into Lake Erie.

Lake Ontario is the smallest of the Great Lakes, but it forms an important link in the Great Lakes–St. Lawrence Waterway. It is the first of the Great Lakes that international ships enter.

▲ A coal freighter on Lake Erie (*upper*) Ferryboats on Lake Michigan (*lower*)

▼ Sailing is popular on Lake Michigan.

Great Lakes Boats

The Great Lakes are home to many different kinds of vessels. Ore carriers are long, low ships that transport 70,000 tons of raw material at a time. The sturdy, flat-bottomed boats called barges carry big and heavy loads, such as coal or logs. Tugboats are small but powerful vessels that push or pull large ships and barges. Tankers have compartments below decks so that they can transport different kinds of cargo.

Ships on the lakes carry human cargo, too. Ferryboats take passengers to various destinations, and sailboats skim the waters of the lakes.

Protecting the Great Lakes

The Great Lakes are valuable for shipping, commercial fishing, and recreation. They also provide water for drinking and manufacturing. But the waters of the lakes have become polluted by chemicals from industries and by wastes from nearby cities.

▲ The water in the Great Lakes is tested regularly for pollution.

Today the United States and Canadian governments are working together to improve the quality of the water in the lakes. The two countries are funding programs to restore the purity of the Great Lakes so that the lakes will be safe for the fish and plants that inhabit them. Groups of people are also interested in protecting the Great Lakes. Their goal is to prevent pollution before it starts.

SHOW WHAT YOU KNOW!

REFOCUS
COMPREHENSION

1. Where is the St. Lawrence Seaway?

2. Why is Chicago an important port?

THINK ABOUT IT
CRITICAL THINKING

Why did the United States and Canada work together to build the Great Lakes–St. Lawrence Waterway?

STATE CHECK
ACTIVITY

Find out about a lake in your state. Then make a table in which you compare that lake with one of the Great Lakes.

SUMMING UP

1 DO YOU REMEMBER . . .
COMPREHENSION

1. What are the chief landforms in the Midwest and Great Plains region?

2. What makes Nicodemus, Kansas, a special place?

3. What were some of the occupations, or jobs, of the people in Prairietown?

4. Why is steel needed?

5. How do the Great Lakes help link the Midwest and Great Plains region to the Atlantic Ocean?

2 SKILL POWER
USING AN ATLAS

An atlas helps you discover information about a place. Choose one place in the world that you would like to know more about. Team up with a partner. Together, use maps in an atlas to learn more about your chosen places, such as their locations, boundaries, elevations, and climates. Share your findings with your classmates.

3 WHAT DO YOU THINK?
CRITICAL THINKING

1. What has helped the Midwest and Great Plains region become our country's breadbasket?

2. If you had been living in Prairietown in 1836, what might you have liked most about your life? Why?

3. Might Lewis and Clark have been able to reach the Pacific Ocean without the help of Sacajawea? Explain your answer.

4. What might happen if the locks in the St. Lawrence Seaway did not work properly?

5. Do you expect that the United States and Canada will continue to work together on problems that affect both countries? Why?

4 SAY IT, WRITE IT, USE IT
VOCABULARY

Write a letter to a friend to tell some new and interesting things that you learned about the Midwest and Great Plains region. Name at least three new things that you think would surprise your friend. Include as many of the key terms as you can.

apprentice	livestock
barter	lock
Conestoga wagon	orchard
cottage industry	ore carrier
grain elevator	refine
iron ore	tributary

5 GEOGRAPHY AND YOU
MAP STUDY

Use the map below to answer these questions.

1. Which Canadian port city is on Lake Ontario?

2. Name the port city that ships pass on their way from Cleveland, Ohio, to Detroit, Michigan.

3. Which port city is farther east—Chicago, Illinois, or Detroit, Michigan?

4. On which of the Great Lakes is Duluth, Minnesota?

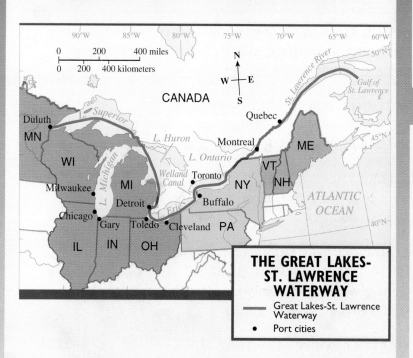

**THE GREAT LAKES-
ST. LAWRENCE
WATERWAY**
— Great Lakes-St. Lawrence Waterway
• Port cities

6 TAKE ACTION
CITIZENSHIP

Think about the importance of keeping bodies of water like the Great Lakes clean and safe. With a partner make a booklet in which you explain how people can help protect a body of water or waterway in your community or state.

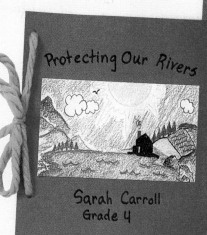

7 GET CREATIVE
LANGUAGE ARTS CONNECTION

If you were invited to participate in a state fair, what would you like to exhibit? Draw yourself at the state fair. Create a sign, describing what is great about your exhibit.

LOOKING AHEAD Find out in the next chapter how the **Midwest** and **Great Plains** region links to other parts of the country.

MIDWEST AND GREAT

The Midwest and Great Plains region is rich in natural resources, key industries, and great cities. Learn how this region shares its wealth with other regions and the world.

CONTENTS

This boy is wearing a uniform from Nebraska's Cornhuskers football team. Find out Nebraska's connection to corn on page 199.

PLAINS LINKS NEAR AND FAR

The following books give you information about how the Midwest and Great Plains region is connected to other regions and to the world. Read one that interests you and fill out a book-review form.

READ AND RESEARCH

Discovering Maps: A Children's World Atlas
by Alma Graham and Robert Thomas (Hammond, 1995)
The maps in this atlas will help you find where your state is located. The distribution maps will show you which products come from your area and how many people live there. *(reference)*

Corn Belt Harvest by Raymond Bial (Houghton Mifflin Co., 1991)
Explore the Corn Belt region of the United States, where much of the world's corn is grown. From its planting to picking, you will follow the growing of corn through colorful photographs. *(nonfiction)*

Rand McNally Skyscrapers: A Fold-out Book
by Nicholas Harris, illustrated by Stephen Conlin
(Rand McNally & Co., 1995)
As you unfold the pages of this amazing book, you will take a tour of the John Hancock Center in Chicago, the seventh tallest skyscraper in the world. You will also learn about other tall buildings around the world. *(nonfiction)*

Australia by Peter Crawshaw, illustrated by Ann Savage
(Silver Burdett Press, 1988)
Explore Australia and discover its land, history, people, and industries. Let the book's illustrations guide you on your trip. *(nonfiction)*

SKILL POWER — Reading Graphs

Knowing how to read graphs will help you compare information in a quick and easy way.

UNDERSTAND IT

A graph is a drawing that uses pictures, circles, bars, or lines to give information. A graph can compare information about people, places, goods, and many other things.

A graph usually has a title that tells what the graph is comparing. Labels on the graph give more detailed information.

Look at the *bar graph* on this page. What is the title? What are the labels? Notice the abbreviations of the state names along the bottom of the graph. The numbers along the left side show how many millions of bushels of corn are produced in each state.

Which state has the tallest bar? This means that more corn is grown in this state than in any other state. Put your finger at the top of the bar for Illinois. Move your finger to the left. The corn grown in Illinois in one year is more than 1,200 million bushels.

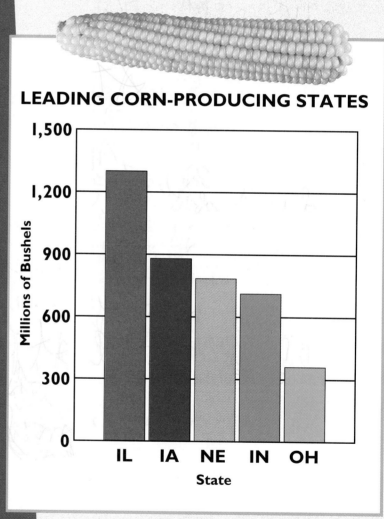

LEADING CORN-PRODUCING STATES

Millions of Bushels

1,500
1,200
900
600
300
0

IL   IA   NE   IN   OH

State

▲ This graph shows the five states that grow the most corn in the United States. Which state grows more corn—Iowa or Nebraska?

The population of Minnesota has increased since 1930. In which year did Minnesota have the largest number of people?

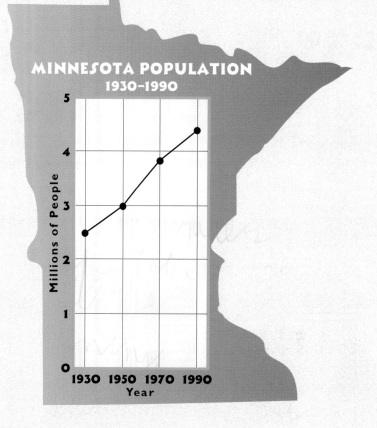

MINNESOTA POPULATION
1930–1990

Millions of People

5
4
3
2
1
0

1930 1950 1970 1990
Year

EXPLORE IT

Using the bar graph on the opposite page, compare production of corn in the five states shown. Which state is the second largest producer of corn? Which state produced less than 600 million bushels?

Next, turn your attention to the graph on this page. This graph is a *line graph*. A line graph shows how things have changed over a period of time.

How many people were living in Minnesota in 1950? What happened to the population of the state of Minnesota between 1950 and 1990? Did the population of Minnesota get larger or smaller between 1930 and 1990?

TRY IT

On a sheet of paper, write two questions that can be answered by reading the bar graph on page 196. Develop two questions that can be answered by reading the line graph above. Use the questions asked in Understand It and Explore It as models. Trade your paper with a partner. Use the graphs to answer your partner's questions.

SKILL POWER SEARCH

Look through the chapter for two other graphs. What is each comparing? Be sure to read the titles and labels.

Setting the Scene

KEY TERMS

feedlot
meatpacking
process
mill
service industry
insurance

A REGION OF CONNECTIONS

FOCUS *The Midwest and Great Plains region is connected to the rest of the country and to the world through its manufacturing and service industries.*

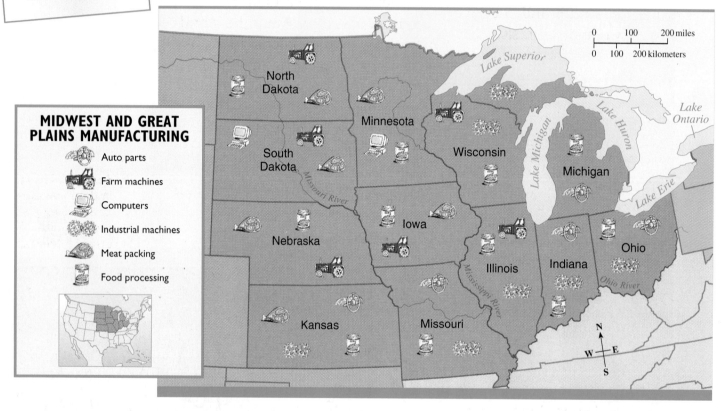

MIDWEST AND GREAT PLAINS MANUFACTURING

- Auto parts
- Farm machines
- Computers
- Industrial machines
- Meat packing
- Food processing

Meatpacking

Find Kansas and Nebraska on the map above. These states lead the region in the production of beef. The beef comes from cattle that graze on prairie grasses in the summer and on special feed in the winter. When the cattle are about a year old, they are sent to **feedlots** for about four months. Here cattle are fattened up before slaughter and the processing of their meat in a **meatpacking** plant.

People in Kansas and Nebraska work in these plants to prepare meats for people to buy. Omaha, Nebraska, is an important feedlot and meatpacking city in the region.

 feedlot Large fenced-in pen in which cattle are fed

 meatpacking The process of preparing meat for people to eat

Food Processing

The Midwest and Great Plains region processes many foods. Wisconsin has some of the largest dairy farms in the country. Nearby processing plants take in fresh milk and turn it into butter and cheese.

Illinois, Iowa, and Nebraska are the top three states for growing corn. Kansas is the leading wheat-producing state in the country. In these states are mills that grind wheat and corn into cereals and flour for breads. Kansas City, Kansas, is a major milling center.

Factories that prepare vegetables and put them into cans for sale in stores are called canneries. Ohio, Indiana, Illinois, and Iowa have many large canning factories. Many canned vegetables come from canneries in Des Moines, Iowa.

Manufacturing in the Region

Farmers need special machinery, tools, and other supplies in order to do their work. Missouri factories produce many of the fertilizers and chemicals that farmers use on their fields. The fertilizers help the crops grow, and the chemicals protect the plants from destructive insects.

Tractors, harvesting equipment, and farm trucks are manufactured in Illinois, Iowa, North Dakota, South Dakota, and Nebraska. Find these places on the map on page 198. Most of these pieces of heavy equipment are sold to the region's farmers. The rest are shipped to farmers in other parts of the country and throughout the world.

Michigan and Ohio factories use steel produced in the region to make many kinds of cars, trucks, and school buses. In Illinois, Indiana, Kansas, and Missouri, factories produce bulldozers and railroad cars. These products are shipped by rail and truck to people throughout the United States.

▼ Automobile factories in the Midwest and Great Plains region produce up to 75 cars per hour.

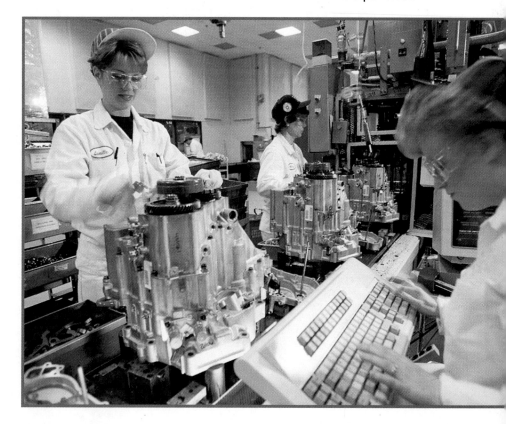

 process To make something step by step
mill Place where grains are ground into flour

Making Popcorn

HOW POPCORN IS MADE

Many Americans love popcorn! Each year over 17 billion quarts of popped popcorn are eaten in the United States. That's 68 quarts for every man, woman, and child!

Most of the corn for this popcorn comes from farms in the Midwest and Great Plains region. A lot must happen before we have popcorn to pop. Farmers have to grow a special type of corn for popcorn. This corn is different from the corn on the cob that you eat or corn that is fed to farm animals.

After the special ears of corn have been harvested, they are stored in huge buildings called corncribs. Each corncrib holds 4 million pounds of corn. There the corn dries slowly for many months.

Next, the corn kernels are taken off each cob and cleaned to remove dust and chaff, the covering around a kernel. The kernels are sorted by size and weight in special machines.

Then, the kernels travel down a conveyor belt where an inspector picks out kernels that are too dry to pop. Next, the good kernels are packed in bags or jars. Before these are sent to stores, another inspector pops some finished packages as a test for quality.

1 Dried ears of corn are removed from corncribs.

2 Corn husks are stripped in husking machines.

3 Corn kernels are sorted by size and weight.

4 The best kernels are packaged in bags and jars.

5 Some corn kernels are popped as a test for quality.

Service Industries

Not all people in the Midwest and Great Plains region work on farms or in factories. Many have jobs in **service industries**. Among those who have service jobs are teachers, doctors, bank tellers, store clerks, truck drivers, and restaurant cooks. People all over the United States work in many different kinds of service industries.

The Midwest and Great Plains region is well-known for its service industries in the medical profession. For a long time, doctors from around the world have sent their patients to famous medical centers in Illinois, Minnesota, Missouri, and Ohio. These health centers employ many doctors, laboratory workers, nurses, pharmacists, and other medical specialists.

Many Kinds of Services

In Michigan, where automobiles are a major product, many people are employed in service work. Some people work on ideas for new cars. Some develop ways to sell the most current car models. Others answer people's questions on "customer service" phone lines.

Some of the largest **insurance** companies have their main offices in Nebraska, Kansas, and Ohio. Insurance companies originally chose the Midwest and Great Plains region because of its central location in the United States.

The same is true for some large banks, which have their main offices in North Dakota, South Dakota, Iowa, and Minnesota. The banks handle the money of people across the country.

THE REGION AT WORK

Millions of People

18
16
14
12
10
8
6
4
2
0

Service   Manufacturing   Agriculture

Kinds of Work

☆ **service industry** Business that has to do with work that helps people
insurance Protection against loss or damage

THE MIGHTY MISSISSIPPI

FOCUS *The Midwest and Great Plains is a region of rivers and cities. The Mississippi, Missouri, and Ohio rivers form a natural transportation system.*

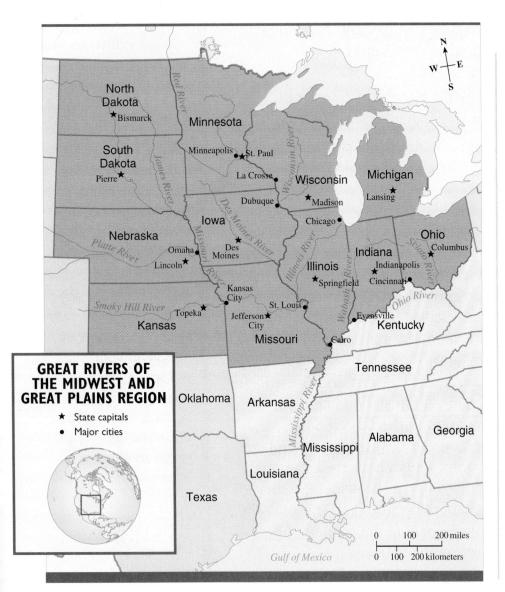

GREAT RIVERS OF THE MIDWEST AND GREAT PLAINS REGION

★ State capitals
● Major cities

The Great Mississippi

The Mississippi River begins in the state of Minnesota. It flows for more than 2,000 miles before emptying into the Gulf of Mexico at New Orleans in Louisiana. Trace with your finger the course of the Mississippi on the map at the left.

Along the Mississippi River, numerous cities and towns have thrived because of their locations on the river. Great cities in the Midwest and Great Plains region—such as St. Louis, Minneapolis, and LaCrosse—have become major river ports and centers of trade.

A Region of Rivers

A smaller river that flows into a larger river is called a tributary. The Mississippi has 250 tributaries. The Ohio River is the major tributary on the eastern side of the Mississippi. The Ohio River flows for 981 miles south from Pittsburgh, Pennsylvania, and joins the Mississippi at Cairo, Illinois. Find the Ohio River on the map on page 202.

The major tributary on the western side of the Mississippi is the Missouri River. The **source of the river** is in Montana. The Missouri flows southward until it joins the Mississippi near St. Louis, Missouri. Look at the map and name the cities you would pass as you travel down the Missouri River to St. Louis.

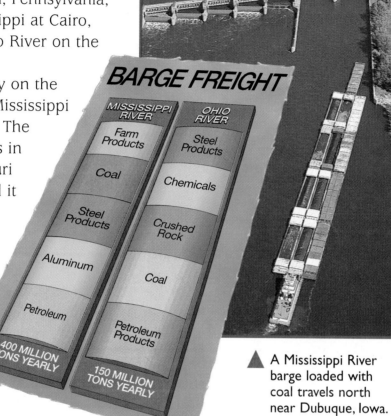

BARGE FREIGHT

MISSISSIPPI RIVER	OHIO RIVER
Farm Products	Steel Products
Coal	Chemicals
Steel Products	Crushed Rock
Aluminum	Coal
Petroleum	Petroleum Products
400 MILLION TONS YEARLY	150 MILLION TONS YEARLY

▲ A Mississippi River barge loaded with coal travels north near Dubuque, Iowa.

Barge Transportation

Barges on the Mississippi, Ohio, and Missouri rivers carry corn, soybeans, and other agricultural products from farms in the Midwest and Great Plains region to other regions in the United States. Some of these farm products arrive in New Orleans for shipment to other countries of the world. Mississippi River barges carry more than 400 million tons of cargo each year.

Nearly all of the freight on the Ohio River is shipped on barges. About half of the total is coal that is shipped southwest from Ohio and Pennsylvania to where the river meets the Mississippi. Here the coal is moved north by barge on the Mississippi River to manufacturing plants and steel mills in Illinois, Minnesota, and Wisconsin.

 source of a river The place where a river begins

SHOW WHAT YOU KNOW!

REFOCUS
COMPREHENSION

1. Name a river that is a tributary of the Mississippi River.

2. What are some products that are shipped on barges on the Mississippi River?

THINK ABOUT IT
CRITICAL THINKING

Explain why many barges on the Mississippi carry agricultural products.

STATE CHECK
ACTIVITY

Identify an important river in your state. Find out what things are transported up and down the river.

★ **KEY TERMS**
elevated train
cargo plane

A VISIT TO CHICAGO

FOCUS *Chicago offers a visitor many places to visit and opportunities to learn about its history and people.*

A Chicago Journal

Yesterday my mom gave me some great news—next week our family is going to Chicago, Illinois, to visit Grandma and Grandpa. I'm so excited about the trip that I've decided to keep a journal to share with my class when I return.

Thursday

Dad gave me a book about Chicago. I found out that it is a city on the southwestern shore of Lake Michigan. It's the third largest city in the United States, with about 2,784,000 people.

I read that Chicago became a city in 1837. At that time there were only wooden cottages and small hotels called rooming houses for about 4,200 people. Chicago was a trading post for settlers heading west across the prairies. Traders came to Chicago to send furs and other goods to customers back east.

Friday

Today in class, my teacher told me that Chicago has been a rail center for over 100 years. Railroad cars brought cattle to Chicago from southern and western ranches. The animals were killed, packaged as food, and then shipped throughout the country.

Most of the houses in Chicago in 1871 were made of wood. Even the roads were made of wood. That year a fire swept through the city, destroying thousands of buildings.

POPULATION OF CHICAGO 1900–1990

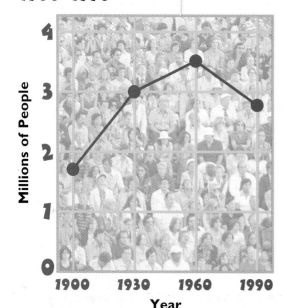

Millions of People

1900   1930   1960   1990
Year

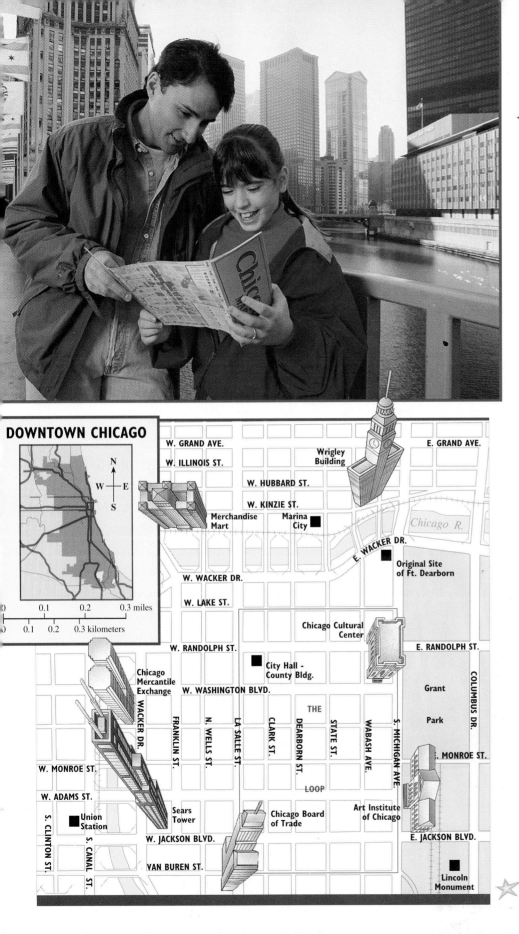

Elizabeth and her father stop on Michigan Avenue above the Chicago River as they check their map of downtown Chicago.

DOWNTOWN CHICAGO

N
W←→E
S

0	0.1	0.2	0.3 miles
0	0.1	0.2	0.3 kilometers

W. GRAND AVE.
W. ILLINOIS ST.
E. GRAND AVE.
W. HUBBARD ST.
W. KINZIE ST.
Wrigley Building
Merchandise Mart
Marina City
Chicago R.
E. WACKER DR.
Original Site of Ft. Dearborn
W. WACKER DR.
W. LAKE ST.
Chicago Cultural Center
W. RANDOLPH ST.
E. RANDOLPH ST.
Chicago Mercantile Exchange
City Hall - County Bldg.
W. WASHINGTON BLVD.
Grant Park
WACKER DR.
FRANKLIN ST.
N. WELLS ST.
LA SALLE ST.
CLARK ST.
DEARBORN ST.
STATE ST.
WABASH AVE.
S. MICHIGAN AVE.
COLUMBUS DR.
THE
LOOP
E. MONROE ST.
W. MONROE ST.
W. ADAMS ST.
S. CLINTON ST.
S. CANAL ST.
Union Station
Sears Tower
Chicago Board of Trade
Art Institute of Chicago
W. JACKSON BLVD.
E. JACKSON BLVD.
VAN BUREN ST.
Lincoln Monument

A Visit Downtown

Monday

Today we arrived at Union Station, one of Chicago's busiest railroad stations. Dad bought me a city map to show me where the Loop is located. The Loop has a series of **elevated trains** that loop around 35 blocks of downtown office buildings and stores. The trains carry people into and out of the city of Chicago.

As we left Union Station, I saw the 110-story Sears Tower, which is the world's tallest building. Then we drove to the Merchandise Mart, a huge indoor mall. Next, we stopped to see the Wrigley Building. It is brightly lighted at night.

We had a snack of Chicago pizza near Grant Park before deciding to visit the Field Museum. This is the biggest natural history museum in the region. There is even an aquarium nearby. We ended up at the Art Institute of Chicago. It has some exhibits just for kids. It's no wonder that 8 million people visit Chicago each year.

⭐ ***elevated train*** A train that rides above ground on a bridgelike structure

Chicago Neighborhoods

Tuesday

Tomorrow we are going to drive to some of the neighborhoods of Chicago. My guidebook says that people from many different countries settled in Chicago in the 1800s. This was because there were many jobs here. People settled in three sections of Chicago—the North Side, West Side, and South Side.

The book says many Polish immigrants settled in the North Side of the city. Grandpa told me that the area still has a lot of Polish restaurants and bakeries. People from Greece and Italy mostly settled in the West Side. The South Side of Chicago, more than half of the city, is the biggest section in area and population. It once was the home of many Irish and German settlers. It is now the home of African Americans, Chicago's largest group of people.

Wednesday

I told Grandma all that I had learned about the many different groups of immigrants who came to Chicago in the early 1900s. She told me that the city has many museums where I can learn about the people who came to Chicago from 16 different countries.

We visited two of these museums. At the Ukrainian National Museum, I saw beautifully decorated eggs called pysanky (PIHS-ahn kih). At the Hellenic Museum and Cultural Center, we saw an exhibit on immigrants from Greece. Grandpa told me that there is always a parade or festival going on in Chicago. He said that on Saint Patrick's Day, people actually dye the Chicago River green!

▼ Polish American children wear native dress as they march down Michigan Avenue in Chicago.

◀ Eggs decorated with colorful designs by Ukrainian artists are world famous.

▲ The terminal at O'Hare Airport is a busy place, with over 850,000 planes arriving or departing yearly.

Trading Center

Thursday

I watched a television program tonight that said Chicago is the largest transportation center in the United States. Oceangoing ships cross the Great Lakes to get to Chicago. In the port of Chicago, there are 84 different places where ships can dock, load, and unload. The port handles more than 20 million tons of freight every year.

I decided I'd better look up some facts on Chicago for my journal. I found out that trains and trucks carry more goods into and out of Chicago than anywhere else in the United States. Trucking companies in the area transport more than 30 million tons of freight each year. The city's railroad lines handle more than 20 million tons yearly.

Rank	City Airport	Total Passengers per Year
1	Chicago	65,077,508
2	Dallas/Ft. Worth	49,970,180
3	London	49,898,526
4	Los Angeles	47,844,794
5	Atlanta	47,088,487
6	Tokyo	41,562,084

Busiest Airports in the World

Friday

We flew out of O'Hare Airport today. I read in my Chicago book that O'Hare is the busiest airport in the world. More people fly into and out of this airport than anywhere else. Huge **cargo planes** share O'Hare with jumbo passenger jets.

As our plane took off, I looked down at the crowded expressways. I saw one of the many trains that cut across the city. I looked back on the downtown part of the city with Lake Michigan in the background. Goodbye, Chicago!

★ **cargo plane** A plane that transports only freight

SHOW WHAT YOU KNOW!

REFOCUS
COMPREHENSION

1. How many tons of cargo does the port of Chicago handle?

2. What body of water forms part of the boundary of Chicago?

THINK ABOUT IT
CRITICAL THINKING

Why did Chicago develop into such a large city over time?

STATE CHECK
ACTIVITY

In the States Almanac on pages 342–397, find three historic sites in your state. Write about one of these sites in your state scrapbook.

KEY TERMS
meat processing
drover

THE CATTLE BUSINESS— UNITED STATES AND AUSTRALIA

FOCUS *Cattle raising and meat processing are large industries of both the Midwest and Great Plains region and Australia—a country halfway around the world.*

U.S. Cattle Raising

Raising beef cattle is big business in the western part of the Midwest and Great Plains region. In Kansas, Nebraska, North Dakota, and South Dakota on large ranches—sometimes 100,000 acres or more in size—beef cattle are raised. In Kansas alone, over six million cattle graze on grasslands in the northern part of the state.

Aside from raising cattle, a large part of the cattle business includes preparing, packaging, and transporting meat from beef cattle. As the map on this page shows, no other region of the United States has more **meat processing** plants than the Midwest and Great Plains region. That's because it is less costly to process meat close to the areas where cattle are raised. The processed beef is then transported by truck or by ship for sale elsewhere in the country.

meat processing The steps by which meat is separated into its usable parts, packaged, and distributed

Cattle Raising in Australia

On the other side of the world in the country of Australia, there are flat grasslands similar to those of our Midwest and Great Plains region. Several thousand cattle ranches take up more than one quarter of the land in Australia. These ranches, called stations or runs, average 120 square miles in

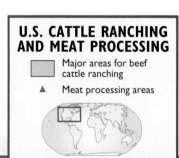

U.S. CATTLE RANCHING AND MEAT PROCESSING
- Major areas for beef cattle ranching
- ▲ Meat processing areas

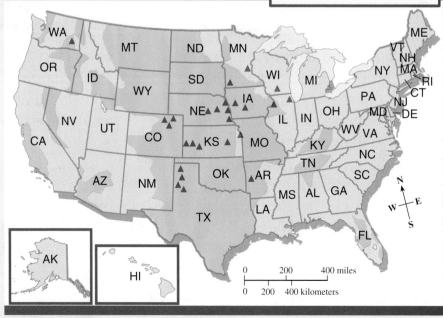

208

 Australian cowboys, called drovers, move the herd.

size. The largest runs are in the Northern Territory and Queensland. Find these areas on the map below.

The stations or runs of Australia are huge. On some runs, cowboys on horseback, called **drovers**, keep track of the cattle. On others, herders drive modern trucks.

★ **drover** A person who drives cattle or sheep

Look at the map on this page to find where many of Australia's meat processing plants are located. Compare this map to the map on page 208. What conclusions can you make about raising beef cattle and processing meat in the United States and Australia?

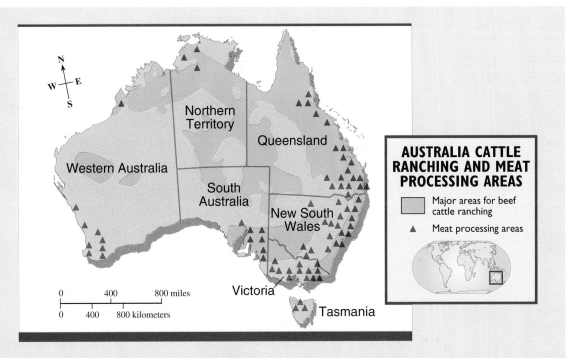

Northern Territory

Queensland

Western Australia

South Australia

New South Wales

Victoria

Tasmania

AUSTRALIA CATTLE RANCHING AND MEAT PROCESSING AREAS

▢ Major areas for beef cattle ranching

▲ Meat processing areas

0   400   800 miles
0   400   800 kilometers

SHOW WHAT YOU KNOW!

REFOCUS
COMPREHENSION

1. In which states of the Midwest and Great Plains region are there large cattle ranches?

2. What is the average size of a cattle run in Australia?

THINK ABOUT IT
CRITICAL THINKING

What are some similarities between the cattle business in the Midwest and Great Plains region and the cattle business in Australia?

STATE CHECK
ACTIVITY

Find out if there are any kinds of ranches in your state. Make a special-purpose map to show where those ranches are located.

SUMMING UP

1. Name three manufacturing industries in the Midwest and Great Plains region.

2. What are the steps involved in processing corn for popcorn?

3. Name three facts about the Mississippi River that you learned in this chapter.

4. Name three groups of people who have settled in Chicago.

5. What makes the western part of the Midwest and Great Plains region so good for raising beef cattle?

3 **WHAT DO YOU THINK?**
CRITICAL THINKING

1. Why is food processing in the Midwest and Great Plains region a major industry?

2. Why have so many cities and towns grown along the Mississippi River?

3. Why did many immigrants from countries in Europe settle in Chicago?

4. What makes Chicago an important transportation center?

5. Describe some of the resources and products that the Midwest and Great Plains region has to offer to other parts of the world.

2 **SKILL POWER**
READING GRAPHS

In this chapter, you learned how to read graphs to compare and contrast information. Can you find more examples of useful graphs? Team up with a partner. Look for graphs in newspapers, magazines, almanacs, encyclopedias, and other information sources. Share what you find.

4 **SAY IT, WRITE IT, USE IT**
VOCABULARY

In your state scrapbook write a paragraph about one state in the Midwest and Great Plains region. Include as many of the key terms as you can. Share your paragraph with your classmates.

cargo plane	meat processing
drover	mill
elevated train	process
feedlot	service industry
insurance	source of a river
meatpacking	

5 GEOGRAPHY AND YOU
MAP STUDY

Use the map below to answer these questions.

1. Which street is between Clark Street and State Street?

2. Which streets are between Franklin Street and Dearborn Street?

3. Which street is City Hall closer to— Van Buren Street or La Salle Street?

4. How might you get from Union Station to City Hall?

DOWNTOWN CHICAGO

0   0.1   0.2   0.3 miles
0   0.1   0.2   0.3 kilometers

W. RANDOLPH ST.

Chicago Mercantile Exchange

City Hall - County Bldg.

W. WASHINGTON BLVD.

THE

WACKER DR.

FRANKLIN ST.

N. WELLS ST.

LA SALLE ST.

CLARK ST.

DEARBORN ST.

STATE ST.

W. MONROE ST.

W. ADAMS ST.

LOOP

S. CLINTON ST.

S. CANAL ST.

Union Station

Sears Tower

Chicago Board of Trade

W. JACKSON BLVD.

VAN BUREN ST.

N
W   E
S

6 TAKE ACTION
CITIZENSHIP

Whether you live in a big city like Chicago or in a small town, it is important to know about where you live. Learn about your community's businesses, industries, and special places of interest. Volunteer for a community project. This will help you feel like part of your community. You'll be proud of what is happening there.

7 GET CREATIVE
LANGUAGE ARTS CONNECTION

Work with some classmates to plan and publish a magazine about your city or town. Your magazine can have articles, poems, interviews, reviews, and photographs. The magazine can also tell about different businesses and industries, places to visit, and restaurants. Distribute copies of your magazine to other classes and to people in your community.

LOOKING AHEAD

Next you'll travel to the Southwest region and learn about its land and people.

The Southwest

The Southwest region includes only four states—Texas, Oklahoma, Arizona, and New Mexico. Yet in land area, this region is large. In this chapter, you will find out what makes the region special.

▼ Do you know what this girl is planting? Find out on page 218.

CONTENTS

Region

These books tell about people, events, and places that are important to the Southwest region. Read one that interests you and fill out a book-review form.

READ AND RESEARCH

Justin and the Best Biscuits in the World by Mildred Pitts Walter (Random House, 1991)
When Justin visits his grandfather's ranch, he gets to try his hand at being a cowboy. He also learns about his great-great-grandpa, a cowboy who drove herds of cattle on the trails from Texas to Kansas. *(fiction)*
•*You can read a selection from this book on page 232.*

Chile Fever: A Celebration of Peppers by Elizabeth King (Dalton Children's Books, 1995)
Have you ever eaten nachos with chile peppers? Have you ever wondered where those chiles come from? Read about Hatch, New Mexico, to find out about the crop that makes this town the Chile Pepper Capital of the World. *(nonfiction)*

The Desert Is Theirs by Byrd Baylor, illustrated by Peter Parnall (Simon & Schuster Books for Young Readers, 1995)
Living in a desert is not always easy, but the Papago desert people love their land and respect the plants and animals that live there with them. *(poetry)*

Pueblo Storyteller by Diane Hoyt-Goldsmith, photographs by Lawrence Migdale (Holiday House, 1991)
Ten-year-old April tells you her story of life in a pueblo village near Santa Fe, New Mexico. Learn about the traditions that have been passed down through generations in her family. *(nonfiction)*

SKILL POWER

Recognizing Fact and Opinion

Knowing the difference between a fact and an opinion can help you evaluate information that you hear and read.

UNDERSTAND IT

If you ask a friend to tell you about a book, your friend might say, "This book is the best adventure ever written! It's about a cowboy in the old Southwest."

The first statement that your friend made is a personal opinion. An *opinion* is what someone *thinks* is true. The second statement is a fact. A *fact* is a statement that can be checked and proved to be true.

A lot of the information that you hear and read contains facts and opinions. Both kinds of statements can help you understand something. But you need to be able to tell the difference between the two. Then you can decide whether to believe the information.

EXPLORE IT

Get together with one or two classmates to study the song and photograph shown on these two pages. What facts can you learn about the life cowboys led on the range? What opinions about the life of a cowboy does the song express? What opinions about the life of a cowboy might you form from the photograph?

Home on the Range
Cowboy song from the United States

Oh, give me a home
   where the buffalo roam,
Where the deer and the
   antelope play,
Where seldom is heard
   a discouraging word,
And the skies are not
   cloudy all day.

In 1890, a trail photographer catches some cowboys having their midday meal.

TRY IT

Now that you know the difference between a fact and an opinion, look again at the photograph on this page. What kind of song might you write, based on what you see in the photograph? What facts would you include? What opinions might you include?

Work with a partner to write a song about cowboys that expresses both facts and opinions. Choose a way to show which parts of the song are facts and which parts are opinions. Then sing or recite your song to the class. Ask your classmates to identify at least one fact and one opinion in your song.

SKILL POWER SEARCH *As you read this chapter, list five interesting facts that you find.*

Setting the Scene

KEY TERMS

erode
mesa
panhandle
pueblo
adobe
nuclear energy

An Amazing Land

FOCUS *The Southwest region has unusual landforms and a varied climate. Many people of this region live and work on large farms and ranches.*

The Region's Boundaries

Tucked away in the southwestern part of our country are four large states—Texas, Oklahoma, New Mexico, and Arizona. These states form the Southwest region of the United States.

You can see on the map below that three of the states in the Southwest region form most of our boundary with Mexico. The Rio Grande is an international river,

because it flows along most of the boundary between the United States and Mexico.

The Rio Grande is formed high in the Rocky Mountains, where rainfall is plentiful. The river then flows downhill, across the Southwest region, and empties into the Gulf of Mexico.

Another boundary of the Southwest region is the Gulf of Mexico. Beneath this body of water

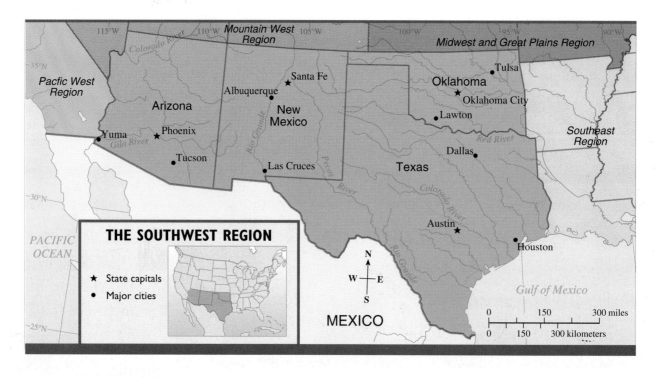

THE SOUTHWEST REGION

★ State capitals
● Major cities

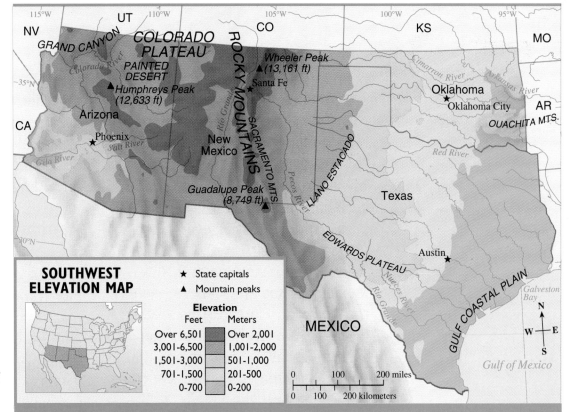

SOUTHWEST ELEVATION MAP

★ State capitals
▲ Mountain peaks

Elevation

Feet	Meters
Over 6,501	Over 2,001
3,001–6,500	1,001–2,000
1,501–3,000	501–1,000
701–1,500	201–500
0–700	0–200

off the coast of Texas are valuable oil deposits.

The Colorado River flows along much of the western boundary of the Southwest region. The swift waters of this river have been **eroding**, or cutting through, layers of red, pink, and orange rock for millions of years. This is how the Colorado River formed the Grand Canyon in northwestern Arizona. Find the Colorado River and the Grand Canyon on the map above.

erode To wear away the earth's surface by wind, running water, ice, or waves

Unusual Landforms

Over time, the wind, rain, and rivers of the Southwest have cut away large areas of soil and rock. Some of the landforms that have

The Rio Grande flows through Big Bend National Park in Texas. The fox is one kind of animal that lives in the park.

been left behind after centuries of erosion look like huge blocks that might have dropped out of the sky onto the land below.

These landforms are called **mesas** (MAY suhz). They are made of very hard rock layers—too hard to be worn down easily, even after years of eroding.

In northern Arizona and New Mexico, mesas are scattered across the Colorado Plateau. This area is high, but the land is flat on the surface. It has many canyons that have been created by rivers such as the Colorado River.

Southern Arizona and New Mexico have several mountain ranges. The ranges are close together and have rugged peaks. Between these ranges are large flat areas called basins. This part of the Southwest region is called the Basin and Range area.

Panhandles and Plains

Did you notice on the map on page 216 that northwestern Oklahoma and northwestern Texas have sections of land that jut out past the main parts of the state boundaries? These sections are called **panhandles** because they look like the handles of pans.

The panhandles and most of western Texas and Oklahoma are on the Great Plains. The plains are covered with thick grasses, some tall and some short. These are dry places, but enough rain falls to

There are many kinds of cactuses. Most grow in hot, dry regions, such as the Southwest.

★ *mesa*   A wide flat-topped hill or mountain with steep sides that rises from a plain

★ *panhandle*   A narrow strip of land extending from a larger land area

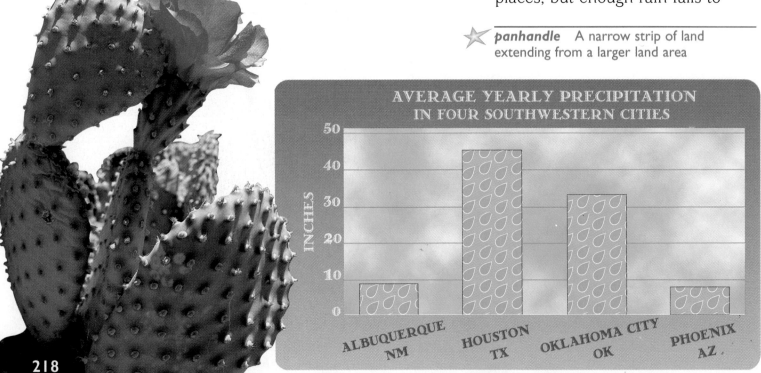

AVERAGE YEARLY PRECIPITATION
IN FOUR SOUTHWESTERN CITIES

INCHES

50

40

30

20

10

0

ALBUQUERQUE NM   HOUSTON TX   OKLAHOMA CITY OK   PHOENIX AZ

keep the grasses growing along with blankets of colorful wildflowers.

The Region's Climate

Mountains play an important role in the climate of parts of the Southwest region. High in the mountains of northwestern New Mexico and northern Arizona, winter temperatures can be low. In other areas of the Southwest region, winter temperatures can also be quite low. For example, on winter days in Oklahoma City, the temperature may not even reach 50°F, and nights can bring freezing temperatures.

Summer brings warm sunny days to most of the Southwest region. In the southern areas of the Southwest, summer heat is intense. In Phoenix, Arizona, summer temperatures often reach over 100°F.

The part of Texas along the Gulf of Mexico is much rainier than the Great Plains area of western Texas. Houston, Texas, which is near the coast, receives over 46 inches of rainfall per year. Amarillo, a city in the Texas Panhandle, receives about 21 inches of rainfall each year.

Ancient Adobe

Before air conditioning was invented, how did people survive the heat in parts of the Southwest region? Several thousand years ago, Native Americans of northern Arizona and New Mexico lived in "apartment" houses in communities called **pueblos** (PWEB lohz) like the one shown above.

The Native Americans used clay bricks called **adobe** (uh DOH bee) to build their homes. Adobe stays cool even during hot sunny days. Thick walls and small windows also kept the daytime heat out of their homes.

▲ Early adobe "apartment" houses can still be seen in Taos, New Mexico.

▼ This painting by Native American artist Peter Ray James shows adobe houses.

★ **pueblo** A large adobe structure in the Southwest built for housing a number of families

★ **adobe** A mixture of straw and clay shaped into blocks and sun-dried to use as bricks

◁ Farmers in Texas grow more watermelons than farmers in any other state.

Research in New Mexico

Rockets have been used for hundreds of years. Today, many scientists use rockets for exploration and research in the atmosphere and in space. In 1969, rockets carried astronauts to the first landing on the moon.

New Mexico is the chief place in the United States for research into rocketry. In Albuquerque (AL buh-kur kee), New Mexico, there is a large research laboratory where rockets for exploring space are designed and built. Scientists conduct experiments with **nuclear energy** (NOO klee ur EN ur jee) to improve travel into space by rockets.

New Mexico also offers scientists a place to launch rockets for testing. The many open spaces in the northwestern part of the state, far from busy cities, make good testing grounds for rockets.

Farming in the Southwest

Many people think that cotton is grown only in the Southeast region. But about one third of the cotton produced in our country comes from the Southwest. Texas alone produces one quarter of all the cotton grown in our country.

Wheat, too, is a major crop of the Southwest region. Oklahoma is the major wheat producer in the region, followed closely by Texas and Arizona.

Citrus fruits are grown on farms in Arizona and along the Rio Grande. Arizona produces such products as broccoli, onions, cauliflower, and honeydew melons.

New Mexico is known for its chile peppers. Each year Hatch, a New Mexico town near the Rio Grande, celebrates a chile festival.

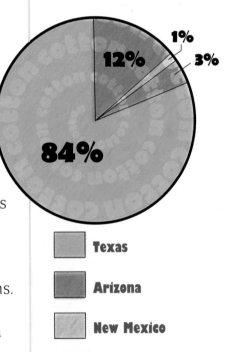

Income From Cotton in the Southwest Region

1%
3%
12%
84%

☐ Texas
☐ Arizona
☐ New Mexico
☐ Oklahoma

⭐ **nuclear energy**   Energy that is released when the structure of atoms is changed

Southwest

◄ A flight director at Mission Control uses a computer to communicate with astronauts in space.

A Space Center in Texas

The Lyndon B. Johnson Space Center attracts thousands of visitors each year. The center opened in 1964 at a location about 25 miles from downtown Houston, Texas. At the Johnson Space Center, astronauts are trained, spacecraft are designed, and missions into space are directed. The space center is also the location of the space shuttle program of the National Aeronautics and Space Administration, or NASA. Many scientists and astronauts work at the Johnson Space Center.

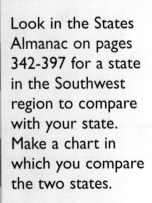

▲ A moon rock brought to Earth by an Apollo mission

You can visit NASA's visitor center at the Johnson Space Center. There you can see spacecraft that have orbited Earth, work with exhibits, and watch space program films. If you are there when engineers are not busy, you can take a tour of Mission Control, the heart of America's space program.

Metals and Minerals

FOCUS *Many people have gone to the Southwest region to find natural resources, such as metals and oil. Natural resources have helped the region grow.*

The Search for Gold

In 1540, a Spanish explorer named Francisco Coronado traveled north from Mexico in search of gold. He had heard stories about treasures in the Seven Cities of Cíbola (SEE buh luh) in what is now the Southwest region. Coronado didn't find those cities because they didn't exist.

▼ Copper ore, or rock, is first ground into tiny particles before it is used to make copper wiring.

But valuable resources in the form of metals did exist beneath the ground in that region. Gold, silver, and copper were just some of the metals that the earth held.

Valuable Resources

The map below shows that many different kinds of metals and minerals are found in the

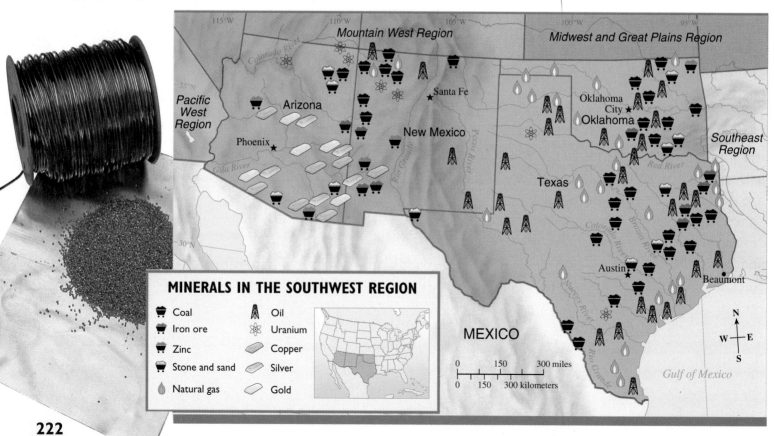

MINERALS IN THE SOUTHWEST REGION

- Coal
- Iron ore
- Zinc
- Stone and sand
- Natural gas
- Oil
- Uranium
- Copper
- Silver
- Gold

Mountain West Region
Midwest and Great Plains Region
Pacific West Region
Arizona
Santa Fe
Oklahoma City
Oklahoma
Phoenix
New Mexico
Southeast Region
Texas
Austin
Beaumont
MEXICO
Gulf of Mexico

0   150   300 miles
0   150   300 kilometers

Southwest region today. For example, silver, gold, and copper are mined chiefly in Arizona. More than half the copper mined in the United States comes from Arizona. Copper is used for making pennies and especially for wires that carry electricity in such items as telephone cables, refrigerators, radios, and televisions.

Miners in Texas dig for three other natural resources—coal, oil, and iron ore. Miners in Oklahoma dig coal and quarry stone.

The largest deposit of uranium in the United States lies in New Mexico. Uranium is used in nuclear power plants as a source of energy for producing electricity.

COPPER PRODUCTION IN THE UNITED STATES

13%
23%
64%

ARIZONA   NEW MEXICO

OTHER STATES

A Great Discovery

Cattle ranching and farming were the major industries in the Southwest region for many years. Then, in 1901, a huge deposit of oil was discovered at Spindletop, near Beaumont, Texas. The first well gushed oil 200 feet into the air. At the close of the year, production of oil at the Spindletop oil field was nearly 4 million barrels. By 1902, it was producing more than one quarter of all the oil in the United States. Today, there are still 50 producing oil wells at Spindletop.

With the discovery of oil at Spindletop, thousands of people rushed to Texas. They hoped to buy land that contained oil, and they found new jobs in the oil fields. Other industries, such as shipping, developed around the discovery of oil. The economy of the Southwest was changed forever.

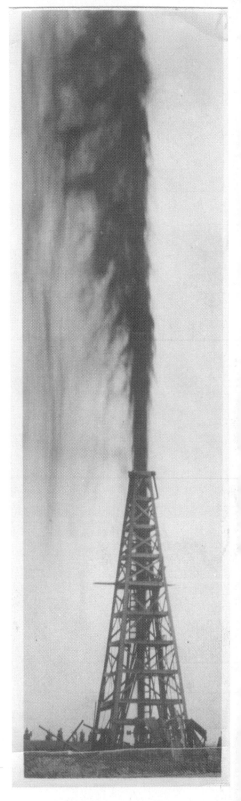

Oil rises high into the air at Spindletop oil field near Beaumont, Texas, on January 10, 1901.

1

Pumping oil

Finding Oil

How does **crude oil** get from thousands of feet underground to a gas station? An oil company might first hire a **geologist** (jee AHL-uh jihst) to help locate areas where oil might be trapped underground. But the only way to find out for sure is to drill into the earth.

First a derrick, or steel tower, is built where the geologists think the oil might be. A sharp point on the end of a turning drill pipe cuts a hole in the ground and through the rock. Usually the natural pressure is strong enough to force the oil to the surface. If the pressure is not strong enough, pumps are used to force the oil to the surface.

2

Refining oil

Once the oil reaches the top of the well, it passes through a machine called a separator, which removes the gases and water. Then this crude oil can be pumped into huge tanks, where it is stored until it is transported to a **refinery**.

At the Refinery

Pipelines, tanker trucks, or railroad cars carry the crude oil to a refinery. There the crude oil is heated until much of it turns into vapor, or thick mist. Then the hot oil vapor passes into a tower where it turns into liquid again. Different products, including gasoline and heating oil, can now be made.

The gasoline produced at the refinery is loaded into tanker trucks and driven to gas stations. Underground storage tanks hold the gas until it is pumped into vehicles.

⭐ **crude oil** The oil that comes directly from the ground, before it is refined
geologist A scientist who studies the rocks that make up Earth

⭐ **refinery** A building with machines that change a natural resource to make it pure or to make different products from it

Transporting oil

3

Using oil

4

Many of the items people use in sports are made from petrochemicals. ▶

Using Petrochemicals

Scientists recombine the different liquids and gases separated from oil in many ways. The new substances made from oil or natural gas are called **petrochemicals**.

Today, petrochemicals supply us with thousands of things we use every day. Petrochemicals are used in making paints, plastics, and clothing. The pictures on this page show you some of the many things made from petrochemicals.

People began making petrochemicals around 1915. In the 1940s, when the United States started to run out of natural materials such as rubber and silk, scientists used petrochemicals to create substitutes. They made a substance much like natural rubber,

and they invented nylon to replace silk. Plastic containers replaced those made of tin and glass.

Some cities in the Southwest region began to grow rapidly with the petrochemical industry. The petrochemical industry has helped Tulsa, Oklahoma, become one of the fastest-growing cities in the United States. And Houston, Texas, has become the fourth largest city in the United States. Both of these cities are located in major oil-producing regions.

 petrochemical A chemical that comes from oil or natural gas

SHOW WHAT YOU KNOW!

REFOCUS
COMPREHENSION

1. Why did many people move to Texas in 1901?

2. What caused Tulsa, Oklahoma, and Houston, Texas, to grow rapidly?

THINK ABOUT IT
CRITICAL THINKING

How might the Southwest region be different today if Spanish explorers had found gold there?

STATE CHECK
ACTIVITY

In the States Almanac on pages 342-397, find three cities in your state. Make a chart in which you list each city, its population, and its location in the state.

March of Time

1609 TO 1889

Four Firsts in the Southwest

FOCUS *Follow four interesting events that shaped the history of the Southwest region.*

FIRST CITY IN NEW MEXICO

The state of New Mexico was once a part of the country of Mexico. In 1609, the governor of the northern part of Mexico established a settlement in what is now Sante Fe, New Mexico. The settlement was built on the ruins of a Native American village. Santa Fe was far from other towns. About every three months, wagons delivered supplies from Mexico City to the few hundred people who lived in Santa Fe. Little by little the town began to grow.

When New Mexico became a state in 1912, Santa Fe became the capital city. Although Santa Fe has been a state capital for less than 100 years, it has been a center of government since 1609.

FIRST FORT IN ARIZONA

In the 1600s, Spanish explorers who lived in Mexico began to move northward into what is now the southwestern part of the United States. Often the Spaniards clashed with Native Americans who lived on land the Spaniards wished to settle.

The Spaniards wanted to live peacefully with the Native Americans. So they built towns where the Native Americans could live. The Spaniards also built presidios (prih SIHD ee ohz), or forts. In 1776, a presidio was built where the city of Tucson, Arizona, now stands. The presidio at Tucson became the center of a little town where Spaniards and Native Americans lived peacefully.

1609 Santa Fe is founded

1776 Fort Tucson is established

1836 Alamo is attacked

1889 Oklahoma land runs start

| 1600 | 1620 | 1640 | 1770 | 1790 | 1810 | 1830 | 1850 | 1870 | 1890 |

FIRST DEFEAT, THEN VICTORY FOR TEXAS

In 1718, Spaniards established a mission, or settlement, on the San Antonio River in what is now the state of Texas. They named the mission Mission San Antonio de Valero. The mission later became a fort and was known as the Alamo.

In 1836, the Alamo became the "Cradle of Texas Liberty" when a group of Texans defended the fort against an attack by the Mexican army. David "Davy" Crockett was among the brave Americans who fought for the freedom of Texas at the Alamo and who died there. The cry "Remember the Alamo" inspired others who fought for and won the independence of Texas from Mexican rule.

FIRST LAND RUN IN OKLAHOMA

At noon on April 22, 1889, about 50,000 people lined up near the south-central boundary of Kansas. The United States government was opening to settlers 2 million acres of land in what would become the state of Oklahoma. When a signal was given, everyone took off in a race called a land run. Some people raced across the boundary on horseback. Some rode in wagons, and some walked. The first person to reach a parcel of land claimed it simply by pounding a stake into the ground. By the end of the day, where there had been open space, there now were settlers.

SHOW WHAT YOU KNOW!

REFOCUS
COMPREHENSION

1. Why did Spanish explorers build towns in what is now the southwestern part of the United States?

2. Why is the Alamo important in the history of Texas?

THINK ABOUT IT
CRITICAL THINKING

How did land runs help the Southwest region grow?

STATE CHECK
ACTIVITY

Find out about a famous first in your state. Write about the event in your state scrapbook.

227

4

Then and Now

★ **KEY TERMS**

ranch
brand
vaquero
chaparral
stampede

LITERATURE

Justin and the Best Biscuits in the World

Ranching and the Cowboys

FOCUS *The first European settlers in the Southwest region came from Mexico. They brought herds of cattle and horses with them. Later, cattle raising became a major business in the Southwest region.*

The First Ranches

As Spanish settlers moved northward from Mexico in the 1700s, they brought herds of cattle and horses with them. The large open areas of dry, grassy land in the Southwest region provided good pasture for these animals.

By the late 1700s, there were many **ranches** in the Southwest region, especially in Texas. Some ranch herds numbered in the tens of thousands. In the mid-1800s, people from the eastern part of the United States were settling in the Southwest. These people started their own ranches in the area.

Ranches grew bigger and bigger over time. The owners needed workers to round up the cattle, **brand** them, and move them from one pasture to another. The people who did those jobs became known as cowboys.

▼ Cowboys move cattle from place to place so that the herd will have enough grass to eat.

★ **ranch** A large farm with grazing land for raising horses, cattle, or sheep

★ **brand** To burn an identification mark on the hide of an animal with a hot iron

▲ A saddle, a wide-brimmed hat, spurs, and a lariat—these are part of a cowboy's gear.

The First Cowboys

Early cowboys who looked after herds of cattle were called **vaqueros** (vah KER ohz). *Vaquero* comes from the Spanish word *vaca*, which means "cow." Many vaqueros were Native Americans. Some were Africans who had been brought north by Spaniards as slaves.

Some vaqueros were Spaniards and Mexicans who had settled on small ranches in the Southwest region. Most cowboys were young men. Many were even teenagers.

Clothing and Gear

A cowboy's clothes helped him work. He wore cotton shirts to stay cool in the summer and wool shirts for warmth in the winter. A wide-brimmed hat shaded him from the hot sun. A rawhide strand held the hat firmly in place. To cover his nose and mouth on a dusty ride, he had only to pull up the bandanna tied around his neck. Leather chaps protected his legs from the thorns of the **chaparral** (chap uh RAL).

Not all cowboys had boots. Many wore ordinary shoes, sandals, or even were barefoot when riding horses. With or without boots, however, the cowboy always strapped spurs to his heels. Spurs helped him control his horse.

The cowboy's gear made his work easier. One important piece of equipment was a strong lariat (LAR ee ut). Lariats were made of 4 to 12 strands of cowhide braided together. The lariat was as thick as

 vaquero A Spanish word for "cowboy"

 chaparral A thick growth of shrubs or thorny bushes

A cowboy poses for his picture in his trail gear. ▶

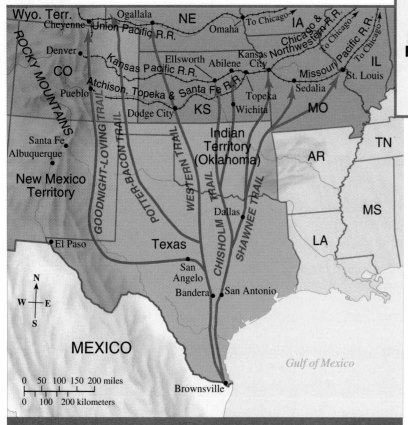

CATTLE TRAILS
IN THE SOUTHWEST
REGION, 1865-1885
→ Cattle trails
╫ Railroads
• Cities

To get their herds to market, ranchers had to move the cattle to towns that were on railroad lines. The cattle were packed into railroad cars and transported north or east.

Cowboys began the cattle drive by rounding up the cattle and branding them. Usually six to eight cowboys, plus a cook, a trail boss, and someone to care for the horses, moved the herd of cattle.

The team was on the trail for weeks. They traveled only about 15 miles in a full day, and many trails were more than 700 miles long.

Life on the Trail

Cattle driving was hard and dangerous work. Cowboys faced poisonous snakes, floods, and lightning. Storms often scared the cattle into stampedes. One or two frightened animals would run away, causing the entire herd to panic and charge out of control. Cowboys had to gallop in front of the cattle and turn them around.

a man's little finger and about 30 to 35 feet long.

Perhaps the cowboy's most important piece of equipment was his leather saddle. The saddle provided comfort on long rides. And it gave the cowboy greater control of his horse than riding bareback.

The Cattle Drive

By 1865, ranchers realized they would get more money for their cattle if they sold them in the northern and eastern parts of the United States.

▼ A chuck wagon carried the many items needed on a cattle drive.

⭐ **stampede** A sudden rush of a herd of frightened animals, such as cattle or horses

One of the best-known cattle trails was the Chisholm (CHIHZ um) Trail from south Texas to the railroad in Abilene (AB uh leen), Kansas. On a trail named the Goodnight-Loving Trail, cattle were moved to the railroad at Cheyenne (shy AN), Wyoming, and on to western ranges. Trace the routes of these cattle trails on the map on page 230.

By 1890, cattle drives had all but stopped. People would no longer pay the high prices for cattle. And many ranchers had fenced their lands, so herds had trouble traveling north.

Ranching Today

Ranching has changed in some ways since the days of the cattle drives, but in other ways it has not changed. Raising cattle still requires a lot of space. Most of the land of a ranch is used for grazing. Land is also used for growing grass and other plants that are dried for use as feed for the animals during the winter.

Today, most ranchers employ workers called ranch hands. The ranch hands do ride horses, as vaqueros once rode, and sometimes they use lariats. But many ranch hands use helicopters rather than horses to move the cattle from one pasture to another. And they rely on the latest technology to make the best use of their time.

Cattle in the Southwest Region Today

Rank	State	Number of Cattle
1	Texas	15,000,000
2	Oklahoma	5,000,000
3	New Mexico	1,000,000
4	Arizona	900,000

Workers on a cattle and sheep ranch near San Angelo, Texas, are rounding up cattle.

231

Justin and the Best Biscuits in the World

by Mildred Pitts Walter

Justin is going to visit his grandfather, who owns a ranch. Thoughts of seeing real cowboys and learning how to handle real horses fill his mind.

Later that evening Justin packed his duffle bag. He polished his cowboy boots and shined his silver cowboy belt buckle. He was so excited about going with Grandpa he couldn't sleep.

He turned restlessly on his bed, thinking about the festival and the rodeo. He thought of the horses at Grandpa's ranch. Three of them in all. One was called Cropper after the horse of the famous cowboy Bill Pickett. Another horse, a dapple gray, got his name from Grandpa. Grandpa said the horse talked to him, so he named him Palaver. Black Lightning, the youngest of the three, belonged to Justin whenever Justin visited the ranch. Justin called him Black and called Palaver, Pal.

For as long as he could remember, the Q-T Ranch had been in his mother's family. Justin's Great-Great-Grandfather Ward

232

had been a cowboy who rode cattle trails taking cattle to market, out of Texas into Kansas. Those trips lasted many weeks, sometimes months. People in the East depended upon cowboys to put beef on their tables.

Then the railroads spread across the country linking the East and the West. Cowboys were no longer needed to drive cattle. So, many of them settled in the West. Great-Great-Grandpa Ward settled in Missouri. He founded a ranch with a hundred and sixty acres. The place was so quiet and tranquil, he named it the Q-T Ranch.

Now Justin's house creaked in the stillness. Everyone else was asleep. Justin lay on his bed imagining himself riding upon a horse under a dark starlit sky.

Thousands of cattle rested close by. He listened to their breathing. Cowboys lay on blankets scattered about on the ground. Justin carefully guided his horse around the men. Snores of some rattled in the darkness while some slept without a sound of breathing.

The chuck wagon that carried supplies and the cook's utensils stood farther ahead on the trail. A big box attached to the wagon held the iron rods that fitted over a firepit, and a table.

During his visit, Justin learns to do many things. You can find out about his prize-winning biscuits by checking this book out of your school or public library.

SHOW WHAT YOU KNOW!

REFOCUS
COMPREHENSION

1. Why is the Southwest region a good place for ranching?

2. Where did the Goodnight-Loving Trail begin and end?

THINK ABOUT IT
CRITICAL THINKING

Why was a chuck wagon an important part of a cattle drive?

STATE CHECK
ACTIVITY

Trace a route from your home to a Texas city through which a cattle trail once ran. Refer to the maps on pages 402–403 and 230. Describe your trip in your state scrapbook.

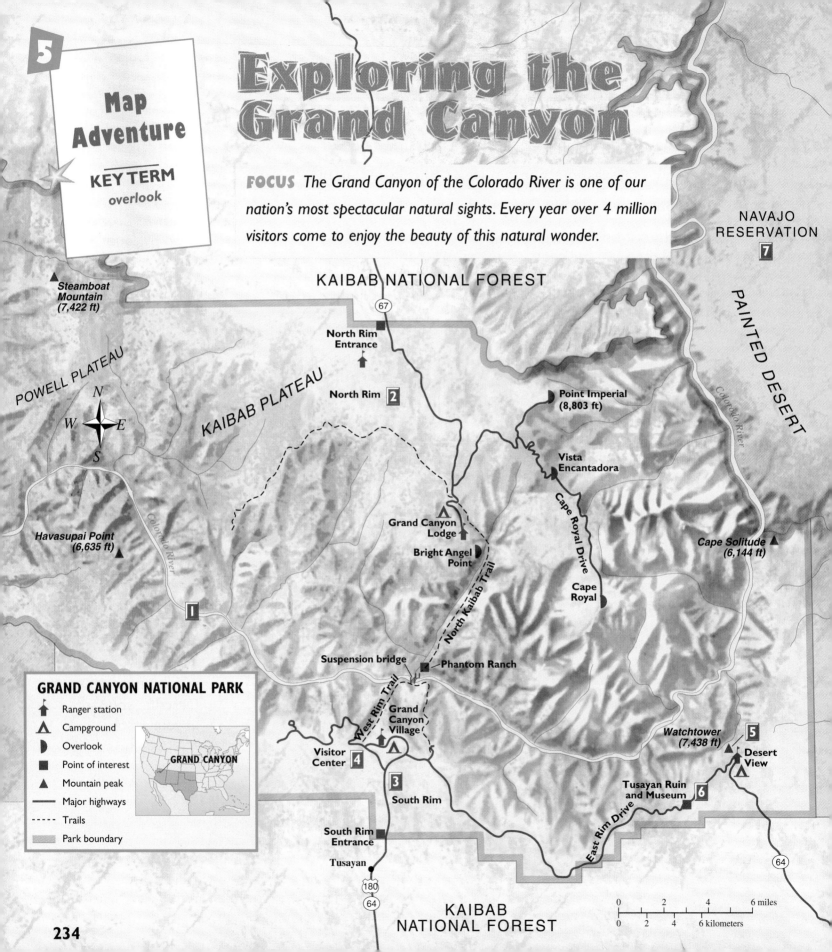

Map Adventure

KEY TERM
overlook

Exploring the Grand Canyon

FOCUS *The Grand Canyon of the Colorado River is one of our nation's most spectacular natural sights. Every year over 4 million visitors come to enjoy the beauty of this natural wonder.*

NAVAJO RESERVATION **7**

KAIBAB NATIONAL FOREST

▲ *Steamboat Mountain (7,422 ft)*

POWELL PLATEAU

67

North Rim Entrance

North Rim **2**

KAIBAB PLATEAU

PAINTED DESERT

Colorado River

Point Imperial (8,803 ft)

Vista Encantadora

Havasupai Point (6,635 ft) ▲

Colorado River

Grand Canyon Lodge

Bright Angel Point

Cape Royal Drive

Cape Royal

Cape Solitude (6,144 ft) ▲

1

North Kaibab Trail

Suspension bridge

Phantom Ranch

West Rim Trail

Grand Canyon Village

Watchtower (7,438 ft) ▲ **5** Desert View

GRAND CANYON NATIONAL PARK

Visitor Center **4**

3

South Rim

East Rim Drive

Tusayan Ruin and Museum **6**

🧍 Ranger station

△ Campground

◗ Overlook

■ Point of interest

▲ Mountain peak

— Major highways

---- Trails

▒ Park boundary

GRAND CANYON

South Rim Entrance

Tusayan

180
64

64

KAIBAB NATIONAL FOREST

| 0 | 2 | 4 | 6 miles |

| 0 | 2 | 4 | 6 kilometers |

Adventure in the Grand Canyon!

Picture yourself standing at the top of a steep cliff and looking straight down. Far below, you see the Colorado River. This river has carved out a canyon on its way southward. Take a journey through this world-famous natural wonder—the Grand Canyon.

Map Key

1 The Colorado River This river has been cutting through the canyon for millions of years.

2 The North Rim The North Rim of the canyon is part of the Kaibab Plateau. This rim is the site of Point Imperial *overlook*, the highest place in the whole canyon.

3 The South Rim The South Rim is the site of Grand Canyon Village. From this site, you can hike or ride a mule down to the canyon floor.

4 Visitor Center Here you can see exhibits and watch a slide show about the landforms, animals, and people of the canyon.

5 Watchtower This three-story tower has an observatory where you can view the canyon for many miles.

6 Tusayan Ruin and Museum Here you can walk among the ruins of an Anasazi pueblo and learn how these Native Americans lived.

7 The Navajo Reservation This reservation is home to the Navajos (NAHV uh hohz), who make up one of the largest Native American nations today. Part of their reservation borders the eastern edge of Grand Canyon National Park.

 overlook A place to view scenery

MAP IT

1. You are at the Visitor Center. A ranger tells you that the Watchtower is the place to see a great view of the canyon. In what direction will you go to reach the Watchtower? How many miles will you need to travel?

2. You climb up to the tower's observatory. What desert can you see if you look to the northeast? What major river will you see below?

3. You stop for a rest at Phantom Ranch before heading to Bright Angel Point. What trail will you hike to reach Bright Angel? In what direction will you travel?

4. Your tour bus is parked at Grand Canyon Lodge. When it's time to leave, the bus leaves the park through the North Rim Entrance. On which highway are you traveling? How far is it from the Lodge to the North Rim Entrance?

EXPLORE IT

You decide to write a postcard to a friend telling about your adventures in the canyon. Include information about the many overlooks and mountain peaks in the Grand Canyon. Give the location and height of each.

SUMMING UP

1 DO YOU REMEMBER...
COMPREHENSION

1. Name three landforms in the Southwest region.

2. Name three metals mined in the Southwest region.

3. What is special about Sante Fe, New Mexico?

4. Why is the Southwest region a good place for raising cattle?

5. What famous site was carved by the Colorado River?

2 SKILL POWER
RECOGNIZING FACT AND OPINION

In this chapter, you learned how to recognize facts and opinions. Team up with a partner. Together choose two photographs from this book. Write two facts and two opinions about each photograph. Then share your statements with another pair of students. Ask them to decide whether each statement is a fact or an opinion.

3 WHAT DO YOU THINK?
CRITICAL THINKING

1. How is the southern boundary of the Southwest region like the northern boundary of the New England region?

2. How might the Southwest region be different today if oil had not been discovered there?

3. Were land runs a fair way of opening what is present-day Oklahoma to settlement? Explain your answer.

4. How might ranching in the Southwest region be different in the future from ranching there today?

5. How is the Grand Canyon a mixture of what is old and what is new?

4 SAY IT, WRITE IT, USE IT
VOCABULARY

Suppose you are part of a cattle drive in 1870. In your state scrapbook, write a paragraph describing one day on the cattle drive. Write about what you see and do, what you wear, and what food you eat. Include as many of the key terms as you can.

adobe	mesa	pueblo
brand	nuclear energy	ranch
chaparral	overlook	refinery
crude oil	panhandle	stampede
erode	petrochemical	vaquero
geologist		

5 GEOGRAPHY AND YOU
MAP STUDY

Use the map below to answer these questions.

1. Where did the Goodnight-Loving Trail begin?

2. Which trail ended in Ogallala, Nebraska?

3. Which trail led cattle to Abilene, Kansas?

4. On which railroad was Dodge City?

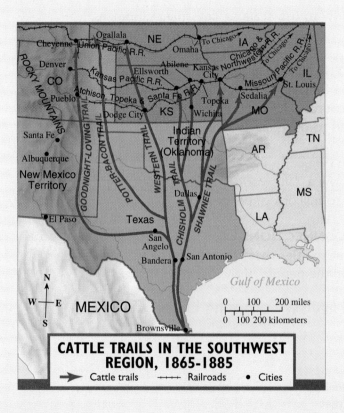

CATTLE TRAILS IN THE SOUTHWEST REGION, 1865-1885
➤ Cattle trails   ⊢⊢⊢⊢ Railroads   • Cities

6 TAKE ACTION
CITIZENSHIP

SAVING ENERGY AT HOME

SHUT THE DOOR   TURN OFF WATER

It takes energy to move a car or bus. It takes energy to warm or cool your home. Most of that energy depends on oil, coal, or natural gas. There are large supplies of natural resources to make energy, but the resources will not last forever.

With a group of classmates, make a poster that shows ways in which you can conserve, or save, energy. One example is to close all windows and outer doors in your home in cold weather. Place your poster in your school library for others to read.

7 GET CREATIVE
MATHEMATICS CONNECTION

Ask a classmate to join you on a trip along a cattle trail. Choose a trail that you would like to follow, using the map on page 230. Then use the scale of miles on the map to estimate the length of the trail.

Estimate how many days you might be on the trail in traveling from Texas northward to a city on a railroad line. Remember that cowboys traveled about 15 miles in one day.

L👀KING AHEAD
In the next chapter, find out more about the Southwest's resources and the region's connections to Mexico.

Southwest Links

The Southwest region has a variety of landforms as well as plentiful natural resources. Learn how people of this region use and share these resources with people around the world.

CONTENTS

Many kinds of melons are grown in the Southwest region and in Mexico. Find out about other products that are grown in these two areas on pages 250 and 251.

Near and Far

These books tell about people, events, and places that are important to the Southwest region. Read one that interests you and fill out a book-review form.

READ AND RESEARCH

Katie Henio: Navajo Sheepherder **by Peggy Thomson, photographs by Paul Conklin** (Dutton Children's Books, 1995)
Katie Henio is a Navajo sheepherder from New Mexico. Read about her Navajo way of life and her love of the outdoors. *(nonfiction)*

Family Pictures: **Cuadros de familia**
by Carmen Lomas Garza (Children's Book Press, 1992)
The author's story and paintings tell about her childhood in Kingsville, Texas. In both English and Spanish, she shares day-to-day family experiences that are so much a part of her Mexican American culture. *(nonfiction)*

Dams **by Andrew Dunn** (Thomson Learning, 1993)
Do you know how a dam is built? Through the book's photographs, drawings, and maps, you can learn about dams around the world, including Hoover Dam in the Southwest region. *(nonfiction)*

Grand Canyon **by Patrick Cone** (Carolrhoda Books, 1994)
Explore the plateaus and deep gorges of the Grand Canyon to learn about the plants and animals that live there. Breathtaking photographs reveal the beauty of this natural wonder. *(nonfiction)*

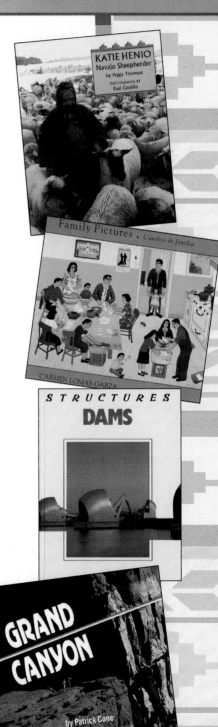

Skill POWER Using Scale

Knowing how to use a map scale will help you understand distances between places on a map.

UNDERSTAND IT

A map can show where places or things are located. But maps cannot show places and things in their true size. To represent size, maps are drawn to scale. This means that the places and distances shown on maps are smaller than their real size.

A certain number of inches on a map stands for a certain number of real feet or miles. When size or distance is shown this way, the map is drawn to scale. The map scale tells the real size or distance between places.

Scale is also used to make copies of things in smaller sizes. For example, many model airplanes are built to a scale of about 50 to 1. If you built a 1-foot-long model of an airplane, then the length of the real airplane is 50 times 1 foot, or 50 feet.

EXPLORE IT

Place a ruler under the scale for Map A on page 241. On this map scale, 1 inch equals 100 miles. Next, place your ruler in a straight line between Taos (TAH ohs) and Albuquerque. How many inches do you measure between the two cities? (If you measured about 1 inch, you are correct.) To determine the mileage from Taos to Albuquerque, multiply 1 x 100. Taos is about 100 miles from Albuquerque.

Now, on Map B, measure the distance between Taos and Albuquerque with your ruler. The distance with your ruler is less than on Map A. But using the scale on Map B, the number of miles between the two cities is the same as on Map A.

Copies of planes, boats, trains, and racing cars in smaller sizes are called scale models.

TRY IT

Measure the distance between Roswell and Las Cruces (las KROO sihs) on Map A. How many miles are between the two cities?

How many miles are between Roswell and Las Cruces on Map B? Be sure to use the map scale.

Remember that if your ruler shows $\frac{1}{2}$ inch, then the number of miles represented is one half the number of miles for 1 inch.

Write your findings on a sheet of paper. Then compare your answers with those of a partner.

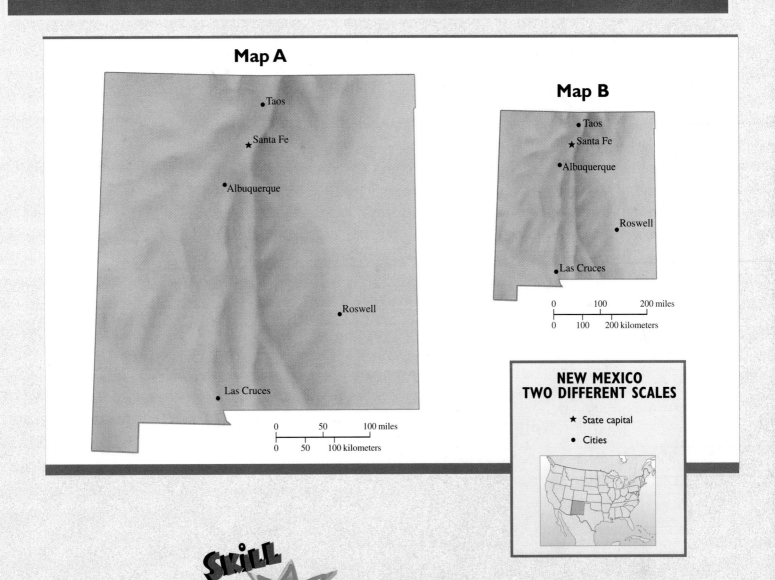

Map A

Taos

★ Santa Fe

Albuquerque

Roswell

Las Cruces

0   50   100 miles

0   50   100 kilometers

Map B

Taos

★ Santa Fe

Albuquerque

Roswell

Las Cruces

0   100   200 miles

0   100   200 kilometers

**NEW MEXICO
TWO DIFFERENT SCALES**

★ State capital

• Cities

SKILL POWER SEARCH

Look at the scales for two maps in chapters you have read. List the name of each map and the measurement and number of miles for each scale.

Setting the Scene

KEY TERMS

petrified
cavern
national park system
natural gas
soot

Resources for a Nation

FOCUS *The Southwest region has many natural wonders, from caverns to deserts. The land, its people, and varied resources make this a rich region of the country.*

Wonders of Nature

Millions of people from around the world visit the Southwest region each year. Many visitors come to see the region's varied landforms of breathtaking beauty.

Look at the photograph below to see Monument Valley on the state boundary of Arizona and Utah. The 1,000-foot-high towers of red sandstone rise from the land like tall monuments. Over thousands of years, the force of the wind has carved out these wonders of nature.

Southwest National Parks

Many of the Southwest's natural wonders are found in national parks. A national park is an area of land set aside as public property by the national government. The aim is to preserve the land in its natural beauty so that people can enjoy it.

As you can see in the chart below, there are five national parks

Southwest National Parks

Park	State	Year Established	Size in Acres
Big Bend	Texas	1944	801,163
Carlsbad Caverns	New Mexico	1930	46,753
Grand Canyon	Arizona	1919	1,218,375
Guadalupe Mountains	Texas	1972	76,293
Petrified Forest	Arizona	1962	94,189

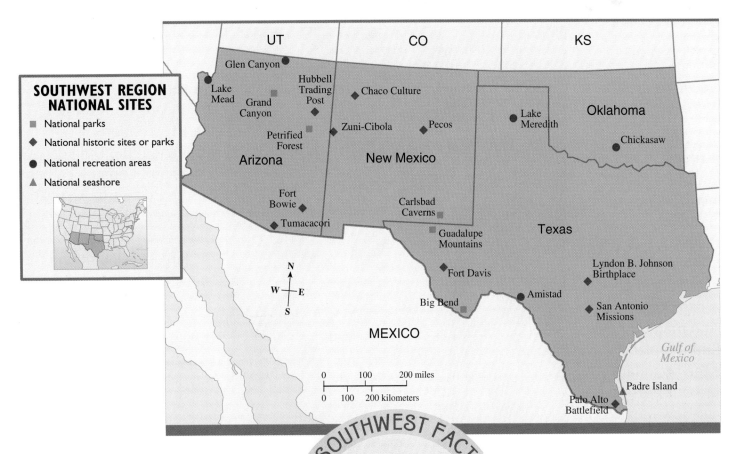

SOUTHWEST REGION NATIONAL SITES

- ■ National parks
- ◆ National historic sites or parks
- ● National recreation areas
- ▲ National seashore

UT • Glen Canyon • Lake Mead • Hubbell Trading Post • Grand Canyon • Chaco Culture • Petrified Forest • Zuni-Cibola • Arizona • Fort Bowie • Tumacacori

CO

KS

Oklahoma • Lake Meredith • Chickasaw

New Mexico • Pecos • Carlsbad Caverns • Guadalupe Mountains

Texas • Lyndon B. Johnson Birthplace • Fort Davis • Amistad • San Antonio Missions • Big Bend

MEXICO

Gulf of Mexico • Padre Island • Palo Alto Battlefield

N W E S

0 100 200 miles
0 100 200 kilometers

in the Southwest region. Each park has something special. For example, Arizona's Petrified Forest contains the world's largest amount of **petrified** wood. The wood is from trees that grew there about 150 million years ago. Over time, the trees fell into clay and sand, and the wood was replaced by minerals.

Summer is the time when many people visit the **caverns** at the Carlsbad Caverns National Park in New Mexico. Above ground, the park covers 46,753 acres. Below ground, over 70 caves make up the longest underground system of caverns in the world. The explored area is 23 miles long, of which 3

SOUTHWEST FACT

The most popular national park in the Southwest region is Grand Canyon National Park. More than 4 million people visit this park each year.

▼ A piece of petrified wood

miles are open to the public. One of the most impressive sights is the 750-foot-deep Big Room. It is the largest cave in the park. Millions of bats leave the caverns each day at twilight to search for food.

A Larger Park System

National parks are part of the **National Park System**. Other kinds of parks in this system include national historic sites, national recreation areas, and national seashores. Find the Hubbell Trading Post National Historic Site on the map above. The site preserves the history of Native Americans of the Southwest region.

⭐ **petrified** Having turned to stone
cavern A large cave

⭐ **national park system** The group of parks set aside by the government that have importance to the nation

243

Native American Traditions

Native Americans have a rich history in the Southwest region. The ancestors of the Pueblo Indians lived here thousands of years ago. The Navajos came in the 1500s. Other groups came later.

On the map on page 243, find the place where the boundary lines of the states of Arizona, New Mexico, Utah, and Colorado meet. This place is called Four Corners. It is the site of the Navajo Reservation, the largest Native American reservation in the United States. About 150,000 Native Americans live on the 16-million-acre reservation.

▲ A painting by a Native American artist for the 1994 Red Earth Festival

Every year, Native Americans from more than 100 nations throughout the United States and Canada, gather for the Red Earth Festival held in Oklahoma City, Oklahoma. This festival is the largest celebration of Native American heritage in the country.

Settlers From Europe

Many Southwesterners have Native American roots. Others can trace their roots to European settlers, such as those from Spain. Centuries ago, Spanish explorers claimed land in the Southwest for Spain. They established forts, built towns, and set up ranches. Various cities in the Southwest received names from the

NATIVE AMERICANS
IN THE SOUTHWEST REGION TODAY

STATE	NATIVE AMERICAN POPULATION	NATIVE AMERICAN PEOPLES
Oklahoma	252,100	Cherokees, Creeks, Choctaws, Cheyennes, Kiowas
Arizona	203,000	Navajos, Apaches, Tohono O'Odham, Hopis
New Mexico	134,100	Apaches, Navajos, Zunis
Texas	64,300	Alabama-Coushattas, Tiguas, Kickapoos

Spanish language such as El Paso and San Antonio, Texas. Spaniards introduced horses and cattle to the Southwest. Over time, cattle ranching developed into a major industry in this region. The introduction of cattle and horses also led to some of the Southwest's most popular attractions—rodeos, livestock exhibits, and horse shows.

Roots in Mexico

When Mexico gained its independence from Spain in 1821, parts of the Southwest region became part of Mexico. People who then lived in the region were under the government of Mexico.

In the early 1800s, English-speaking people from the eastern part of the United States came to settle in the Southwest region. These American settlers brought their language and traditions with them, such as the Fourth of July. They thought of themselves as Americans, even though they had to obey the laws of Mexico.

Disputes between the government of Mexico and the new settlers resulted in a war fought in Texas in 1836. The

Americans won the war, and Texas became independent from Mexico. In 1845, Texas became the 28th state of the United States.

Today, many people in the Southwest trace their ancestry back to these American settlers of Texas. But others trace their family roots back to Mexico or Spain.

In 1846, Mexico and the United States fought against each other in a war. After the United States won this war in 1848, the Rio Grande was established as the official boundary between our country and Mexico.

Newcomers Today

People continue to move into the Southwest region. Some come from Mexico or Canada. Other people come from different parts of the United States. Many newcomers are older people who find that the warm climate helps them enjoy healthier lives.

Some people also come to the region to take jobs in companies that have chosen the Southwest as a good place to do business. Among the items that these companies produce are aircraft, rocket parts, and computers.

POPULATION GROWTH IN THE SOUTHWEST REGION

1970
1990

Population in Millions

New Mexico   Oklahoma   Arizona   Texas

State

Where Energy Is Used in the United States

Homes 20%

Transportation 27%

Businesses 15%

Factories 38%

Energy Needs

Energy is released when machines—the engines in cars or factory machines—burn natural resources, such as oil, coal, and **natural gas**. Look at the chart on this page to see where energy is used today in the United States.

As you read in Chapter 11, the Southwest region supplies the nation with crude oil, which is transported by trucks and pipelines across the United States. The Southwest also supplies the country with most of its natural gas. But what is natural gas?

⭐ **natural gas** A flammable gas found with oil deposits

Natural Gas

If you have a barbecue grill at home, you may already be using natural gas. Natural gas includes propane and a number of other gases. The main gas is called methane (METH ayn). These gases are found deep within the earth along with oil.

For a long time, natural gas was considered to be of little value. Oil companies would let the gas burn off as they pumped oil from deep below the earth's surface.

Today, natural gas is second only to crude oil as an important fuel and as a source of energy. Of all the energy used daily in the United States, natural gas provides about one quarter of our needs.

Because natural gas produces little **soot**, it is now being used more in cities that have a lot of air

⭐ **soot** Black powder that is formed when certain things burn

A pipeline worker checks on the flow of gas through a natural gas pipeline.

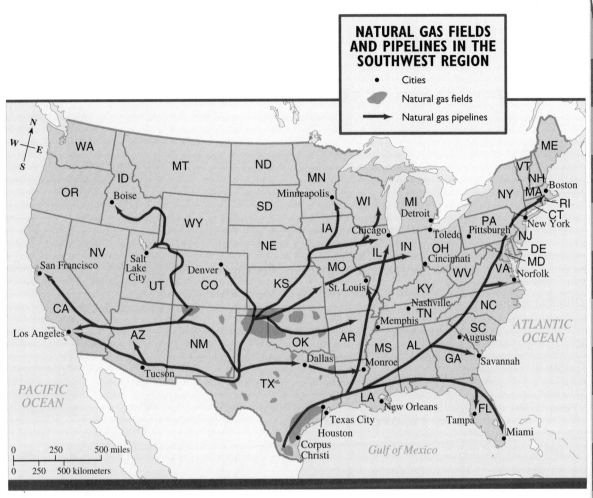

NATURAL GAS FIELDS AND PIPELINES IN THE SOUTHWEST REGION

- Cities
- Natural gas fields
- Natural gas pipelines

SHOW WHAT YOU KNOW!

REFOCUS
COMPREHENSION

1. What is a national park?

2. Why do people continue to move to the Southwest region today?

THINK ABOUT IT
CRITICAL THINKING

Why is the use of pipelines a good way to transport natural gas?

STATE CHECK
ACTIVITY

Find out if your state has any national parks or national historic sites. Locate the parks and sites on a map and record your findings in your state scrapbook.

pollution. More than 30,000 vehicles in the United States now run on natural gas fuel.

Natural Gas Pipelines

A natural gas pipeline is a series of pipes that allow gas to travel by land over thousands of miles. There are 1.2 million miles of natural gas pipelines in the United States. As you can see from the map above, the use of pipelines is the major way in which gas is sent from the rich natural gas fields of the Southwest to the rest of the country. Most of these pipes are placed under the ground. Pumps along the way keep the gas moving.

More natural gas pipelines are being planned for the future. That's because pipelines are durable and easy to maintain. These new pipelines will extend from the Southwest region to growing cities on both coasts of the United States.

Spotlight

KEY TERMS

dam
reservoir
hydroelectricity
aqueduct

Water for a Dry Land

FOCUS *Much of the Southwest is dry land in need of water. Look at some of the ways people have built dams and aqueducts to control the supply of water.*

How Dams Work

Much of the Southwest region is very dry. In many places, less than 20 inches of rain falls in a year. Most of this rain falls during a few days in the spring, causing rivers to overflow their banks.

During the rest of the year, the sun bakes the land of the Southwest, and water is scarce. To control flooding and store rainwater for later use, the people of the Southwest have built a number of **dams**. A dam is a barrier, or wall, placed across a river.

Water collects behind the wall of a dam in a lake called a **reservoir** (RES ur vwahr). A steady supply of water flows from the reservoir for use in cities and on farms that are downstream from the dam.

Dams do more than control the water supply. The force of water that flows through a dam provides energy to large machines called turbines. These turbines then produce **hydroelectricity**. People use this form of energy to light and heat homes, and run factories. In some places, dams also create places where people can swim and enjoy water sports.

The Hoover Dam

Hoover Dam is on the Arizona-Nevada boundary. It was the first of many dams to be built on rivers of the Southwest region. The dam, made of concrete, was completed in 1936. It holds back the waters of the mighty Colorado River. At 726 feet high and 1,244 feet long, Hoover Dam is one of the largest concrete dams in the world.

Lake Mead, the reservoir behind Hoover Dam, is more than 100

▲ Large turbines inside Hoover Dam produce enough energy for 500,000 homes.

---

dam A barrier preventing water flow
reservoir A place where water is collected

hydroelectricity Electricity produced by the power of rapidly moving water

◄ Lake Mead, behind Hoover Dam, is the largest constructed U.S. reservoir.

miles long. The lake supplies water to more than 1 million acres of farmland in the states of Arizona, Nevada, and California.

Transporting Water

Parker Dam and its reservoir, Lake Havasu, are also on the Colorado River between Arizona and California. This dam and its reservoir are located 145 miles downstream from Hoover Dam. Lake Havasu provides water for the 242-mile-long Colorado River Aqueduct. This major **aqueduct** (AK wuh dukt) delivers 1 billion gallons of water each day to the Los Angeles area in California. Five pumping stations have to lift the water 1,617 feet over the mountains between the Colorado River and the western coastal plain.

The Amistad Dam on the Rio Grande is another famous Southwest dam. It was completed in 1969 as a joint project of the United States and Mexico. The dam controls the water that is used to irrigate more than 3 million acres of farmland on both sides of the Rio Grande.

▲ Dams in the Southwest provide water to irrigate fields of crops, such as these along the Gila River in Arizona.

★ **aqueduct** A structure of pipes or an artificial channel used to transport water

SHOW WHAT YOU KNOW!

REFOCUS
COMPREHENSION

1. What are two reasons for building dams?

2. Name two major rivers of the Southwest region on which dams have been built.

THINK ABOUT IT
CRITICAL THINKING

Compare Hoover Dam in Arizona with Amistad Dam in Texas. How are they similar?

STATE CHECK
ACTIVITY

Prepare a report about water control in your state. Have dams been built on rivers of the state? What is the purpose of each dam?

Global Connections

KEY TERMS

fiesta
tariff
economist

Our Neighbor Mexico

FOCUS *The people of northern Mexico and the people of our Southwest region share a common geography, climate, and culture.*

Cities on the Boundary

The northern part of Mexico is dry, and most of its land is flat. The climate here is the same as in the southern areas of Texas, Arizona, and New Mexico. The Rio Grande forms 1,240 miles of the international boundary between the United States and Mexico. On both sides of this boundary, people grow cotton, wheat, and fruits such as melons in irrigated fields. Here you'll also find large cattle ranches.

Pairs of Cities

Pairs of cities have grown up along this boundary. Find Laredo, Texas, on the map on this page. If you cross the Rio Grande here, you'll enter the Mexican city of Nuevo Laredo (NWAY voh lah RAY-doh). In Arizona, just south of Tucson, you can leave Nogales, Arizona, and enter Nogales, Mexico.

People travel between the United States and Mexico through these cities every day—to work, shop, and visit friends and relatives. You can hear both Spanish and English being spoken as people meet and conduct business on both sides of the boundary.

THE U.S.-MEXICO BOUNDARY

— International boundary
— Major highways
• Cities

Children from Mexico and the United States celebrate Washington's Birthday in a parade in Nuevo Laredo, Mexico.

Sharing Traditions

People who live in the Southwest region enjoy many elements of Mexican culture. Mexican celebrations, called **fiestas**, include birthdays, town parades, and holidays. Fiestas that celebrate the cultures of both Mexico and the United States are also found in the Southwest, especially in towns along the Rio Grande.

People of both countries also enjoy some of the same foods. Tacos, chili, and enchiladas have their origin in Mexico. Tex-Mex food is the American version of these traditional foods of northern Mexico. Tex-Mex foods are now among the most popular foods in the United States.

Trade Agreement

Often countries charge **tariffs**, or taxes, on imported goods. These tariffs make the products from other countries more expensive. In 1994, Mexico, Canada, and the United States agreed not to charge tariffs on goods exchanged between the three countries. This trade agreement is called the North American Free Trade Agreement. We refer to the agreement by the first letter of each word—NAFTA.

The countries became stronger trading partners by being able to send goods freely to one another. Officials and **economists** in each country hope that all three countries will benefit from NAFTA. Each country will profit by selling more products to its trading partners. Because the states of the Southwest region are gateways, or entry points, to Mexico, these states hope to gain much by NAFTA.

---

 fiesta   A holiday or celebration

---

tariff A tax on goods that come into or go out of a country

economist   A person who studies the ways people use goods and services

SHOW WHAT YOU KNOW!

REFOCUS
COMPREHENSION

1. What are two things that people who live on the Mexico–United States boundary have in common?

2. What is a tariff?

THINK ABOUT IT
CRITICAL THINKING

Why have cities located on the Rio Grande grown in population?

STATE CHECK
ACTIVITY

Find the U.S. map in the Atlas on page 402. Find out which states share a boundary with Canada or Mexico.

SUMMING UP

1 DO YOU REMEMBER...
COMPREHENSION

1. Name three national parks to visit in the Southwest region.

2. Name three groups of people who have settled in the Southwest region.

3. What natural resources does the Southwest region supply to the country?

4. What are two benefits of building dams?

5. Name two things that Mexicans and Americans living near the Rio Grande have in common.

2 SKILL POWER
USING SCALE

In this chapter, you learned how to use scale on a map to estimate distances between places. Locate a map in an encyclopedia, a travel guide, or an atlas. Photocopy the map and make up three questions about distances between different places on the map. Exchange your map and questions with a partner. Have your partner use the map scale to answer the questions. Answer your partner's questions in the same way.

3 WHAT DO YOU THINK?
CRITICAL THINKING

1. Why does the national government spend money on national parks?

2. How does the Red Earth Festival preserve the heritage and culture of Native Americans?

3. Why is natural gas so important to the energy needs of the United States?

4. How would life be different for people in the Southwest region if there were no dams?

5. For the people of Mexico and the Southwest, what are the benefits of sharing cultures?

4 SAY IT, WRITE IT, USE IT
VOCABULARY

You are visiting the Southwest region. Write a letter to a friend at home, telling what you have seen. Try to include as many of the following key terms as you can.

aqueduct	national park system
cavern	natural gas
dam	petrified
economist	reservoir
fiesta	soot
hydroelectricity	tariff

CHAPTER 12

5 GEOGRAPHY AND YOU
MAP STUDY

Use the map below to answer these questions.

1. What state is the city of El Paso in?

2. Into what body of water does the Rio Grande empty?

3. What is the Mexican city across the boundary from Brownsville, Texas?

4. What three states of the Southwest region share land boundaries with Mexico?

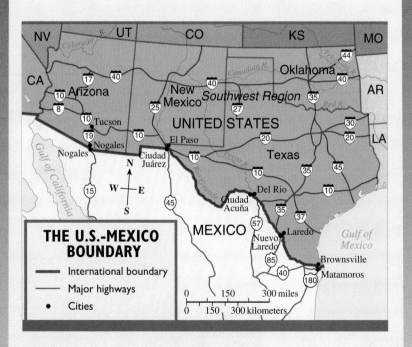

THE U.S.-MEXICO BOUNDARY
- International boundary
- Major highways
- Cities

6 TAKE ACTION
CITIZENSHIP

As a young person, you can be a good citizen by preserving the environment. Find information about groups in your community that work to preserve our land and water. With your class, make a resource book about these groups. Identify ways you can help save our land and water.

7 GET CREATIVE
LANGUAGE ARTS CONNECTION

Look at the designs of these Native American baskets. Design a basket pattern of your own. Paint your design and cut it out to paste into your state scrapbook. Then write a descriptive caption for the basket pattern you designed.

LOOKING AHEAD Get ready to climb the Rockies and learn about the Mountain West region in the next chapter.

HEADING
West

How Can Two Regions of the United States Have So Much Variety?

From sandy beaches and palm trees to the snow-capped Rocky Mountains, you'll find out about the great variety in land, climate, and people that make up the Mountain West and the Pacific West regions of the United States.

MOUNTAIN WEST

The Mountain West region was once a land where many people went to find adventure. In this chapter, you will find out what is special about the region today.

Rangers help to protect our national parks. Read about Yellowstone National Park on pages 276 and 277.

CONTENTS

REGION

These books tell about people and events in the Mountain West region. Read one that interests you and fill out a book-review form.

READ AND RESEARCH

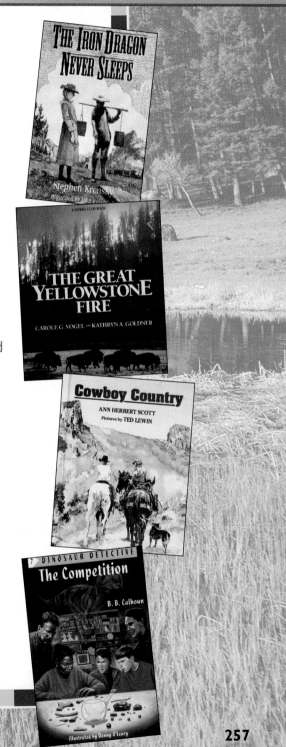

The Iron Dragon Never Sleeps by Stephen Krensky, illustrated by John Fulweiler
(Bantam Doubleday Dell Books for Young Readers, 1994)
Find out how Winnie's opinion of the transcontinental railroad changes when she learns about the working conditions of the Chinese laborers. *(historical fiction)*
• *You can read a selection from this story on page 268.*

The Great Yellowstone Fire by Carole G. Vogel and Kathryn A. Goldner (Little, Brown & Co., 1990)
The wildfires that burned out of control in 1988 had many people worried about Yellowstone and other forest areas. Discover what followed the great fires. *(nonfiction)*

Cowboy Country by Ann Herbert Scott, illustrated by Ted Lewin (Houghton Mifflin Co., 1993)
Visit Nevada with an old-time cowboy as your guide. Ride a pony through Devil's Canyon, camp out under the stars, and hear many stories about cowboy life. *(fiction)*

The Competition by B. B. Calhoun, illustrated by Danny O'Leary (W.H. Freeman & Co., 1995)
Fenton Rumplemayer helps his father's dig team solve a dinosaur puzzle in a competition. Can they figure out the name of the mystery dinosaur? *(fiction)*

Writing an outline

Knowing how to write an outline helps you organize information and see how main ideas and details fit together.

Title

Roman numeral for main idea

Capital letter for supporting idea

Capital letter to start each new idea

The Rocky Mountains of North America

I. The Rocky Mountain Chain

   A. Extends from Alaska to New Mexico

   B. Is more than 3,000 miles long

   C. Is made up of several ranges

II. Plant and animal life in the Rockies

   A. Pine, spruce, and fir trees

   B. Daisy, columbine, and Indian paintbrush plants

   C. Black bears, deer, elk, foxes, moose

   D. Bluebirds, robins, owls, eagles

   E. Rainbow trout and graylings

III. Economic activities in the Rockies

   A. Raising cattle and sheep

   B. Farming

   C. Lumbering and mining

   D. Tourism

UNDERSTAND IT

An outline is a written plan for organizing information. You can use an outline as a way to organize information that you have read or as a plan for writing a research report.

In an outline, the main ideas are listed in a certain order. Supporting ideas, or details, are listed under the main ideas that they help to explain.

Main ideas are identified with Roman numerals. Details are identified with the capital letters *A*, *B*, *C*, and so on. Each main idea and supporting idea listed begins with a capital letter. Every outline has a title.

EXPLORE IT

The outline gives information about the Rocky Mountains. Now use the outline to answer some questions.

1. How many main ideas does the outline have?

2. What is the first main idea? What are the other main ideas?

3. How many details support the first main idea? How many details support the second main idea?

4. What do the details tell you about the Rocky Mountains?

You can write an outline yourself. Just remember that each section of an outline should be an idea you can write a separate paragraph about.

TRY IT

Select a magazine article or an entry in an encyclopedia and write an outline for the selection. Share your outline with classmates. Ask them questions about your outline to see how well they understand the information you have outlined.

This student is planning an outline for an article that she read in a magazine. ▶

SKILL POWER SEARCH As you read through the chapter, notice how sections are organized by looking at headings and main ideas of paragraphs.

1

Setting the Scene

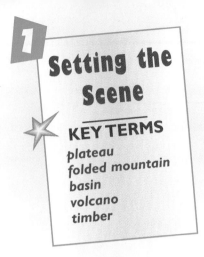

KEY TERMS

plateau
folded mountain
basin
volcano
timber

A Land of Peaks, Plateaus, and Plains

FOCUS *Fewer people live in the Mountain West region than in any other region of the United States. But the region has many attractions and resources.*

A Mountainous Region

Six rugged states make up the Mountain West region of the United States. These states are Montana, Idaho, Wyoming, Nevada, Utah, and Colorado, as shown on the map at the right. They have some of the highest mountains in our country. But they also have flat **plateaus** and broad plains.

One thing the Mountain West region does not have is a coast along an ocean. The Mountain West is located within the continent of North America. However, many small rivers and streams of the region join larger rivers that flow to the Pacific Ocean. Some rivers and streams join the Mississippi River as it flows to the Gulf of Mexico.

The region's name—Mountain West—tells you that this region's chief landform is mountains. The

Rocky Mountains form a long, high range that runs through five states in the region. Smaller ranges of these mountains have their own names. For example, the Sawatch (suh WAHCH) Range is in central Colorado. Mount Elbert, the highest

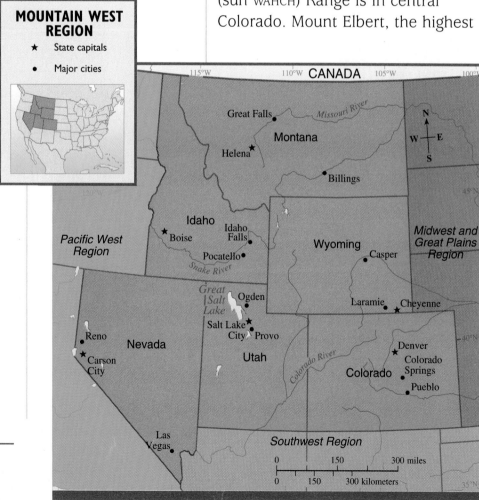

MOUNTAIN WEST REGION

★ State capitals

• Major cities

---

plateau A large level area that is raised above the surrounding land

260

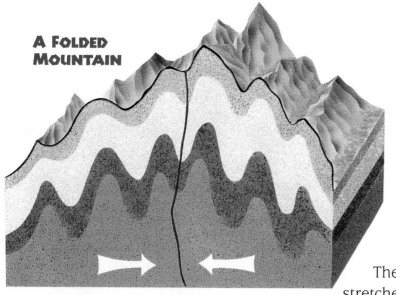

A FOLDED MOUNTAIN

Folded mountains form when masses of rock are squeezed from opposite sides.

A geologist is examining a sample of quartz, a mineral that is plentiful in the Mountain West.

peak of the Rocky Mountains, is in the Sawatch Range. Find Mount Elbert on the map on page 262.

Folded Mountains

Some of the smaller ranges of mountains are a kind called **folded mountains**. They were formed when the earth's surface was raised and pushed by heat and pressure from deep inside the earth. As the earth's surface was pushed together, it folded in places like an accordion. Lands that were pushed up became folded mountains.

Other Landforms

Another landform of the region is a **basin** called the Great Basin. Most of Nevada and parts of Utah are in the Great Basin. Much of the Great Basin is very dry.

The Colorado Plateau stretches into southern Colorado and Utah from the Southwest region. The high land has been cut into valleys and canyons by rivers and wind.

Another plateau of the Mountain West region is the Columbia Plateau, in southwestern Idaho. The Snake River has cut through this plateau and made a wide, fertile valley.

The eastern edges of Montana, Wyoming, and Colorado are part of the Great Plains. These grasslands are covered with farms and cattle ranches.

Denver, Colorado, is a major city on the Great Plains. It is located on the South Platte River, which flows out of the Rocky Mountains and onto the Great Plains.

folded mountain A mountain formed when rock layers are squeezed together
basin A bowl-shaped area of land almost entirely surrounded by mountains

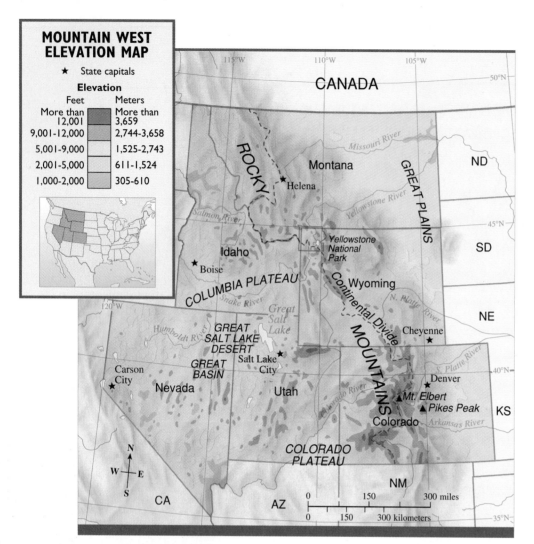

MOUNTAIN WEST ELEVATION MAP

★ State capitals

Elevation

Feet	Meters
More than 12,001	More than 3,659
9,001–12,000	2,744–3,658
5,001–9,000	1,525–2,743
2,001–5,000	611–1,524
1,000–2,000	305–610

▲ Bighorn sheep (*top*) live at high elevations in the Mountain West. Beavers (*center*) live at middle elevations, and roadrunners (*bottom*) live at low elevations.

Comparing Mountains

How do the Rocky Mountains compare with the Appalachians, our country's other major mountain chain? For one thing, the Rockies have higher peaks. Dozens of peaks in the Rockies reach over 10,000 feet. Mount Elbert has an elevation of 14,433 feet. Mount Mitchell, the highest peak in the Appalachians, rises 6,684 feet.

The Rockies are also younger than the Appalachians. Wind, rain, and rivers have had less time to erode the Rockies into lower mountains, like the Appalachians.

In some places in the Rocky Mountains, heat builds up deep under the earth's surface. Pressure from this heat pushes the land up, creating a large mountain called a **volcano**. The volcano can sometimes erupt in a spray of steam or rocks and ashes. Volcanic eruptions do not occur today in the Appalachian Mountains.

 volcano An opening in the earth out of which steam and melted rock may pour

262

Rich in Resources

The Mountain West is a region that has a little bit of everything in its natural resources. Mountain slopes have forests with tall, strong trees. Forests have plenty of open space in which to spread and grow. The cutting and transporting of **timber** provides jobs for many people of the region. Making lumber, paper, pencils, and other wood products are important manufacturing industries, especially in Idaho and Montana.

The mountains also provide many minerals and sources of energy. The crushing and folding that created the mountains also formed valuable minerals out of underground rocks. Nevada and Idaho are the most important sources of gold and silver in the country. Utah produces large amounts of copper. Coal and oil are valuable products of Wyoming and Colorado.

Farming and Industries

In river valleys, plains, and other flat areas in the region, agriculture is big business. Farmers raise large crops of wheat, barley, potatoes, and sugar beets. Sheep and cattle ranches are scattered throughout the region. Montana and Wyoming are among the leading sheep-ranching states in our country.

Many farm products are sold to nearby food-processing plants, where the products may be frozen or canned. Food processing is a big industry in the Mountain West.

To do their work, people need tools, machinery, and supplies such as paper and computers for keeping records. For that reason, many industries in the Mountain West region produce these goods.

▼ A shepherd is herding sheep near Telluride, Colorado.

timber Trees, when they are considered a source of lumber

263

A Growing Region

Compared with other regions, the Mountain West has a small population. But the states of this region, especially Nevada and Colorado, are growing fast. The climate, the scenery, and the jobs available in the Mountain West are attractive to people from other states.

The Mountain West offers outdoor fun too. For a real adventure, some people like to go white-water rafting or mountain climbing. They can be in a warm desert in the morning and skiing on mountain slopes in the afternoon. With so many interesting things to do, many people find the Mountain West a great place to live and work.

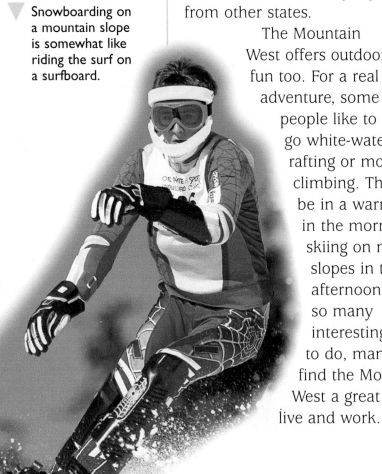

Snowboarding on a mountain slope is somewhat like riding the surf on a surfboard.

Utah's Largest City

More than 150 years ago, a group of people led by Brigham Young left their homes in Illinois

and moved westward. They were members of the Mormon Church. They were looking for a place where they might freely practice their religion.

When the Mormons reached the edge of the Great Basin, they decided to settle near the Great Salt Lake. Their community located at the foot of the Wasatch Mountains became Salt Lake City. The Mormons planned their new city carefully. The heart of the city was

MOUNTAIN WEST

Temple Square, where the city's main streets met.

Many of the Mormons were farmers. The valley around the Great Salt Lake had rich soil that was good for growing crops.

Today, Great Salt Lake Valley is an important center for manufacturing in the Mountain West. Copper goods and computer software are just two products made there.

Falcons in Idaho

In 1995, the U.S. Fish and Wildlife Service announced that peregrine falcons (PER uh grihn FAWL kunz) in the United States were no longer in danger of extinction. For years the falcons' eggs were not hatching because their shells were very thin and would break before the babies were ready to hatch. Little by little, falcons disappeared in the eastern part of the United States and their numbers diminished in the Mountain West region.

Scientists found that when falcons ate insects containing a powerful chemical called DDT, the birds produced eggs with very thin shells. People such as members of the Peregrine Fund in Boise (BOI see), Idaho, decided to help the few falcons that were left. They worked hard to find where the falcons were building nests. They carefully collected many falcon eggs with thin shells and cared for them until the young hatched. They fed and protected the young birds until they could be released into the wild. The efforts of the people in Boise have paid off. Today there are several thousand peregrine falcons throughout the United States.

2

March of Time

1806
TO
1885

LITERATURE
The Iron
Dragon Never
Sleeps

REACHING NEW GOALS

FOCUS *Learn about some of the people and events that are important in the history of the Mountain West region.*

THE EQUALITY STATE

At one time, only men in the United States were allowed to vote in local, state, and national elections. In 1869, Wyoming was first to grant women the right to vote. At that time, Wyoming was not yet a state. It was called the Territory of Wyoming.

In 1924 in Wyoming, Nellie Tayloe Ross was elected the first woman governor in the United States. Wyoming earned one of its nicknames—the Equality State—because it recognized that women and men had equal rights.

A DISCOVERY

Pikes Peak stands 14,110 feet above sea level in the Rocky Mountains, in central Colorado. Zebulon Pike, a lieutenant in the United States Army, and his men first sighted the snow-covered mountain peak in 1806 while they were looking for the source of the Arkansas River. Pike and some of his men tried to scale the peak, but they were unable to do so. Later the mountain peak came to be known as Pikes Peak.

A RAILROAD ACROSS OUR COUNTRY

May 10, 1869, was an important day in the history of transportation in the United States. On that day, workers drove a golden spike into the last railroad tie that joined two railroad lines at Promontory (PRAHM un tawr ee), Utah.

In 1862, the Central Pacific Railroad Company started building east from Sacramento, California. That same year, the Union Pacific Railroad Company started building west from Omaha, Nebraska, where a railroad from the East had stopped. When the two railroads were joined, in 1869, people could finally travel across the United States by train.

THE FIRST NATIONAL PARK

On March 1, 1872, Yellowstone National Park became the first national park in the world. President Ulysses S. Grant signed an act on that day that set Yellowstone aside as a "public park or pleasuring ground for the benefit and enjoyment of the people."

Most of Yellowstone National Park is in Wyoming, although narrow strips of the park spread into Idaho and Montana. It is larger than the states of Delaware and Rhode Island combined.

Yellowstone is known for its geysers (GYE zurz). These fountains of steam and water are forced above ground by volcanic gases. There are more than 200 geysers in Yellowstone. Old Faithful is the most famous geyser in the park. It erupts more than 12 times each day.

A SCHOOL FOR NATIVE AMERICAN CHILDREN

Sarah Winnemucca always wanted to help Native American children learn English and gain other skills that would help them progress. She was a Paiute (PYE yoot) who was born about 1844 in what is now the state of Nevada. She learned to speak English when she served as a guide for United States government officials in the area.

In 1885, she opened a school near today's Lovelock, Nevada. She taught there for three years before she became ill and was no longer able to teach.

The Iron Dragon Never Sleeps

by Stephen Krensky

Eli Tucker is a mining engineer who is helping to build the transcontinental railroad. His wife, Marjorie, and their daughter, Winnie, come to visit him in Cisco, California. Here, Winnie learns about a group of workers from China known as the Celestials because they call their home in China the Celestial Kingdom.

He shook his head and stabbed his mashed potatoes.

"What's the matter, dear?" asked Marjorie.

Eli shrugged. "Oh, it's just the tunnel. My crew spent the whole day blasting. We were trying to enlarge the heading. And how far did we get? One foot!" He slowly crushed a roll between his fingers. "Solid rock can be so—so stubborn."

"I'm sure it is, Eli," said Marjorie. "But don't take it out on the rolls."

"The Celestials work hard, don't they?" asked Winnie.

"Sure do," said her father. "Why, they even beat a crew of

THE IRON DRAGON
NEVER SLEEPS

Stephen Krensky
Illustrated by John Fulweiler

Welsh miners brought over special from Europe. I don't know where they get their energy." He sipped his coffee. "Maybe it's their baths."

Winnie looked confused. "Baths?" She disliked them almost as much as vegetables.

"Yes, baths." Her father took a bite of roast beef. "The Celestials are very organized. They've divided themselves into small groups. At night the group cook prepares a large boiler of hot water. Then the Celestials fill empty powder kegs with the water and take sponge baths."

"A bath every night?" Winnie was amazed. It sounded like torture.

"Every night," her father repeated. "Then they put on fresh clothes to eat supper."

Her mother eyed Winnie's dusty frock. "You know, Winnie," she said, "you could learn a lot from the Chinese."

When the Chinese workers on the railroad object to the conditions under which they are forced to work, Winnie faces a serious decision. You can learn about her decision by checking this book out of your school or public library.

SHOW WHAT YOU KNOW!

REFOCUS
COMPREHENSION

1. What happened at Promontory, Utah, in 1869?

2. Where is Yellowstone National Park located?

THINK ABOUT IT
CRITICAL THINKING

Why were Chinese laborers hired to work on the transcontinental railroad?

STATE CHECK
ACTIVITY

Read about a woman in the history of your state. In your state scrapbook, explain why she is important.

Map Adventure

GHOST TOWNS OF THE MOUNTAIN WEST

FOCUS From the mid-1800s to the early 1900s, thousands of treasure-seekers came to the Mountain West to find their fortune. Today, you can visit towns that were built in the region and were later abandoned by miners and dreamers.

GHOST TOWNS OF THE MOUNTAIN WEST

=== Interstate highways

90 Interstate highway route numbers

★ State capitals

• Other cities

⚒ Ghost towns

Montana
- Garnet
- Bearmouth
- Granite
- Florence
- Helena ★
- Elkhorn
- Castle
- 5
- Nevada City
- Gilmore

Idaho
- Bay Horse
- Boise ★
- Silver City
- 4

Oregon

Washington

North Dakota
94

South Dakota
90

Wyoming
- South Pass City
- Cheyenne ★
25

Nebraska
80

Nevada
- Unionville
- Galena
- 3
- Virginia City
- Carson City ★
- Rawhide
- Berlin
- Pine Grove
- Aurora
- Belmont
- Candelaria
- Ward Charcoal Ovens
- Gold Point
- Rhyolite

California
5

Utah
- Great Salt Lake
- Salt Lake City ★
- Mercur
- Spring Canyon
- Sego
- 2
- Silver Reef
- Grafton

Colorado
- Silver Plume
- Denver ★
- Kokomo
- Marble
- St. Elmo
- Animas Forks
- Alta
- 1

Kansas
70

Arizona

New Mexico

Texas

ROCKY MOUNTAINS

Missouri River
Yellowstone River
Snake River
Green River
Colorado River
North Platte River
South Platte River
Arkansas River
Red River

76

| 0 | 50 | 100 | 150 | 200 miles |
| 0 | | 100 | | 200 kilometers |

N W E S

Mining for Treasure

Thousands of **prospectors** came to the Mountain West when gold or silver was discovered there. They set up camps that quickly grew into towns. When the gold or silver ran out, the people moved on. Today, most of these abandoned towns, called **ghost towns**, have few or no buildings left standing.

Map Key

1 **Silver Plume, Colorado** This town was built in a swampy valley during the 1870s. Only a few of the mines are working today, but any resident will proudly show you around.

2 **Silver Reef, Utah** This is the only place where silver was found in sandstone, a kind of rock used for building. Many stone and brick buildings still stand here today.

3 **Virginia City, Nevada** Between 1859 and 1938, $900 million worth of gold and silver was mined here. At its height, the town was home to about 30,000 people. Today, about 750 people live there.

4 **Silver City, Idaho** Visitors to Silver City see a well-planned town with stores, hotels, barns, and even a school. Mining here ended in 1942 with the closing of the last silver mine.

5 **Elkhorn, Montana** Several empty frame buildings still stand in this once famous mining town. In the 1880s and 1890s, its chief mine produced about $14 million in silver.

⭐ **prospector** A person who explores or searches for valuable ores or oil
ghost town The remains of a settlement that people have abandoned

MAP IT

1. You begin your tour of ghost towns in Denver, Colorado. Your first stop is Silver Plume. On what highway do you travel? When was this town built?

2. You cross the state boundary into Utah and head for Silver Reef. What highways do you take?

3. Your next stop is Virginia City, Nevada. What state capital is nearby?

4. Now you head for Silver City, Idaho. Which route is the most direct? What can you see in Silver City?

5. You want to visit Elkhorn, Montana, in the Rocky Mountains. In which direction do you travel?

EXPLORE IT

Choose one of the ghost towns on the map. Plan a trip there from your home, using an atlas as a guide. Note the highways you would take and the major cities you would pass.

THE MILE HIGH CITY

FOCUS *Denver, Colorado, is located on the eastern edge of the Rocky Mountains. It is an important manufacturing and transportation center for the Mountain West region.*

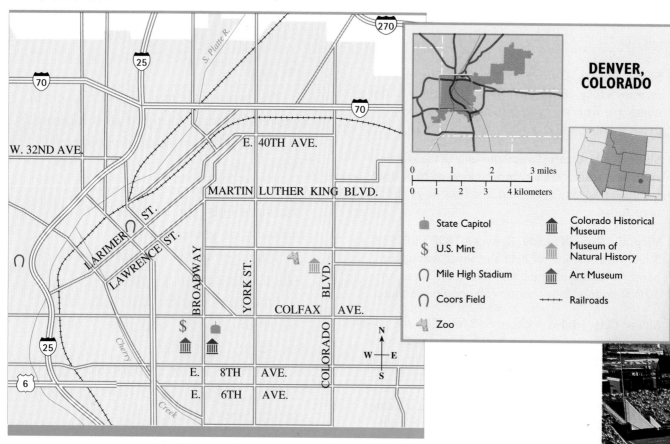

DENVER, COLORADO

🏛 State Capitol	🏛 Colorado Historical Museum
$ U.S. Mint	🏛 Museum of Natural History
∩ Mile High Stadium	🏛 Art Museum
∩ Coors Field	┼┼┼┼ Railroads
🦒 Zoo	

A Mountain West City

Denver, the capital of Colorado, is the largest city in the Mountain West. It is located just east of the Rocky Mountains. From almost anywhere in the city, people can see the Rockies.

Denver is called the Mile High City because of its **altitude**. The city takes its nickname from the fact that the dome of its capitol building in the center of the city is 5,280 feet, or one mile, above sea level.

⭐ *altitude* Height above sea level

Downtown Denver

The South Platte River flows through Denver. It is joined by Cherry Creek in the downtown section, where a civic center has been built. The map on page 272 shows part of downtown Denver.

Find the state capitol on the map. Across from the state capitol is the Denver Art Museum. Here is one of the finest collections of Native American art in the world.

Now find the city's Museum of Natural History on the map. The museum has a variety of exhibits of interesting animals. For another

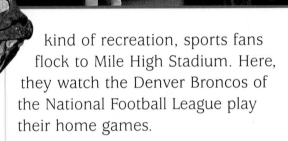

You can see parts of dinosaur skeletons at the Denver Museum of Natural History.

kind of recreation, sports fans flock to Mile High Stadium. Here, they watch the Denver Broncos of the National Football League play their home games.

How Denver Grew

Prospectors founded Denver in 1858, when gold was discovered in Cherry Creek. In 1870, the Denver Pacific Railroad was completed. It joined the Union Pacific line in Cheyenne, Wyoming. Another railroad, the Kansas Pacific, reached Denver soon after. The two lines brought more people and more trade into the town.

Denver continued to grow when supplies were brought in by train. The supplies were repackaged into smaller bundles for shipment west along mountain trails by horseback or on small wagons. People built warehouses where they stored

The Colorado Rockies, a major league baseball team, plays its home games in Coors Field in Denver.

goods. They also built factories to process the gold and other minerals mined near Denver.

After the Gold Rush

As the gold rush ended, prospectors discovered silver near Denver. When silver mining slowed down, many towns near Denver closed. Residents moved away, and the deserted former settlements became known as ghost towns. Denver residents kept their town going. They made their living from cattle and sheep ranching, farming, and commerce.

The railroad and the warehouses that early residents built in Denver helped the town grow. It became an important distribution, transportation, and trade center for the Mountain West region.

Today, there are more than 1,500 manufacturing plants in and around Denver. Many of them process foods, such as beef, wheat, and corn. Some plants produce medical and scientific instruments.

The United States government plays a larger role in the economy of Colorado than it does in most other states. Denver is the headquarters of more federal offices than any other city in the United States, except Washington, D.C. Since 1966, the area has housed the North American Aerospace Defense Command, which tracks the paths of satellites and spacecraft.

Making Money

In the United States and most other countries, only the federal government can manufacture money. Our country's first federal **mint** was opened in Philadelphia, Pennsylvania, in 1792, and is still operating. Now there are mints also in Denver, Colorado; San Francisco, California; and West Point, New York. These mints only make coins. Our paper money, called bills or notes, is made in Washington, D.C., and Fort Worth, Texas.

mint A place where the government makes coins

This ghost town shows how early mining towns in the Mountain West might have looked.

▲ Two U.S. minted coins

If you look carefully at the two quarters shown on this page, you will see that the letter P is engraved on one coin and the letter D on the other. The letters mean that the coin at the left was made at the United States Mint in Philadelphia and the coin at the right was made at the United States Mint in Denver.

The Mint in Denver

The Denver mint was opened for business in 1863. Gold from nearby areas was brought to the mint, weighed and valued, then melted and shaped into gold bars.

In 1906 the Denver mint began making coins—half dollars, quarters, dimes, nickels, and pennies. It now produces about three fourths of all the coins in the United States. The Denver mint produces nearly 5 billion pennies each year.

Specially issued coins to commemorate, or remember, certain occasions are also minted in Denver. For example, a coin to commemorate the 1996 Summer Olympics in Atlanta, Georgia, was minted in Denver.

Tours of the Denver mint are free. Visitors see how different designs are pressed into blank coins. One press at the Denver mint is set aside for visitors. They can stamp their own Denver mint souvenir medals.

Number of Coins Made Yearly at the Denver Mint

Millions of Coins: 0, 100, 200, 300, 400, 500, 600, 700

Type of Coins: Nickels, Dimes, Quarters

SHOW WHAT YOU KNOW!

REFOCUS
COMPREHENSION

1. Why is Denver called the Mile High City?

2. What types of coins are made at the Denver mint?

THINK ABOUT IT
CRITICAL THINKING

How did Denver's location help it to become a gateway to the west?

STATE CHECK
ACTIVITY

How are your community and Denver alike or different? Write about the similarities or differences in your state scrapbook.

YELLOWSTONE FOR THE FUTURE

FOCUS *Yellowstone National Park is one of the biggest tourist attractions in the entire United States. With so many visitors each year, the park faces many challenges.*

Visiting Yellowstone

Yellowstone National Park offers visitors a variety of activities, such as hiking, horseback riding, canoeing, and cross-country skiing. There are many kinds of animals to see in Yellowstone, including elk, grizzly bears, and bighorn sheep. Visitors are forbidden to feed the animals in Yellowstone, but they can enjoy watching the animals in their natural environment. The

Yellowstone gets too many visitors! With so many people, the park can be damaged. I think only a certain number of people should be allowed in the park each year.

I don't think that Yellowstone should limit the number of visitors each year. The park was put aside for all people to enjoy whenever they wish.

many acres of land provide these animals with a spacious home, making the park an important **preserve** in the United States.

With so many visitors, it's difficult for park rangers to protect the natural environment from being damaged. The park also faces high costs for maintaining its heavily used roads and other facilities.

To keep the park safe, clean, and beautiful for future generations, Yellowstone Park officials must make some tough decisions.

⭐ **preserve** A place where fish and wild animals are protected

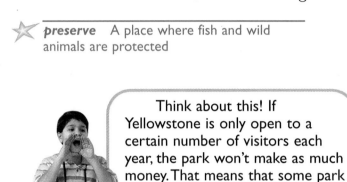

Think about this! If Yellowstone is only open to a certain number of visitors each year, the park won't make as much money. That means that some park workers might lose their jobs.

OK—I see your point. Maybe the park can make some new rules to protect the land and its wildlife without limiting the number of visitors.

YOU DECIDE . . .

- Do you think Yellowstone National Park should limit the number of visitors who can come every year?

- Should more rules be made to protect the park?

- What are your suggestions for protecting Yellowstone National Park?

SHOW WHAT YOU KNOW!

REFOCUS
COMPREHENSION

1. Name three things that people can do at Yellowstone.

2. Name one expense of keeping up Yellowstone National Park.

THINK ABOUT IT
CRITICAL THINKING

Why is feeding animals in Yellowstone forbidden?

STATE CHECK
ACTIVITY

Plan a trip from your home to Yellowstone. In your state scrapbook, describe the route that you would take and draw a map of the route from your home to the park.

SUMMING UP

1 DO YOU REMEMBER...
COMPREHENSION

1. What states make up the Mountain West region?

2. How did Wyoming earn the nickname the Equality State?

3. What brought prospectors to the Mountain West region?

4. Why did Denver continue to grow after many nearby towns became deserted settlements?

5. Name three facts that you learned about Yellowstone National Park.

3 WHAT DO YOU THINK?
CRITICAL THINKING

1. Would the Mountain West region have grown even if gold and silver had not been discovered? Why or why not?

2. Why are people interested in visiting ghost towns?

3. Why is the United States Mint in Denver important to the economy of the state?

4. What ideas do you have for protecting Yellowstone National Park for future generations?

5. Will the Mountain West region attract even more people in the future? Why or why not?

2 SKILL POWER
WRITING AN OUTLINE

In this chapter, you learned how to write an outline to organize information and to see how main ideas and details fit together. Are you ready to write another outline? Choose one lesson you have read in this book. Review the headings and main ideas. Also look for details. Organize the information in an outline. Then share your outline with classmates.

4 SAY IT, WRITE IT, USE IT
VOCABULARY

Suppose you had lived in a town that became a ghost town in the Mountain West. Write a paragraph in which you describe your life in the town before it became a ghost town. In your paragraph use as many of the key terms as you can.

altitude	plateau
basin	preserve
folded mountain	prospector
ghost town	timber
mint	volcano

5 GEOGRAPHY AND YOU
MAP STUDY

Use the map below to answer these questions.

1. What is the capital of Idaho?

2. What is similar about the location of Great Falls, Montana, and Billings, Montana?

3. Which city is farther west—Casper, Wyoming, or Pueblo, Colorado?

4. Through which states shown on the map does the Snake River flow?

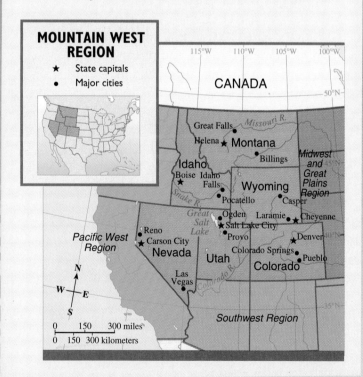

MOUNTAIN WEST REGION
- ★ State capitals
- ● Major cities

6 TAKE ACTION
CITIZENSHIP

STAY ON BIKE PATH

You have read about Yellowstone National Park and that it has to be protected for everyone's use. With a partner, think of ways that you can protect a park in your community or state. Make a brief list of your suggestions. Compare your list with lists made by other students. Perhaps as a class you might combine the best suggestions from all the lists and send one list to your community or state park service.

File Edit Draw Paint Type Window
Poster 1

7 GET CREATIVE
COMPUTER CONNECTION

With a partner, create a travel poster about the Mountain West region on a classroom or library computer. Review all the things the region has to offer. You might illustrate your poster by drawing or using a graphics program if you have one.

LOOKING AHEAD
Explore in the next chapter the kinds of work that people in the Mountain West do.

Mountain West

The Mountain West region has many special features—lofty mountain peaks, dry deserts, and broad plains. In this chapter, you'll learn more about how people live and work in the Mountain West, and how they connect to the world around them.

CONTENTS

◀ This girl is holding a pan like those used in the 1800s to find gold in Mountain West streams. Learn more about the search for gold on page 290.

Links Near and Far

These books tell about people, events, and places that are important to the Mountain West region. Read one that interests you and fill out a book-review form.

READ AND RESEARCH

Rand McNally Children's Atlas of the United States
edited by Elizabeth Fagan Adelman (Rand McNally & Co., 1995)
Read about each of the Mountain West states in this colorful atlas, with its individual state maps, photographs, drawings, and charts. Find out why early settlers came to each state and how people who live there today make their living. *(nonfiction)*

Idaho by **Kathy Pelta** (Lerner Publications Co., 1995)
Discover how much of the world's grain and other useful items are produced in Idaho and sent to places around the world. *(nonfiction)*

Familiar Rocks and Minerals by the staff of **Chanticleer Press** (Alfred E. Knopf, 1988)
Gold, silver, and copper are some of the minerals mined today in the Mountain West. This guide contains photographs and descriptions of these and other minerals found in North America. *(nonfiction)*

Ticket to Canada by Celia Barker Lottridge, illustrated by **Wendy Wolsak Frith** (Silver Burdett Press, 1995)
At first Sam Ferrier is not happy about moving from his family's Iowa farm to the Canadian prairie in 1915. As time passes, however, Sam discovers some exciting and frightening surprises. *(fiction)*

SKILL POWER

Comparing and Contrasting

Knowing how to compare and contrast gives you a better understanding of people and places all over the world.

UNDERSTAND IT

In what ways is your school similar to other schools in the area? Is it about the same size as other schools? Do other schools have a cafeteria or lunchroom like the one in your school? When you find out how places and things are alike, you are comparing them. Maybe there are ways in which your school is different from other schools. Noticing differences between two or more things is called contrasting.

Comparing and contrasting the ways in which people live in different parts of the world help you understand them better. For example, how is the job of a potato farmer in Idaho similar to the job of a potato farmer in Ireland? Both of these people have the same kind of job—farming. How are their jobs similar? How does their farming differ?

EXPLORE IT

Pictures can help you compare and contrast things. In the pictures below, the people are sheepherding in two different parts of the world. The picture at the left shows sheepherding in Idaho. The other picture shows sheepherding in India. Compare these two photos. What similar things do you see in them? What differences do you see?

Herding sheep in Idaho

Herding sheep in India

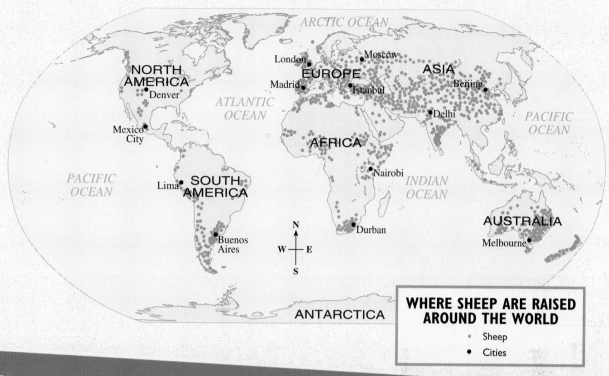

NORTH
AMERICA
Denver

Mexico
City

PACIFIC
OCEAN

ATLANTIC
OCEAN

London
Madrid
EUROPE
Istanbul
Moscow

ASIA
Beijing

Delhi

PACIFIC
OCEAN

ARCTIC OCEAN

AFRICA

Lima
SOUTH
AMERICA

Buenos
Aires

Nairobi
INDIAN
OCEAN

Durban

N
W   E
S

AUSTRALIA
Melbourne

ANTARCTICA

WHERE SHEEP ARE RAISED AROUND THE WORLD

- Sheep
- Cities

TRY IT

There are many sheep ranches located around the world. Some countries, however, raise more sheep than do other countries. The countries that raise more sheep produce more wool. For example, China is the world's leading sheep-raising country. Because of the great number of sheep raised, China is the biggest producer of wool in the world.

Look at the map above. It shows where sheep are raised around the world. You can compare the amount of sheep raised in various countries by using the information found on the map.

See if you can answer this question by looking at the map. Are more sheep raised in South America or in North America?

Use the cities found on the map as clues to help you identify different countries of the world. Now select two countries and compare the information found on the map about the number of sheep raised in each country.

SKILL POWER SEARCH

Compare and contrast two pictures in this chapter. How are the pictures alike? How are they different?

283

1 **Setting the Scene**

⭐ **KEY TERMS**

water vapor
rain shadow
Continental Divide
metropolitan area
county
sheriff

Mountain West Links

FOCUS *Tall mountains, dry deserts, and broad plains influence how people live and work in the Mountain West region.*

Mountains Affect Weather

Most winds, or air masses, travel from west to east across the middle section of the Northern Hemisphere. Winds on the West Coast of the United States carry moisture gathered from the Pacific Ocean.

However, mountains often block these damp winds from traveling smoothly across an area. For example, the Cascade Mountains and the Sierra Nevada Mountains form barriers to winds traveling east. As the winds rise over these mountains, the air cools off. At cooler temperatures, air holds less **water vapor**. Some of this water vapor falls to the ground in the form of rain or snow. This precipitation falls on the western slopes of these mountain ranges.

The winds that cross the mountains are then too dry to drop much precipitation on the eastern slopes. This is why most of Nevada and western Utah are very dry—as you can see from the map on this page.

⭐ **water vapor** Water in the atmosphere

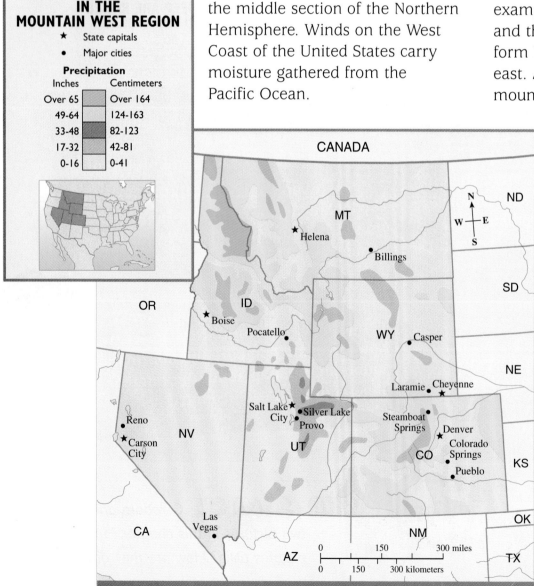

ANNUAL PRECIPITATION IN THE MOUNTAIN WEST REGION

★ State capitals
• Major cities

Precipitation

Inches		Centimeters
Over 65		Over 164
49-64		124-163
33-48		82-123
17-32		42-81
0-16		0-41

Over the Rockies

Heading eastward, the winds meet even taller barriers—the Rocky Mountains. The winds rise, cool off, and again lose moisture collected from rivers and lakes below. Because of this, western parts of Colorado and northeastern Utah get more than 40 inches of precipitation yearly.

After passing over the Rocky Mountains, the winds blow down onto the Great Plains. Now the winds are dry again. In some areas east of the Rocky Mountains, just enough rain falls to keep grasses growing to feed beef cattle.

Rain Shadow

To explain the difference in precipitation between the western sides of mountains and the eastern sides, we say that mountains create a rain shadow. Places located on the western side of a mountain usually receive a lot of precipitation. One example is Silver Lake, Utah, with 42 inches of precipitation yearly. Places on the eastern side, in the rain shadow, are much drier. Denver, Colorado, gets 15 inches of precipitation each year.

▲ Some ski resorts such as Steamboat Springs, Colorado, are located on the western side of a mountain.

Living in a Rain Shadow

Rain shadow affects the lives of people in the Mountain West. To grow crops in a rain shadow, farmers must irrigate their fields. Much of this water comes from the region's rivers. For example, the Snake River—which flows through Idaho, Wyoming, and Washington—supplies much of the water that Idaho farmers use to grow potatoes, the state's major crop.

★ **rain shadow** A region of reduced rainfall on the side of a mountain that is facing away from the wind

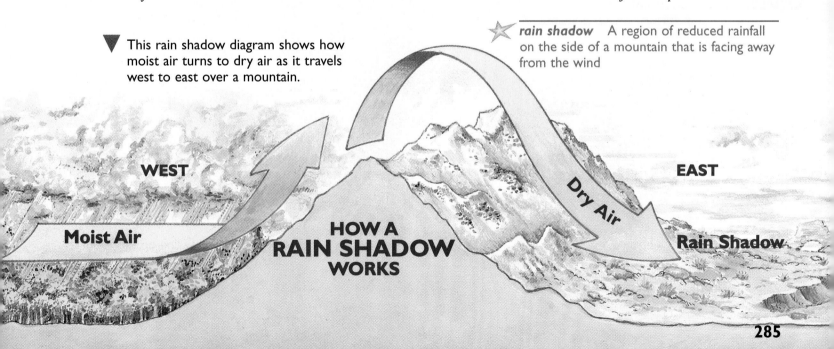

▼ This rain shadow diagram shows how moist air turns to dry air as it travels west to east over a mountain.

WEST

Moist Air

HOW A RAIN SHADOW WORKS

Dry Air

EAST

Rain Shadow

The Continental Divide

When snow melts or rain falls on mountainsides, the water flows downhill and forms streams. Streams that form on the eastern slopes of the Rocky Mountains flow into rivers that eventually reach the Atlantic Ocean or the Gulf of Mexico. Rivers that originate on the western slopes empty into the Pacific Ocean. The line of mountain ridges that separates rivers that flow eastward from those that flow westward is the Continental Divide.

The Missouri River, for example, flows eastward from the Continental Divide. Its waters join the Mississippi River and end up in the Gulf of Mexico. The Snake River twists its way west from its source on the western side of the divide. It then joins the Columbia River, which flows into the Pacific Ocean.

Continental Divide The highest points of land that separate rivers and streams flowing eastward from those flowing westward

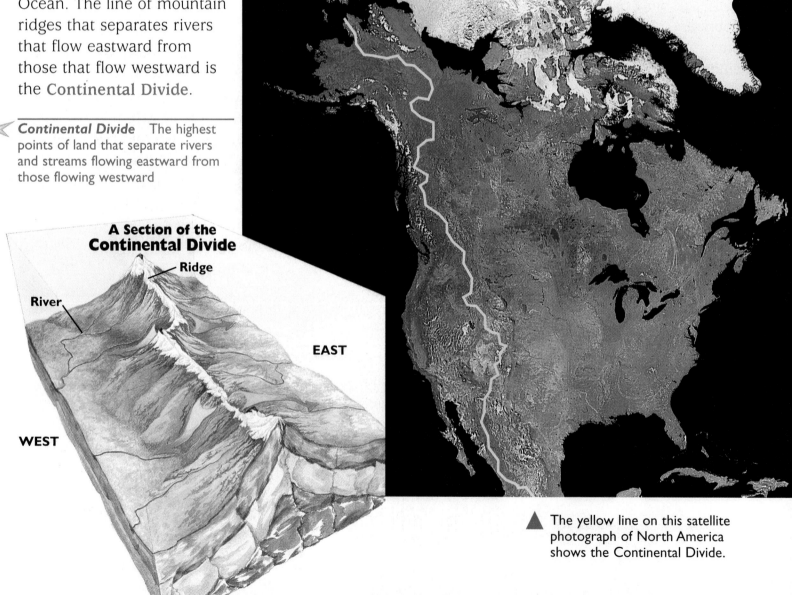

A Section of the Continental Divide

Ridge

River

EAST

WEST

▲ The yellow line on this satellite photograph of North America shows the Continental Divide.

286

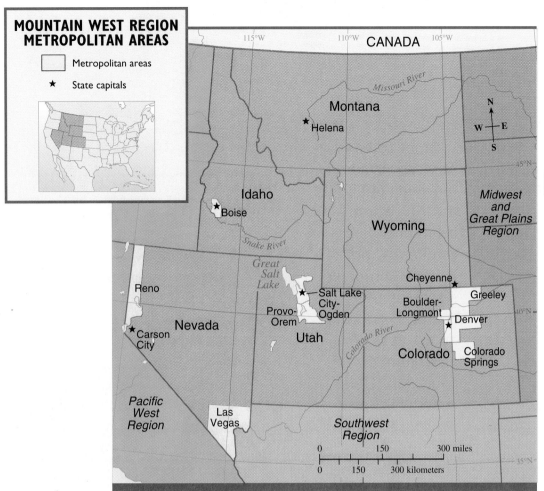

MOUNTAIN WEST REGION METROPOLITAN AREAS

- ☐ Metropolitan areas
- ★ State capitals

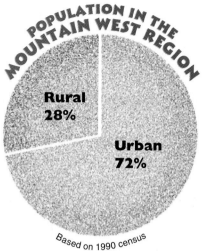

POPULATION IN THE MOUNTAIN WEST REGION

Rural 28%

Urban 72%

Based on 1990 census

Where People Live

The land on either side of the Continental Divide has some of the highest mountain peaks in the region. Much of the land is steep and rocky. Only scattered small towns nestle in the valleys between the high mountains.

The deserts of the Mountain West region are as sparsely populated as the area around the mountains. Locate the Great Salt Lake on the map on this page. To the southwest of the Great Salt Lake is a desert called the Great Salt Lake Desert. Few people live in this barren area.

Some people live on the plains of Montana and Wyoming. Many of those people grow crops or raise livestock on isolated farms and ranches.

Cities and Towns

The pie graph on this page shows that most of the people in the Mountain West live in cities and towns. The yellow spaces on the map above show the major **metropolitan areas** of the region. Las Vegas, Nevada, and Denver, Colorado, are the region's fastest-growing metropolitan areas.

 metropolitan area A large city with its surrounding suburbs, towns, and other communities

Living in Counties

The states in the Mountain West region, like most states of the United States, are divided into sections called **counties**. Each county has a government, just as towns, cities, and states do. Residents of a county elect county officials.

The **sheriff** is a county official who helps keep people safe from crime and responds to emergencies when they occur. Other county officials collect taxes, issue documents such as pet licenses, and supervise county recreational areas.

County Services

In states that are sparsely populated, such as Wyoming and Montana in the Mountain West, people often rely on their county for needed services. Some of these services include registering people to vote— and providing emergency services.

County roads link farms, ranches, and small towns in rural areas. The county government oversees snow removal and the repair of county roads and highways.

Other county services include providing public libraries where county residents can borrow books and use computer resources. Many counties also hold annual fairs on agriculture or education. These county fairs give people the chance to get together, share ideas, and have fun.

SOME COUNTY SERVICES IN THE MOUNTAIN WEST

TRANSPORTATION
Repairs county roads and bridges
Removes snow from roads

PARKS AND RECREATION
Runs county parks
Holds county fairs
Provides recreation centers

PUBLIC SAFETY
Enforces fire code
Provides ambulance service

ELECTIONS
Registers voters
Tallies final votes

County officials include sheriffs and their assistants who patrol county roads and respond to emergencies.

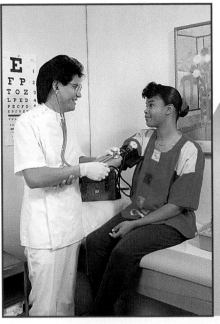

People who provide health care services, such as this nurse, are part of the health care industry.

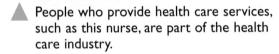

WHERE PEOPLE WORK IN THE MOUNTAIN WEST REGION			
State	Agriculture	Manufacturing	Service
Colorado	49,500	191,000	1,056,000
Idaho	46,000	72,000	338,000
Montana	37,100	23,000	245,000
Nevada	7,900	34,000	578,000
Utah	22,800	116,000	643,000
Wyoming	15,700	10,000	127,000

Where People Work

The table on this page shows the number of people who work in agriculture, manufacturing, and service jobs in each state in the Mountain West. Notice how large the numbers are in the right column for service workers. Like people in other parts of the United States, most workers of the Mountain West are employed in service jobs. They work in stores, government offices, banks, hospitals, schools, and in other places where people provide services.

The Tourist Industry

Many of the jobs in the Mountain West region involve meeting or working with people from other states and countries. That is because the scenery, the outdoor life, and the entertainment centers of the region attract tourists from many places. This tourism industry creates many jobs—especially in vacation spots. Here, hotel and restaurant workers, park rangers, and others are needed to provide tourists with many needed services.

Mining and How It Works

FOCUS *The states of the Mountain West region are rich in silver, gold, uranium, and copper. Finding and mining these precious metals is different today than was mining during the 1800s.*

Mining Towns

In 1859, two prospectors were searching for gold in the hills of Nevada. They dug up some pieces of gold mixed with blue-black clay. The clay was loaded with silver. The mine where this silver and gold were found became known as the Comstock Lode. It led to the founding and development of Virginia City, in western Nevada.

The dream of finding silver and gold brought thousands of people to the Mountain West region in the 1800s. Mining towns grew up overnight at sites where gold or silver had been discovered. Both Denver, Colorado, and Helena, the capital of Montana, started as mining towns. The main street of Helena is even named after an old gold camp—Last Chance Gulch.

The mining pan and pickax were common mining tools in the 1800s.

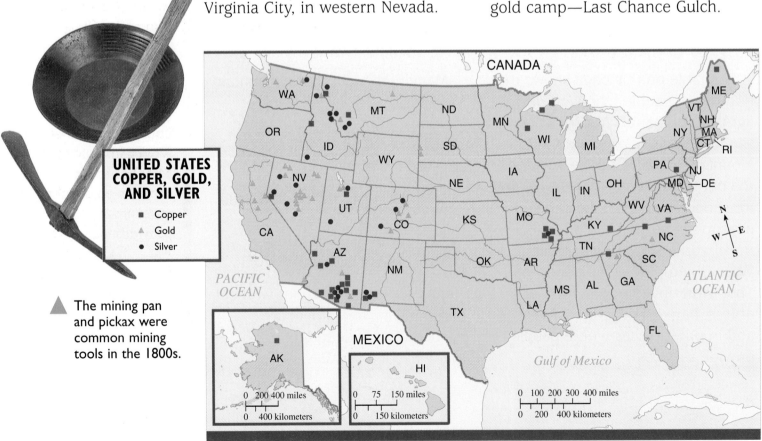

UNITED STATES COPPER, GOLD, AND SILVER
- Copper
- Gold
- Silver

Mining for copper in Utah

Looking for Minerals

Many prospectors in the 1800s looked for minerals that were near the surface of the earth. They used pickaxes and shovels to dig gold out of the ground.

Other prospectors looked for precious minerals in streams. They scooped gravel from the bottom of the stream and poured it into a pan. The prospectors then swirled the pan around to eliminate the water inside. This left only the heavier minerals such as gold and silver in the pan. This kind of mining was called panning.

Mining Today

Today, mining is an important industry in the states of the Mountain West region. More gold and silver are mined in Nevada than in any other state in the nation. Idaho is second in silver mining. On the map on page 290, find two other Mountain West states where silver is mined.

Miners use modern methods to remove minerals from the earth. In **open-pit mining**, large bulldozers strip the top layer of earth from a shallow mineral deposit. Then the miners use powerful machines to scoop up the minerals.

If a mineral deposit is close to the surface and very thick, the dirt on top is first scraped away. Then minerals are dug out of the earth, leaving a deep hole in the ground. This hole is called a **quarry**.

To reach minerals that are deep under the earth's surface, today's miners use machines to dig large tunnels. These tunnels, or shafts, often reach straight down into the earth. Sometimes, tunnels are dug in the side of a hill or a mountain. Then the miners dig sideways to remove the deeply-buried minerals.

 open-pit mining Method of mining in which the soil is stripped from the earth

 quarry A place from which minerals are cut, dug, or blasted

SHOW WHAT YOU KNOW!

REFOCUS
COMPREHENSION

1. What tools did prospectors use to look for gold in the 1800s?

2. What are some modern methods for taking minerals from the earth?

THINK ABOUT IT
CRITICAL THINKING

Besides the chance to mine for gold, why would people go to a booming mining town?

STATE CHECK
ACTIVITY

Look in the States Almanac on pages 342–397 to find out about minerals that may be mined in your state or nearby states. Record your findings in your state scrapbook.

Canada's Western Provinces

FOCUS *The rich lands of Canada's western provinces provide a wealth of valuable resources similar to those found in the Mountain West region.*

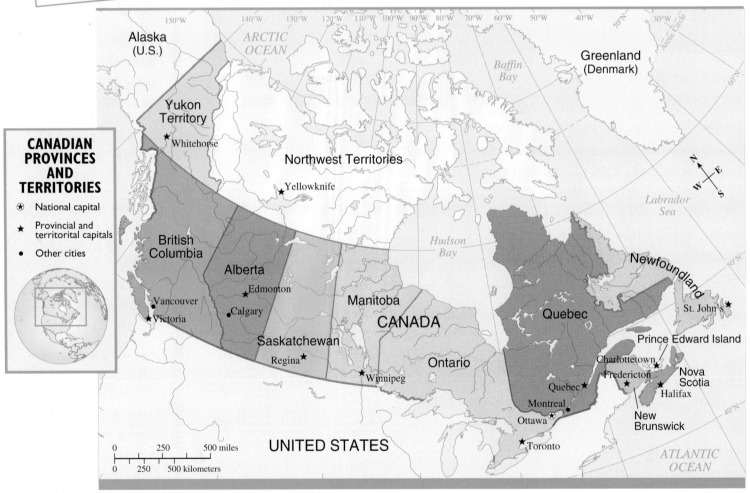

Canada's Provinces

Canada is a large nation with ten provinces, or divisions, similar to states in the United States. Canada also has two territories. The names of these provinces and territories are shown on the map above. Most Canadians live in the southern part of the country.

⭐ **province** A division of Canada similar to a state in the United States

A farmer mows down a field of wheat in the province of Saskatchewan.

Three Canadian provinces—Saskatchewan (sas KACH uh wahn), Alberta, and British Columbia—share boundaries with states of our Mountain West region. The land in the southern part of these provinces and the land of the Mountain West region share two features. Both areas have rich soil for growing certain crops, such as wheat and hay. Both areas also contain grasslands—ideal places in which to raise cattle. Alberta has grasslands similar to those that cover most of North Dakota and the eastern sections of Wyoming and Montana.

Farms and Ranches

Saskatchewan has more farmland than any other province in Canada. Here, wheat is the chief crop raised. In fact, Saskatchewan is the greatest wheat-growing region in North America. Farmers here also raise crops of barley, rye, and corn.

More beef cattle is raised in Alberta than any other province in Canada. Ranchers in this province also raise hogs, sheep, and dairy cattle.

Mountain Resources

Just as the discovery of gold brought prospectors to the Mountain West region in the 1800s, the discovery of gold in the mountains of British Columbia lured many people to this Canadian province. Today, British Columbia still has gold and silver mines. Coal, zinc, and lead are also mined in the southeastern part of the province. There are also many large coal deposits in Alberta.

Loggers harvest timber in forests in the mountains of Alberta and British Columbia. Forests cover nearly one half of British Columbia. This province produces nearly three fourths of Canada's lumber.

logger A person who cuts trees for lumber

SHOW WHAT YOU KNOW!

REFOCUS
COMPREHENSION

1. Name the three provinces that share boundaries with the Mountain West.

2. What are the major industries of Saskatchewan, Alberta, and British Columbia?

THINK ABOUT IT
CRITICAL THINKING

Besides farming, ranching, and mining, how might Canada's western provinces be similar to states in our Mountain West region?

STATE CHECK
ACTIVITY

List the industries that are important to Canada's western provinces. Which of these industries are important in your own state?

SUMMING UP

1 DO YOU REMEMBER . . .
COMPREHENSION

1. Why does Nevada get so little rainfall?

2. What is the line of high mountain ridges called that goes through the Rocky Mountains?

3. What are two examples of services that county governments provide?

4. What are two methods of mining today in the Mountain West region?

5. What is the chief crop raised in Saskatchewan?

2 SKILL POWER
COMPARING AND CONTRASTING

In this chapter, you learned how to compare things that are alike. You also learned to contrast things that are different. Draw a Venn diagram similar to the one on page 82. Then, work with a partner to find two things that you can compare from this chapter. Record your information on the Venn diagram. Share your findings with the rest of the class.

3 WHAT DO YOU THINK?
CRITICAL THINKING

1. What influence do the Rocky Mountains have on the work people do in the Mountain West region?

2. Why do many people in rural areas of the Mountain West rely on county services?

3. Why is Nevada a faster growing state in population than Idaho?

4. How would life in the Mountain West region be different without mining?

5. What do people living in Saskatchewan, Alberta, and British Columbia have in common with people living in the Mountain West states?

4 SAY IT, WRITE IT, USE IT
VOCABULARY

Write a paragraph that summarizes what you have learned about the Mountain West region in this chapter. Use as many of the following key terms as you can.

Continental Divide	province
county	quarry
logger	rain shadow
metropolitan area	sheriff
open-pit mining	water vapor

5 GEOGRAPHY AND YOU
MAP STUDY

Use the map below to answer these questions.

1. What are the two metropolitan areas in the state of Nevada?

2. Which two states have no metropolitan areas?

3. Which state has the greatest number of metropolitan areas?

4. What are the names of the metropolitan areas in Utah?

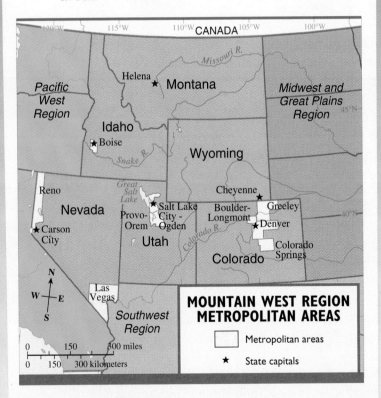

MOUNTAIN WEST REGION
METROPOLITAN AREAS

☐ Metropolitan areas
★ State capitals

6 TAKE ACTION
CITIZENSHIP

In this chapter, you learned that a county provides various services to its residents. The telephone book lists county offices. Record a list of these offices. Then work with a partner to research the services that two of these county offices provide. Write a paragraph about each county office. As a class, combine the descriptions to make a booklet about county services.

7 GET CREATIVE
SCIENCE CONNECTION

Scientists use a rain gauge to measure rainfall in the Mountain West. You can make one, too. Ask an adult to help you cut the top off a plastic soda bottle. Place the bottle, open side up, in a secure spot outside. After a rainfall, use a ruler to measure the rain in the bottle. Compare your measurement with those of other classmates.

LOOKING AHEAD Get ready to travel great distances as you explore the states of the Pacific West region.

Pacific West

The Pacific West region is the only region in the United States in which all the states are not connected. Learn how the states in this region are alike and different.

CONTENTS

▼ This boy is counting the rings in a section of a tree trunk. Find out about logging on page 307.

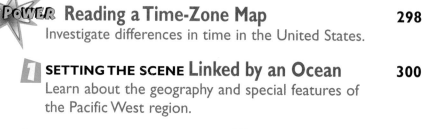 

Region

These books help you to know more about the environments of the Pacific West region. Read one that interests you and fill out a book-review form.

READ AND RESEARCH

Bound for Oregon **by Jean Van Leeuwen, pictures by James Watling** (Dial Books for Young Readers, 1994)
In 1852, the Todd family left their home in Arkansas to find a better life in the Oregon Territory. Find out if their long and dangerous journey on the Oregon Trail leads them to their goal. *(historical fiction)*
•*You can read a selection from this story on page 310.*

The Big Storm **by Bruce Hiscock** (Macmillan Children's Books, 1993)
Follow the path of a powerful spring storm that began off the coast of California in 1982. Find out what happened as great winds blew the storm across the United States. *(nonfiction)*

Kate on the Coast **by Pat Brisson, illustrations by Rick Brown** (Macmillian Publishing Co., 1992)
Read Kate's letters to a friend telling about her many adventures in the Pacific West—hiking near Mount Saint Helens, exploring Hawaii's island of Oahu, and visiting a historic park in Alaska. *(fiction)*

A Child's Alaska **by Claire Rudolf Murphy, photographs by Charles Mason** (Alaska Northwest Books, 1994)
Let the colorful photographs in this book take you on a journey through the adventures that this state has to offer. *(nonfiction)*

SKILL POWER

Reading a Time-Zone Map

Understanding how to use a time-zone map helps you find what time it is anywhere on Earth.

UNDERSTAND IT

Look at a clock. What time is it now? Did you know it is now a different time in some parts of the United States?

Earth is constantly rotating from west to east. As it turns, the sun's rays touch different places. One part of the earth gets darker while another part gets lighter. Every morning, the sun lights up Washington, D.C., three hours before it shines on Washington State.

EXPLORE IT

Look at the map on the next page. Of the eight time zones shown on the map, six of those time zones are in the United States. The time zones are named as follows.

1. Eastern   4. Pacific

2. Central   5. Alaska

3. Mountain   6. Hawaii-Aleutian

Now look at the clock in each time zone on the next page. The time in each zone is different by 1 hour from the zone next to it. When it is 9 A.M. in the Eastern Time Zone, it is 8 A.M. in the Central Time Zone. When it is 7 A.M. in the Mountain Time Zone, what time is it in the Pacific Time Zone?

◀ You can see why Earth is divided into time zones by shining a light on a rotating globe.

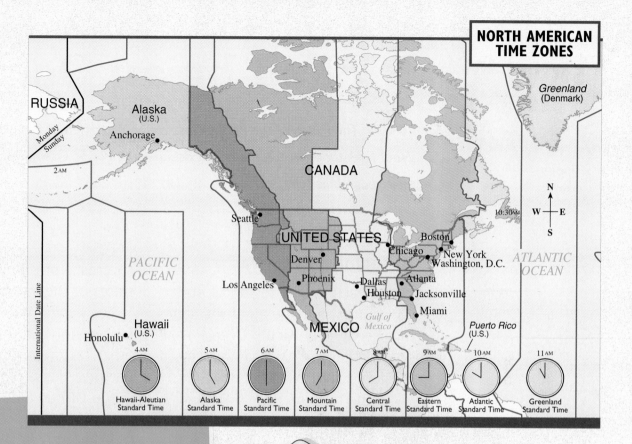

NORTH AMERICAN TIME ZONES

RUSSIA

Monday / Sunday

2 AM

Alaska (U.S.)

Anchorage

CANADA

Greenland (Denmark)

10:30 AM

N
W · E
S

Seattle

UNITED STATES

Boston

Chicago

New York
Washington, D.C.

PACIFIC OCEAN

Denver

Atlanta

ATLANTIC OCEAN

International Date Line

Los Angeles

Phoenix

Dallas
Houston

Jacksonville

Miami

Hawaii (U.S.)

Honolulu

MEXICO

Gulf of Mexico

Puerto Rico (U.S.)

4 AM	5 AM	6 AM	7 AM	8 AM	9 AM	10 AM	11 AM
Hawaii-Aleutian Standard Time	Alaska Standard Time	Pacific Standard Time	Mountain Standard Time	Central Standard Time	Eastern Standard Time	Atlantic Standard Time	Greenland Standard Time

TRY IT

Use the map above to play a travel game with a group of your classmates. As a group, make about 20 "go to" cards. On each card write one direction similar to the directions at the right. Shuffle the cards. Then take turns choosing a card. As each student in turn reads aloud the direction on the card he or she has chosen, have group members decide which city they would go to by looking at the map on this page.

- Go to the time zone in which your state is located.

- Go to a city that is in the same time zone as Denver, Colorado.

- Go to a city that is 1 hour earlier than Washington, D.C.

- Go to a city that is 2 hours earlier than Seattle, Washington.

- Go to a city that is 2 hours later than Los Angeles, California.

SKILL POWER SEARCH

As you read this chapter, think about how differences in time affect the Pacific West region. For example, how might time differences affect a telephone call between California and New York?

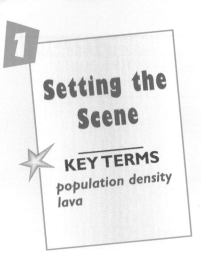

Linked by an Ocean

FOCUS *The states of the Pacific West region are different in several ways. What links them together is a vast ocean—the Pacific Ocean—as well as their geographic features.*

A Region of Contrasts

The Pacific West region of our country is made up of the states that border the Pacific Ocean. These states are Alaska, Washington, Oregon, California, and Hawaii.

On the map on page 301, find Alaska, our largest state. The Pacific West also includes a chain of 8 small islands and 124 even smaller islands that make up the state of Hawaii. This is one example of the contrasts, or differences, in the states of the Pacific West.

The Pacific West region reaches farther north and south than any other region in our country. Point Barrow, Alaska, is the closest place in the United States to the North Pole. The most southern point in the United States is in Hawaii. It is Ka Lae (kah LAH ay), a cape at the southern end of Hawaii, the largest island in Hawaii.

▼ A sea turtle is one of nature's wonders on the California coastline.

Comparing Population

Another contrast is in population. Some parts of the Pacific West region are crowded, but other parts are not. We can measure how crowded a place is by finding its **population density**. The more people there are in a certain area, the higher the population density.

California has a population density of 191 people per square mile. Alaska has a population density of 1 person per square mile. Of the five Pacific West states, California has the highest population density, and Alaska has the lowest population density.

Comparing Elevation

The Pacific West also includes our country's highest and lowest points. The lowest place in the United States is in Death Valley, California. It is actually 282 feet below sea level.

The highest place in the United States and in all of North America is Mount McKinley in Alaska. It has an elevation of 20,320 feet. Mount McKinley is more than three times as high as Mount Washington in the White Mountains of the New England region.

 population density   The average number of people per unit of an area, such as a square mile, in a country or state

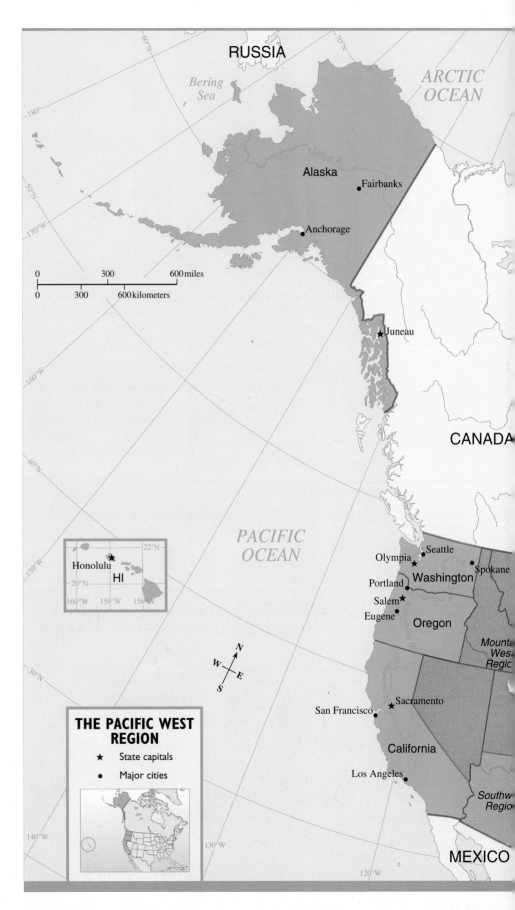

THE PACIFIC WEST REGION

★ State capitals

● Major cities

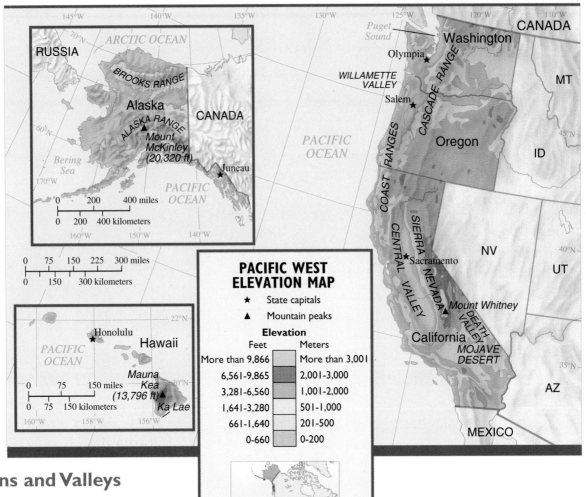

PACIFIC WEST
ELEVATION MAP

★ State capitals
▲ Mountain peaks

Elevation

Feet	Meters
More than 9,866	More than 3,001
6,561-9,865	2,001-3,000
3,281-6,560	1,001-2,000
1,641-3,280	501-1,000
661-1,640	201-500
0-660	0-200

Mountains and Valleys

A long chain of mountains called the Coast Ranges extends along the Pacific Ocean all the way from Alaska to southern California. The mountains of this chain hug the Pacific Coast through Washington, Oregon, and California.

Inland there is another chain of mountains. It is called the Cascade Range in the north and the Sierra Nevada (see ER uh nuh VAD uh) in the south. The Cascade Range almost cuts Washington and Oregon in half from north to south. The Sierra Nevada stretches through most of California.

There are two main mountain ranges in Alaska—the Brooks Range and the Alaska Range. Find these mountain ranges on the map on this page.

Between the mountain ranges of the Pacific West region are several valleys. California's Central Valley is the largest valley of the Pacific West region. This long, narrow valley runs 460 miles from north to south and is up to 60 miles wide.

The Willamette (wih LAM iht) Valley is the second largest valley of the Pacific West. It is in the northwestern corner of Oregon.

An Island State

Of all the states in our country, the only state made up of islands is Hawaii. The Hawaiian island chain covers a wide area of the Pacific Ocean. But the eight islands of greatest size and importance to the state are located within a few hundred miles of one another.

Steep mountains are the chief landform of Hawaii. Some of the mountains seem to rise directly out of the Pacific Ocean. Like California, Hawaii has valleys, too.

The Region's Climate

You have read on pages 284 and 285 that tall mountains create a rain shadow. The mountains are one reason the Pacific Coast receives a lot of precipitation. The Coast Ranges force winds from the Pacific Ocean to drop much of their moisture along the

Bearberry shrubs with their bright red leaves grow in Denali National Park in Alaska.

A lemon tree in California

coast. As a result, northern California gets about 80 inches of precipitation on its coastal slopes each year. Western Washington and Oregon get about 130 inches of rainfall.

When winds come down into the valleys of central Washington, Oregon, and California, they don't carry as much water. Rainfall in these areas is less than 20 inches a year.

Crops of the Region

You might think that little would grow in the Pacific West region. Yet more vegetables and fruits are grown in the Central Valley of California than in any of our other states. In the valleys of Washington and Oregon, vegetables such as potatoes and carrots and fruits such as apples and cherries thrive. The irrigation water from the valley's rivers provides farmers with enough water to grow many crops.

Farming is important in Alaska, too. The state's southern coast is warmed by the Pacific Ocean. Hay, potatoes, and vegetables such as carrots and cabbage grow well there.

Hawaii has warm temperatures year-round. There are many sugar cane and pineapple plantations in Hawaii. Hawaii is the only state in the United States in which coffee is grown.

A Volcano in Hawaii

Every now and then Kilauea (kee-lou AY uh) volcano in Hawaii releases a river of hot, liquid rock called lava. Sometimes the lava flows out of an opening in the side of Kilauea and inches its way down the slope. When this hot lava reaches the Pacific Ocean, it hisses and steams as it enters the cold ocean water.

At other times, Kilauea hurls fiery boulders and rocks into the air. At night this makes a display that looks like a magnificent fireworks show.

⭐ **lava**   Hot liquid rock at or close to Earth's surface

Pacific West Salmon

On many rivers in Oregon and Washington there are dams that produce electricity. But the dams on the rivers create problems for salmon. These fish swim long distances up the rivers from the Pacific Ocean to lay their eggs in protected places. With dams in the way, the salmon could not get to their nesting grounds.

Special constructions—called fish ladders—solved this problem. Around a dam, a series of steps was built with river water in each step. Salmon were now able to leap up the steps of the fish ladder to get to the top of the dam. Then they could continue their swim upstream again in the river itself.

▲ The steps of a fish ladder help salmon swim upstream.

Kilauea volcano is in Hawaii Volcanoes National Park on the island of Hawaii. ▶

Pacific West

In the Beverly Cleary Sculpture Garden for Children, fans salute the author with signs naming characters from her books.

SHOW WHAT YOU KNOW!

REFOCUS
COMPREHENSION

1. How is the Pacific West region different from all the other regions in the United States?

2. Which state in the Pacific West has the lowest population density?

THINK ABOUT IT
CRITICAL THINKING

Name two ways that Alaska and Hawaii are alike.

STATE CHECK
ACTIVITY

Choose two states in the Pacific West to compare with your state for leading products. Find the information in the States Almanac on pages 342–397.

People who live near Kīlauea never know for sure whether their houses and cars will be buried under one of these lava flows. But usually they have warning and can leave with their pets and belongings.

Ramona, Henry, and Ribsy

Like people everywhere, the people of Portland, Oregon, are proud of their city. Recently, they showed their pride in their city by honoring Beverly Cleary, a writer who grew up in Portland. You may have read a book by this author.

Between 1950 and 1984, Beverly Cleary wrote 15 books about some imaginary children growing up in Portland. Ramona Quimby, her friend Henry Huggins, and Henry's dog, Ribsy, are some of the characters Beverly Cleary created for her books.

Now you can see Ramona and Henry in larger-than-life-size bronze statues at the Beverly Cleary Sculpture Garden for Children in Grant Park. The garden is located in the neighborhood where Ramona and Henry live.

Portland was already a beautiful city before the Sculpture Garden was built. But now it's a city that is special to Beverly Cleary fans.

Spotlight

KEY TERMS
logging
wood pulp

A Region of Remarkable Forests

FOCUS *The Pacific West is the leading lumber-producing region in the United States. The region is well-known for the amazing size of many of the trees.*

An Important Resource

One of the most important natural resources of the Pacific West region is its forests. From Alaska in the far north to California in the south, thick forests cover many areas of the Pacific West.

Logging has always been important to the economy of the Pacific West region. Today, the Pacific West region produces more lumber than any other region in the United States.

Some of the trees in the Pacific West forests grow to an amazing size. The giant sequoia (sih KWOI uh) trees that grow in northern California are the largest trees on Earth. They are among the oldest living things, too. Some are 3,000 years old.

Sequoia trees may grow to heights of 300 feet and over. In a city, a tree of 300 feet would be as high as a 30-story building.

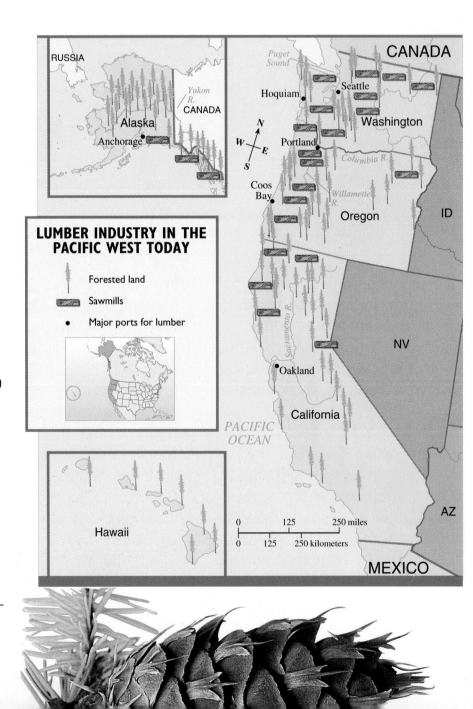

LUMBER INDUSTRY IN THE PACIFIC WEST TODAY

- Forested land
- Sawmills
- Major ports for lumber

logging Cutting down trees and taking the logs to a sawmill

Scientists can learn the age of a tree by counting its rings. ▶

Where the Forests Are

Oregon leads the nation in lumber production. One fifth of all the lumber produced in the United States comes from forests that line the Pacific coast of Oregon.

Washington is second to Oregon in lumber production. Pine, hemlock, and Douglas fir trees grow all along the western coast of that state.

Forests cover nearly one half of California. Redwoods grow in a narrow band along the northern coast, where there are many sawmills and wood factories. Pine trees stand tall at the foothills of the mountains in the eastern part of California.

Some of the forests in Alaska are in the interior of the state. These forests are hard to get to because there are few good roads in that part of the state. Most of Alaska's lumber comes from forests in the panhandle, along the southern coast. Ketchikan (KECH ih kan) and Sitka, two of the largest cities in the region, have sawmills and factories that process wood pulp.

Protecting Our Forests

State and federal laws help to save the great forests of the Pacific Northwest. When logging companies harvest wood, they must leave some trees standing so that the trees can reseed the area. Many companies grow trees from seeds and carefully replant the seedlings in logged areas.

★ **wood pulp**   A mixture of ground wood and chemicals used to make paper

Students learn about planting and protecting a tree. ▶

SHOW WHAT YOU KNOW!

REFOCUS
COMPREHENSION

1. Where do the largest trees on Earth grow?

2. Why is most of Alaska's lumber harvested in forests along the coast of the panhandle?

THINK ABOUT IT
CRITICAL THINKING

In addition to being a source of lumber, why are forests valuable?

STATE CHECK
ACTIVITY

In the States Almanac on pages 342–397, look for the town with the smallest population in the Pacific West region. Compare the population with that of the smallest town in your state.

The Way West

FOCUS *Learn about some people who traveled to the Pacific West region and some events that helped the region to grow.*

DISCOVERING A RIVER

Robert Gray was an American sea captain. In 1787, he sailed from Boston Harbor, in Massachusetts, for the Pacific Northwest. He bought sea otter pelts, or skins, from the Native Americans who lived in the region. Later he sold the pelts in China for tea.

In 1791, Gray returned to the Pacific Northwest. On May 12, 1792, he discovered a river that flowed between what are now the states of Oregon and Washington. Gray named the river in honor of his ship, the *Columbia*.

GOLD IN CALIFORNIA!

In 1849, people from all over the United States and even from other countries hurried to California. News that gold had been discovered the year before near Sacramento, California, had at last reached the eastern part of the United States and parts of Europe.

The gold seekers who rushed west in 1849—more than 80,000 people—became known as forty-niners. A few struck gold, but most did not.

THE OREGON TRAIL

In the spring of 1843, nearly 1,000 people left Independence, Missouri, and headed west on the Oregon Trail. They had heard of the rich farmland in the Pacific Northwest and wanted to claim a share of the land. The settlers crossed prairies, deserts, rivers, and mountains to reach their destination. Other people followed the Oregon Trail well into the 1850s.

| 1792 | 1843 | 1849 | 1867 | 1910 | 1959 |
| Gray finds Columbia River | People head west on the Oregon Trail | Gold rush in California | Alaska is purchased | Angel Island is opened | Alaska and Hawaii become our 49th and 50th states |

| 1790 | 1810 | 1830 | 1850 | 1870 | 1890 | 1910 | 1930 | 1950 | 1970 |

PURCHASE OF ALASKA

About 150 years ago, the country of Russia owned the land that is now our state of Alaska. Between 1799 and 1861, Russian and American fur traders built a fur trading business there.

In 1867, William Seward (soo ward), the United States' secretary of state, purchased Alaska from Russia for $7,200,000. At first, many Americans thought that Alaska was only a vast, ice-covered land. Then people began to value Alaska's many natural resources. These included fish, gold, and timber.

Since then, oil and other valuable minerals have been found in Alaska. On January 3, 1959, Alaska became our 49th state.

ANGEL ISLAND

By 1882, there were nearly 400,000 Chinese immigrants in the United States. Most lived in San Francisco, California, and worked in mines and on railroads. Because the Chinese worked for low wages, some people believed they took jobs away from other workers. This led the United States government to limit Chinese immigration.

In 1910, a center was opened to receive the limited number of Chinese people coming to the United States. The center, on Angel Island in San Francisco Bay, became known as the West Coast Ellis Island. Ellis Island in New York received European immigrants between 1892 and 1954.

OUR 50TH STATE

On August 21, 1959, Hawaii became the 50th state of the United States. Hawaii was once an independent kingdom, ruled by kings and a queen.

The Polynesian language of the early Hawaiian people was made up of the 12-letter alphabet shown above.

A E H
I K L
M N O
P U W

309

Bound for Oregon

by Jean Van Leeuwen

Jean Van Leeuwen

BOUND FOR OREGON

pictures by James Watling

It is 1852 and the Todd family leave their home in Arkansas to travel by covered wagon on the Oregon Trail.

A moment later the captain blew a loud blast on his silver trumpet. Whips cracked and drivers shouted. For a few minutes the wagons milled around in seeming confusion. Then slowly they began to string out in an orderly line, facing west.

We were on our way.

To me it was a beautiful sight: the line of white-covered wagons stretching out in front of us, the moving wave of cattle, the riders sitting tall and straight on their horses. And Father's whip curling over the heads of our oxen as he shouted, "Gee, Buck! Gee, Ben!"

Soon we crossed over the border from Missouri into Kansas. We were out on the wild prairie. In all my imaginings I had never dreamed that there could be so much space, wide and flat and empty. The sky seemed bigger here, like an enormous bright-blue lid set down over the earth. Green-gold grass waved on every side, bobbing and nodding in the constant wind. Yellow-chested larks flew up from their nests on the ground as we passed by. Here and there the grass was dotted with spring flowers, pink and purple, yellow and blue. I breathed in their perfume as I walked along. Though I had never seen an ocean, these great shimmering waves of grass reminded me of what one must be like. They rippled and rolled, up small hills and down, and on and on as far in front of us and behind as I could see.

Traveling in a large wagon train was much different than traveling alone, we soon found out. There was all the dust raised by so many feet and turning wheels. The dust was worse when the wind blew, and especially for those unlucky families at the rear of the train. Because of this a rule was made that the wagon in the lead one day had to drop all the way back the next, giving everyone an equal turn.

What challenges and happy surprises do the Todd family face on the journey? You can find out by checking this book out of your school or public library.

SHOW WHAT YOU KNOW!

REFOCUS
COMPREHENSION

1. Who were the forty-niners?

2. How is Hawaii different from all our other states?

THINK ABOUT IT
CRITICAL THINKING

Why did the Todd family set out on the Oregon Trail in the spring?

STATE CHECK
ACTIVITY

Find in the States Almanac, on pages 342–397, when your state became part of the U.S. How many years longer than Hawaii has it been a state?

KEY TERMS
meteorologist
jet stream

Meet a Meteorologist

FOCUS *The weather very often affects our daily lives. Meteorologists work 24 hours a day, seven days a week to tell us what the weather will be in our future.*

▲ Sharon Alden uses a computer to watch weather changes all over the world.

What Is a Meteorologist?

Weather reports tell us if it will be cloudy or sunny in the coming days or if we need to watch out for snowstorms or rainstorms. To get this weather information, we rely on **meteorologists** (meet ee ur-AHL uh jihsts). These are people who are trained to study weather and make forecasts so that we know what the weather will be.

Sharon Alden is a meteorologist in Fairbanks, Alaska. She became interested in meteorology because she loved looking at cloud patterns. To learn the skills she uses, Ms. Alden attended college. Many of the classes she took were in math and science.

In her work, Ms. Alden studies weather maps of the United States created by the National Weather Service, or NWS. In addition, Ms. Alden studies weather maps and weather charts of Alaska to predict the weather in and around Fairbanks. Then she writes forecasts that are sent to local newspapers and television stations.

Ms. Alden also writes forecasts for airlines. Pilots and air-traffic controllers use the information to help in forecasting visibility. Fog, snow, and ice conditions might affect whether planes can land or take off.

meteorologist A person who studies changes in the atmosphere

◀ This barometer graphs pressure changes in the atmosphere.

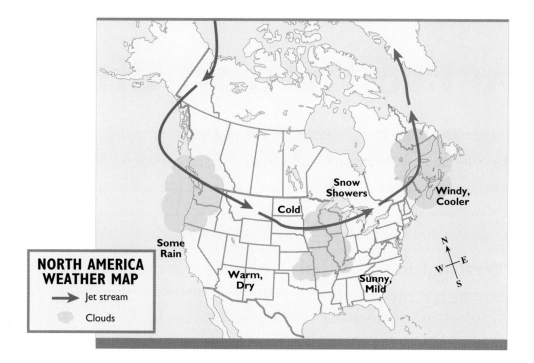

NORTH AMERICA WEATHER MAP
→ Jet stream
Clouds

Snow Showers
Cold
Windy, Cooler
Some Rain
Warm, Dry
Sunny, Mild

N
W E
S

Weather Tools

Meteorologists use many different kinds of tools for help in predicting the weather. One tool that has been used for hundreds of years is a barometer (buh RAHM ut ur). A barometer measures air pressure. Changes in air pressure signal changes in weather.

Some of the newest tools used in weather forecasting are weather satellites and computers. Satellites in space take pictures of the earth and record information about the weather. This information is organized and analyzed by computers. Ms. Alden uses the information, along with her own observations, to predict the weather.

An old barometer ▶

Tracking a Storm

In the fall and the winter, storms often develop over the Pacific and Arctic oceans. These storms then move east and south to affect the weather in the United States.

The map above shows the path of a narrow band of fast-moving air called a **jet stream**. These "rivers of air" help to steer weather systems across the earth's surface. The jet stream shown on the map is pulling cold air into its path as it moves to the south and to the east from the Arctic Ocean.

Meteorologists study the paths of jet streams. Information about the jet streams helps meteorologists such as Ms. Alden forecast the weather.

★ **jet stream** A high speed wind that moves around the earth at high altitudes

SHOW WHAT YOU KNOW!

REFOCUS
COMPREHENSION

1. Why do we depend on weather forecasts?

2. How might the weather in the Pacific West region affect the weather in other regions?

THINK ABOUT IT
CRITICAL THINKING

How does the weather affect your everyday life?

STATE CHECK
ACTIVITY

Over the next three days, record a forecast for your part of your state. Make a chart in which you compare the forecast with the actual weather.

Five Pacific West Cities

FOCUS *Several cities in the Pacific West region are well-known throughout the United States. Five cities in the region are of special interest to many people.*

Seattle, Washington

Seattle is a city that attracts many people. It is nestled between Puget Sound and Lake Washington, a 24-mile stretch of fresh water. The city extends across a number of hills, some of them 500 feet high. But they are small compared with the mountains to the west and to the east of the city.

Each year, Seattle's natural harbor welcomes about 2,000 cargo vessels. Many products from the city's surrounding forests and farms are shipped to ports in Alaska and faraway China and Japan. In recent years, Seattle has prospered from the manufacture of jet airplanes, missiles, and space vehicles.

The Space Needle, built as the symbol of Seattle's 1962 World's Fair, still stands. It represents the city's present-day, forward-looking attitude.

Seattle has become known as one of the most desirable places in the United States to live. The city's large park system includes open areas, playgrounds, and a zoo. And the mountains and water around Seattle offer year-round opportunities for recreation.

Visitors to Seattle, Washington, ▶ tour Pioneer Square and learn some history of the city.

A statue of a pioneer stands atop the capitol in Salem, Oregon.

Salem, Oregon

Salem is the capital and the third largest city of Oregon. It is located in the heart of the rich farmland of the Willamette River valley in northwestern Oregon.

Many of the pioneer families who traveled the Oregon Trail across the Great Plains and the Rocky Mountains ended their journeys near present-day Salem. Atop the state capitol is a tower topped by a bronze statue of a pioneer. The statue is a tribute to all the pioneers who carved Oregon out of the wilderness.

Today, Salem is the center of the state government. It is also the market for many crops grown in the surrounding Willamette Valley. Farmers who raise flower bulbs, fruits, seed crops, and vegetables sell them in Salem.

Los Angeles, California

More people live in Los Angeles than in any other city in the United States except New York. And the city continues to grow! The people of Los Angeles come from many different cultures. Some are descendants of Spanish settlers. Others have parents or grandparents who came to the city from Mexico. Some residents' ancestors lived in countries in Africa. Others have come from countries in Asia, such as Japan and China.

Los Angeles is not really one city. It is a combination of communities, each with its own stores, offices, schools, and government buildings.

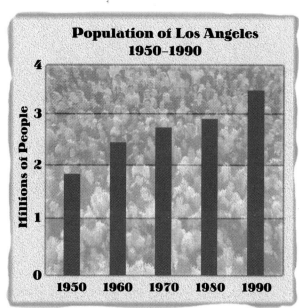

Population of Los Angeles 1950–1990

315

A **freeway** system joins all the neighborhoods of Los Angeles. The first freeway, the Pasadena Freeway, was opened in 1940. Now, miles and miles of freeways allow drivers to crisscross the city to get to jobs and schools and home again.

Something else that joins the people of Los Angeles is their awareness of **earthquakes**. In Los Angeles, schools hold earthquake drills as well as fire drills. The students are taught to duck under their desks whenever an earthquake is felt. The desks would help to protect them if a school building shakes during an earthquake.

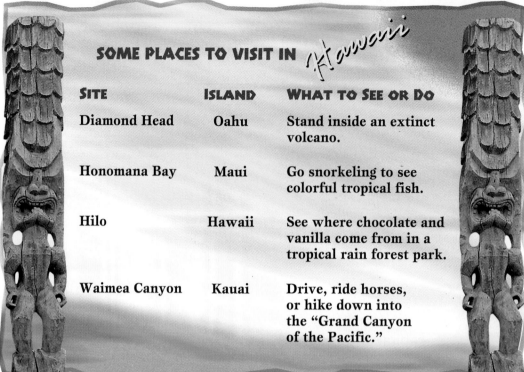

SOME PLACES TO VISIT IN *Hawaii*		
SITE	**ISLAND**	**WHAT TO SEE OR DO**
Diamond Head	Oahu	Stand inside an extinct volcano.
Honomana Bay	Maui	Go snorkeling to see colorful tropical fish.
Hilo	Hawaii	See where chocolate and vanilla come from in a tropical rain forest park.
Waimea Canyon	Kauai	Drive, ride horses, or hike down into the "Grand Canyon of the Pacific."

Honolulu, Hawaii

Honolulu is on Oahu (oh AH-hoo), the busiest of the eight main Hawaiian islands. Honolulu is the capital of Hawaii and the largest city in the state. The city has spectacular views of blue water and sandy beaches on one side and mountain peaks on the other. These features, along with a warm and sunny climate, make Honolulu a popular vacation spot.

Most Hawaiians speak English, but there are some words in the Hawaiian language that people continue to use today. Often, visitors to Honolulu like to learn a few words in Hawaiian. *Aloha* (ah-LOH huh) is a Hawaiian greeting or a farewell. *Mahalo* (mah HAH loh) means "thank you."

The Hawaiian language was brought to the islands several thousand years ago. It was used by people who sailed to Hawaii from other islands in the central Pacific Ocean called Polynesia (pahl uh NEE zhuh).

---

freeway An express highway with limited entrances and exits; it has no tolls
earthquake A shaking and trembling of the earth's crust

Anchorage, Alaska

About half of all the people who live in the state of Alaska live in or around Anchorage (ANG kur ihj). Anchorage is located in south-central Alaska in the shadow of the Chugach (CHOO gach) Mountains, as shown in the picture below.

Anchorage is a fairly new city. It was established in 1914 as a construction camp for workers who were building the Alaska Railroad. It served as a port through which workers entered and left Alaska.

Anchorage is still the head-quarters of the Alaska Railroad. The city is connected by railroad to Fairbanks in the north and to Seward in the south.

Alaska, which is the largest state in the United States in land area, has fewer miles of highway than Vermont, which is the eighth smallest state in land area. But most Alaskan roads lead into and out of Anchorage.

Each year, hundreds of people meet in downtown Anchorage to watch the start of the annual Iditarod (eye DIHT uh rahd) Trail Sled Dog Race. The Iditarod is the longest sled dog race in the world. Racers speed from Anchorage along a narrow trail through wilderness to Nome, which is 1,200 miles to the northwest.

SHOW WHAT YOU KNOW!

REFOCUS
COMPREHENSION

1. Why are people attracted to Seattle, Washington?

2. Why was Anchorage, Alaska, established?

THINK ABOUT IT
CRITICAL THINKING

In which of these five cities would you most like to live? Why?

STATE CHECK
ACTIVITY

Choose one of the states in the Pacific West and compare its state flag with the flag of your state. Find the information you need in the States Almanac on pages 342–397.

6 Citizenship

KEY TERMS
pollutant
smog

Respecting the Environment

FOCUS *Los Angeles is one city that has problems with air pollution. By studying the causes of these problems, we can find ways to reduce the amount of pollution in our air.*

The Air We Breathe

Air is an invisible mixture of gases that surround the earth. When harmful substances are released into the air, air pollution occurs. Substances that dirty our environment are called **pollutants**.

Automobiles create most of the world's air pollution. The engine of a car or truck burns gasoline, which releases pollutants into the air. Waste from factories, chemicals, and bug sprays are other pollutants.

Some kinds of air pollution are visible. For example, you may have seen smoke coming from the backs of trucks or black clouds rising from the smokestacks of factories.

Often, though, we can't see the pollution that goes into our air. Many pollutants from coal, oil, and natural gas are invisible but are also harmful to our environment.

Air Pollution

People first became aware of the dangers of air pollution in Los Angeles, California. Air pollution is a major concern in Los Angeles due to the city's location.

As air blows eastward, the cold water of the Pacific Ocean cools the

---

pollutant Something that makes something else impure, as a harmful chemical that gets into the air

318

Sources of Air Pollution

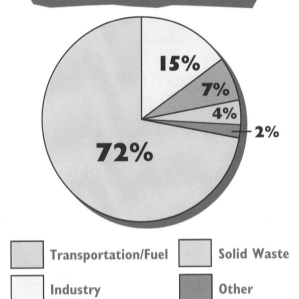

15%

7%

4%

2%

72%

- Transportation/Fuel
- Solid Waste
- Industry
- Other
- Agriculture

lower layers of air. Warm, dry air above the land serves as a lid, preventing the cool air from rising. These conditions trap pollutants and keep them from rising. The pollutants collect in the air and turn into a thick haze called **smog**.

Solutions to Air Pollution

The United States government has passed laws to help reduce air pollution. Gasoline does not contain as much lead as it once did, so now it creates less pollution. Some states, such as Oregon, have passed their own strict laws to help protect the environment. On some state highways, there are High Occupancy Vehicle (HOV) lanes. Only vehicles with at least two occupants are permitted to travel in these lanes. This cuts down the number of cars on our highways.

Air pollution affects everyone. To reduce air pollution, all the states need to work together. One of the best things you can do to reduce air pollution is to carpool with others whenever you can.

⭐ **smog** The combination of smoke and fog in the air

SHOW WHAT YOU KNOW!

REFOCUS
COMPREHENSION

1. What are three kinds of pollutants?

2. Why does Los Angeles have air pollution problems?

THINK ABOUT IT
CRITICAL THINKING

How does pollution affect our health?

STATE CHECK
ACTIVITY

In your state scrapbook, describe what your community might do to reduce air pollution.

SUMMING UP

DO YOU REMEMBER . . .
COMPREHENSION

1. Why is there more precipitation along the coast in the Pacific West than farther inland?

2. Name two ways that states and logging companies help forests in the Pacific Northwest survive.

3. Why did many early settlers head for what is now Oregon in the 1840s and 1850s?

4. Why do people in the eastern parts of the United States pay attention to Alaska's weather?

5. Why doesn't the wind blow away the smog from Los Angeles?

2
SKILL POWER
READING A TIME-ZONE MAP

Use the time-zone map on page 299 to answer these questions.

1. In what time zone is Arkansas?

2. In what time zone is Hawaii?

3. Name two states in the Eastern Time Zone.

4. If it's 3:00 P.M. in Colorado, what time is it in Florida?

5. If it's 2:00 A.M. in New York, what time is it in California?

3
WHAT DO YOU THINK?
CRITICAL THINKING

1. What are some things that Alaska and Hawaii share?

2. In addition to its natural resources, how is Alaska valuable today?

3. Why does a meteorologist today depend on modern technology?

4. Would you say that location is important for a city's growth? Why?

5. List two advantages and two disadvantages of living in one of the cities described on pages 314 to 317.

4
SAY IT, WRITE IT, USE IT
VOCABULARY

Think of yourself as a TV meteorologist in Los Angeles. Write a report in which you predict the weather for three days. Include as many of the following key terms as you can in your report.

earthquake	meteorologist
freeway	pollutant
jet stream	population density
lava	smog
logging	wood pulp

5 GEOGRAPHY AND YOU
MAP STUDY

Use the map below to answer these questions.

1. What is a major port for lumber in California?

2. What is a major port for lumber in Alaska?

3. On what river is Portland, Oregon?

4. Which part of Washington has the most forest land?

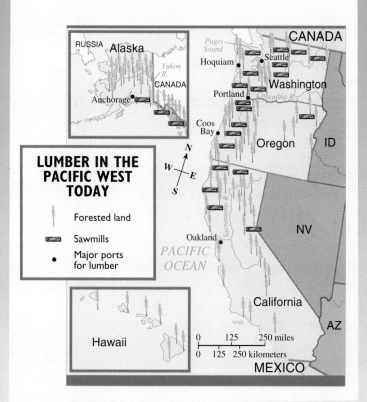

LUMBER IN THE PACIFIC WEST TODAY

| Forested land
| Sawmills
| • Major ports for lumber

6 TAKE ACTION
CITIZENSHIP

We take pride in members of our community who achieve success. Think of someone in your community who has accomplished something important. Design a plaque to honor the person. Draw your plaque in your state scrapbook.

7 GET CREATIVE
SCIENCE CONNECTION

Is the weather in your community or state affected by an ocean, mountains, or lakes? To what areas of the country or world do meteorologists look to predict the weather in your region? Create a map, showing a weather report for your region. Watching TV weather reports or reading newspaper reports will give you some ideas for your map.

LOOKING AHEAD Find out in the next chapter how manufacturing and trade link the Pacific West to other regions.

PACIFIC WEST LINKS

The Pacific West region sends many of its natural resources and manufactured products across the country and to the growing nations of the Pacific Rim. Many people from these same Pacific Rim countries are choosing the Pacific West region as their new home.

CONTENTS

◀ The Pacific West region is a leader in many agricultural products. On page 326, find out about other types of goods the region produces.

NEAR AND FAR

These books give you some interesting and little-known facts about states in the Pacific West region and about one Pacific Rim country—Japan. Read one that interests you and fill out a book-review form.

READ AND RESEARCH

Japan by Deborah Tyler (Silver Burdett Press, 1993)
Did you know that some of the products that you use come from Japan? Trace the history of this important industrial nation and learn about its influence on the United States. *(nonfiction)*

Monarchs by Kathryn Lasky, photographs by Christopher G. Knight (Harcourt Brace & Co., 1993)
After learning about the life cycle of monarch butterflies, you will trace their migration. Meet some people in California and Mexico who welcome and protect the butterflies at the end of their journey each fall. *(nonfiction)*

It Happened in America: True Stories from the Fifty States by Lila Perl, illustrated by Ib Ohlsson (Henry Holt & Co., 1992)
This book contains interesting stories about all the states. You'll enjoy reading about Liliuokalani, the last Hawaiian queen, as well as other stories about states in the Pacific West region. *(nonfiction)*

SKILL POWER

Understanding Cause and Effect

Understanding the connections between cause and effect helps you understand why and how things happen.

UNDERSTAND IT

Have you ever heard about an earthquake on the news? If you have, you know how damaging earthquakes can be. Highway bridges, buildings, and other structures can collapse, causing a great deal of destruction. The earthquake and the damage have a cause-and-effect relationship—one thing (the earthquake) causes another thing (the damage) to happen.

EXPLORE IT

By asking yourself what happened (the effect) and why it happened (the cause), you can better understand what you read. Watch for words such as *because, therefore, so,* and *as a result*. These words may be clues that there are cause-and-effect relationships in your reading. What clue words can you find in the following paragraph that tell you about a cause-and-effect relationship?

On January 17, 1994, a powerful earthquake struck the city of Los Angeles. As a result, many buildings were damaged. Because of the earthquake, stores and schools remained closed for days.

◀ The earthquake on January 17, 1994, toppled this parking garage in the Northridge area of Los Angeles, California.

With a group of your classmates, try playing a cause-and-effect game. First, make a chart like the one below. Under the box labeled "Effect," write a sentence about a funny or interesting event that has happened to you. In the chart below, the sentence "My frozen yogurt melted before I could eat it" is in that box. Now read your sentence to your group. Ask the group to guess the cause of your event. Could the event have had more than one cause?

Other members of your group will write sentences for their own charts. Take turns finding causes to those events.

CAUSE-AND-EFFECT GAME

CAUSE	EFFECT
It was a hot day.	My frozen yogurt melted before I could eat it.
You waited too long before eating it.	
You put the yogurt on top of a heater.	

SKILL POWER SEARCH *Search through this chapter to find other examples of cause and effect. Make a chart to show the causes and the effects.*

TRANSPORTATION IN THE PACIFIC WEST

FOCUS *The Pacific West region produces many valuable products that are sent to market by trucks, trains, planes, ships, and pipelines.*

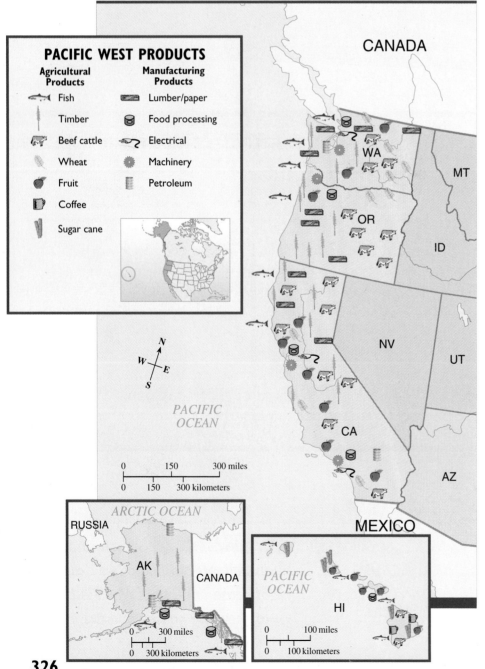

PACIFIC WEST PRODUCTS

Agricultural Products		Manufacturing Products	
🐟	Fish	🥫	Lumber/paper
🌲	Timber	🥫	Food processing
🐄	Beef cattle	〰️	Electrical
🌾	Wheat	🌼	Machinery
🍎	Fruit	🛢️	Petroleum
☕	Coffee		
🎋	Sugar cane		

CANADA

WA

MT

OR

ID

NV

UT

N
W E
S

PACIFIC OCEAN

CA

AZ

0   150   300 miles

0   150   300 kilometers

ARCTIC OCEAN

RUSSIA

AK

CANADA

0   300 miles

0   300 kilometers

MEXICO

PACIFIC OCEAN

HI

0   100 miles

0   100 kilometers

Food and Wood Products

You have already learned that the Pacific West region produces a great variety of both agricultural products and manufactured goods. Look at the map at the left to see where many of the agricultural areas and industries are located within the Pacific West region.

The climate allows plentiful harvests of fresh products, such as citrus fruits and vegetables. The region has many factories in which these products are prepared as either canned or frozen foods.

For example, Hawaii's top three agricultural products are sugar cane, pineapples, and coffee. Each of these foods is processed and then sent to all parts of the country.

The region is also known for its wood products. Lumber mills in Washington, Oregon, and Alaska saw just-cut trees, called timber, into boards and beams for the building industry. Other factories make paper from timber.

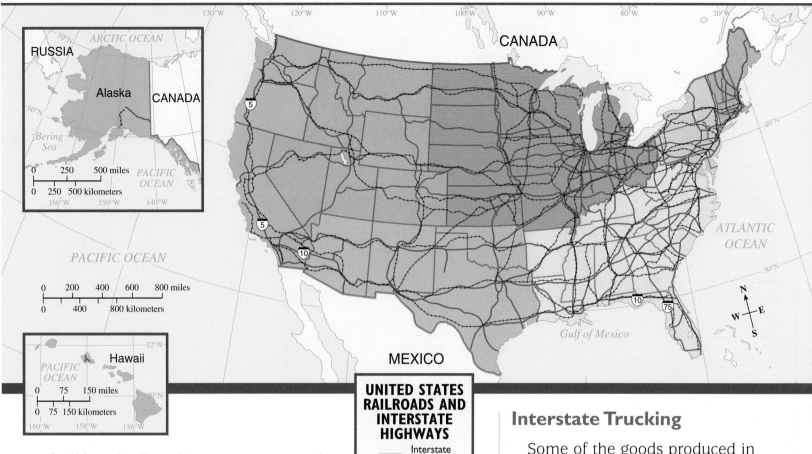

United States Railroads and Interstate Highways

Legend:
— Interstate highways
┅┅ Railroads

California Products

California is not only the top agricultural state in the country but also the top manufacturing state. More goods are manufactured in California than in any other state. These goods are mostly products of modern science and engineering—computers, scientific instruments, and television equipment.

Southern California is the nation's leading aircraft assembly center. Airplanes, missiles, and spacecraft are made here. Because southern California has a warm, dry climate, new airplanes can be flown and tested throughout the year.

Interstate Trucking

Some of the goods produced in the Pacific West region are transported by trucks and railways to stores and factories. As you can see on the map above, many major roads, called **interstate highways**, crisscross the country. These highways connect all seven regions of our country. More than 1 million large trailer trucks travel these highways each day—transporting goods to and from the regions.

In the Pacific West states, interstate highway I-5 links towns and cities in a north-south route. Railroads follow a similar path.

One interesting fact about highways is the way that they are numbered. Interstate highways

 interstate highway A major road that goes from one state to another

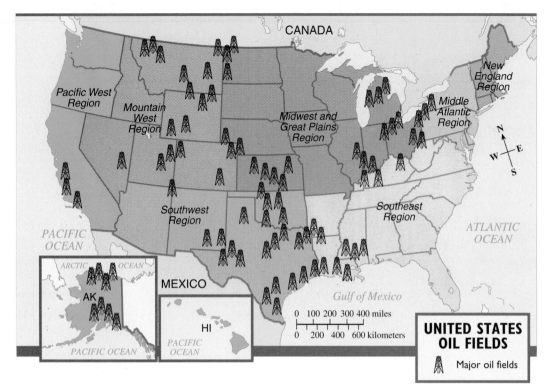

Pacific West Region

Mountain West Region

Pacific West Region

CANADA

Midwest and Great Plains Region

New England Region

Middle Atlantic Region

Southwest Region

Southeast Region

ATLANTIC OCEAN

PACIFIC OCEAN

ARCTIC OCEAN

AK

MEXICO

HI

PACIFIC OCEAN

PACIFIC OCEAN

Gulf of Mexico

0 100 200 300 400 miles

0   200 400 600 kilometers

UNITED STATES OIL FIELDS

Major oil fields

that have north-south routes, such as I-75, have odd numbers. Interstate highways that follow east-west routes, such as I-10, have even numbers.

Ship and Airplane Links

The Pacific Ocean has always been the major transportation link for Hawaii. Most of the goods that are moved between Hawaii and mainland United States are carried in oceangoing vessels. Barges are often used to move goods between the islands and along the coasts. They carry goods, such as sugar cane, pineapples, and crude oil.

Most of Hawaii's visitors, however, arrive by air. Honolulu International Airport is one of the busiest airports in the United

States. Many commercial airlines handle travel between the islands.

Airplanes are important in Alaska, too. Pilots called bush pilots fly passengers and freight in small airplanes to and from remote places. Some airplanes are equipped with floats or skis to land and take off on water or snow where other forms of transportation cannot go.

Alaska depends on the other states for most goods except for some farm products. Most of the goods shipped to Alaska come by ship or by ocean barges. The port at Seattle, Washington, is an important link between Alaska and the other states.

▼ An oceangoing cargo ship, packed with containers, docks at the port of Oakland, California.

The Trans-Alaska Pipeline extends for 800 miles, across three mountain ranges and areas of earthquake activity.

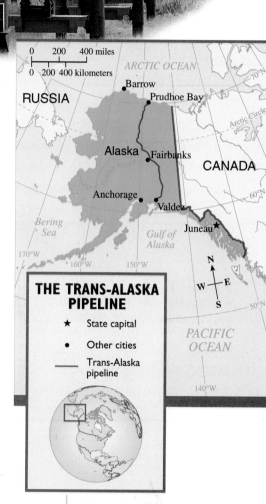

Alaskan Oil

Oil is an energy source that we use in large amounts to heat our homes and fuel our cars, trucks, and airplanes. Many plastic products are also made from oil.

Oil fields in the United States are found in Texas and Oklahoma as well as in Alaska, California, and other states. Look at the map on page 328 to see where oil fields are located in the United States.

Alaska's Prudhoe (PROOD oh) Bay area is one of the major oil-producing regions in the world. It has been estimated that the crude oil located in this area could fill nearly 10 billion barrels.

Prudhoe Bay is located on the Arctic Ocean. In that very cold area, ice prevents the movement of ships for much of the year. So it is not possible to use oil tankers to move oil from Prudhoe Bay. Scientists needed a way to get the oil to a port that ships could use all year. The answer was a pipeline over land.

The Trans-Alaska Pipeline

The Trans-Alaska Pipeline is an 800-mile-long pipeline that carries oil from Prudhoe Bay south to the ice-free port of Valdez (val-DEEZ), Alaska. The pipeline transports more than 2 million barrels of crude oil each day. Look at the map on this page to see the path this oil takes.

Since the pipeline was completed in 1977, Valdez has become the third busiest port in the United States. This is because of the large number of tankers that leave the port loaded with crude oil.

Some tankers carry the oil south to refineries in the Pacific West region. Some travel as far as the Gulf of Mexico with their precious cargo. Other tankers transport large quantities of oil to Japan.

THE TRANS-ALASKA PIPELINE

★ State capital

• Other cities

— Trans-Alaska pipeline

Environmental Concerns

The Trans-Alaska Pipeline took a lot of planning to make it safe. In the early 1970s, when the pipeline was being developed, some people in Alaska were concerned about harmful effects to the environment. What if the pipes broke and damaging oil spilled out over the land? What if the oil ended up in the rivers and lakes of Alaska?

The engineers planning the pipeline had to answer these concerns. The climate of Alaska makes it difficult to build things in the ground, especially during the winter months, when the ground is frozen solid. In the spring, the ground thaws and becomes soft. This could allow pipes under the ground to shift. The shifting might cause pipes to break and spill oil where they were joined.

Building a Safe Pipeline

Planners of the Trans-Alaska Pipeline built many miles of the pipeline above the ground. As the diagram shows, they elevated the pipeline by attaching it to large support beams that were sunk deep into the frozen ground.

Special chemicals were placed in each beam to help keep the ground around it frozen. The chemicals directed any heat from under the

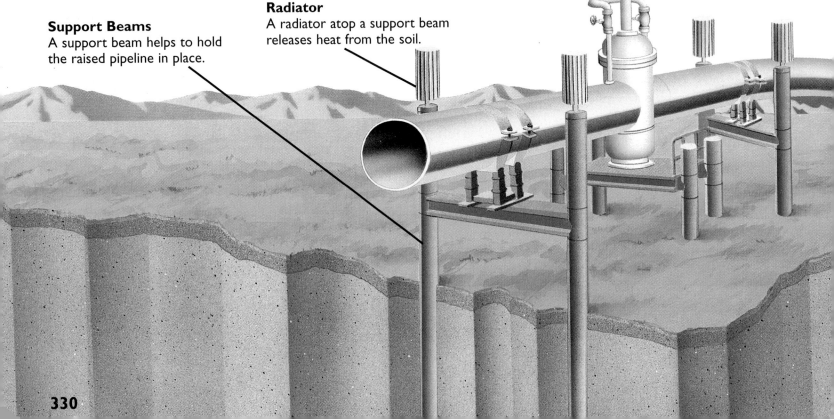

Valve
A valve is designed to shut down in 4 minutes if there is an oil leak.

Support Beams
A support beam helps to hold the raised pipeline in place.

Radiator
A radiator atop a support beam releases heat from the soil.

Volunteers worked hard to clean oil off birds after the *Exxon Valdez* oil spill.

Oil Spills

Accidents can happen when oil is transported. In 1989, a tanker carrying oil ran aground in shallow waters just off the port of Valdez, Alaska. Eleven million gallons of oil polluted the water and beaches near Valdez.

The clean-up job was huge. Hundreds of volunteers worked day and night cleaning up the thick, sticky oil. The volunteers washed the oil-covered rocks, birds, and other animals.

The oil spill at Valdez led to the creation of special emergency teams for oil spills. These clean-up and rescue teams are ready around the clock to respond quickly to an oil spill, even one as large as the spill at Valdez, Alaska.

ground up the beams and out the radiators on top of the beams.

Engineers also decided to build parts of the pipeline under the ground. The pipes that were laid under the ground were placed far below the layers of soil that freeze and thaw throughout the year. These sections of the pipeline do not shift when the soil thaws.

The pipeline is buried under the ground in places where it might block the movement of such animals as caribou.

SHOW WHAT YOU KNOW!

REFOCUS
COMPREHENSION

1. What are three top products of Hawaii?

2. In building the Trans-Alaska Pipeline, what did engineers do to make the pipeline safe?

THINK ABOUT IT
CRITICAL THINKING

Why are good systems of transportation important to the Pacific West region?

STATE CHECK
ACTIVITY

Research the interstate highway and railway systems in your state. In your state scrapbook, make a map that shows where these are located.

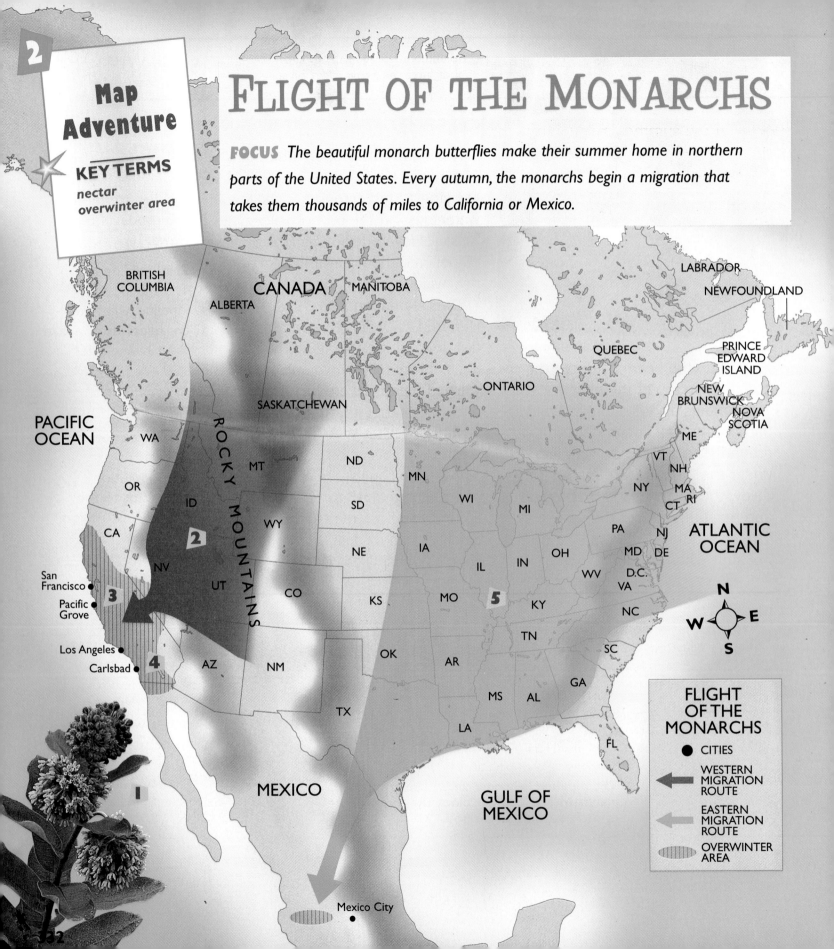

Map Adventure

KEY TERMS

nectar
overwinter area

FLIGHT OF THE MONARCHS

FOCUS The beautiful monarch butterflies make their summer home in northern parts of the United States. Every autumn, the monarchs begin a migration that takes them thousands of miles to California or Mexico.

BRITISH COLUMBIA

CANADA

MANITOBA

ALBERTA

LABRADOR

NEWFOUNDLAND

QUEBEC

PRINCE EDWARD ISLAND

SASKATCHEWAN

ONTARIO

NEW BRUNSWICK

NOVA SCOTIA

PACIFIC OCEAN

WA

ME

ROCKY MOUNTAINS

MT

ND

MN

VT

NH

OR

ID

WY

SD

WI

MI

NY

MA

RI

CT

2

CA

NV

PA

NJ

ATLANTIC OCEAN

IA

IL

IN

OH

MD

DE

San Francisco ●

UT

NE

WV

D.C.

VA

3

CO

KS

MO

5

KY

Pacific Grove ●

NC

Los Angeles ●

TN

Carlsbad ●

4

AZ

NM

OK

AR

SC

GA

N

W   E

S

MS

AL

TX

LA

FL

1

MEXICO

GULF OF MEXICO

FLIGHT OF THE MONARCHS

● CITIES

◀ WESTERN MIGRATION ROUTE

◀ EASTERN MIGRATION ROUTE

▨ OVERWINTER AREA

Mexico City ●

Adventure With the Migrating Monarchs

In the summer months, monarch butterflies form two large groups—one group east of the Rocky Mountains and the other group west of the Rockies. During the summer, they sip **nectar** out of flowers and lay their eggs. As autumn approaches, these butterflies fly to warmer climates for the winter. Think of looking up into the sky and seeing a cloud of bright orange, black, and white butterflies. Let's see where they go.

Map Key

1 Milkweed plant This juicy plant is the only place a monarch butterfly will lay its eggs and the only food a monarch caterpillar will eat.

2 Western migration routes In the summer months, most western monarchs can be found on the milkweed plants in the forests and valleys of Idaho and Montana. Before winter, they migrate to more than 10 different spots in sunny California.

3 Pacific Grove This city is a popular **overwinter area** in California for millions of western monarchs. The city of Pacific Grove celebrates the arrival of the monarchs each year with parades and community activities.

4 Carlsbad This city on the coast of southern California is another popular overwinter area each year for millions of monarchs.

5 Eastern migration routes Eastern monarchs travel over 1,800 miles to a site in Mexico. Some monarchs follow the coastlines of the eastern and southern United States.

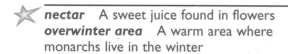

nectar A sweet juice found in flowers
overwinter area A warm area where monarchs live in the winter

MAP IT

1. It is summer, and you are a scientist searching for western monarchs. What states should you visit? What mountain range would you be near?
2. It is autumn, and the western monarchs will be migrating south to their overwinter areas. Find the cities in California where you are likely to see monarchs during the winter months.
3. It is autumn, and you are following the migration of the eastern monarchs. What large bodies of water do some monarchs fly near?
4. It is winter, and you want to visit the main overwinter area of the eastern monarchs. What large city is this area near?

EXPLORE IT

Now that you have studied the migration routes of western and eastern monarchs, describe what is similar about both routes. Then describe the differences in both routes in your state scrapbook.

Global Connections

LOOKING TO THE PACIFIC RIM

FOCUS *The Pacific Rim is a region of many countries that share boundaries with the Pacific Ocean. Most of these countries are strong trade partners.*

The Pacific Rim

When you look at a globe, you can see that the Pacific Ocean is vast. Many countries and thousands of islands have the Pacific Ocean as a natural boundary.

The **Pacific Rim** is the name given to some countries that occupy the land around the Pacific Ocean. They form what might be called the rim, or an edge, of the Pacific Ocean.

Countries that form one rim of the Pacific Ocean include Canada, the United States, and Mexico. The largest countries on the opposite rim of the Pacific Ocean are China and Australia. Japan, South Korea, and the two island nations of the

Philippines and Taiwan (tye WAHN) are also part of the Pacific Rim.

Find on the map on this page some other countries that share a boundary with the Pacific Ocean. Name the states in the United States that have a boundary on the Pacific Ocean.

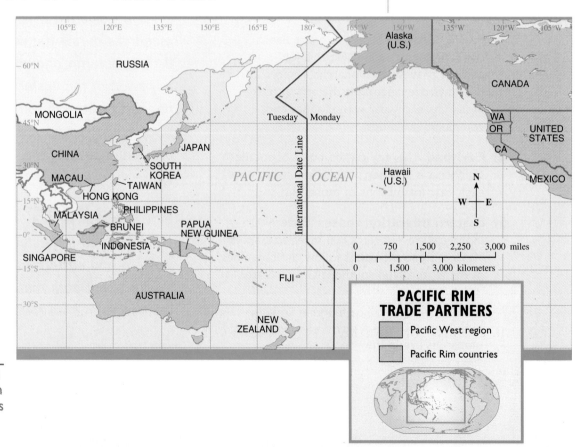

PACIFIC RIM TRADE PARTNERS

☐ Pacific West region

☐ Pacific Rim countries

Pacific Rim Some countries surrounding the Pacific Ocean that are strong trade partners

LOS ANGELES
MONDAY, 4:00 P.M.

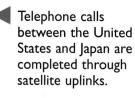

Telephone calls between the United States and Japan are completed through satellite uplinks.

COMMUNICATION ACROSS THE PACIFIC

TOKYO, JAPAN
TUESDAY, 9:00 A.M.

Business Links

The many countries of the Pacific Rim are linked by more than just the Pacific Ocean. These countries have strong ties to one another through trade and business. The countries across the Pacific from the United States include some of the fastest-growing countries in the world. Countries such as Japan, Taiwan, and South Korea are strong economic powers and have large *financial* centers.

Pacific Rim countries contain one third of all the people in the world. This has created a huge market for the buying and selling of goods.

The pictures above show a woman in Los Angeles talking by telephone with businesspeople in Tokyo, Japan. It is 4 P.M., on Monday. In Tokyo, the time is 9 A.M., on Tuesday.

What causes the difference in time? Since Los Angeles and Tokyo are far apart, they are in different time zones. You know that as you move east, you must add one hour for each time zone you cross. As you move west, you must subtract one hour for each time zone you cross.

International Date Line

Exactly halfway around the world from the prime meridian, or 0° longitude, is the international date line. Located at 180°, this line marks where each day begins.

The date to the west of the international date line is one day later than the date just to the east of the line. Find the international date line on the map on page 334.

⭐ *financial* Having to do with money

The dragon is part of every Chinese New Year parade, which is celebrated sometime between January 20 and February 20.

Imports and Exports

The United States imports from countries of the Pacific Rim more than $150 billion worth of goods each year. In turn, the United States exports many different kinds of goods to these countries.

Of all the Pacific Rim countries, the United States carries on the most trade with Japan. And Japan, in turn, exports many of its products to the United States. The drawing below shows the chief products that the United States and Japan trade.

Not far from Japan is the country of South Korea, another strong Pacific Rim trading partner. The United States exports to South Korea aircraft, oil, and construction equipment. Among the products that the United States imports from South Korea are carpets and footwear, especially sneakers.

Australia is another strong trading partner with the United States. Australia sends to the United States meat, wool, and minerals such as coal. The United States exports to Australia crude oil, office equipment, cars, and petrochemicals.

Pacific Links

Cities in the Pacific West region, such as Seattle, San Francisco, and Los Angeles, have grown with the increase in Pacific trade. Raw

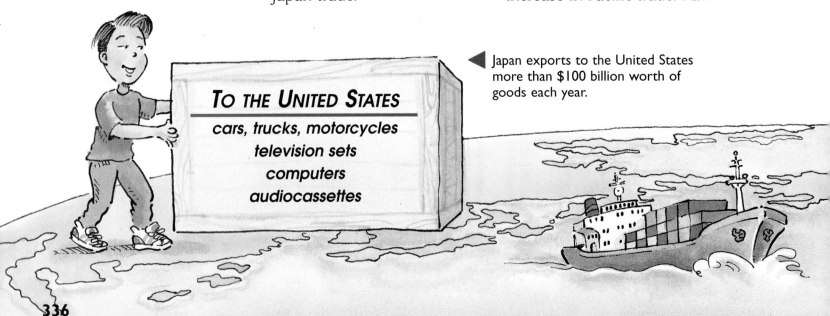

TO THE UNITED STATES
cars, trucks, motorcycles
television sets
computers
audiocassettes

Japan exports to the United States more than $100 billion worth of goods each year.

materials are moved by ship from ports in Seattle, Washington, and Oakland, California, to ports in Japan, China, and South Korea.

In these faraway countries the raw materials are made into manufactured goods and then shipped back to the Pacific West ports for distribution in the United States.

New Americans

Many people from the Pacific Rim countries visit the United States each year. Some decide to settle permanently in this country, bringing with them the traditions and languages of their homelands.

Many of these newcomers decide to live, work, and raise their families in the Pacific West region. Hawaii is home to many

Japanese, Chinese, and Korean immigrants. Immigrants from these countries have also settled in California in the cities of San Francisco, Los Angeles, and San Diego. Recently other groups of people have come from the countries of Thailand, Vietnam, Cambodia, and the Philippines.

New Americans from Pacific Rim countries work hard to make better lives for themselves in the United States. Like other immigrants in earlier times, today's newcomers add their own special heritage to the country we all call home--the United States of America.

The United States exports to ▶ Japan more than $45 billion worth of goods each year.

TO JAPAN

aircraft
computer parts
wheat and corn
cotton
fish
lumber
iron ore
petrochemicals
steel products

SHOW WHAT YOU KNOW!

REFOCUS
COMPREHENSION

1. What are the main exports that the United States sends to Japan?

2. From which countries have recent immigrants come to settle in Hawaii?

THINK ABOUT IT
CRITICAL THINKING

Other than trade, what ties might link the people of the Pacific Rim countries?

STATE CHECK
ACTIVITY

Choose a fact about your state that you would like to share with a new American from a Pacific Rim country. In your state scrapbook, write why you chose the fact.

SUMMING UP

1 DO YOU REMEMBER . . .
COMPREHENSION

1. What is the name for the nations that have a boundary on the Pacific Ocean?

2. Why was a pipeline built from Prudhoe Bay to Valdez, Alaska?

3. In what country is the overwinter area for eastern monarchs?

4. Name three manufactured goods that the United States imports from Japan.

5. Name important ports in the Pacific West region.

2 SKILL POWER
CAUSE AND EFFECT

Write a cause for each of these effects.

1. Airplanes are an important form of transportation in Alaska.

2. Part of the Trans-Alaska Pipeline was built above the ground.

3. Western monarchs are found in California during winter months.

4. Crude oil washed ashore near Valdez in the state of Alaska.

3 WHAT DO YOU THINK?
CRITICAL THINKING

1. Why is it better to transport goods to Hawaii by ship rather than by plane?

2. How did the builders of the Trans-Alaska Pipeline show concern for the environment?

3. What benefits are there for the people of Pacific Grove, California, in the annual return of the monarchs?

4. Why does Japan import lumber from the Pacific West region of the United States?

5. How might people in the United States welcome people from other Pacific Rim countries?

4 SAY IT, WRITE IT, USE IT
VOCABULARY

Work with a group of classmates to create your own glossary for these key terms. Write a definition for each word and use it in a sentence about the Pacific West region.

financial

interstate highway

nectar

overwinter area

Pacific Rim

5 GEOGRAPHY AND YOU
MAP STUDY

Use the map below to answer these questions.

1. On what ocean is Prudhoe Bay located?

2. What cities are on the Trans-Alaska Pipeline route?

3. What port is at the southernmost end of the Trans-Alaska Pipeline?

4. On what body of water is Valdez, Alaska?

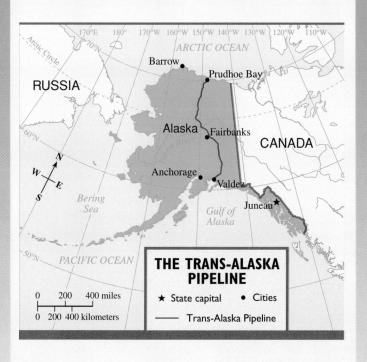

6 TAKE ACTION
CITIZENSHIP

In this chapter you have read about recent immigrants to the United States. Many have become American citizens. Reflect on what ties us together as Americans and what the words of the Pledge of Allegiance mean. Share your thoughts with the rest of the class.

7 GET CREATIVE
SCIENCE CONNECTION

In this chapter, you studied the migration of monarch butterflies. Other insects, fish, and mammals migrate also. Some of these animals include eels, terns, salmon, and caribou. Choose one animal and research its movements. Make a map that shows the migration route. Explain the reasons for the migration and note any special problems the animal has to overcome on its journey.

LOOKING BACK If you could now visit any of the seven regions of the United States, what region would you choose and why?

EXPLORE REFERENCE

CONTENTS

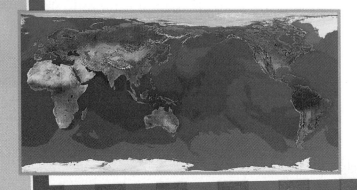

SECTION

RESEARCH AND REFERENCE

These books will help you understand our country's regions and the states within each region. When you study about another country, you can find information about its natural wonders.

Kids Learn America: Bringing Geography to Life With People, Places & History by Patricia Gordon and Reed C. Snow (Williamson Publishing Co., 1991)
While learning more about the people, places, and special events in each of our states, you will have fun doing the many projects and activities in this book.

State Flags: Including the Commonwealth of Puerto Rico by Sue R. Brandt (Franklin Watts, 1992)
Did you know that each state has its own flag? Read the story that tells how each flag was made and what each flag's symbols mean. Why not begin with your own state?

The Children's Atlas of Natural Wonders by Joyce Pope (The Millbrook Press, 1995)
You've explored many natural wonders in the regions of the United States. Find out more about these wonders and others as you tour different continents of the world.

Alabama

The Heart of Dixie

Became the 22nd state on December 14, 1819

State Bird
Yellowhammer

Fabulous Facts!

- Huntsville is nicknamed Rocket City USA. Scientists here made the rockets that launched the first astronauts to the moon. At the U.S. Space Camp, students can train as astronauts do.

- Rosa Parks, an African American, was arrested for refusing to give up her bus seat to a white man in 1955. As a result, Martin Luther King, Jr., led the first civil rights protest in Montgomery.

- At Tuskegee Institute, George Washington Carver, an African American scientist, developed more than 300 products from the peanut, including ink, soap, shaving cream, and a kind of instant coffee.

- The Heisman Trophy is named after Auburn University coach John Heisman. It is given each year to the top college football player in the country.

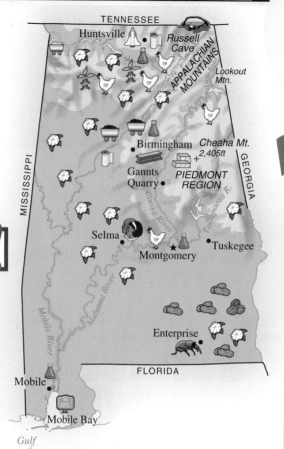

Map labels: TENNESSEE · Huntsville · Russell Cave · Lookout Mtn. · APPALACHIAN MOUNTAINS · GEORGIA · Birmingham · Cheaha Mt. 2,405ft · Gannts Quarry · PIEDMONT REGION · MISSISSIPPI · Coosa River · Tallapoosa R. · Selma · Montgomery · Tuskegee · Alabama River · Mobile River · Enterprise · FLORIDA · Mobile · Mobile Bay · Gulf of Mexico

Key

Capital ★Montgomery

Three largest cities
1. Birmingham
2. Mobile
3. Montgomery

Smallest town
   Gannts Quarry
   Population 2

Geography
+ Highest elevation
  Cheaha Mountain
    2,405 ft above sea level
Appalachian Mountains
Piedmont Plateau
Little River (runs its entire course on top of Lookout Mountain)

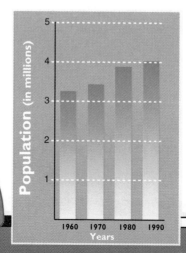

This flag shows a crimson cross shaped like an **X** on a white field. It reminds people in Alabama of the Battle Flag of the Confederacy, which their soldiers carried during the Civil War.

Economy
A leading state in
- broiler chickens
- peanuts
- cotton
- pecans
- bauxite, marble

Important products
- steel
- chemicals
- paper products
- coal
- soybeans

Historic Sites
- Mobile Bay
- Enterprise (boll weevil)
- Russell Cave
- Selma (march to Montgomery)
- Huntsville

Fresh Water Used
2,000 gallons/day/person (average)

Garbage
5,310,000 tons per year
15% recycled

Population (in millions)

Years	Population
1960	~3.2
1970	~3.4
1980	~3.9
1990	~4.0

AK

The Last Frontier

Became the 49th state on January 3, 1959

State Bird
Willow Ptarmigan

Key

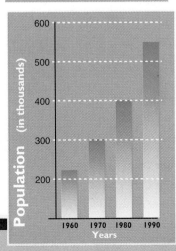

Capital ★Juneau

Three largest cities
1. Anchorage
2. Fairbanks
3. Juneau

Smallest town
Bettles
Population 50

Geography

+ Highest elevation Mt. McKinley (the highest peak in United States)
  20,320 ft above sea level
- Coastline—the longest of all coastal states: 6,640 miles long
- Glaciers—100,000
- Volcanoes—world's largest chain of active volcanoes
- Mountains—has the country's 16 highest
- Lakes—has more than 3,000,000

Map labels:
ARCTIC OCEAN
BROOKS RANGE
CANADA
Bettles
Nome
Fairbanks
Yukon River
ALASKA RANGE
+ Mt. McKinley 20,320 ft
Bering Sea
Anchorage
Klondike Gold Rush National Historical Park
Skagway
Juneau
Pribiloff Islands
Prince William Sound
Kayak Island
Kodiak Island
PACIFIC OCEAN
Sitka
Ketchikan
Aleutian Islands

This flag was a contest entry by 13-year-old Benny Benson before Alaska became a state. He wrote, "The blue field is for the Alaska sky and the forget-me-not, a flower that grows in Alaska. The North Star is for the future state of Alaska, the most northerly in the Union. The Dipper is for the Great Bear—symbolizing strength."

Fabulous Facts!

- Alaska is the top fishing state. About 6 billion pounds of fish and seafood are caught yearly. This is about one pound per person on Earth.

- The largest of all the states, Alaska, once belonged to Russia. The United States bought it in 1867 for two cents per acre. The total cost was $7.2 million.

- Fairbanks hosts a famous baseball game played on June 21 at night with no lights. It is called the Midnight Sun Game. The first pitch is thrown at 11 P.M., and the game ends at 2 A.M.

- Saxman, near Ketchikan, has the world's largest collection of authentic Indian totem poles.

Economy

First in the nation in
- petroleum reserves
- salmon and other fishing
- mining zinc

A leading state in
- gold
- natural gas
- uranium
- forest products
- canning
- furs

Historic Sites

- Kayak Island
- Ketchikan (totem poles)
- Klondike Gold Rush National Historical Park
- Kodiak Island
- Sitka

Fresh Water Used
517 gallons/day/person (average)

Garbage
500,000 tons per year
6% recycled

Population (in thousands) chart — Years: 1960, 1970, 1980, 1990 (scale 200–600)

Arizona

The Grand Canyon State

Became the 48th state on February 14, 1912

State Bird
Cactus Wren

AZ

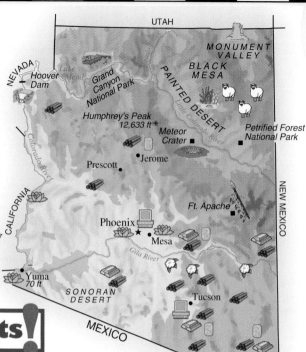

UTAH

NEVADA
Hoover Dam
Lake Mead
Grand Canyon National Park
Colorado River
CALIFORNIA
Humphrey's Peak 12,633 ft +
Jerome
Prescott
Meteor Crater
MONUMENT VALLEY
BLACK MESA
PAINTED DESERT
Little Colorado River
Petrified Forest National Park
NEW MEXICO
Ft. Apache
Phoenix ★
Mesa
Gila River
Yuma 70 ft
SONORAN DESERT
Tucson
MEXICO

Key

Capital ★ Phoenix
Three largest cities
1. Phoenix
2. Tucson
3. Mesa
Smallest town
Jerome
Population 402

Geography
+ Highest elevation
Humphrey's Peak
12,633 ft above sea level
– Lowest point
Colorado River in Yuma County
70 ft above sea level
Grand Canyon National Park
Petrified Forest National Park
Black Mesa
Sonoran Desert

Fabulous Facts!

- Arizona is the top copper-mining state. It produces 2 billion pounds of the metal each year, more than the rest of the 50 states combined.

- Meteor Crater was formed about 50,000 years ago when a giant meteorite struck Earth. It is nearly one mile across and 570 ft deep. The dust in the crater is like that on the moon, and astronauts train here for moon landings.

- Tucson is known as the Astronomy Capital of the World. No other place on Earth has as many telescopes in one area. About 30 are on mountain peaks.

- The largest cactus in the nation is the saguaro which thrives in deserts here. Its blossom is Arizona's state flower.

The star is copper-colored because Arizona mines more copper than any other state. The 13 rays of the sun stand for the first 13 states. The rays are red and yellow, the colors of Spain, which once controlled the region. Blue is used on the lower half because it is the state color.

Fresh Water Used
1,790 gallons/day/ person (average)

Garbage
4,200,000 tons per year
5% recycled

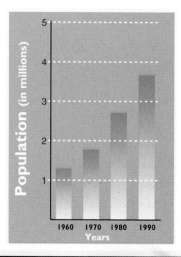

Population (in millions)

5
4
3
2
1

1960 1970 1980 1990
Years

Economy
First in the nation in
mining copper and turquoise
A leading state in
computers
cotton
sheep
lettuce
gold and silver

Historic Sites
Fort Apache
Hoover Dam
Meteor Crater
Monument Valley
Painted Desert

Arkansas

The Land of Opportunity

Became the 25th state on June 15, 1836

State Bird Mockingbird

Map labels

MISSOURI

Pea Ridge • Blue Eye
OZARK PLATEAU
BOSTON MTNS.
Blanchard Caverns
Ft. Smith
+ Magazine Mtn. 2,753 ft
OUACHITA MTNS.
North Little Rock
Little Rock
Hot Springs National Park
Crater of Diamonds State Park
OKLAHOMA
TENNESSEE
White River
Mississippi River
Arkansas River
MISSISSIPPI
GULF COASTAL PLAIN
Ouachita River
TEXAS
Texarkana
55 ft
LOUISIANA

Key

Capital ★Little Rock

Three largest cities
1. Little Rock
2. Fort Smith
3. North Little Rock

Smallest town
Blue Eye
Population 34

Geography

+ Highest elevation
  Magazine Mountain
  2,753 ft above sea level

− Lowest point
  Ouachita River in Ashley-Union Counties
  55 ft above sea level

Ozark Plateau
Ouachita Mountains
Gulf Coastal Plain
Arkansas River

Economy

First in the nation in
🐔 broiler chickens
🌾 rice
⛏ mining bromine

A leading state in
🌿 soybeans
🍇 grapes
🥜 pecans
🌱 cotton

Important product
🛢 natural gas

Historic Sites

🔺 Blanchard Caverns
🏞 Hot Springs National Park
🔫 Pea Ridge

A diamond is at the center of the flag because Arkansas is the only place in North America where diamonds have been discovered and mined. The 25 stars around the diamond show that Arkansas was the 25th state to join the Union. The star at the top shows Arkansas was one of the Confederate States of America during the Civil War. The other three stars stand for the three countries that controlled Arkansas: Spain, France, and the United States.

ARKANSAS

Fabulous Facts!

- Arkansas grows more rice and raises more chickens than any other state.

- Daisy G. Bates, a civil rights leader, was born here. She led nine African American students into all-white Central High School in Little Rock in 1957 to help integrate the school.

- At Crater of Diamonds State Park, visitors are allowed to search the open fields for diamonds and keep any diamond they find that weighs under five carats.

- Texarkana is a city divided by the Arkansas-Texas state line. It has two city governments but only one post office building, which actually stands in both states.

- Arkansas has a state musical instrument. It is the fiddle.

Population graph

Population (in millions)

2.5
2.0
1.5
1.0
0.5

1960 1970 1980 1990
Years

Garbage
2,154,000 tons per year
25% recycled

Fresh Water Used
3,330 gallons/day/person (average)

California

The Golden State

Became the 31st state on September 9, 1850

State Bird
California Valley Quail

Fabulous Facts!

- California has more people and manufactures more goods than any other state.

- The tallest, largest, and oldest trees grow here. Redwoods grow more than 300 ft tall; giant sequoias have trunks more than 25 ft in diameter; some bristlecone pines are more than 4,000 years old.

- Sally Ride, the first U.S. woman in space, was born here in 1951. In 1983 she flew on the space shuttle *Challenger*.

- Mickey Mouse was created by Walt Disney here. Mickey still looks the same as he appeared in his first cartoon, "Steamboat Willie," in 1928.

- California has a state reptile. It is the California desert tortoise.

Fresh Water Used
1,180 gallons/day/person
(average)

Garbage
45,000,000 tons per year 25% recycled

OREGON
Ft. Ross
Sutter's Mill
Sacramento
Amador City
San Francisco
Sacramento River
SIERRA NEVADA
Yosemite Falls
NEVADA
San Jose
PACIFIC OCEAN
SAN ANDREAS FAULT
Mt. Whitney
14,494 ft
Death Valley
282 ft below sea level
La Brea Tar Pits
Los Angeles
MOJAVE DESERT
ARIZONA
San Diego de Alcalá
San Diego
MEXICO

CA

Key

Capital ★Sacramento
Three largest cities
1. Los Angeles
2. San Diego
3. San Jose
Smallest town
Amador City
Population 188

Geography
+ Highest elevation
  Mt. Whitney
  14,494 ft above sea level
- Lowest point
  Death Valley
  (lowest in the nation)
  282 ft below sea level

Sierra Nevada
Yosemite Falls
Mojave Desert
San Andreas Fault

California's flag is called the Bear Flag. It is based on a flag created in 1846 by a small group of American rebels, when California was still under Mexican rule. The grizzly bear stands for courage.

CALIFORNIA REPUBLIC

Economy
First in the nation in

milk | lemons
lettuce | cantalope
strawberries | carrots
grapes | broccoli
processed tomatoes
eggs
tuna
boron
airplanes

Historic Sites

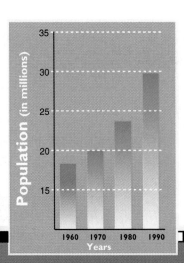

Fort Ross | Sutter's Mill
La Brea Tar Pits
San Francisco
San Diego de Alcalá

Population (in millions)

35
30
25
20
15

1960 1970 1980 1990
Years

The Centennial State

Became the 38th state on August 1, 1876

State Bird
Lark Bunting

Key

Capital ★Denver

Three largest cities
1. Denver
2. Colorado Springs
3. Aurora

Smallest town
Bonanza
Population 8

Geography
+ Highest elevation
  Mt. Elbert
  14,433 ft above sea level
− Lowest point
  Arkansas River in
  Prowers County
  3,350 ft above sea level

Rocky Mountains
Great Plains
Colorado River
Royal Gorge
Pikes Peak

Economy
A leading state in
- scientific equipment
- meatpacking
- wool
- hay
- wheat
- sugar beets
- beef cattle

Historic Sites
- Bent's Old Fort
- Cherry Creek
- Mesa Verde
- Moffat Tunnel
- Union Colony (Greeley)

The large red C stands for *Colorado*, which means "red" in Spanish, and for Colorado's nickname, Centennial State. It became a state in 1876—the centennial, or 100th anniversary, of the Declaration of Independence. The yellow circle represents the gold that was discovered in 1858. Blue stripes stand for the sky, and white stands for snow on the Rocky Mountains.

Fabulous Facts!

- In concrete vaults at Fort Collins, the United States Department of Agriculture (USDA) preserves seeds from nearly every plant known. If the supply of a certain food were to die off, there are seeds to start again.

- More than 50 kinds of dinosaurs lived in western Colorado. There is even a town named Dinosaur.

- Even in areas of Colorado where there is no snow, people still ski or sled. At Great Sand Dunes National Monument, some sand dunes are more than 700 ft tall, the tallest in North America. People ski or sled down the dunes.

- The view from Pikes Peak in 1893 inspired Katharine Lee Bates to write "America the Beautiful."

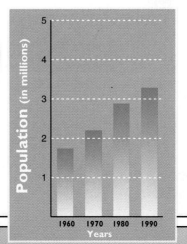

Fresh Water Used
3,850 gallons/day/person (average)

Garbage
2,800,000 tons per year
18% recycled

Population (in millions)

Years	Population
1960	~1.75
1970	~2.2
1980	~2.9
1990	~3.3

Map labels
WYOMING · NEBRASKA · UTAH · ARIZONA · NEW MEXICO · OKLAHOMA · KANSAS

Dinosaur · Yampa River · White River · Fort Collins · Greeley · Moffat Tunnel · Denver · Aurora · Cherry Creek · South Platte River · GREAT PLAINS · Mt. Elbert 14,433 ft · Pikes Peak · Colorado River · Colorado Springs · Gunnison River · Arkansas River · Bonanza · Bent's Old Fort · 3,350 ft · Mesa Verde · Great Sand Dunes National Monument · ROCKY MOUNTAINS

The Constitution State

Became the 5th state on January 9, 1788

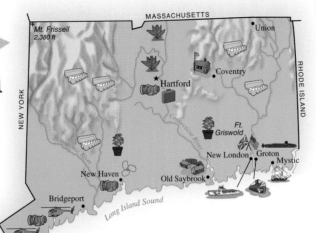

MASSACHUSETTS

Mt. Frissell 2,380 ft

NEW YORK

RHODE ISLAND

Union

Coventry

★ Hartford

Ft. Griswold

Connecticut River

Housatonic River

New London · Groton
Mystic

New Haven

Old Saybrook

Bridgeport

Long Island Sound

CT

**State Bird
Robin**

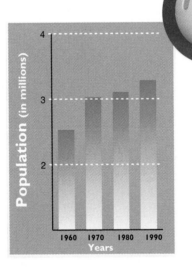

The blue background is for a cloudless sky. On it is a white shield with three vines, each bearing three bunches of purple grapes. The vines represent the three original colonies that made up Connecticut. The state motto is beneath the shield.

Fabulous Facts!

- Connecticut is headquarters to more than 150 insurance companies. Hartford, nicknamed the Insurance Capital of the World, has been an insurance center for almost 200 years.

- The first woman to receive a patent was Mary Hies of South Killingly in 1809. She invented a weaving machine.

- The state was also home to the nation's first bicycle factory, built in 1877, and the world's first nuclear-powered submarine, launched in 1954. Lollipops and the Wiffle® ball were invented here.

Population (in millions)

4

3

2

1960 1970 1980 1990
Years

Key

Capital ★Hartford
Three largest cities
1. Bridgeport
2. Hartford
3. New Haven
Smallest town
   Union
   Population 613

Geography
+ Highest elevation
   Mt. Frissell (on south slope at state line)
   2,380 ft above sea level
Long Island Sound
Connecticut River
Housatonic River

Economy
A leading center for
- insurance companies
- helicopters
- jet aircraft engines
- propellers
- submarines

Important products
- eggs
- greenhouse flowers and nursery plants
- tobacco

Historic Sites
- Coventry
- Fort Griswold
- New London
- Old Saybrook
- Groton
- Mystic

Garbage
2,905,000 tons per year
23% recycled

Fresh Water Used
325 gallons/day/person (average)

The First State

Became the 1st state on December 7, 1787

Key

Capital ★Dover

Three largest cities
1. Wilmington
2. Dover
3. Newark

Smallest town
 Henlopen Acres
 Population 106

Geography

+ Highest elevation Ebright Road at Delaware/Pennsylvania state line
  448 ft above sea level

Coastline 28 miles long

Economy

A leading state in
- banking
- corporations
- chemical management and research
- automobile production

Important products
- chemicals
- broiler chickens
- green peas
- crabs

Historic Sites
- Brandywine Creek
- Delaware Bay
- Fort Delaware
- Lewes
- New Castle (Fort Casimir)

THE FIRST STATE
23561
DELAWARE

**State Bird
Blue Hen
Chicken**

DECEMBER 7, 1787

The diamond stands for Delaware's early nickname, The Diamond State, because Delaware was considered a jewel in colonial times. The wheat, corn, and ox stand for agriculture; the sailing ship stands for the shipping industry. The colonial blue and buff colors are for the coats General George Washington and some regiments wore during the Revolutionary War. December 7, 1787, is the date that Delaware became the first state.

Fabulous Facts!

- About one half of the largest companies in the United States have their headquarters here. However, many do most of their business outside of Delaware. It is easier and less expensive for a company to become a corporation here than in most other states.

- Delaware's northern boundary is a perfect curve, called Twelve Mile Circle. All points along that part of the boundary are exactly twelve miles from the dome of the Court House in New Castle. They were marked in 1701.

- The first log cabins in North America were built here by Swedish settlers in 1638.

- Delaware has a state insect. It is the ladybug.

Population (in thousands)
800
600
400
1960 1970 1980 1990
Years

Fresh Water Used
1,540 gallons/day/person (average)

Garbage
1,100,000 tons per year 27% recycled

Map labels: PENNSYLVANIA, Twelve Mile Circle, Ebright Road 448 ft, Wilmington, Brandywine Creek, Newark, New Castle, Ft. Delaware, Delaware Bay, Lepsic River, Dover, MARYLAND, Murderkill River, Lewes, Henlopen Acres, Nanticoke River, MARYLAND

Florida

The Sunshine State

Became the 27th state on March 3, 1845

State Flower
Orange Blossom

ALABAMA
345 ft+
ALABAMA
GEORGIA
★Tallahassee
Olustee
Jacksonville
St. Augustine
Daytona Beach
Gulf of Mexico
Kennedy Space Flight Center
Orlando
Pelican Island
Tampa
Orchid
Sarasota
Lake Okeechobee
ATLANTIC OCEAN
Big Cypress Swamp
Ft. Lauderdale
Everglades
Miami
Key West
Florida Keys

FL

Fabulous Facts!

- Florida farmers grow about four fifths of the nation's oranges and grapefruits. Each year about 40 billion oranges are harvested, about 8 for each person on Earth.

- The first federal wildlife refuge in the nation was established by President Theodore Roosevelt in 1903 at Pelican Island.

- Automobiles can be driven on the firmly packed sand at Daytona Beach. Tides have beaten the beach to the hardness and smoothness of a highway.

- Florida is the flattest and lowest state in the nation. That is because millions of years ago it was sea bottom.

- Florida has a state marine mammal. It is the manatee.

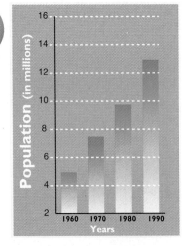

In the center of the flag is the state seal. It shows a Seminole woman, the rising sun, a palm tree, and a steamboat; all are associated with Florida. The diagonal red bars on a white field are a reminder of the Battle Flag of the Confederacy.

Fresh Water Used
582 gallons/day/person (average)

Garbage
23,561,000 tons per year
36% recycled

Population (in millions)

Years	Population
1960	~5
1970	~7.5
1980	~10
1990	~13

Key

Capital ★Tallahassee
Three largest cities
1. Jacksonville
2. Miami
3. Tampa
Smallest town
    Orchid
    Population 19

Geography
Highest elevation
Walton County
    345 ft above sea level
Coastline—1,350 miles long
Big Cypress Swamp
Everglades
Florida Keys

Economy
First in the nation in

oranges	tomatoes
grapefruit	
tangerines, limes	
sugar cane	
phosphate	

A leading state in
- fishing
- shrimp
- houseplant cultivation
- tourism
- beef cattle

Manatee

Historic Sites
- Ft. Lauderdale
- Kennedy Space Flight Center
- Key West
- Olustee   Sarasota
- St. Augustine   Orlando

Georgia

The Empire State of the South

Became the 4th state on January 2, 1788

State Bird
Brown Thrasher

Key

Capital ★Atlanta

Three largest cities
1. Atlanta
2. Columbus
3. Savannah

Smallest town
Edge Hill
Population 22

Geography
+ Highest elevation
  Brasstown Bald
  Mountain
  4,784 ft above sea level
Blue Ridge Mountains
Okefenokee Swamp
Golden Isles
Altamaha River

Economy
First in the nation in
 peanuts
pecans
clay
granite production

A leading state in
peaches
eggs
broiler chickens

Historic Sites
 Chickamauga
Dahlonega
Etowah Mound, Cartersville
St. Simons Island
Warm Springs

Map labels: TENNESSEE, NORTH CAROLINA, Chickamauga, APPALACHIAN MTNS., BLUE RIDGE MTNS., +Brasstown Bald Mtn. 4,784 ft, Dahlonega, Cartersville, Etowah Mound, Chattahoochee River, SOUTH CAROLINA, ★Atlanta, ALABAMA, Warm Springs, Edge Hill, Columbus, Flint River, Savannah, Altamaha River, Golden Isles, ATLANTIC OCEAN, St. Simons Island, OKEFENOKEE SWAMP, FLORIDA

This flag was adopted in 1956. One part shows the Battle Flag of the Confederacy. The other part features the state seal in the center. The date, 1776, represents Georgia's signing the Declaration of Independence. The three columns represent the three branches of government.

Fabulous Facts!

- Georgia leads all the states in the production of peanuts. Almost 2 billion pounds are grown each year.

- Juliet Gordon Low lived here when she began the Girl Scouts of the U.S.A. in 1912. Her property in Savannah was the organization's first headquarters.

- Gullah is a unique language spoken by descendants of African American slaves living on the barrier islands. It is a combination of 17th century English and West African languages.

- Atlanta was selected to host the Olympic Games in the summer of 1996.

Population (in millions) — bar graph

Years	1960	1970	1980	1990
Population	~4	~4.5	~5.5	~6.5

Garbage
8,500,000 tons per year
12% recycled

Fresh Water Used
816 gallons/day/person (average)

Hawaii

HI

The Aloha State

Became the 50th state on August 21, 1959

State Bird
Nene (Hawaiian Goose)

Map labels

WAIMEA CANYON
Menehune Fish Pond
Niihau
Waimea Bay
Kauai
Oahu
KOOLAU RANGE
Kailua
Pearl Harbor
Molokai
Honolulu
Nuuanu Pali
Maunaloa
Maui
Lanai
Kahoolawe
Kukuihaele
Pu'u Wekiu, Mauna Kea+ 13,796 ft
Hilo
Wailuku River
Kealakekua Bay
Hawaii
MAUNA LOA VOLCANO

Key

Capital ★Honolulu

Three largest cities
1. Honolulu
2. Hilo
3. Kailua

Smallest town
Kukuihaele
Population 97

Geography

+ Highest elevation
Pu'u Wekiu on Mauna Kea
13,796 ft above sea level

Koolau Range
Mauna Loa Volcano
Wailuku River
Waimea Canyon

Fabulous Facts!

- Airplanes are important in Hawaii because flying is the quickest and easiest way to travel from one island to another.

- Hawaii once had its own kings and queens. It was an independent monarchy.

- A future Hawaiian island is the Loihi Seamount, a volcano about a half mile under water. It might emit enough lava to surface in 30,000 years.

- The Hawaiian alphabet contains only 12 letters—*a, e, h, i, k, l, m, n, o, p, u*, and *w*.

The flag was designed by the first king of Hawaii, Kamehameha I. It has eight stripes of red, white, and blue, which stand for the eight main islands. The flag of Great Britain is shown in the upper left corner. This is to honor that country's friendship, which began when Captain James Cook visited the islands in 1778.

Economy

First in the nation in
- coffee—the only state that grows it
- pineapples
- bananas

A leading state in
- sugar cane
- pineapple processing

Important product
- leis

Historic Sites

- Pearl Harbor
- Kealakekua Bay
- Menehune Fish Pond
- Nuuanu Pali
- Waimea Bay

Garbage
2,000,000 tons per year
17% recycled

Fresh Water Used
1,070 gallons/day/person (average)

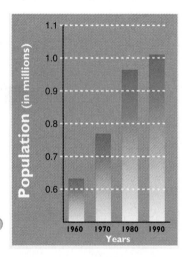

Population (in millions) chart — Years: 1960, 1970, 1980, 1990 (scale 0.6 to 1.1)

ID

The Gem State

Became the 43rd state on July 3, 1890

State Flower Syringa

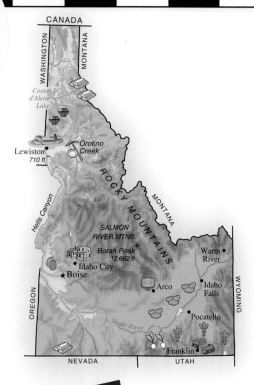

CANADA
WASHINGTON | MONTANA
Coeur d'Alene Lake
Lewiston 710 ft
Orofino Creek
ROCKY MOUNTAINS
Hells Canyon
Snake River
SALMON RIVER MTNS.
Borah Peak 12,662 ft
Idaho City
★Boise
Arco
Warm River
Idaho Falls
Pocatello
Snake River
Franklin
OREGON | NEVADA | UTAH | WYOMING

Key

Capital ★Boise

Three largest cities
1. Boise
2. Pocatello
3. Idaho Falls

Smallest town
Warm River
Population 11

Geography
+ Highest elevation
Borah Peak
12,662 ft above sea level
− Lowest point
Snake River in
Nez Perce County
710 ft above sea level
Rocky Mountains
Hells Canyon
Coeur d'Alene Lake
Salmon River Mountains

Economy

First in the nation in
 potatoes
 garnets

A leading state in
 silver
 barley
 plums
sugar beets

Historic Sites
Franklin
Arco
Orofino Creek
Lewiston
 Idaho City

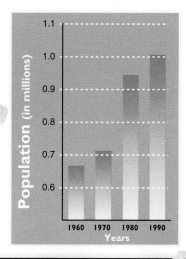

The blue flag has the state seal pictured in the center. The woman represents liberty, justice, and equality. The miner stands for Idaho's mineral resources. The pine tree and farmer represent the forestry and farming industries. The elk's head represents wildlife.

Fabulous Facts!

- Nearly one third of all potatoes in the United States are grown in Idaho.

- As a 16-year-old high school student in Rigby, Philo T. Farnsworth developed the image dissector, which led to the creation of television.

- Idaho lies halfway between the North Pole and the equator.

- The longest main street in the nation is 33 miles long. It runs through Island Park.

- Idaho has a state horse. It is the appaloosa.

Population (in millions)
1.1
1.0
0.9
0.8
0.7
0.6
1960 1970 1980 1990
Years

Fresh Water Used
19,600 gallons/day/person (average)

Garbage
866,000 tons per year 10% recycled

Illinois

The Land of Lincoln

Became the 21st state on December 3, 1818

State Flower
Native Violet

Fabulous Facts!

- Chicago's O'Hare International Airport has the most passenger arrivals and departures of any airport in the world.

- The first metal-frame skyscraper in the world was built in Chicago in 1884. It was 10 stories tall. Now, Chicago has one of the tallest buildings in the world, the Sears Tower, which is 110 stories tall.

- The original Ferris wheel was built in Chicago in 1893. The wheel was so huge that more than 2,000 people could ride on it at one time.

Garbage
15,000,000 tons per year
19% recycled

Fresh Water Used
1,570 gallons/day/person
(average)

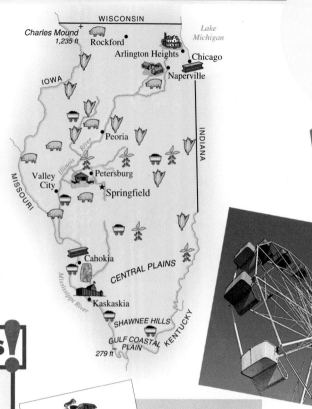

WISCONSIN
Charles Mound 1,235 ft
Rockford
Lake Michigan
Arlington Heights
Chicago
Naperville
IOWA
Illinois River
Peoria
INDIANA
Valley City
Petersburg
Springfield
MISSOURI
Cahokia
CENTRAL PLAINS
Kaskaskia
Mississippi River
SHAWNEE HILLS
GULF COASTAL PLAIN
279 ft
KENTUCKY

The center of the state flag pictures the state seal. The eagle stands for the United States. The state motto is written on the streamer. Thirteen stars and 13 stripes on the shield represent the original 13 states. The sun rising over the prairie stands for the progress made since statehood.

ILLINOIS

Economy

A leading state in

 corn

 soybeans

 hogs

 steel

 coal

Historic Sites

 Cahokia

 Kaskaskia

 Petersburg

 Arlington Heights

 Naperville

Population (in millions)

Years	Population
1960	10.0
1970	11.1
1980	11.4
1990	11.4

(chart axis: 11.5, 11.0, 10.5, 10.0)

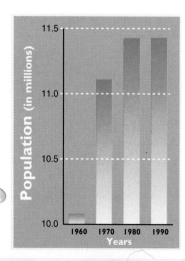

Indiana

The Hoosier State

Became the 19th state on December 11, 1816

State Flower Peony

Key

Capital ★Indianapolis

Three largest cities
1. Indianapolis
2. Fort Wayne
3. Evansville

Smallest town
New Amsterdam
Population 30

Geography
+ **Highest elevation**
  Franklin Township
  1,257 ft above sea level
− **Lowest point**
  Ohio River in
  Posey County
  320 ft above sea level

Wabash River

Economy

First in the nation in
 steel
 corn for popping

A leading state in
 coal mining
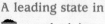 turkeys
corn
 musical instruments
 wheat

Historic Sites
 Vincennes
Gary
 New Harmony
 South Bend
 Lafayette
 Noblesville (Conner Prairie)

Map

Lake Michigan
MICHIGAN
Gary
South Bend
Ft. Wayne
ILLINOIS
Wabash River
Lafayette
1,257 ft +
OHIO
Noblesville
Speedway
Indianapolis
Oolitic
Vincennes
New Amsterdam
KENTUCKY
New Harmony
Evansville
320 ft
Ohio River

Indiana's blue state flag features a golden torch. The flame stands for liberty and knowledge for everyone. The 19th and largest star, above the torch, represents Indiana, the 19th state.

Fabulous Facts!

- Each year the state makes 40 billion pounds of steel. That is enough to build 20 million automobiles.

- Most of the limestone used to build the Empire State Building, in New York City, came from the Empire Hole, near Oolitic.

- The famous Indianapolis 500 automobile race is held in the town of Speedway every Memorial Day weekend.

Population (in millions)

5.5
5.0
4.5
4.0

1960 1970 1980 1990

Years

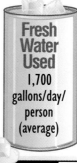

Fresh Water Used 1,700 gallons/day/ person (average)

Garbage 5,600,000 tons per year 19% recycled

Iowa

The Hawkeye State

Became the 29th state on December 28, 1846

**State Flower
Wild Rose**

MINNESOTA

SOUTH DAKOTA

+ 1,670 ft

Sioux City

NEBRASKA

Missouri River

YOUNG DRIFT PLAINS

Des Moines River

Marquette

WISCONSIN

Dubuque

Cedar Rapids

Amana Colonies

Amana

Davenport

Des Moines

Mississippi River

DISSECTED TILL PLAINS

Tabor   Delphos

ILLINOIS

MISSOURI

Keokuk

480 ft

Fabulous Facts!

- Sioux City processes more popcorn than any other city in the United States.

- The first successful electric car was invented around 1891 by William Morrison of Des Moines. It held six passengers and traveled 20 miles per hour.

- The red apple called Delicious was first grown here in the 1880s.

Garbage
2,744,000 tons per year
16% recycled

Fresh Water Used
1,030 gallons/day/ person (average)

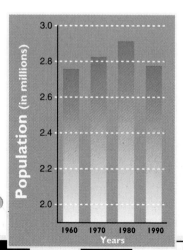

Iowa's state flag is similar to that of France. Both have three vertical stripes—one red, one white, and one blue. France once owned this area but sold it to the United States in 1803 as part of the Louisiana Purchase. The eagle is from the state seal, and the state motto is on the streamer.

IOWA

Key 🔑

Capital ★Des Moines

Three largest cities

1. Des Moines
2. Cedar Rapids
3. Davenport

Smallest town
Delphos
Population 18

Geography

+ Highest elevation
  Northern boundary of Osceola County
  1,670 ft above sea level

− Lowest point
  Mississippi River in Lee County
  480 ft above sea level

Dissected Till Plains
Young Drift Plains

Economy

First in the nation in

🐷 hogs and pigs

🌱 soybeans

A leading state in

🌽 corn   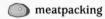 meatpacking

🐑 sheep

🥛 milk

⚙️ farm machinery

🌾 oats

Historic Sites

🏛️ Amana Colonies

📺 Tabor

🗼 Dubuque

Keokuk

Marquette

Population (in millions)

Bar graph showing population for years 1960, 1970, 1980, 1990 (in millions, range 2.0 to 3.0)

Years

The Sunflower State

Became the 34th state on January 29, 1861

NEBRASKA
Lebanon • geographical center of the mainland U.S.
Republican River
Ft. Leavenworth • Kansas City
SMOKY HILLS
Saline River
Topeka ★
+ Mt. Sunflower 4,039 ft
COLORADO
Abilene
Lawrence
Arkansas River
Dodge City
FLINT HILLS
Wichita
Verdigris River
MISSOURI
RED HILLS
Freeport
679 ft
OKLAHOMA

State Flower
Sunflower

Key

Capital ★Topeka
Three largest cities
1. Wichita
2. Kansas City
3. Topeka
Smallest town
Freeport
Population 11

Geography

+ Highest elevation
Mt. Sunflower in
Wallace County
4,039 ft above sea level
− Lowest point
Verdigris River in
Montgomery County
679 ft above sea level
Flint Hills
Red Hills
Smoky Hills

Economy

First in the nation in
🌾 wheat
sorghum
✈ light airplanes
beef meatpacking
helium

A leading state in
hay   pigs
beef cattle   salt
petroleum and natural gas

Historic Sites

Dodge City
Lawrence
Abilene
Fort Leavenworth

KANSAS

A sunflower is pictured near the top of the Kansas state flag because it is the state flower and because Kansas is nicknamed the Sunflower State. The design below it is from the state seal. The thirty-four stars show that Kansas is the 34th state. The farmer plowing indicates that agriculture has been important to the state.

Fabulous Facts!

- In Wichita, four large aircraft manufacturers build almost 60% of the nation's aircrafts.

- Amelia Earhart of Atchison was the first woman to fly solo across the Atlantic Ocean. She disappeared with her plane in 1937 as she attempted to fly around the world.

- The geographical center of the 48 contiguous states is in Kansas. A group of citizens hired engineers to determine its location. A limestone column marks the spot, which is in a pasture two miles west of Lebanon.

- The American buffalo is the state animal.

Population (in millions)

Years	Population
1960	2.13
1970	2.25
1980	2.36
1990	2.48

Fresh Water Used
2,460 gallons/day/ person (average)

Garbage
3,500,000 tons per year
8% recycled

Kentucky

The Bluegrass State

Became the 15th state on June 1, 1792

State Flower
Goldenrod

Daniel Boone

Fabulous Facts!

- The vault in the Bullion Depository, in Fort Knox, contains more than 6 billion dollars in gold bullion. This represents a large part of the gold owned by the United States government.

- Daniel Boone explored much of Kentucky. He and a group of settlers founded Boonesborough. The trail he blazed is called the Wilderness Road.

- One of the most popular songs is "Happy Birthday." It was written in 1893 by Kentucky teachers Mildred and Patty Hill, who were sisters.

The navy-blue flag pictures the state seal. On it a frontiersman and a statesman are shaking hands to show they can help everyone by working together. Goldenrod, the state flower, is at the lower half of the picture.

Garbage
3,750,000 tons per year 15% recycled

Fresh Water Used
1,170 gallons/day/ person (average)

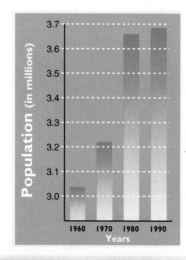

Population (in millions)

3.7
3.6
3.5
3.4
3.3
3.2
3.1
3.0

1960 1970 1980 1990

Years

Key

Capital ★Frankfort

Three largest cities
1. Louisville
2. Lexington
3. Owensboro

Smallest town
Dycusburg
Population 41

Geography

+ Highest elevation
  Black Mountain
  4,139 ft above sea level

− Lowest point
  Mississippi River in
  Fulton County
  257 ft above sea level

Land Between The Lakes
Appalachian Mountains
Cumberland Plateau

Economy

First in the nation in
 burley tobacco

A leading state in
 coal
 racehorses
 trucks

Historic Sites

 Fort Knox
 Harrodsburg
 Cumberland Gap
 Burkesville
 Booneville

358

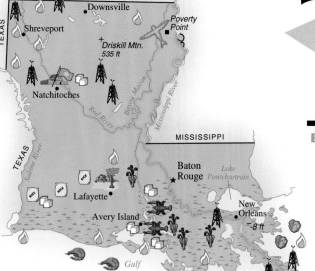

The Pelican State

Became the 18th state on April 30, 1812

State Flower
Magnolia

Key

Capital ★Baton Rouge
Three largest cities
1. New Orleans
2. Baton Rouge
3. Shreveport
Smallest town
Downsville
Population 101

Geography
+ Highest elevation
  Driskill Mountain
  535 ft above sea level
− Lowest point
  New Orleans
  8 ft below sea level
Mississippi Delta
Lake Pontchartrain
Mississippi River
Red River

The state flag features the pelican. It is the state bird, and Louisiana is known as the Pelican State. The picture features a mother pelican in a nest, feeding her young. This shows the state cares for its people and resources.

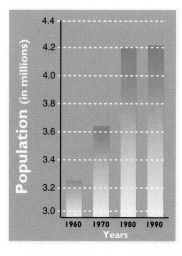

Economy

First in the nation in
 crayfish
shrimp
common salt

A leading state in
oysters   sugar cane
petroleum   rice
natural gas

Historic Sites
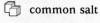 Lafayette
 Poverty Point
 Natchitoches

Fabulous Facts!

- More crayfish are produced here than anywhere else in the world. About 87% of all crayfish produced in the United States comes from Louisiana.

- Louisiana played a major role in the United States space program. The Saturn rocket that launched the astronauts to the moon in 1969 was built in New Orleans.

- Hot pepper sauce was first made here in 1868 with seeds brought from Tabasco, Mexico. It is still made on Avery Island. It is used to spice Cajun and Creole dishes.

Population (in millions) vs **Years**
4.4, 4.2, 4.0, 3.8, 3.6, 3.4, 3.2, 3.0
1960 1970 1980 1990

Garbage
3,323,000 tons per year
8% recycled

Fresh Water Used
2,200 gallons/day/person (average)

359

Maine

The Pine Tree State

Became the 23rd state on March 15, 1820

State Bird
Chickadee

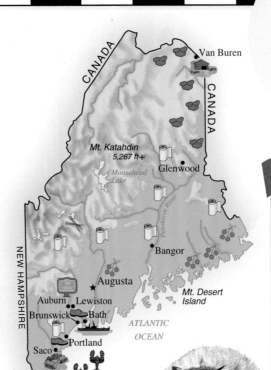

CANADA
CANADA
NEW HAMPSHIRE

Van Buren

Mt. Katahdin
5,267 ft+

Moosehead Lake

Glenwood

Penobscot River

Bangor

Augusta

Auburn   Lewiston
Brunswick   Bath
Saco   Portland

York

Mt. Desert Island

ATLANTIC OCEAN

Fabulous Facts!

- Maine makes more toothpicks than any other state. It produces 50 billion per year, which is more than 100 million per day.

- More than 90% of the state is covered with forests. This is the highest percentage of any state.

- Harriet Beecher Stowe wrote *Uncle Tom's Cabin* in 1851 while living in Brunswick.

- The official state cat is the Maine coon cat.

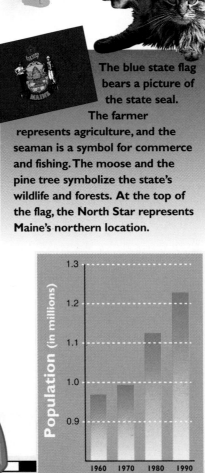

The blue state flag bears a picture of the state seal. The farmer represents agriculture, and the seaman is a symbol for commerce and fishing. The moose and the pine tree symbolize the state's wildlife and forests. At the top of the flag, the North Star represents Maine's northern location.

Key

Capital ★Augusta

Three largest cities
1. Portland
2. Lewiston
3. Bangor

Smallest town
Glenwood
Population 2

Geography

+ Highest elevation
Mt. Katahdin
5,267 ft above sea level

Penobscot River
Mt. Desert Island
Moosehead Lake

Economy

First in the nation in
- lobsters
- blueberries
- toothpicks
- paper products

A leading state in
- potatoes
- shoes

Historic Sites
- Auburn
- York
- Saco
- Bath (shipbuilding)
- Van Buren

Fresh Water Used
433 gallons/day/person (average)

Garbage
1,293,000 tons per year
33% recycled

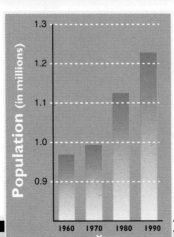

Population (in millions)

1.3
1.2
1.1
1.0
0.9

1960 1970 1980 1990
Years

MD

PENNSYLVANIA

WEST VIRGINIA

ALLEGHENY MTNS.

Potomac River

Hancock

Backbone Mtn. 3,360 ft

Antietam

BLUE RIDGE MTNS.

Baltimore

Columbia

Ft. McHenry

Silver Spring

Annapolis

Kent Island

VIRGINIA

DELAWARE

District Of Columbia

Port Tobacco

St. Marys City

Chesapeake Bay

Assateague Island

VIRGINIA

Maryland

The Old Line State

Became the 7th state on April 28, 1788

State Bird
Baltimore Oriole

Key

Capital
★Annapolis

Three largest cities
1. Baltimore
2. Silver Spring
3. Columbia

Smallest town
    Port Tobacco
    Population 21

Geography
+ Highest Elevation
    Backbone Mountain
        3,360 ft above sea level
Chesapeake Bay
Assateague Island
Potomac River
Allegheny Mountains
Blue Ridge Mountains
Patuxent River

The flag pictures the coats of arms of two families related to Lord Baltimore, who helped found the state. The black and yellow colors and design are for the Calvert family. The red and white colors and design represent the Crossland family.

Fabulous Facts!

- Maryland is well known for its crabs and oysters. It is the number-one state in the sale of soft-shell crabs.

- Mary Pickersgill sewed by hand a huge flag of the United States. It measured 30 ft by 42 ft and flew over Fort McHenry during the War of 1812. This flag inspired Francis Scott Key to write "The Star-Spangled Banner."

- Maryland has a state dog. It is the Chesapeake Bay retriever.

- The official state sport is jousting. This is featured at the annual Renaissance Festival in Crownsville.

Economy

First in the nation in
    🦁 sale of soft-shell crabs

A leading state in
    🐔 broiler chickens
    🐚 oysters   🦀 blue crabs

Historic Sites
    Antietam
    Assateague Island
    Kent Island
    St. Marys City

Population (in millions)

5.0
4.5
4.0
3.5
3.0

1960 1970 1980 1990
Years

Fresh Water Used
307 gallons/day/ person (average)

Garbage
5,200,000 tons per year
26% recycled

361

MA

The Bay State

Became the 6th state on February 6, 1788

State Bird
Chickadee

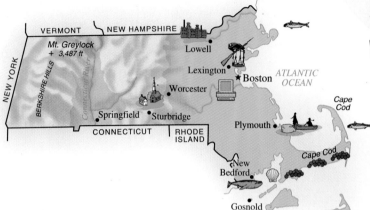

Key 🔑

Capital ★Boston
Three largest cities
1. Boston
2. Worcester
3. Springfield
Smallest town
Gosnold
Population 42

Geography
+ Highest elevation
  Mt. Greylock
    3,487 ft above sea level
Cape Cod
Berkshire Hills
Connecticut River

Fabulous Facts!

- Massachusetts grows about half the nation's cranberries: about 200 million pounds, or 90 billion berries per year.

- Susan B. Anthony, a women's rights leader, was born here in 1820. She was arrested in 1872 for voting.

- Basketball was invented in 1891 in Springfield.

- Dr. Seuss, author of many famous children's books, was born here. His real name was Theodor Seuss Geisel.

The flag shows a Native American on a blue shield. He has an arrow pointing down, which stands for peace. The star means that Massachusetts was one of the original 13 colonies. Above the shield an arm holds a sword. This represents the state motto, By the sword we seek peace.

Economy
First in the nation in
🐚 scallops
A leading state in
🫐 cranberries
💻 computers
🐟 fishing

Historic Sites
⚓ Plymouth
🏛 Lexington
🏚 Sturbridge
🏭 Lowell
🐟 New Bedford

Cranberries

Garbage
6,750,000 tons per year
32% recycled

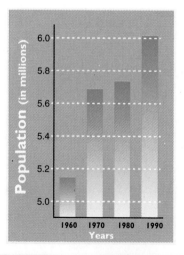
Population (in millions)
6.0
5.8
5.6
5.4
5.2
5.0
1960 1970 1980 1990
Years

Fresh Water Used
338 gallons/day/person (average)

MI

Michigan

The Wolverine State

Became the 26th state on January 26, 1837

State Flower
Apple Blossom

Map labels

Isle Royale
Lake Superior
Copper Range
Mt. Arvon +1,979 ft
CANADA
Sault Ste. Marie
WISCONSIN
Upper Peninsula
Mackinac Island
Mackinaw City
Lake Michigan
Lake Huron
Grand Rapids
Lower Peninsula
Eagle
Holland
Lansing
Warren
Detroit
Dearborn
Battle Creek
INDIANA
OHIO
571 ft
Lake Erie
CANADA

Key

Capital ★Lansing

Three largest cities
1. Detroit
2. Grand Rapids
3. Warren

Smallest town
  Eagle
  Population 103

Geography
+ Highest elevation
  Mt. Arvon
    1,979 ft above sea level
− Lowest point
  Lake Erie
    571 ft above sea level
Upper Peninsula
Lower Peninsula
Copper Range
Isle Royale

Economy

First in the nation in
- automobile production
- tart cherries
- cucumbers for pickles

A leading state in
- breakfast cereals
- dried beans
- iron ore
- milk
- steel production

Historic Sites
- Sault Ste. Marie
- Dearborn
- Mackinac Island
- Holland
- Mackinaw City

The state flag is based on the state seal. It shows three mottoes. The eagle represents the United States. The elk and moose represent the state. The man is pictured with his hand raised as a sign of peace.

TUEBOR
CIRCUMSPICE

Fabulous Facts!

- Factories in Michigan produce about 1/4 of all cars and trucks made in the United States.

- Ralph J. Bunche, who was the first African American to win the Nobel Peace Prize, was born here. He helped found the United Nations.

- Battle Creek is the number-one city in the world for producing breakfast cereals.

Population graph

Population (in millions)

9.4
9.2
9.0
8.8
8.6
8.4
8.2
8.0
7.8

1960 1970 1980 1990
Years

Fresh Water Used
1,250 gallons/day/person (average)

Garbage
13,700,000 tons per year
20% recycled

Minnesota

The Gopher State

Became the 32nd state on May 11, 1858

State Bird
Common Loon

CANADA
Lake of the Woods
NORTH DAKOTA
CANADA
Upper Red Lake
Lower Red Lake
Lake Itasca
Grand Rapids
Mesabi Range
Eagle Mt. 2,301 ft
Lake Superior
600 ft
Red River of the North
Mississippi River
WISCONSIN
Tenney
Fort St. Anthony
Minneapolis
Bloomington
St. Paul
Minnesota River
Mississippi River
Pipestone
SOUTH DAKOTA
IOWA

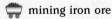
Gopher

Key

Capital ★St. Paul
Three largest cities
1. Minneapolis
2. St. Paul
3. Bloomington

Smallest town
Tenney
Population 7

Geography
+ Highest elevation
  Eagle Mountain
  2,301 ft above sea level
Lowest point
  Lake Superior
– 600 ft above sea level
Red Lake
Mesabi Range

Fabulous Facts!

- Minnesota provides about 80% of the nation's iron ore.

- In 1889, William Mayo and his two sons founded the Mayo Clinic in Minnesota. It is a world-known medical center.

- A fountain shaped like a giant spoon and cherry is featured at the Minneapolis Sculpture Garden. It is $51\frac{1}{2}$ ft high.

- Minnesota has more than 15,000 lakes.

The state flag shows a farmer plowing and a Native American hunting. The three dates shown are important days in Minnesota's history. The nineteen stars mean that Minnesota was the 19th state added to the Union after the original 13.

Economy

First in the nation in
- mining iron ore
- sugar beets

A leading state in
- beef meatpacking
- flour
- milk, butter, and cheese
- hogs
- corn
- soybeans

Historic Sites
- Grand Rapids
- Lake Itasca, source of Mississippi River
- Pipestone
- Fort St. Anthony

Sugar beets

Garbage 4,600,000 tons per year 44% recycled

Fresh Water Used 748 gallons/day/person (average)

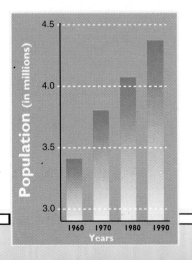
Population (in millions)
4.5
4.0
3.5
3.0
1960 1970 1980 1990
Years

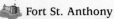

Mississippi

The Magnolia State

Became the 20th state on December 10, 1817

State Flower
Magnolia

Key

Capital ★Jackson

Three largest cities

1. Jackson
2. Biloxi
3. Greenville

Smallest town
Satartia
Population 58

Geography

+ Highest elevation
Woodall Mountain
806 ft above sea level
Mississippi River
Yazoo River
Pearl River
Delta
Tennessee River Hills

Economy

First in the nation in
🐟 farm-raised catfish

A leading state in

🦐 shrimp   🌿 soybeans
🌱 cotton   🪵 lumber
🐔 broiler chickens
🌾 rice
🚢 shipbuilding

Historic Sites

🏠 Ocean Springs
🏛 Vicksburg
🏚 Pascagoula
🏛 Natchez
🏯 Greenwood
⛪ Tinsley

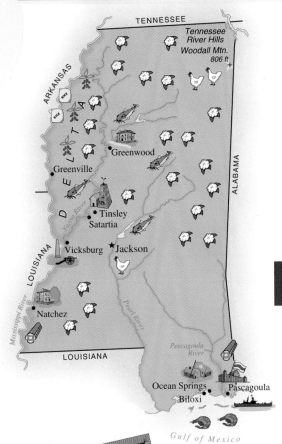

The upper left corner of the flag shows the Battle Flag of the Confederacy. The bars of red, white, and blue are the colors of the United States flag.

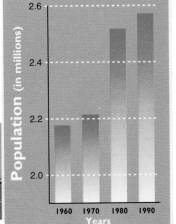

Fabulous Facts!

- Mississippi leads the country in raising catfish. They are raised and cared for in former cotton fields that were flooded.

- The very first Memorial Day, originally called Decoration Day, was celebrated in Columbus as a holiday in 1866, after the Civil War.

- Pascagoula River is known as the Singing River. At one point along the river, the water makes mysterious music that sounds like a swarm of bees in flight.

- Steamboats travel up and down the Mississippi River.

Population (in millions) — Years 1960, 1970, 1980, 1990

Fresh Water Used
1,290 gallons/day/person
(average)

Garbage
2,200,000 tons per year
11% recycled

Missouri

The Show Me State

Became the 24th state on August 10, 1821

State Flower
Hawthorn

Map

NEBRASKA
IOWA
ILLINOIS

St. Joseph
Florida
Missouri River
Independence
Kansas City
Washington
St. Louis
OSAGE
PLAINS
Jefferson City
Ste. Genevieve
KANSAS
Springfield
Taum Sauk Mtn. 1,772 ft
St. Francois Mountains
Mississippi River
OKLAHOMA
OZARK PLATEAU
St. Francis River
TENNESSEE
KENTUCKY
ARKANSAS
230 ft

Pony Express rider

Fabulous Facts!

- The world's largest producer of corncob pipes is Washington, Missouri. Factories there make about 7,000 corncob pipes each day.

- In 1860 a mail service called the Pony Express began. Riders on horseback took mail between St. Joseph, Missouri, and Sacramento, California. It took ten days.

- Mark Twain, author of *The Adventures of Tom Sawyer*, was born here. His real name was Samuel Langhorne Clemens. *Mark twain* was a river term that meant a water depth of 12 ft.

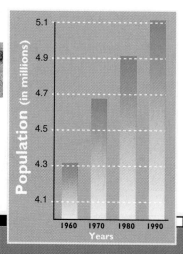

The red, white, and blue bars of the state flag stand for loyalty to the Union. A picture of the state seal is in the center. It shows two grizzly bears. They represent courage. The twenty-four stars mean that Missouri became the 24th state.

Garbage
5,600,000 tons per year
17% recycled

Fresh Water Used
1,150 gallons/day/person (average)

Population (in millions)

5.1
4.9
4.7
4.5
4.3
4.1

1960 1970 1980 1990
Years

Key

MO

Capital
★ Jefferson City

Three largest cities
1. Kansas City
2. St. Louis
3. Springfield

Smallest town
Florida
Population 2

Geography
+ Highest elevation
Taum Sauk Mountain
1,772 ft above sea level

− Lowest point
St. Francis River in Dunklin County
230 ft above sea level

Ozark Plateau
Osage Plains
St. Francois Mountains

Economy

First in the nation in

 lead

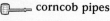 corncob pipes

A leading state in

 corn

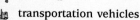 soybeans

 breeding mules

 transportation vehicles

 flour

 hogs

beef cattle

hats

greeting cards

Historic Sites

 St. Joseph

Ste. Genevieve

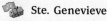 Independence

366

MT

The Treasure State

Became the 41st state on November 8, 1889

Key

Capital ★Helena

Three largest cities
1. **Billings**
2. **Great Falls**
3. **Missoula**

Smallest town
Ismay
Population 20

Geography
+ **Highest elevation**
  Granite Peak
  12,799 ft above sea level
− **Lowest point**
  Kootenai River in Lincoln County
  1,800 ft above sea level
Rocky Mountains
Great Plains

Economy
First in the nation in
- gem sapphires
- platinum

A leading state in
- Christmas trees
- silver, gold, lead
- cattle ranching
- coal
- copper
- wheat

Historic Sites
- Hamilton
- Virginia City
- Little Bighorn
- Butte (copper)
- Grasshopper Creek (gold)
- Glacier National Park
- Yellowstone National Park

Map labels: CANADA, Kootenai R. 1,800 ft, Glacier National Park, Flathead Lake, ROCKY MOUNTAINS, Great Falls, Missouri River, GREAT PLAINS, NORTH DAKOTA, Missoula, Helena, Butte, Hamilton, Billings, Yellowstone River, Ismay, SOUTH DAKOTA, Granite Peak 12,799 ft, Little Bighorn, Grasshopper Creek, Virginia City, WYOMING, Yellowstone National Park, Grasshopper Glacier, IDAHO

State Bird
Western Meadowlark

MONTANA

The state flag pictures the state seal on a field of blue. It show mountain scenery. Montana is a Spanish word that means "mountain." The pick stands for mining, and the plow stands for farming.

Fabulous Facts!

- More gem sapphires are found here than in any other state. Visitors can dig for them and keep what they find.

- Butte has been called the Richest Hill on Earth. Between 1864 and 1983, 20 billion pounds of copper were mined here.

- Large numbers of grasshoppers became trapped and frozen in a glacier long ago. It is called Grasshopper Glacier, near Granite Peak.

- The state animal is the grizzly bear.

Population graph (in thousands): 1960, 1970, 1980, 1990 — Years. Values range 650 to 800.

Fresh Water Used
11,600 gallons/day/person (average)

Garbage
790,000 tons per year
6% recycled

Nebraska

The Cornhusker State

Became the 37th state on March 1, 1867

State Flower
Goldenrod

Fabulous Facts!

- Farms make up 95% of the state's area, more than any other state.

- One of the world's first rodeos was held in North Platte in July 1882. It starred its founder, William "Buffalo Bill" Cody.

- The first Arbor Day was celebrated here in 1872. More than 1 million trees were planted on that day.

The state flag pictures the state seal on a field of blue. It shows a blacksmith, a settler's cabin, a steamboat, and a train. The Rocky Mountains are in the background, although they are not in Nebraska.

Economy

First in the nation in

   highest percent of land used for farming

A leading state in

   beef cattle   soybeans

   food processing

   corn

   hogs

Historic Sites

   Bellevue (oldest town)

   Fort Atkinson

   Beatrice

   Brownville (river port)

   Grand Island (railroad town)

Fresh Water Used
5,660 gallons/day/
person (average)

Garbage
1,650,000 tons per year
19% recycled

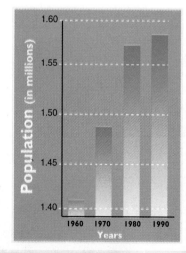

Population (in millions)

1.60
1.55
1.50
1.45
1.40

1960 1970 1980 1990
Years

NV

Nevada

The Silver State

Became the 36th state on October 31, 1864

State Bird
Mountain Bluebird

Map labels:
OREGON | IDAHO
CALIFORNIA
UTAH
Humboldt River
Pyramid Lake
Reno
Virginia City
Lake Tahoe
Carson City
Gabbs
Austin
GREAT BASIN
Boundary Peak 13,140 ft
Rhyolite
CALIFORNIA
Devil's Hole
Las Vegas
Henderson
Paradise Valley
Hoover Dam
Lake Mead
Colorado River
ARIZONA
479 ft

Key

Capital ★Carson City

Three largest cities
1. Las Vegas
2. Reno
3. Henderson

Smallest town
Gabbs
Population 367

Geography
+ Highest elevation
  Boundary Peak
  13,140 ft above sea level
− Lowest point
  Colorado River in Clark County
  479 ft above sea level

Great Basin
Lake Tahoe
Humboldt River

Hoover Dam

Economy

First in the nation in
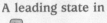 gold
 silver
 mercury

A leading state in
 turquoise

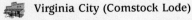
Gold nugget

Historic Sites
 Virginia City (Comstock Lode)
Austin
Hoover Dam
Rhyolite (ghost town)

A large silver star is in the upper left corner of the blue flag. It represents silver, the state metal. The words *Battle Born* mean that Nevada became a state during the Civil War.

Fabulous Facts!

- Tourism is the most important source of income for the state. Every year, 30 million visitors enjoy Nevada, spending $7 billion a year.

- Many of the state's sheepherders and cowboys are Basques from the French and Spanish Pyrenees. They were attracted to the mountain villages and farms.

- Several rare species of fish live here. They include the cui-ui, found only in Pyramid Lake, and the Devil's Hole pupfish, found only in Devil's Hole.

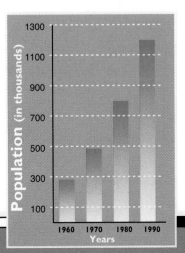

Population (in thousands) — Years: 1960, 1970, 1980, 1990

Fresh Water Used
2,780 gallons/day/person (average)

Garbage
2,420,000 tons per year
17% recycled

369

The Granite State

Became the 9th state on June 21, 1788

State Bird
Purple Finch

Fabulous Facts!

- Paper companies own more than a half million acres of land here.

- New Hampshire became the first of the 13 colonies to declare its independence from Great Britain on January 5, 1776.

- Two famous astronauts were born here—Alan B. Shepard, Jr., and Christa McAuliffe.

- Sarah Josepha Hale was born here in 1788. She wrote the poem "Mary's Lamb," which became a famous nursery rhyme.

- The state animal is the white-tailed deer.

Fresh Water Used
378 gallons/day/person (average)

Garbage
1,032,000 tons per year
16% recycled

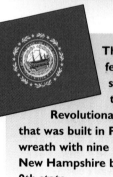
Old Man of the Mountains

Map labels
CANADA
Mt. Washington 6,288 ft
WHITE MOUNTAINS
Hart's Location
Old Man of the Mountains
Flume
VERMONT
MAINE
Lake Winnipesaukee
Merrimack River
Connecticut River
Cornish Flat
Concord
Dover
Portsmouth
Manchester
ATLANTIC OCEAN
Nashua
MASSACHUSETTS

The state flag features the state seal. It pictures the *Raleigh*, a Revolutionary War warship that was built in Portsmouth. The wreath with nine stars represents New Hampshire becoming the 9th state.

NH

Key

Capital ★Concord
Three largest cities
1. Manchester
2. Nashua
3. Concord
Smallest town
Hart's Location
Population 33

Geography
+ Highest elevation
Mt. Washington
6,288 ft above sea level
Coastline, the shortest of all 50 states, 13 miles long
White Mountains
Old Man of the Mountains
Lake Winnipesaukee
Flume (deep narrow valley)
Connecticut River

Economy
A leading state in
🍯 maple syrup
Important products
🥛 milk
💻 computers
🧻 paper goods
🧱 granite

Historic Sites
🏛 Strawbery Banke (Portsmouth)
Dover   Cornish Flat
Mt. Washington (cog railway)

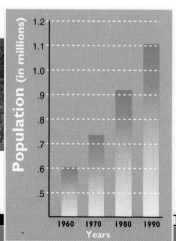

Population (in millions)
1.2
1.1
1.0
.9
.8
.7
.6
.5
1960 1970 1980 1990
Years

The Garden State

Became the 3rd state on December 18, 1787

State Bird
Eastern Goldfinch

Map labels

High Point 1,803 ft
KITTATINNY MTNS.
APPALACHIAN VALLEY
NEW YORK
Pahaquarry
Delaware Water Gap
NEW JERSEY HIGHLANDS
Paterson
Morristown
Hudson River
PIEDMONT PLATEAU
Newark
Jersey City
Menlo Park
Batsto Historic Village
Sandy Hook Bay
PENNSYLVANIA
Princeton
Delaware River
Trenton
ATLANTIC COASTAL PLAIN
ATLANTIC OCEAN
DELAWARE
PINELANDS
Atlantic City
Delaware Bay
Cape May

Key

Capital ★Trenton

Three largest cities
1. Newark
2. Jersey City
3. Paterson

Smallest town
Pahaquarry
Population 8

Geography
+ Highest elevation
High Point
1,803 ft above sea level
Pinelands
Kittatinny Mountains
Delaware Water Gap
Appalachian Valley

Economy

First in the nation in
- chemical production
- medicines

A leading state in
- peaches
- tomatoes
- blueberries
- cranberries
- clams

Historic Sites
- Morristown
- Menlo Park
- Princeton
- Atlantic City
- Sandy Hook Bay
- Batsto Historic Village

State Flag

The color of the state flag is the color General George Washington and his troops wore during the Revolutionary War. The picture is from the state seal. The women represent liberty and farming. The horse's head represents strength and speed in peace and war.

Fabulous Facts!

- New Jersey is one of the top ten manufacturing and food-packaging states.

- General George Washington and his troops crossed the icy Delaware River by boat on December 25, 1776. The next day his forces surprised and defeated enemy soldiers in Trenton, who were busy celebrating the holiday.

- Thomas Edison invented the light bulb here in 1879. He also invented wax paper and a talking doll.

Population (in millions)

Years	Population
1960	6.0
1970	7.15
1980	7.35
1990	7.75

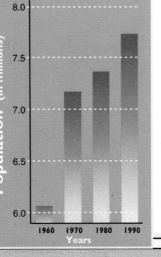

Garbage
7,400,000 tons per year
41% recycled

Fresh Water Used
287 gallons/day/person (average)

New Mexico

The Land of Enchantment

Became the 47th state on January 6, 1912

State Bird
Roadrunner

NM

Map

COLORADO
OK
Wheeler Peak
13,161 ft
Grenville
Los Alamos
Taos
Pueblo Bonito
Santa Fe Trail
Santa Fe
ROCKY MOUNTAINS
Pecos River
Albuquerque
GREAT PLAINS
TEXAS
ARIZONA
Rio Grande
Alamogordo
Las Cruces
Carlsbad Caverns
2,842 ft
TEXAS
MEXICO
Red Bluff Reservoir

Chilies

Key

Capital ★Santa Fe

Three largest cities
1. Albuquerque
2. Las Cruces
3. Santa Fe

Smallest town
Grenville
Population 30

Geography
+ Highest elevation
  Wheeler Peak
  13,161 ft above sea level
- Lowest point
  Red Bluff Reservoir
  2,842 ft above sea level

Rocky Mountains
Great Plains
Rio Grande
Pecos River
Carlsbad Caverns

Fabulous Facts!

- Cattle and sheep ranching are important here. With about 2 million farm animals, New Mexico has more livestock than people.

- In the 1100s the Anasazi, ancestors of Pueblo Indians, had an advanced civilization. They built houses with many stories, grew corn and cotton, and trained dogs for hunting.

- A black bear cub was rescued from a forest fire in Lincoln National Forest in 1950. Firefighters named him Smokey Bear, and he became the symbol of forest fire prevention.

The ancient sun symbol of the Zia Pueblo Indians is featured on the state flag. It stands for friendship and peace. The sun is red, and the background is gold. Both are colors of Spain's flag. Spain once ruled this area.

Fresh Water Used
2,300 gallons/day/person (average)

Garbage
1,880,000 tons per year
9% recycled

Population Graph

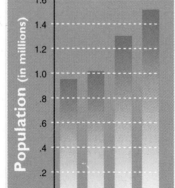

Population (in millions)

1.6
1.4
1.2
1.0
.8
.6
.4
.2

1960 1970 1980 1990

Years

Economy

First in the nation in
🌶 chilies
P potash

A leading state in
⛽ natural gas
🛢 oil
copper
⚛ atomic research
☢ uranium

Historic Sites
🏺 Taos
Alamogordo
🚂 Santa Fe Trail
Los Alamos
Pueblo Bonito

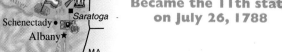

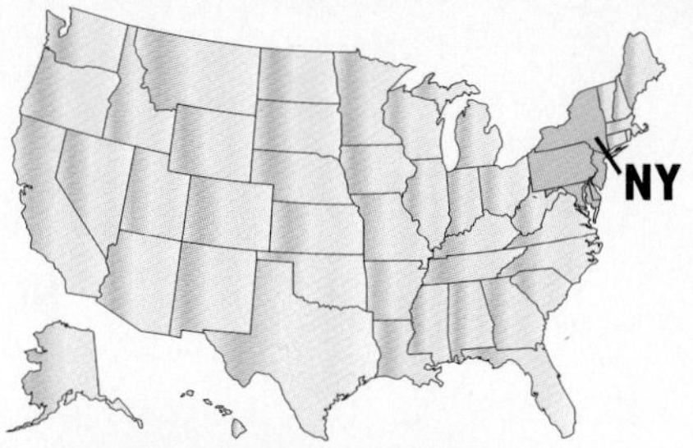
NY

New York

The Empire State

Became the 11th state on July 26, 1788

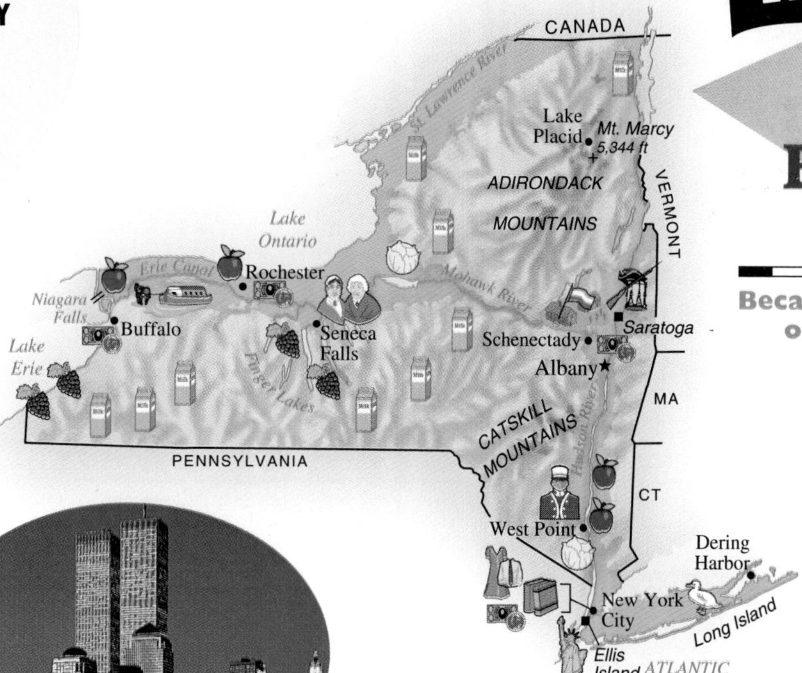
CANADA
St. Lawrence River
Lake Placid
Mt. Marcy 5,344 ft
ADIRONDACK MOUNTAINS
VERMONT
Lake Ontario
Erie Canal
Rochester
Niagara Falls
Buffalo
Lake Erie
Seneca Falls
Finger Lakes
Mohawk River
Schenectady
Saratoga
Albany
MA
CATSKILL MOUNTAINS
Hudson River
PENNSYLVANIA
CT
West Point
Dering Harbor
New York City
Long Island
Ellis Island
ATLANTIC OCEAN

Key

Capital ★Albany

Three largest cities

1. New York City
2. Buffalo
3. Rochester

Smallest town

Dering Harbor
Population 28

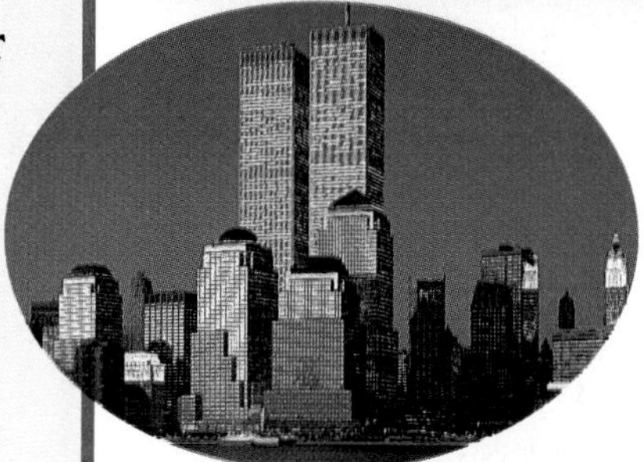

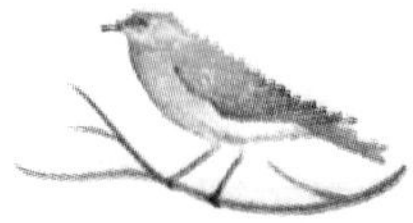

State Bird
Bluebird

Geography

\+ Highest elevation Mt. Marcy
5,344 ft above sea level

Adirondack Mountains
Catskill Mountains
Finger Lakes
Long Island
Niagara Falls

Fabulous Facts!

- New York City is the nation's leading financial center. About 724,000 New Yorkers work in finance and business.
- Sojourner Truth was born a slave here about 1797. She was the first African American to speak publicly against slavery. Her real name was Isabella Baumfree.
- The Winter Olympic Games have been held here twice at Lake Placid, in 1932 and in 1980.

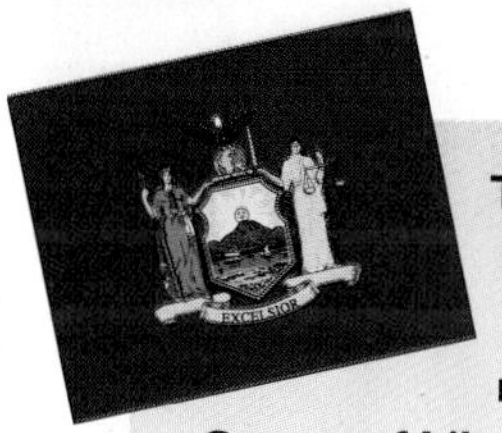
EXCELSIOR

The state flag pictures two women. One reminds us of the Statue of Liberty. The other stands for equal treatment of all people under the law.

Economy

First in the nation in

- clothing manufacturing
- books
- banking
- cabbages
- raising ducks

A leading state in

- milk
- apples
- grapes

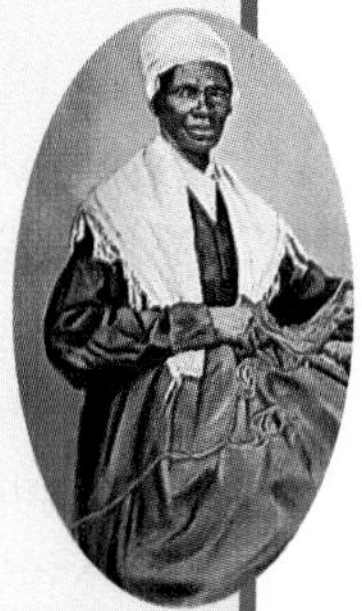

Historic Sites

- Saratoga
- Schenectady
- Seneca Falls
- Ellis Island
- Erie Canal
- West Point

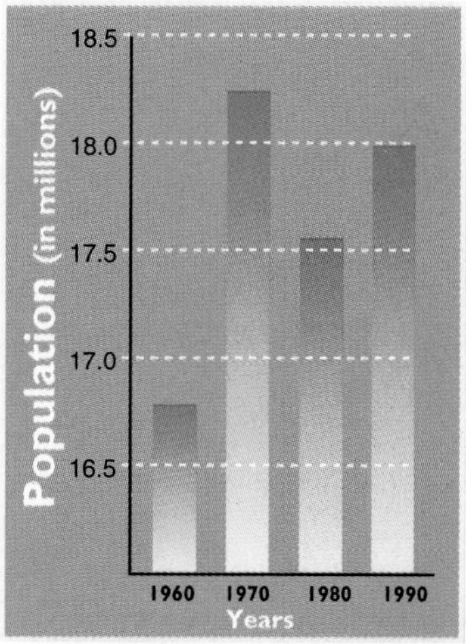
18.5
18.0
17.5
17.0
16.5
Population (in millions)
1960
1970
1980
1990
Years

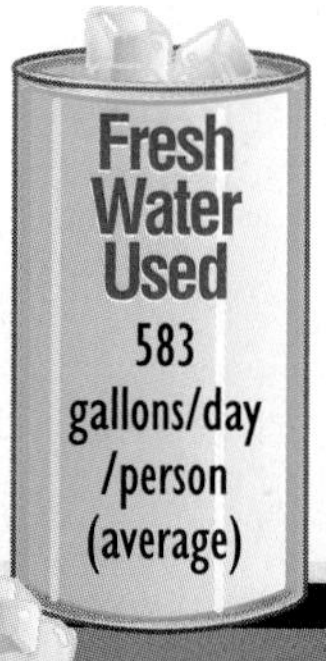
Fresh Water Used
583 gallons/day /person (average)

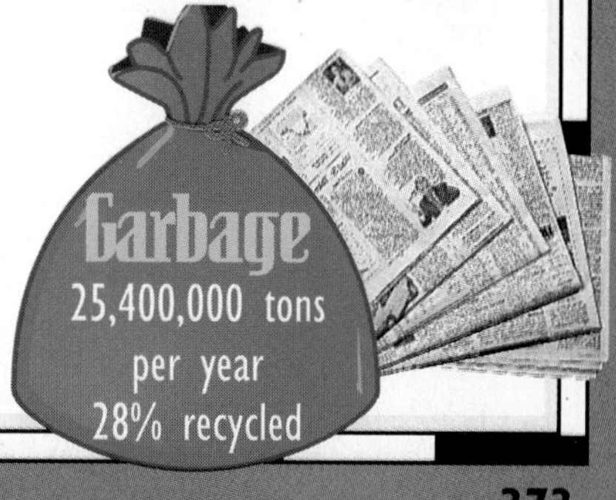
Garbage
25,400,000 tons per year
28% recycled

North Carolina

The Tar Heel State

Became the 12th state on November 21, 1789

State Flower
Flowering Dogwood

Map labels:
VIRGINIA
TENNESSEE
GREAT SMOKY MTNS.
APPALACHIAN MTNS.
BLUE RIDGE MTNS.
+ Mt. Mitchell 6,684 ft
Cherokee
Winston-Salem
Greensboro
Durham
★ Raleigh
Dellview
Charlotte
Greenville
Bath
Roanoke River
Kitty Hawk
Roanoke Island
Outer Banks
GEORGIA
SOUTH CAROLINA
SOUTH CAROLINA
Cape Fear River
Wilmington
ATLANTIC OCEAN

Fabulous Facts!

- One of the largest denim mills in the world is in Greensboro. It produces enough denim each year to go around the world twice.

- Virginia Dare, the first English baby born in America, was born on Roanoke Island on August 18, 1587.

- Part of the Wright brothers' first airplane is on the moon. Astronauts Neil Armstrong and Buzz Aldrin placed it there in 1969, when they became the first people to land on the moon.

Flag text: MAY 20th 1775 N * C APRIL 12th 1776

The state flag displays two dates that are important to the state's history. May 20, 1775, is the date of the Mecklenburg Declaration of Independence from Great Britain. On April 12, 1776, the state allowed its delegates to go to the Continental Congress to vote for independence.

Fresh Water Used
1,350 gallons/day/person (average)

Garbage
7,754,000 tons per year
8% recycled

Key

Capital ★ Raleigh
Three largest cities
1. Charlotte
2. Raleigh
3. Greensboro
Smallest town
Dellview
Population 16

Geography
+ Highest elevation
Mt. Mitchell
6,684 ft above sea level
Blue Ridge Mountains
Great Smoky Mountains
Roanoke River
Outer Banks

Economy
First in the nation in
 tobacco
 sweet potatoes
 hard blue crabs
 turkeys
 textiles
 wooden furniture

Historic Sites
 Bath
 Roanoke Island
 Winston-Salem
Kitty Hawk (Wright brothers)

Bar graph:
Population (in millions)
7
6
5
4
3
2
1
1960 1970 1980 1990
Years

ND

The Flickertail State

Became the 39th state on November 2, 1889

Key

Capital ★ Bismarck

Three largest cities
1. Fargo
2. Grand Forks
3. Bismarck

Smallest town
Hove Mobile Park
Population 2

Geography
+ Highest elevation
  White Butte
  3,506 ft above sea level
− Lowest point
  Red River in
  Pembina County
  750 ft above sea level

Turtle Mountains
Red River Valley
Badlands
Great Plains
Drift Prairie

Economy

First in the nation in

 sunflower seeds
 flaxseed
 barley
dry edible beans
oats
lignite coal

Historic Sites

 Pembina
Tioga (oil)
 Medora
 Garrison Dam
 Mandan (Indian village)

CANADA

TURTLE MOUNTAINS

Tioga
Garrison
Garrison Dam
Medora
White Butte +
3,506 ft
Mandan
Bismarck

Lake Sakakawea
GREAT PLAINS
BADLANDS

MONTANA

DRIFT
PRAIRIE

Sheyenne River
Missouri River

Hove Mobile Park
Pembina — 750 ft
Grand Forks
Fargo

RED RIVER VALLEY
Red River
MINNESOTA

SOUTH DAKOTA

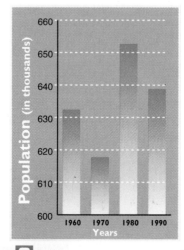

The picture on the state flag is similar to the **Great Seal of the United States.** It shows a bald eagle holding an olive branch. The eagle stands for freedom, and the branch stands for peace.

State Flower
Wild Prairie Rose

Fabulous Facts!

- The Red River Valley has some of the world's richest farmland. The state's economy depends heavily on agriculture.

- Cattle ranching became popular in the late 1800s. Even Theodore Roosevelt owned two ranches here before he became President of the United States.

- North Dakota shares the International Peace Garden with Manitoba, Canada. It is a park that lies in the United States and Canada and honors the friendship between the two countries.

Population (in thousands)
660
650
640
630
620
610
600
1960 1970 1980 1990
Years

Garbage
500,000 tons per year
18% recycled

Fresh Water Used
4,190 gallons/day/person (average)

Ohio

The Buckeye State

Became the 17th state on March 1, 1803

State Flower
Scarlet Carnation

OH

Map labels

MICHIGAN
Lake Erie
Toledo
Cleveland
Akron
PENNSYLVANIA
GREAT LAKES PLAINS
INDIANA
Zoar Village
Campbell Hill 1,549 ft
Coshocton
Columbus
Jacksonburgh
Dayton
Ohio River 455 ft
Cincinnati
Great Serpent Mound
Scioto River
Marietta
WEST VIRGINIA
KENTUCKY

Key

Capital ★ Columbus

Three largest cities
1. Columbus
2. Cleveland
3. Cincinnati

Smallest town
Jacksonburgh
Population 52

Geography
+ Highest elevation
  Campbell Hill
  1,549 ft above sea level
– Lowest point
  Ohio River in Hamilton County
  455 ft above sea level

Scioto River
Great Lakes Plains

Fabulous Facts!

- Ohio is a leading state in manufacturing, farming, and mining.

- One of the best prehistoric structures in the world is the Great Serpent Mound. It is shaped like a giant snake and is four feet tall and more than a quarter mile long.

- In 1869 the Cincinnati Red Stockings became the first professional baseball team in the United States.

- Tomato juice is the state beverage.

Ohio's state flag has an unusual shape. It is called a burgee. The triangles stand for Ohio's hills and valleys. The stripes stand for the roads and waterways. Seventeen stars mean Ohio became the 17th state. The large circle recalls the first letter in the name Ohio.

Economy

First in the nation in
- sandstone
- lime (made from limestone)
- household appliances

A leading state in
- motor vehicles
- coal
- steel
- salt
- corn
- tomatoes
- soybeans
- hogs

Historic Sites
 Marietta (oldest town)
Toledo
Dayton
Coshocton
Akron (rubber)
Zoar Village

Fresh Water Used
1,080 gallons/day/person (average)

Garbage
22,543,000 tons per year
32% recycled

Population (in millions)
11
10.5
10.0
9.5
9.0
1960 1970 1980 1990
Years

The Sooner State

COLORADO
KANSAS
MISSOURI
NEW MEXICO
Black Mesa Mtn. 4,973 ft
PANHANDLE
TEXAS
Enid
Bartlesville
Hoot Owl
GREAT PLAINS
Cimarron River
Tulsa
OZARK PLATEAU
Tahlequah
Guthrie
Oklahoma City
Canadian River
Anadarko
ARKANSAS
Lawton
OUACHITA MTNS.
Red River
289 ft
TEXAS

Became the 46th state on November 16, 1907

State Bird
Scissor-tailed Flycatcher

Key

Capital ★Oklahoma City

Three largest cities
1. Oklahoma City
2. Tulsa
3. Lawton

Smallest town
Hoot Owl
Population 0

Geography
+ Highest elevation
  Black Mesa Mountain
  4,973 ft above sea level
− Lowest point
  Little River in
  McCurtain County
  289 ft above sea level

Ouachita Mountains
Great Plains
Ozark Plateau
Panhandle

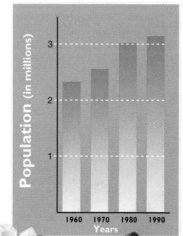

Mistletoe

Economy

First in the nation in
 iodine (useful to clean germs)
 gypsum

A leading state in
 beef cattle   peanuts
 wheat
 oil
 natural gas

Historic Sites
 Guthrie
Bartlesville
Tahlequah (headquarters of the
  Cherokee Nation)
Enid
 Anadarko

The battle shield of an Osage warrior is featured on the state flag. The peace pipe and the olive branch are peace symbols. The flag's background is blue, which is the color of the battle flag carried by Choctaw soldiers who fought for the Union during the Civil War.

OKLAHOMA

Fabulous Facts!

- Oklahoma's oil reserves are among the largest in the nation. Oil pumps operate even from the front lawn of the state capitol.

- Sequoyah, a Cherokee Indian, spent 12 years developing the first alphabet for an Indian language. It was used to publish newspapers and books in the Cherokee language. He lived near Sallisaw.

- On April 22, 1889, at 12 noon, the United States government opened up almost 2 million acres of land to settlers. By evening about 50,000 eager settlers had staked land claims in Oklahoma.

- Oklahoma has an unusual state flower. It is mistletoe.

Population (in millions)
3
2
1
1960 1970 1980 1990
Years

Fresh Water Used
452 gallons/day/person (average)

Garbage
2,500,000 tons per year
12% recycled

Oregon

The Beaver State

Became the 33rd state on February 14, 1859

Map labels: Astoria • Columbia River • WASHINGTON • HELLS CANYON • Portland • Oregon City • Salem • Mt. Hood 11,239 ft • Granite • Baker • Eugene • PACIFIC OCEAN • COAST RANGES • WILLAMETTE VALLEY • CASCADE RANGE • GREAT SANDY DESERT • Crater Lake • IDAHO • CALIFORNIA • NEVADA

State Flower
Oregon Grape

Fabulous Facts!

- Oregon earns more money from making wood products than from any other industry.

- During the mid-1840s, thousands of pioneers traveled west on the Oregon Trail. The trip was 2,000 miles long, from Independence, Missouri, to the Willamette Valley.

- Beverly Cleary, who writes stories for children, was born here. She created Ramona Quimby and Henry Huggins.

Oregon has a two-sided state flag. One side pictures the state seal. The thirty-three stars mean that Oregon was the 33rd state. The covered wagon honors the pioneers who settled the region. A picture of a beaver, the state animal, appears on the reverse side.

STATE OF OREGON 1859

Key

Capital ★Salem

Three largest cities
1. Portland
2. Eugene
3. Salem

Smallest town
Granite
Population 16

Geography

+ Highest elevation
Mt. Hood
11,239 ft above sea level
Crater Lake (deepest lake in the United States)
1,932 feet deep
Hells Canyon
Coast Ranges
Cascade Range
Great Sandy Desert
Willamette Valley

Economy

First in the nation in

 lumber production

 hazelnuts, also called filberts

 grass seeds

 nickel

 pumice

 peppermint oil

A leading state in

 salmon   shrimp

 sheep   potatoes

Historic Sites

Astoria

Oregon City

Baker

Fresh Water Used 2,970 gallons/day/person (average)

Garbage 3,255,000 tons per year 30% recycled

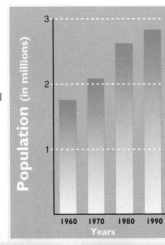

Population (in millions)

3

2

1

1960 1970 1980 1990
Years

The Keystone State

Became the 2nd state on December 12, 1787

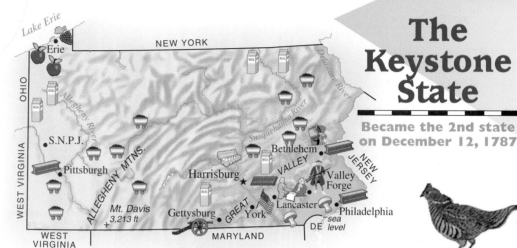

Key

Capital ★Harrisburg

Three largest cities
1. Philadelphia
2. Pittsburgh
3. Erie

Smallest town
S.N.P.J. (Slovenska Narodna Podporna Jednota)
Population 20

Geography
+ Highest elevation
  Mt. Davis
  3,213 ft above sea level
− Lowest point
  Delaware River in Delaware County
  at sea level

Blue Ridge Mountains
Allegheny Mountains
Great Valley

Economy

First in the nation in
- anthracite (hard coal in eastern part of state)
- mushrooms
- chocolate and cocoa products

A leading state in
- bituminous coal
- steel   - apples
- milk   - grapes
- eggs

Historic Sites
- Gettysburg (Civil War battle)
- Valley Forge   - York
- Lancaster   - Bethlehem

State Bird
Ruffed Grouse

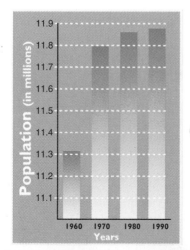

The state flag pictures the state seal, which is supported by two black horses. The sailing ship represents trade. The plow and three wheat sheaves represent farming and agriculture.

Fabulous Facts!

- Each year the United States Mint, in Philadelphia, issues more than 6 billion coins worth about $300 million. Most of the coins are pennies.

- In 1688 the Quakers of Germantown were the first people to protest against slavery in North America.

- The Little League World Series is played here every August.

- The 2,080 pound Liberty Bell rang out in Philadelphia on July 8, 1776, after the Declaration of Independence was signed.

Fresh Water Used
827 gallons/day/person (average)

Garbage
9,500,000 tons per year
20% recycled

Population (in millions)

11.9
11.8
11.7
11.6
11.5
11.4
11.3
11.2
11.1

1960 1970 1980 1990
Years

379

The Ocean State

Became the 13th state on May 29, 1790

State Flower
Violet

MASSACHUSETTS

Blackstone River

Jerimoth Hill 812 ft +

CONNECTICUT

Pawtucket
Providence ★
Cranston
Warwick

MASSACHUSETTS

Narragansett Bay

Portsmouth
Little Compton
Jamestown
Newport

Narragansett

COASTAL LOWLANDS

Block Island Sound

Block Island

RI

Fabulous Facts!

- The Providence area is the leading center in the nation for manufacturing inexpensive jewelry, called costume jewelry. The industry began here in 1794.

- The Arcade, in downtown Providence, is the oldest indoor shopping mall in the United States. Built in 1828, it has three levels and is still in use.

- On May 4, 1776, Rhode Island was the first state to declare its independence from Great Britain.

- Slater Mill, which was built by Samuel Slater in Pawtucket in 1793, has been called the Cradle of American Industry. It was the first water-powered cotton mill in the new nation.

HOPE

The state flag features a gold anchor, which is a symbol of hope and the state motto. The 13 gold stars represent the original 13 colonies.

Fresh Water Used
132 gallons/day/person
(average)

Garbage
1,062,000 tons per year
24% recycled

Key

Capital ★Providence
Three largest cities
1. Providence
2. Warwick
3. Cranston
Smallest town
Block Island
Population 820

Geography
+ Highest elevation
Jerimoth Hill in Providence County
812 ft above sea level
36 islands
Narragansett Bay
Blackstone River

Economy
First in the nation in
 costume jewelry production
 silverware production
Other important activities
 fishing
 poultry
 textiles
 toys

Rhode Island Red, the state bird

Historic Sites
 Pawtucket
 Newport
 Jamestown
 Narragansett

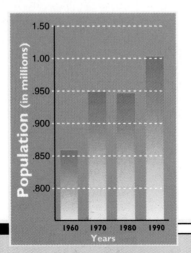

Population (in millions)

1.50
1.00
.950
.900
.850
.800

1960 1970 1980 1990
Years

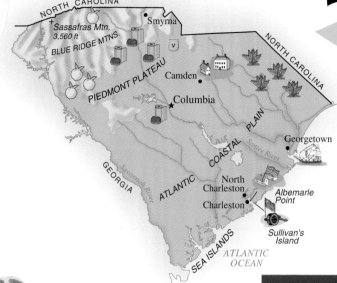

The Palmetto State

Became the 8th state on May 23, 1788

State Bird
Carolina Wren

Key

Capital ★ Columbia

Three largest cities
1. Columbia
2. Charleston
3. North Charleston

Smallest town
Smyrna
Population 57

Geography
+ Highest elevation
Sassafras Mountain
3,560 ft above sea level
Sea Islands
Atlantic Coastal Plain
Piedmont Plateau
Blue Ridge Mountains
Santee River

Economy

First in the nation in
 vermiculite

A leading state in
 textiles
 tobacco
 peaches

Historic Sites
 Albemarle Point
 Sullivans Island
 Georgetown
Camden

Fresh Water Used
1,720 gallons/day/
person (average)

The state flag features a silver crescent and the palmetto tree, which is the state tree. Soldiers of the Revolutionary War wore caps with crescents on them.

Fabulous Facts!

- South Carolina ranks among the leading textile-producing states. There are about 480 textile mills here.

- More battles of the American Revolution took place in South Carolina than in any other state.

- Peggy Parish, a children's author, was born here. She is known for her Amelia Bedelia books.

- A bright red flower from Mexico was brought to the United States by Joel Poinsett of South Carolina. It was named the poinsettia for him.

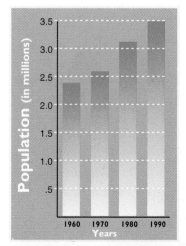

Population (in millions) — Years
1960 1970 1980 1990

Garbage 5,100,000 tons per year 9% recycled

South Dakota

The Mount Rushmore State

Became the 40th state on November 2, 1889

State Bird
Ring-necked Pheasant

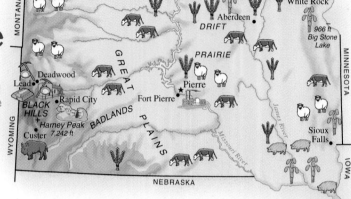

NORTH DAKOTA

MONTANA

White Rock

Aberdeen

DRIFT

966 ft
Big Stone
Lake

PRAIRIE

MINNESOTA

Deadwood
Lead

Pierre

BLACK
HILLS

Rapid City

Fort Pierre

Harney Peak

Custer 7,242 ft

BADLANDS

GREAT PLAINS

Missouri River

James River

Sioux
Falls

WYOMING

IOWA

NEBRASKA

Fabulous Facts!

- The Homestake Mine, in Lead, is one of the largest gold-producing mines in the Western Hemisphere. It produces about $160 million worth of gold a year.

- South Dakota renamed its Columbus Day holiday Native American Day in 1990. Now American Indians are honored instead of Christopher Columbus.

- South Dakota has more buffaloes than any other state. About 8,000 buffaloes roam in various areas in the state. They are pictured on old buffalo nickels.

The state flag features a picture of the state seal. The picture shows the state's early industries. The farmer represents agriculture; the cattle, ranching; the furnace, mining; and the riverboat, commerce. The new state nickname, The Mount Rushmore State, is written at the bottom.

Garbage
840,000 tons per year
20% recycled

Fresh Water Used
851 gallons/day/person
(average)

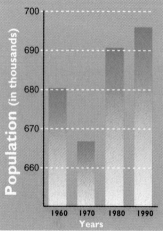

Population (in thousands)

700
690
680
670
660

1960 1970 1980 1990
Years

Key

Capital ★Pierre
Three largest cities
1. Sioux Falls
2. Rapid City
3. Aberdeen
Smallest town
   White Rock
   Population 6

Geography
+ Highest elevation
   Harney Peak
      7,242 ft above sea level
− Lowest point
   Big Stone Lake
      966 ft above sea level
Black Hills
Great Plains
Drift Prairie
Missouri River
Badlands

Economy
First in the nation in
   rye
A leading state in
   gold
   beef cattle
   hogs
   sheep
   spring wheat
   oats

Mount
Rushmore

Historic Sites
   Fort Pierre
   Lead
   Deadwood
   Rapid City
   Custer

The Volunteer State

Became the 16th state on June 1, 1796

State Flower
Iris

Key

Capital ★Nashville

Three largest cities
1. Memphis
2. Nashville
3. Knoxville

Smallest town
Silerton
Population 47

Geography

+ Highest elevation
  Clingmans Dome
  6,643 ft above sea level
− Lowest point
  Mississippi River in
  Shelby County
  178 ft above sea level

Appalachian Mountains
Great Smoky Mountains
Great Valley
Cumberland Plateau
Gulf Coastal Plain

Three stars highlight the state flag. Each represents a different region and landform. East Tennesee has the Great Smoky Mountains. Middle Tennessee has the highlands, and West Tennessee has the lowlands along the Mississippi River.

Economy

First in the nation in

 natural-gemstones production

cultured fresh-water pearls

country music publishing and record companies

A leading state in

chemicals

automobiles

book publishing

zinc

Historic Sites

 Shiloh

Dayton

Oak Ridge

Tennessee Valley Authority

Fabulous Facts!

- Tennessee became a center for making automobiles in the 1980s. Two large manufacturing plants were built near Nashville.

- Part of northeastern Tennessee was once known as the State of Franklin. It existed from 1784–1788 but was not recognized by the United States. It was a state without a country.

- The Tennessee walking horse was developed in Middle Tennessee around 1790.

- The nation's first civil rights museum is in Memphis. It is at the Lorraine Motel, site of the 1968 assassination of Dr. Martin Luther King, Jr.

Fresh Water Used
1,880 gallons/day/ person (average)

Garbage
6,000,000 tons per year 15% recycled

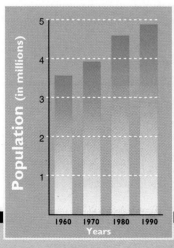

Population (in millions) — 5, 4, 3, 2, 1

Years: 1960 1970 1980 1990

Texas

The Lone Star State

Became the 28th state on Dec. 29, 1845

State Flower
Bluebonnet

Fabulous Facts!

- Texas has about 186,000 farms and more farmland than any other state.

- For almost ten years, beginning in 1836, Texas was a country of its own called the Republic of Texas. It had its own army, navy, money, and postal service.

- The sprawling Dallas-Fort Worth Airport is almost the size of New York's Manhattan Island.

Garbage
25,026,000 tons per year
14% recycled

Key

Capital ★ Austin
Three largest cities
1. Houston
2. Dallas
3. San Antonio
Smallest town
   Mustang
   Population 27

Geography
+ Highest elevation
   Guadalupe Peak
   8,749 ft above sea level
Rio Grande
Rocky Mountains

The Lone Star flag was adopted in 1839. The big white star was first used on flags carried in the 1830s during the Texas Revolution. The color red represents bravery; white, purity; and blue, loyalty.

Economy
First in the nation in
 beef cattle
oil
natural gas
sheep and wool

Historic Sites
The Alamo
Washington-on-the-Brazos
Lyndon B. Johnson Space Center
San Jacinto
Palmito Hill

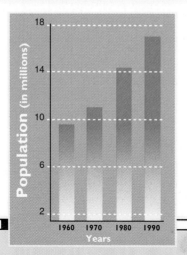

Fresh Water Used
1,180 gallons/day/person
(average)

Population (in millions)

18
14
10
6
2

1960 1970 1980 1990
Years

UT

The Beehive State

Became the 45th state on January 4, 1896

**State Bird
Sea Gull**

Key

Capital ★ Salt Lake City

Three largest cities

1. Salt Lake City
2. West Valley City
3. Provo

Smallest town
   Ophir
   Population 22

Geography

+ Highest elevation
  Kings Peak
     13,528 ft above sea level
− Lowest point
  Beaver Dam Wash Creek
     2,000 ft above sea level

Rocky Mountains
Colorado Plateau
Colorado River
Green River
Great Salt Lake
Great Salt Lake Desert
Bryce Canyon

Economy

First in the nation in
   mink pelts

A leading state in
   salt   barley
   sheep   pears
   cherries

Historic Sites

   Ogden
   Fillmore
   Canyonlands National Park
   Promontory

The state flag pictures the state seal. The beehive on the shield stands for hard work, industry, and the state nickname. The date 1847 is the year the Mormons arrived in Utah.

Fabulous Facts!

- Rocket engines are manufactured here and sold to the United States government.

- Northeast Utah is nicknamed Dinosaurland because thousands of dinosaur bones have been found here.

- The Great Salt Lake is saltier than most oceans. Swimmers can float easily.

- In 1983 a class of fifth-grade students in Utah helped pass a law that made the honeybee the state insect.

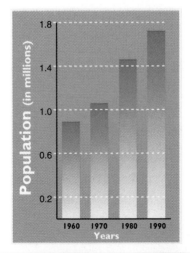

Population (in millions)

1.8
1.4
1.0
0.6
0.2

1960 1970 1980 1990
Years

Garbage
2,000,000 tons per year
13% recycled

Fresh Water Used
2,540 gallons/day/person
(average)

Vermont

The Green Mountain State

Became the 14th state on March 4, 1791

State Bird
Hermit Thrush

Fabulous Facts!

- Each spring, sugar makers tap millions of trees to produce the half million gallons of maple syrup Vermont produces each year.

- In 1777, Vermont passed the first state constitution that prohibited slavery and allowed all men to vote.

- A Vermont law forbids large billboards that hide the state's scenery. Small wooden signs point the way instead.

- Vermont has more than 100 covered bridges. This is more than most states.

Fresh Water Used
1,120 gallons/day/person
(average)

Garbage
700,000 tons
per year
28% recycled

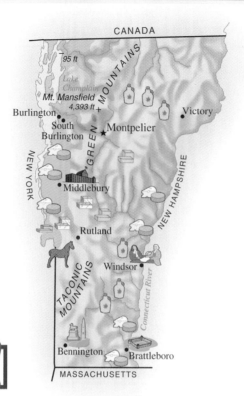

CANADA

95 ft

Lake Champlain

Mt. Mansfield
4,393 ft

Burlington

South Burlington

Montpelier

Victory

GREEN MOUNTAINS

NEW YORK

Middlebury

NEW HAMPSHIRE

Rutland

TACONIC MOUNTAINS

Windsor

Connecticut River

Bennington

Brattleboro

MASSACHUSETTS

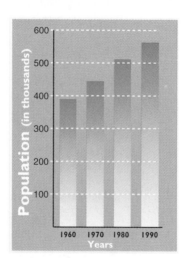

Vermont's flag features the state's coat of arms on a deep-blue background. The cow and bundles of grain represent Vermont's agriculture. The Green Mountains are in the distance.

Key

Capital ★Montpelier
Three largest cities
1. Burlington
2. Rutland
3. South Burlington
Smallest town
Victory
Population 28

Geography
+ Highest elevation
Mt. Mansfield
4,393 ft above sea level
− Lowest point
Lake Champlain
95 ft above sea level
Green Mountains
Connecticut River
Taconic Mountains

Economy
First in the nation in
- maple syrup
- slate
- marble

Important products
- Morgan horses
- cheese
- granite

Historic Sites
- Middlebury
- Brattleboro
- Bennington
- Windsor

Population (in thousands)

600
500
400
300
200
100

1960 1970 1980 1990
Years

Virginia

Old Dominion

Became the 10th state on June 25, 1788

Key

Capital ★Richmond

Three largest cities
1. Virginia Beach
2. Norfolk
3. Richmond

Smallest town
Duffield
Population 52

Geography

+ Highest elevation
  Mt. Rogers
  5,729 ft above sea level

Allegheny Mountains
Blue Ridge Mountains
Chesapeake Bay
Shenandoah Valley
Dismal Swamp
Tidewater
Chincoteague Island

Map labels: MARYLAND, WEST VIRGINIA, ALLEGHENY MTNS., SHENANDOAH VALLEY, BLUE RIDGE MTNS., Arlington, District of Columbia, Chesapeake Bay, Chincoteague Is., Chincoteague, Assateaque Is., TIDEWATER, James River, Richmond, Appomattox, PIEDMONT PLATEAU, Williamsburg, Yorktown, Jamestown, Hampton, Norfolk, Virginia Beach, Dismal Swamp, KENTUCKY, Duffield, Mt. Rogers 5,729 ft, TENNESSEE, NORTH CAROLINA

State Flower
Dogwood

Economy

First in the nation in

⚓ largest United States naval base

A leading state in

🍃 tobacco products

🦃 turkeys

⛏ bituminous coal

🦀 crabs   🦪 oysters

🚢 shipbuilding

Historic Sites

🏛 Jamestown

⚔ Yorktown

🤝 Appomattox

🏘 Williamsburg

🚢 Hampton

🏛 Arlington

The state seal appears on Virginia's deep-blue flag. It pictures a woman who represents Virginia. She has defeated an unfair ruler whose crown has fallen off. This represents the colonies' belief that the British king had treated them unfairly.

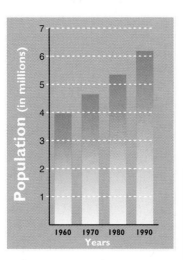

Williamsburg

(Bar graph) Population (in millions) — Years: 1960, 1970, 1980, 1990

Fabulous Facts!

- The largest office building in the world is the Pentagon, in Arlington, where about 25,000 people work.

- The first permanent English settlement in America was founded at Jamestown in 1607.

- Mother of Presidents is a nickname given to Virginia because eight Presidents of the United States were born here.

- Chincoteague Island's wild ponies live on Assateaque Island, in Maryland. Each July, after the ponies are rounded up, they swim to Chincoteague, where they are sold.

Fresh Water Used
762 gallons/day/person (average)

Garbage
8,000,000 tons per year
28% recycled

Washington

The Evergreen State

Became the 42nd state on November 11, 1889

CANADA

San Juan Island

Whidbey Island

PACIFIC OCEAN

Puget Sound

OLYMPIC MOUNTAINS

Redmond
Seattle

Olympia ★
Tumwater

Tacoma

COAST RANGES

CASCADE RANGE

Mt. Rainier 14,410 ft

Mt. St. Helens

Vancouver

Columbia River

OREGON

Grand Coulee Dam

Krupp

Spokane

IDAHO

Snake River

Hanford Works

WA

State Bird
Willow Goldfinch

Olympic National Park

Fabulous Facts!

- Washington leads the states in growing apples. About 5 billion pounds are grown here yearly.

- Bill Gates was born here in 1955. At the age of 19, he founded Microsoft Corp. It is based in Redmond and is a major computer software company.

- Olympic National Park has a large rain forest. This area receives more than 100" of rain each year.

- One of the tallest totem poles in the world is in Kalama.

Washington is the only state with a green flag. The color is for the state's forests. The state seal on the flag features a portrait by Gilbert Stuart of George Washington, for whom the state is named. It is the only state flag with the picture of a President on it.

Garbage
6,513,000 tons per year
38% recycled

Fresh Water Used
1,630 gallons/day/person (average)

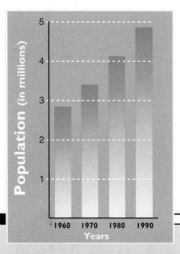

Population (in millions)

5
4
3
2
1

1960 1970 1980 1990
Years

Key

Capital ★Olympia
Three largest cities
1. Seattle
2. Spokane
3. Tacoma
Smallest town
     Krupp
     Population 54

Geography
+ Highest elevation
   Mt. Rainier
      14,410 ft above sea level
Cascade Range
Coast Ranges
Mt. St. Helens
Olympic Mountains
Puget Sound

Economy
First in the nation in
- apples
- sweet cherries
- iris, tulip, and daffodil bulbs
- green peas
- spearmint oil
- aluminum
- clams

A leading state in
- lumber
- airplanes
- salmon and other fish
- computer software
- potatoes

Historic Sites
- San Juan Island
- Whidbey Island
- Vancouver
- Grand Coulee Dam
- Hanford Works
- Tumwater

— WV

West Virginia

The Mountain State

Became the 35th state on June 20, 1863

State Flower
Rhododendron

Wheeling
Moundsville
PENNSYLVANIA
Brandonville
MARYLAND
Shepherdstown
240 ft
Harpers Ferry
Charles Town
Potomac River
Monongahela River
Ohio River
OHIO
ALLEGHENY PLATEAU
Spruce Knob Mtn.
4,861 ft
ALLEGHENY MTNS.
MTNS.
APPALACHIAN
Point Pleasant
Charleston
Huntington
KENTUCKY
Green Bank
Lewisburg
VIRGINIA

Key

Capital ★Charleston

Three largest cities
1. Charleston
2. Huntington
3. Wheeling

Smallest town
Brandonville
Population 47

Geography

+ Highest elevation
Spruce Knob Mountain
4,861 ft above sea level
− Lowest point
Potomac River in Jefferson County
240 ft above sea level

Appalachian Mountains
Allegheny Mountains
Allegheny Plateau
Ohio River
Monongahela River

The state flag pictures the state seal.
The two men represent farming and mining. The rock shows the date that West Virginia became a state. The rifles mean that people were ready to defend their freedom.

Fabulous Facts!

- More glass marbles are manufactured here than in any other state. West Virginia's three marble factories produce more than 1 million marbles each day.

- West Virginia was part of the state of Virginia until the Civil War. People of the northwestern counties broke away from the rest of the state and formed their own government. At first it was called Kanawha.

- The first Mother's Day was celebrated on May 10, 1908, in Grafton. A few months later, on July 5, the first Father's Day was celebrated in Fairmont.

- The black bear is the state animal.

Economy

First in the nation in
🍥 glass marbles

A leading state in
🛒 coal
🍑 peaches
🍎 apples

Important product
🍷 glassware

Historic Sites
🏚 Shepherdstown
⚓ Point Pleasant
🏛 Harpers Ferry
🏠 Lewisburg
🏛 Charles Town

Population (in millions)

2.0
1.9
1.8
1.7

1960 1970 1980 1990
Years

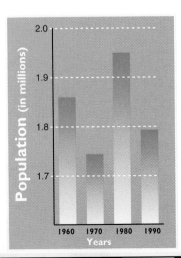

Fresh Water Used
2,560 gallons/day/person
(average)

Garbage
2,000,000 tons per year
12% recycled

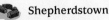

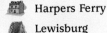

389

Wisconsin

The Badger State

Became the 30th state on May 29, 1848

State Flower Wood Violet

Map labels
Lake Superior
Madeline Island
MICHIGAN
MINNESOTA
Timms Hill +1,951 ft
Peshtigo
Big Falls
Green Bay
Door Peninsula
Green Bay
579 ft
Lake Winnebago
Lake Michigan
Mississippi River
La Crosse
Wisconsin Dells
Wisconsin River
IOWA
Military Ridge
Madison ★
Milwaukee
Racine
Primrose
Kenosha
ILLINOIS

Fabulous Facts!

- Each year, Wisconsin produces 3 billion gallons of milk—one reason the state is called "America's Dairyland."

- Wisconsin has many firsts in the nation. The first kindergarten opened in 1856. The first malted milk was created around 1882. The typewriter was invented in 1867. Facial tissues were first made here in 1917.

- Wisconsin is the first state that required automobiles to have seat belts.

Garbage 5,434,000 tons per year 28% recycled

Fresh Water Used 1,330 gallons/day/person (average)

WISCONSIN 1848

The state flag features the year that Wisconsin became a state and the state seal. A sailor and a miner hold a shield with pictures that represent agriculture, mining, manufacturing, and navigation.

Population (in millions)

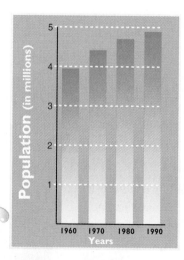

Years	1960	1970	1980	1990

Key

Capital ★ Madison

Three largest cities
1. Milwaukee
2. Madison
3. Green Bay

Smallest town
Big Falls
Population 75

Geography
+ Highest elevation
  Timms Hill
  1,951 ft above sea level
− Lowest point
  Lake Michigan
  579 ft above sea level

Wisconsin Dells
Military Ridge
Lake Winnebago
Door Peninsula

Economy

First in the nation in
- dairy cows
- butter, cheese
- paper
- snap beans
- beets

A leading state in
- milk
- cranberries
- farm machines
- green peas
- canning

Historic Sites
- Primrose
- Peshtigo
- Kenosha
- Racine
- La Crosse
- Madeline Island

The Equality State

Became the 44th state on July 10, 1890

State Flower
Indian Paintbrush

Key

Capital ★Cheyenne

Three largest cities
1. Cheyenne
2. Casper
3. Laramie

Smallest town
Lost Springs
Population 3

Geography
+ Highest elevation
  Gannett Peak
  13,804 ft above sea level
− Lowest point
  Belle Fourche River in
  Crook County
  3,099 ft above sea level

Rocky Mountains
Great Plains
Black Hills
Teton Range
Jackson Hole
Wind River Canyon

Economy
First in the nation in
🛒 coal mining
⚛ uranium

A leading state in
🛢 oil   🌱 sugar beets
💧 natural gas 🧢 wool
🐑 sheep

Historic Sites
⛰ Devils Tower
🐚 Fossil Butte National Monument
💧 Yellowstone National Park
🎩 Cody
📷 Sheridan

On the state flag is a picture of a bison, the state animal, branded with Wyoming's state seal. The woman represents women's rights. The cowboy and miner represent the state's cattle-ranching and mining industries.

Fabulous Facts!

- More coal is mined here than in any other state. About 400 billion pounds of coal are mined here yearly.

- Wyoming is the first state to have a national park, Yellowstone; a national monument, Devils Tower; and a national forest, Shoshone.

- Wyoming is where women first received the right to vote in 1869.

- Wyoming has the fewest people of all the 50 states.

Population (in thousands) chart — Years: 1960, 1970, 1980, 1990

Fresh Water Used
16,700 gallons/day/person (average)

Garbage
504,000 tons per year
5% recycled

The Nation's Capital

Became the capital of the United States in June, 1800

Official Flower
American Beauty Rose
Official Bird
Wood Thrush

Map labels: MARYLAND, PIEDMONT, +410 ft, ATLANTIC COASTAL PLAIN, MARYLAND, VIRGINIA, Vietnam Veterans Memorial, White House, Supreme Court, Lincoln Memorial, Capitol, Washington Monument, Jefferson Memorial, Anacostia River, Potomac River, —1 ft, MARYLAND

DC

Fabulous Facts!

- The Bureau of Engraving and Printing makes the nation's paper money and stamps. Every day about $30 million in paper money is printed in this building.

- The United States had 36 Presidents before the residents of Washington, D.C., were allowed to vote for a President in 1964.

- Washington is the only American city that is not part of any state. It belongs to a separate district, or section, of the United States, called the District of Columbia.

- Unlike most other cities, there are no skyscrapers here. A law limits the heights of buildings in the city.

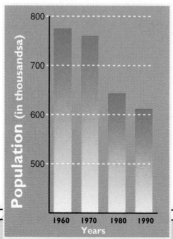

Fresh Water Used
256 gallons/day/person
(average)

The flag was adopted in 1938. Its design is based on the family crest of George Washington's family. It had three red stars and two red bars. The city was named for Washington, who had chosen this site for the capital in 1791.

Key

Geography
+ Highest elevation Tenleytown at Reno Reservoir
  410 ft above sea level
- Lowest point Potomac River
  1 ft above sea level

Atlantic Coastal Plain
Piedmont Plateau
Anacostia River

Economy
Important industries
- federal government
- tourism
- printing and publishing

Historic Sites
- White House
- Capitol
- Washington Monument
- Lincoln Memorial
- Jefferson Memorial
- Supreme Court
- Vietnam Veterans Memorial

Population (in thousandsa)

Bar chart — Population by year:
800, 700, 600, 500
Years: 1960, 1970, 1980, 1990

Garbage
900,000 tons per year
25% recycled

NORTH AMERICA

Atlantic
Ocean

VIRGIN
ISLANDS

PUERTO
RICO

SOUTH
AMERICA

ATLANTIC OCEAN

COASTAL
VALLEYS

Arecibo

COASTAL LOWLANDS

San Juan

Río Grande
de Loíza

El Yunque
Rain Forest

Bayamón

Culebra

Cerro
de Punta
4,389 ft

Utuado
Cordillera Central

COASTAL
VALLEYS

COASTAL

Ponce

LOWLANDS

COASTAL
VALLEYS

Vieques

Caribbean Sea

Island of Enchantment

Became a commonwealth of the United States on July 25, 1952

Commonwealth Flower
Maga
Commonwealth Bird
Reinita

Key

Capital ★San Juan
Three largest cities
1. San Juan
2. Bayamón
3. Ponce

Geography
+ Highest elevation
  Cerro de Punta
  4,389 ft above sea level
Land area 3,515 sq mi
Cordillera Central
Río La Plata
Río Grande de Loíza
Coastal Lowlands
Coastal Valleys
El Yunque Rain Forest

Coqui

The commonwealth flag of Puerto Rico features red and white stripes and a blue triangle. A large white star on the triangle stands for Puerto Rico.

Fabulous Facts!

- About 2,000 factories operate here. They employ about 160,000 workers.

- Christopher Columbus landed here on November 19, 1493.

- At Phosphorescent Bay, millions of tiny plants and animals glow in the water at night.

- Baseball is a national pastime.

- The commonwealth animal is the *coqui*. It is a tan frog that grows to only one inch in length. It has a two-note croak that sounds like a bird.

- The Puerto Rico Paso Fino horse is bred on the island. It is known for its delicate way of walking.

Economy
Important industries
 medicines
 electronic machinery
 food processing
 sugar cane
 coffee
 fishing and lobsters
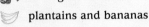 plantains and bananas

Historic Sites
Arecibo
Utuado

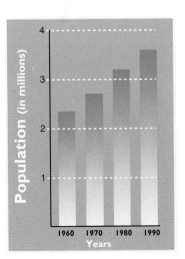

Population (in millions)

4

3

2

1

1960 1970 1980 1990
Years

Fresh Water Used
163 gallons/day/person
(average)

NORTH AMERICA

Atlantic Ocean

VIRGIN ISLANDS

PUERTO RICO

SOUTH AMERICA

St. Croix
St. John
St. Thomas

Became a territory of the United States on March 31, 1917

ATLANTIC OCEAN

BRITISH VIRGIN ISLANDS

Crown Mtn. 1,556 ft +
Charlotte Amalie ★
St. Thomas
Sugar Bay
St. John

Caribbean Sea

Florida
Bahamas
ATLANTIC OCEAN
Cuba
Haiti
Dominican Republic
Jamaica
Caribbean Sea
Puerto Rico
Virgin Islands (U.S.)

Territorial Flower
Yellow Elder or Yellow Cedar

Territorial Bird
Yellow Breast

Frederiksted

St. Croix

Fabulous Facts!

- There are no natural lakes or rivers on the islands. Water can be scarce and people must conserve it.

- Spaniards used the islands to hide their treasure ships from pirates in the 1600s.

- The islands are the only United States possession where people drive on the left side of the road.

The territorial flag features a gold American eagle in the center. It holds a shield of the United States, a green laurel branch, and three arrows. The letters *V* and *I* appear on either side of the eagle.

V I

Key

Capital ★Charlotte Amalie

Geography
+ Highest elevation Crown Mountain on St. Thomas
  1,556 ft above sea level
Land area 133 sq mi
St. Croix
St. John
St. Thomas
Caribbean Sea

Economy
Important industries
- tourism
- oil refining
- aluminum-ore refining
- eggs
- watch factories
- perfume factories

Historic Sites
- Sugar Bay
- Frederiksted

Fresh Water Used
91 gallons/day/person
(average)

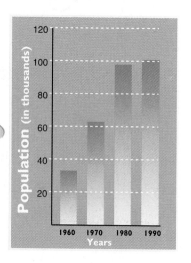

Population (in thousands)

120
100
80
60
40
20

1960 1970 1980 1990
Years

JAPAN
UNITED STATES
HAWAII
Pacific Ocean
GUAM
EQUATOR
AMERICAN SAMOA
AUSTRALIA
NEW ZEALAND

Guam

Hub of the Pacific

Became a territory of
the United States on
August 1, 1950

Territorial Flower
Puti Tai Nobio
(Bougainvillea)

Territorial Bird
Toto **(Fruit Dove)**

PACIFIC OCEAN

Tamuning
Agana ★

Agana River

PACIFIC OCEAN

Agat •

Talofofo River

Mt. Lamlam
1,332 ft +

Ugum River

Umatac Bay

ASIA   NORTH AMERICA

□ Guam

AUSTRALIA

Key

Capital ★Agana

Largest city
   Tamuning

Geography
+ Highest elevation
   Mt. Lamlam
      1,332 ft above sea level

Land area 209 sq mi

Ugum River
Talofofo River
Agana River

The territorial
flag features the
territorial seal
on a blue background.
It pictures a coconut palm tree on
the shore and a seagoing canoe.
The flag is edged with a red
border.

Economy
Important industries

🛩️ United States military
🦜 tourism
🥥 coconuts
🍠 yams
🌿 taro
🐟 tuna fishing

Historic Sites
🏛️ Umatac Bay
🏘️ Agat

Fabulous Facts!

- Tourism is the island's fastest-growing industry. Each year more than 1 million tourists visit here, mostly from Japan.

- About 40% of the Guamanians are Chamorros. These people are descended from the island's first residents, who came from Asia more than 2,000 years ago.

- Guam has two official languages, Chamorro and English.

- Guam has a territorial animal. It is the iguana.

- The territorial motto of Guam is Where America's Day Begins.

- Residents of Guam are citizens of the United States, but they do not vote in presidential elections.

Population (in thousands)

140
120
100
80
60
40
20

1960 1970 1980 1990
Years

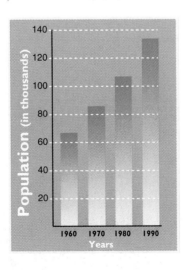

American Samoa

JAPAN
UNITED STATES
MARIANA IS.
PHILIPPINES
MARSHALL IS. HAWAII
GUAM
PALAU
MICRONESIA
Pacific Ocean
INDONESIA
AMERICAN SAMOA
EQUATOR
AUSTRALIA
NEW ZEALAND

Became a territory of the United States on April 17, 1900

Swains Island

PACIFIC OCEAN

Massacre Bay

Pago Pago ★
Tutuila
Aunuu
Pago Pago Bay

Ofu Olosega
Manua Islands Tau
Lata Mountain + 3,160 ft

Rose Island

Territorial Flower
Paogo (Ula-fala)

Territorial Plant
Ava

ASIA   NORTH AMERICA
American Samoa
AUSTRALIA

Fabulous Facts!

- The economy is based on a thriving fishing industry. More than 95% of its exports is canned tuna.

- Most people live in villages, and their lives center around their families. A family unit is called an *aiga*.

- *Kirikiti*, a form of cricket, is a popular sport here. It is played with a hard rubber ball and a three-sided bat. There are teams for both men and women.

- Some local schools use televised instruction.

- Polynesian people lived here for about 2,000 years before Europeans arrived in 1722.

- People born here are not United States citizens and cannot vote in presidential elections.

A white triangle is featured on the right side of the blue territorial flag. An eagle in the triangle holds a yellow *uatogi*, or "war club," which stands for the power of the state, and a *fue*, or "fly switch," which stands for wisdom.

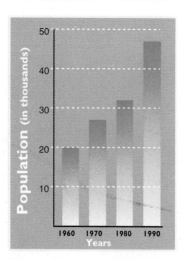

Population (in thousands)

50
40
30
20
10

1960 1970 1980 1990
Years

Key

Capital ★Pago Pago

Geography
+ Highest elevation Lata Mountain on Tau Island
    3,160 ft above sea level
Land area 77 sq mi
7 islands
    Tau
    Tutuila
    Aunuu
    Ofu
    Olosega
    Rose
    Swains

Economy
Important industries
🥫 tuna canning
✂ tourism
🥥 copra (dried coconut)
🧺 handicrafts

Historic Site
🍣 Pago Pago Bay

Commonwealth of the Northern Mariana Islands

Became a commonwealth of the United States on November 4, 1986

Capital ★Saipan
Population 44,000
Geography
14 islands
Land area 184 sq mi
Important Industries
 clothing manufacturing
tourism

The official flag has a blue field. A white star is centered on top of a gray *latte* stone. This is surrounded by a wreath of traditional flowers called *mwåår*.

Fabulous Facts!

- A person born here is a United States citizen at birth.

- The islands are six miles above the Mariana Trench, the deepest known spot in the world's oceans.

Fabulous Facts!

- Kwajalein is one of the largest atolls in the world. Its fringe of reef and land encloses a lagoon that is 840 sq miles.

- Both Marshallese and English are official languages here.

Republic of the Marshall Islands

Became a nation on May 1, 1979*

Capital ★Majuro
Population 43,000
Geography
29 atolls and 5 islands
Land area 70 sq mi
Important Industries
copra processing
handicrafts
tropical aquarium fish

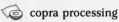

The two rays on the national flag represent the two island chains of the country. White is for the Sunrise Chain, and orange is for the Sunset Chain. The 24 points on the star are for the 24 municipalities.

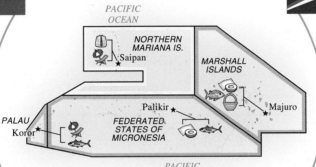

PACIFIC OCEAN

NORTHERN MARIANA IS.
Saipan

MARSHALL ISLANDS

Palikir ★

Majuro

PALAU
Koror ★

FEDERATED STATES OF MICRONESIA

PACIFIC OCEAN

Republic of Palau

Became a nation on October 1, 1994*

The blue background represents the Pacific Ocean. A large yellow moon is in the center because people's lives here depend on the water, tides, and moon.

Capital ★Koror
Population 15,000
Geography
More than 200 islands
Land area 170 sq mi
Important Industries
 fishing
tourism

*The United States gives economic and defense aid to this former Trust Territory under a special agreement.

Fabulous Facts!

- Palauan is the major language spoken here.

- Palau is within the United States postal system.

Fabulous Facts!

- Of the 607 islands, people live on about 100 of them.

- In some areas, families build homes with thatched roofs and walls made from palm branches and local wood.

Federated States of Micronesia

Became a nation on November 3, 1986*

The national flag is blue for the water surrounding the islands. Four large stars represent the four states of Micronesia.

Capital ★Palikir
Population 100,000
Geography
607 islands
Land area 271 sq mi
Important Industries
 fishing
copra processing

ARCTIC OCEAN

Greenland (Den.)

Arctic Circle

Alaska (U.S.)

60°N

ALEUTIAN IS. (U.S.)

CANADA

NORTH

AMERICA

UNITED STATES

See inset below

40°N

AZORES (Port.)

Midway I. (U.S.)

Bermuda (U.K.)

ATLANTIC OCEAN

Tropic of Cancer

HAWAII (U.S.)

MEXICO

20°N

Caribbean Sea

CAPE VERDE

VENEZUELA

GUYANA

SURINAME

French Guiana (Fr.)

COLOMBIA

GALÁPAGOS IS. (Ecuador)

SOUTH

ECUADOR

AMERICA

0° Equator

BRAZIL

PACIFIC OCEAN

WESTERN SAMOA

PERU

AMERICAN SAMOA (U.S.)

FRENCH POLYNESIA (Fr.)

BOLIVIA

TONGA

PARAGUAY

20°S

Pitcairn I. (U.K.)

COOK IS. (N.Z.)

Tropic of Capricorn

CHILE

Easter I. (Chile)

URUGUAY

N

ARGENTINA

W E

S

40°S

FALKLAND IS. (U.K.)

60°S

Antarctic Circle

80°S

UNITED STATES

N

W E

S

30°N

Gulf of Mexico

ATLANTIC OCEAN

25°N

B A H A M A S

Tropic of Cancer

CUBA

20°N

TURKS AND CAICOS IS. (U.K.)

MEXICO

CAYMAN ISLANDS (U.K.)

GREATER ANTILLES

Hispaniola

BR. VIRGIN IS. (U.K.)

HAITI

DOMINICAN REPUBLIC

Puerto Rico (U.S.)

ANTIGUA AND BARBUDA

BELIZE

JAMAICA

VIRGIN ISLANDS (U.S.)

Guadeloupe (Fr.)

GUATEMALA

ST. KITTS AND NEVIS

15°N

Caribbean Sea

DOMINICA

Martinique (Fr.)

HONDURAS

ST. LUCIA

EL SALVADOR

NICARAGUA

NETH. ANTILLES (Neth.)

ST. VINCENT AND THE GRENADINES

LESSER ANTILLES

BARBADOS

ARUBA

GRENADA

10°N

COSTA RICA

TRINIDAD AND TOBAGO

PANAMA

COLOMBIA

VENEZUELA

90°W   85°W   80°W   75°W   70°W   65°W   60°W

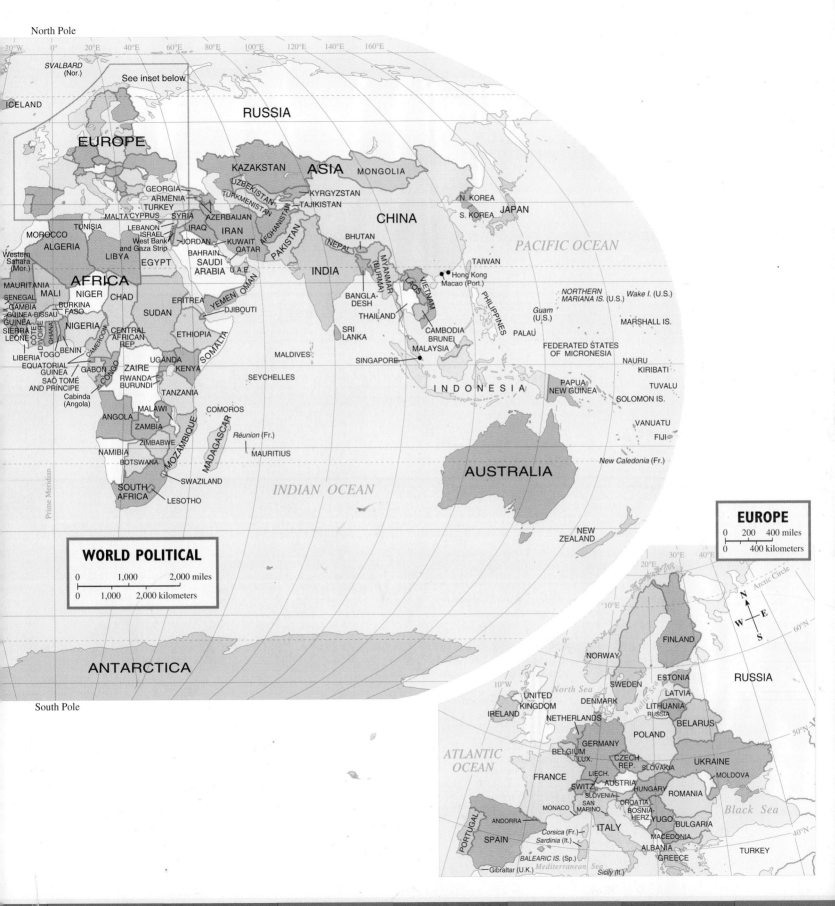

North Pole

SVALBARD
(Nor.)

ICELAND

See inset below

RUSSIA

EUROPE

KAZAKSTAN   ASIA   MONGOLIA

GEORGIA
ARMENIA   KYRGYZSTAN
TURKEY   UZBEKISTAN
MALTA CYPRUS   SYRIA   TURKMENISTAN   TAJIKISTAN
LEBANON   AZERBAIJAN
MOROCCO   ISRAEL   IRAQ   AFGHANISTAN
TUNISIA   West Bank   JORDAN   IRAN
ALGERIA   and Gaza Strip   KUWAIT   PAKISTAN
Western   LIBYA   EGYPT   BAHRAIN   QATAR
Sahara   SAUDI   U.A.E.
(Mor.)   ARABIA   INDIA

CHINA

N. KOREA
S. KOREA   JAPAN

PACIFIC OCEAN

TAIWAN

Hong Kong
Macao (Port.)

MAURITANIA   MALI   NIGER   CHAD
SENEGAL   BURKINA   ERITREA   YEMEN OMAN
GAMBIA   FASO   SUDAN   DJIBOUTI   BANGLA-
GUINEA-BISSAU   GHANA   NIGERIA   DESH
SIERRA   CÔTE   CENTRAL   ETHIOPIA
LEONE   D'IVOIRE   AFRICAN   THAILAND
LIBERIA   BENIN   CAMEROON   REP.
TOGO   SRI
EQUATORIAL   GABON   UGANDA   LANKA
GUINEA   CONGO   ZAIRE   KENYA   SOMALIA
SÃO TOMÉ   RWANDA   MALDIVES
AND PRÍNCIPE   BURUNDI   SEYCHELLES

NEPAL   BHUTAN

MYANMAR   NORTHERN   Wake I. (U.S.)
(BURMA)   MARIANA IS. (U.S.)
LAOS   VIETNAM   Guam
CAMBODIA   (U.S.)   MARSHALL IS.
PHILIPPINES   PALAU
BRUNEI   FEDERATED STATES
MALAYSIA   OF MICRONESIA
SINGAPORE   NAURU
KIRIBATI

AFRICA

Cabinda
(Angola)

ANGOLA   MALAWI
ZAMBIA
ZIMBABWE

TANZANIA   COMOROS   Réunion (Fr.)
MAURITIUS

I N D O N E S I A   PAPUA
NEW GUINEA   TUVALU
SOLOMON IS.

VANUATU
FIJI

NAMIBIA   BOTSWANA
SOUTH   MOZAMBIQUE   MADAGASCAR
AFRICA   SWAZILAND
LESOTHO

INDIAN OCEAN

New Caledonia (Fr.)

AUSTRALIA

WORLD POLITICAL

0   1,000   2,000 miles

0   1,000   2,000 kilometers

NEW
ZEALAND

EUROPE

0   200   400 miles

0   400 kilometers

ANTARCTICA

South Pole

Arctic Circle

FINLAND

NORWAY

ATLANTIC
OCEAN

IRELAND

UNITED
KINGDOM

North Sea

SWEDEN   ESTONIA

DENMARK   LATVIA
LITHUANIA
NETHERLANDS   RUSSIA

RUSSIA

BELARUS

BELGIUM
LUX.   GERMANY   POLAND

FRANCE   LIECH.   CZECH
REP.   SLOVAKIA   UKRAINE

SWITZ.   AUSTRIA   HUNGARY   MOLDOVA
SLOVENIA   ROMANIA
MONACO   SAN   CROATIA
MARINO   BOSNIA-
ANDORRA   HERZ.   YUGO.
PORTUGAL   Corsica (Fr.)   BULGARIA
SPAIN   ITALY   MACEDONIA   Black Sea
Sardinia (It.)   ALBANIA
BALEARIC IS. (Sp.)   GREECE
Gibraltar (U.K.)   Mediterranean Sea   Sicily (It.)   TURKEY

399

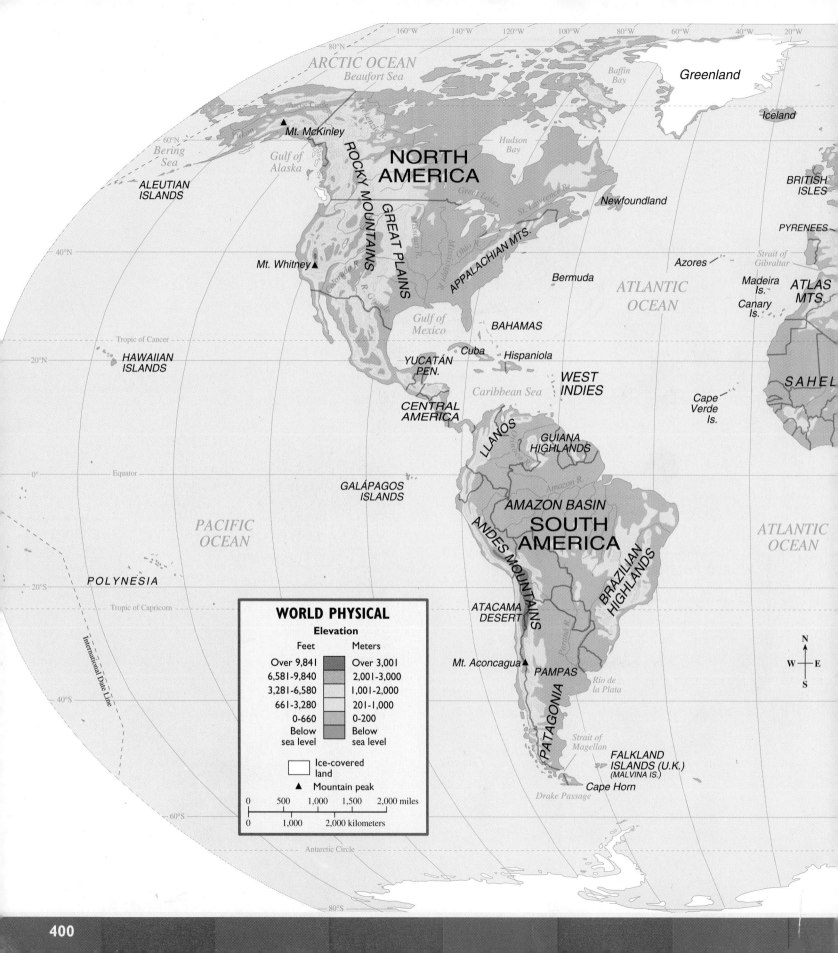

WORLD PHYSICAL

Elevation

Feet	Meters
Over 9,841	Over 3,001
6,581-9,840	2,001-3,000
3,281-6,580	1,001-2,000
661-3,280	201-1,000
0-660	0-200
Below sea level	Below sea level

☐ Ice-covered land
▲ Mountain peak

0   500   1,000   1,500   2,000 miles
0   1,000   2,000 kilometers

ARCTIC OCEAN

SVALBARD

Barents Sea

Novaya Zemlya

SIBERIA

Yenisei R.

Lena R.

Sea of Okhotsk

KAMCHATKA PENINSULA

Ob R.

URAL MTS.

Irtysh R.

ALTAI MTS.

Amur R.

Sakhalin

Volga R.

EUROPE

CARPATHIANS

Ural R.

Aral Sea

ASIA

GOBI

L. Baikal

Sea of Japan

Hokkaido

Danube R.

ALPS

▲ Mt. Blanc

Baltic Sea

BALKAN PEN.

CAUCASUS MTS.

Black Sea

Caspian Sea

Mt. Ararat ▲

Mt. ▲ Damavand

HINDU KUSH

KUNLUN SHAN

TIBETAN PLATEAU

HIMALAYAS

Honshu

Shikoku

Kyushu

North Sea

Mediterranean Sea

Nile R.

ARABIAN PENINSULA

Persian Gulf

Indus R.

THAR DESERT

Ganges R.

▲ Mt. Everest

Huang He

Chang Jiang (Yangtze)

East China Sea

Taiwan

SAHARA

NUBIAN DESERT

Red Sea

DECCAN PLATEAU

Hainan

South China Sea

PHILIPPINE ISLANDS

SUDAN

Arabian Sea

Bay of Bengal

MICRONESIA

AFRICA

GREAT RIFT VALLEY

Zaire (Congo) R.

L. Victoria

▲ Mt. Kenya

▲ Mt. Kilimanjaro

Sri Lanka

MALAY PEN.

Sumatra

Borneo

INDONESIA

Celebes

New Guinea

PACIFIC OCEAN

ZAIRE BASIN

SEYCHELLES

Java

Timor

MELANESIA

Zambezi R.

Madagascar

INDIAN OCEAN

KALAHARI DESERT

Orange R.

GREAT SANDY DESERT

AUSTRALIA

NULLARBOR PLAIN

Darling R.

North Island

Cape of Good Hope

Tasmania

South Island

NEW ZEALAND

ANTARCTICA

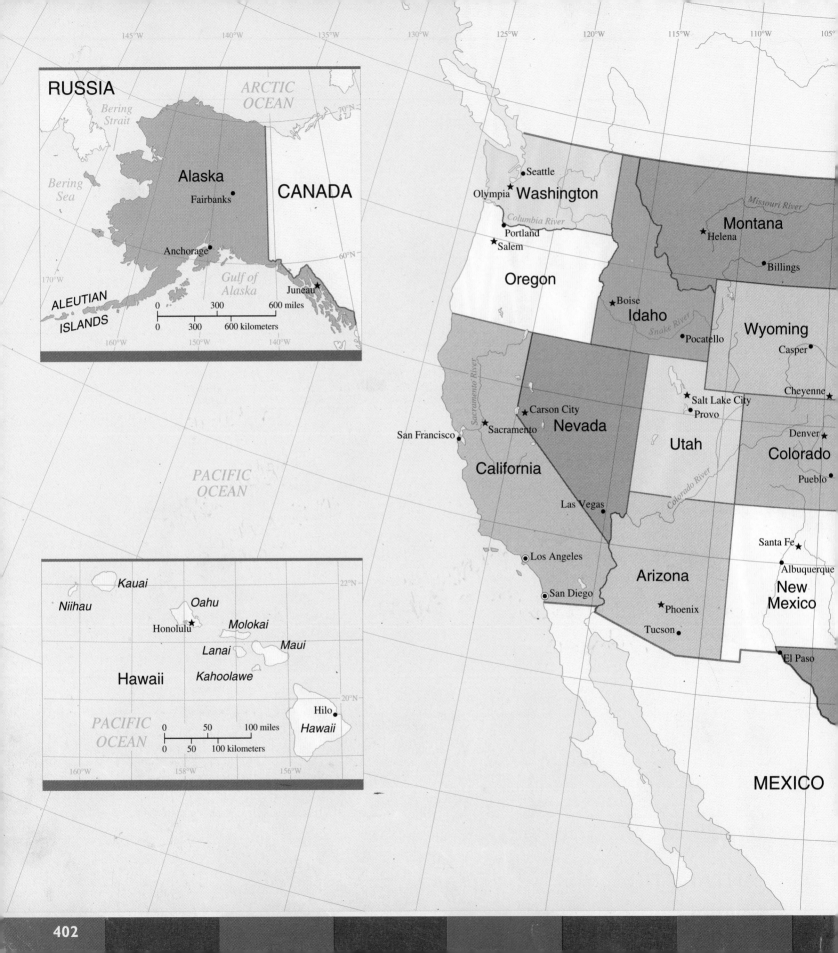

RUSSIA

ARCTIC OCEAN

Bering Strait

Bering Sea

Alaska

CANADA

Fairbanks

Anchorage

Gulf of Alaska

Juneau

ALEUTIAN ISLANDS

0   300   600 miles
0   300   600 kilometers

170°W   160°W   150°W   140°W

70°N

60°N

PACIFIC OCEAN

Kauai

Niihau

Oahu

Honolulu

Molokai

Lanai

Maui

Hawaii

Kahoolawe

22°N

20°N

PACIFIC OCEAN

Hilo

Hawaii

0   50   100 miles
0   50   100 kilometers

160°W   158°W   156°W

145°W   140°W   135°W   130°W   125°W   120°W   115°W   110°W   105°

Seattle

Olympia   Washington

Columbia River

Portland

Salem

Oregon

Missouri River

Montana

Helena

Billings

Boise

Idaho

Snake River

Pocatello

Wyoming

Casper

Cheyenne

Sacramento River

Carson City

Sacramento

San Francisco

Nevada

Salt Lake City

Provo

Utah

Denver

Colorado

Pueblo

California

Las Vegas

Colorado River

Santa Fe

Albuquerque

Los Angeles

San Diego

Arizona

New Mexico

Phoenix

Tucson

El Paso

MEXICO

CANADA

North Dakota
Fargo
Bismarck
Minnesota

South Dakota
Pierre
Sioux Falls

Nebraska
Omaha
Lincoln

Kansas
Topeka
Wichita

Oklahoma
Tulsa
Oklahoma City

Texas
Dallas
Austin
Houston
San Antonio

Minneapolis
St. Paul
Wisconsin
Milwaukee
Madison

Lake Superior

Michigan
Lake Huron

Iowa
Dubuque
Des Moines

Kansas City
Jefferson City

Missouri

Fort Smith
Arkansas
Little Rock

Greenville
Mississippi
Jackson

Louisiana
Baton Rouge
Mobile
New Orleans

Lansing
Detroit

Chicago
Fort Wayne

Illinois
Springfield

St. Louis

Indiana
Indianapolis
Cincinnati

Louisville
Frankfort

Kentucky

Tennessee
Nashville

Memphis

Birmingham
Alabama
Montgomery

Georgia
Atlanta

Tallahassee

Lake Ontario

Lake Erie

Ohio
Columbus

West Virginia
Charleston

Cleveland

Pennsylvania
Pittsburgh
Harrisburg

Washington, D.C.

Virginia
Richmond

Norfolk

North Carolina
Raleigh
Charlotte

South Carolina
Columbia
Charleston

Savannah

St. Lawrence River

Maine
Augusta

Vermont
Burlington
Montpelier
New Hampshire
Manchester
Concord

Albany
New York
Springfield
Buffalo

Boston
Massachusetts
Providence
Hartford
Bridgeport
Rhode Island
Connecticut

New York City
Philadelphia
Trenton
Wilmington
New Jersey
Baltimore
Dover
Annapolis
Delaware

Maryland

ATLANTIC OCEAN

Florida
Tampa

Miami

BAHAMAS

CUBA

Gulf of Mexico

Missouri River
Platte River
Arkansas River
Mississippi River
Red River
Rio Grande
Ohio River

UNITED STATES POLITICAL

⊛ National capital
★ State capitals
◉ Cities with populations over 1 million
• Other cities
━━ National boundaries
── State boundaries

| 0 | 150 | 300 miles |
| 0 | 150 | 300 kilometers |

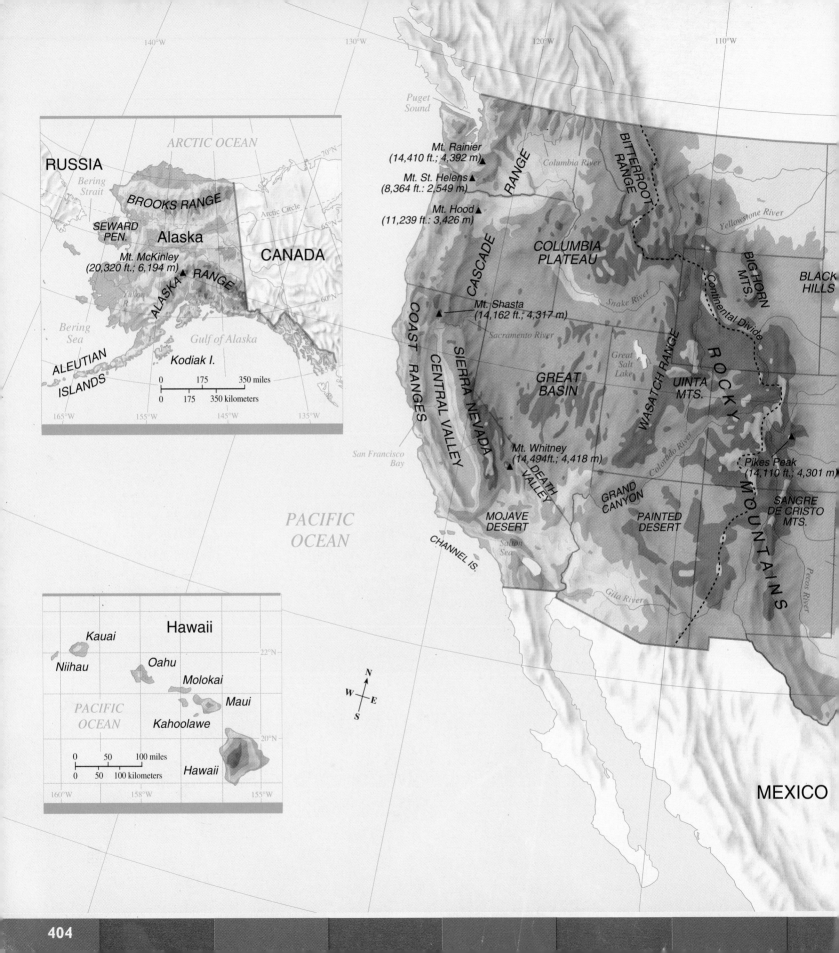

RUSSIA

ARCTIC OCEAN

Bering Strait

BROOKS RANGE

SEWARD PEN.

Alaska

CANADA

Mt. McKinley
(20,320 ft.; 6,194 m) ▲

Bering Sea

ALASKA RANGE

Yukon R.

Gulf of Alaska

ALEUTIAN ISLANDS

Kodiak I.

| 0 | 175 | 350 miles |
| 0 | 175 | 350 kilometers |

PACIFIC OCEAN

Hawaii

Kauai

Niihau

Oahu

Molokai

PACIFIC OCEAN

Maui

Kahoolawe

Hawaii

| 0 | 50 | 100 miles |
| 0 | 50 | 100 kilometers |

Puget Sound

Mt. Rainier
(14,410 ft.; 4,392 m) ▲

Mt. St. Helens ▲
(8,364 ft.: 2,549 m)

Mt. Hood ▲
(11,239 ft.; 3,426 m)

Columbia River

BITTERROOT RANGE

CASCADE RANGE

COLUMBIA PLATEAU

Yellowstone River

BIG HORN MTS.

BLACK HILLS

Continental Divide

Mt. Shasta
(14,162 ft.; 4,317 m)

Snake River

Sacramento River

Great Salt Lake

COAST RANGES

CENTRAL VALLEY

SIERRA NEVADA

GREAT BASIN

WASATCH RANGE

UINTA MTS.

ROCKY MOUNTAINS

San Francisco Bay

Mt. Whitney
(14,494 ft.; 4,418 m)

DEATH VALLEY

Colorado River

Pikes Peak
(14,110 ft.; 4,301 m)

MOJAVE DESERT

GRAND CANYON

PAINTED DESERT

SANGRE DE CRISTO MTS.

CHANNEL IS.

Salton Sea

Gila River

Pecos River

N
W · E
S

MEXICO

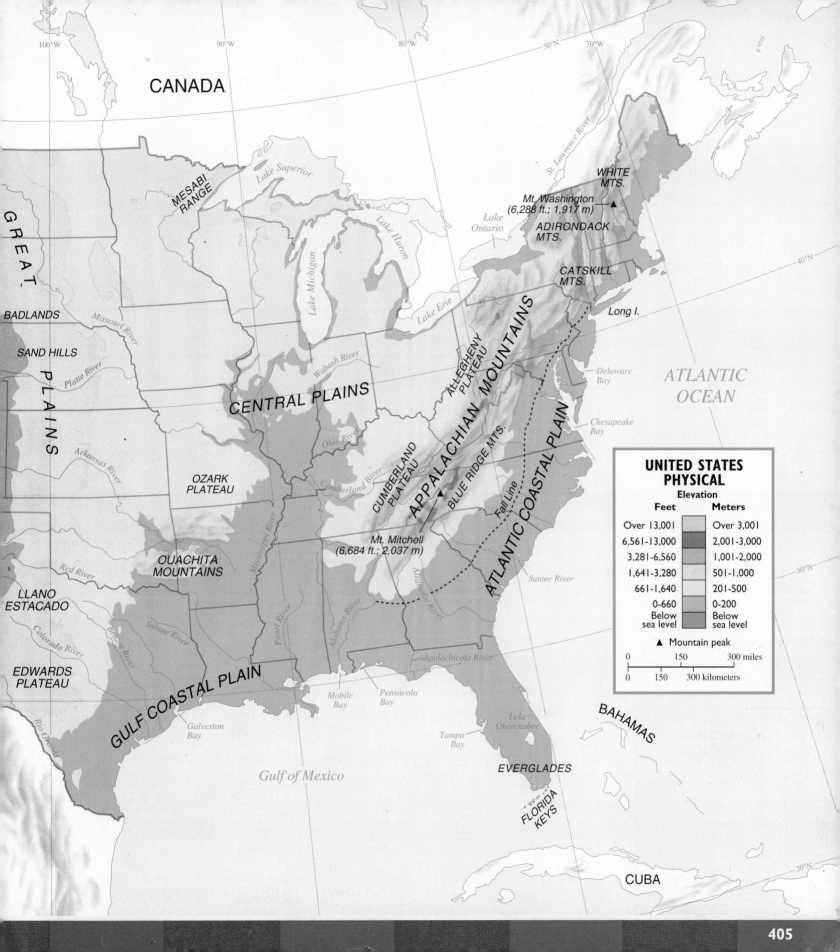

UNITED STATES PHYSICAL

CANADA

MESABI RANGE

Lake Superior

GREAT PLAINS

BADLANDS

SAND HILLS

Missouri River

Lake Michigan

Lake Huron

Platte River

CENTRAL PLAINS

Wabash River

Arkansas River

OZARK PLATEAU

Ohio River

Cumberland River

OUACHITA MOUNTAINS

Red River

Mississippi River

LLANO ESTACADO

Colorado River

Brazos River

Sabine River

Pearl River

EDWARDS PLATEAU

GULF COASTAL PLAIN

Rio Grande

Galveston Bay

Mobile Bay

Pensacola Bay

Gulf of Mexico

Alabama River

Apalachicola River

Tampa Bay

Lake Okeechobee

EVERGLADES

FLORIDA KEYS

BAHAMAS

CUBA

St. Lawrence River

WHITE MTS.

Mt. Washington
(6,288 ft.; 1,917 m)

Lake Ontario

ADIRONDACK MTS.

Lake Erie

CATSKILL MTS.

ALLEGHENY PLATEAU

APPALACHIAN MOUNTAINS

Long I.

Delaware Bay

ATLANTIC OCEAN

Chesapeake Bay

CUMBERLAND PLATEAU

BLUE RIDGE MTS.

Mt. Mitchell
(6,684 ft.; 2,037 m)

ATLANTIC COASTAL PLAIN

Fall Line

Santee River

Altamaha River

UNITED STATES PHYSICAL
Elevation

Feet	Meters
Over 13,001	Over 3,001
6,561–13,000	2,001–3,000
3,281–6,560	1,001–2,000
1,641–3,280	501–1,000
661–1,640	201–500
0–660	0–200
Below sea level	Below sea level

▲ Mountain peak

0   150   300 miles

0   150   300 kilometers

100°W   90°W   80°W   70°W   50°N   40°N   30°N   20°N

ASIA

EUROPE

*Bering
Sea*

ARCTIC
OCEAN

Barrow

*Bering
Strait*

*Beaufort
Sea*

Qaanaaq

Alaska
(U.S.)

Anchorage

Mackenzie R.

*Great
Bear Lake*

*Greenland
(Kalaalit Nunaat)
(Den.)*

*Baffin
Bay*

Whitehorse

Nuuk

*Gulf of
Alaska*

Juneau

Yellowknife

*Great
Slave Lake*

Iqaluit

PACIFIC
OCEAN

*Lake
Winnipeg*

Churchill

*Hudson
Bay*

*Labrador
Sea*

CANADA

Edmonton

Victoria

Vancouver

Calgary

Saskatoon

Goose Bay

Gander

St. John's

Seattle

Spokane

Regina

Winnipeg

Sept-Îles

Portland

Columbia R.

Missouri R.

*Great
Lakes*

ST. PIERRE-
MIQUELON (Fr.)

San Francisco

*Great
Salt Lake*

Minneapolis

St. Paul

Quebec

Montreal

St. John

Salt Lake
City

Milwaukee

Toronto

Ottawa

Halifax

Denver

Omaha

Detroit

Buffalo

Boston

Colorado R.

Chicago

Cleveland

Pittsburgh

New York

Los Angeles

San Diego

Kansas
City

St. Louis

Cincinnati

Philadelphia

Phoenix

Arkansas R.

UNITED STATES

Ohio R.

Washington, D.C.

Norfolk

ATLANTIC
OCEAN

El Paso

Dallas

Memphis

Rio Grande

Mississippi R.

Atlanta

Bermuda
(U.K.)

San Antonio

Houston

New Orleans

Monterrey

MEXICO

Gulf of Mexico

Miami

BAHAMAS

N

Guadalajara

Havana

Nassau

W   E

S

**NORTH AMERICA
POLITICAL**

⊛ National capitals

◉ Cities with populations
    over one million

• Major cities

—— National boundaries

····· State boundaries

0   300   600 miles

0   300   600 kilometers

Clipperton Island
(Fr.)

Mexico City

Orizaba

CUBA

DOMINICAN
REPUBLIC

VIRGIN IS. (U.S.-U.K.)

*CAYMAN
ISLANDS
(U.K.)*

Santiago

HAITI

Puerto
Rico
(U.S.)

ANTIGUA AND
BARBUDA

Belmopan

Port-au-Prince

Santo
Domingo

ST. KITTS
AND NEVIS

Guadeloupe
(Fr.)

BELIZE

JAMAICA

Kingston

DOMINICA

Martinique (Fr.)

GUATEMALA

HONDURAS

ST. LUCIA

Guatemala

Caribbean Sea

BARBADOS

San Salvador

Tegucigalpa

ARUBA

*NETH.
ANTILLES
(Neth.)*

GRENADA

ST. VINCENT AND THE
GRENADINES

EL SALVADOR

NICARAGUA

TRINIDAD
AND TOBAGO

Managua

*Panama
Canal*

San José

PANAMA

COSTA
RICA

Panama

SOUTH AMERICA

ASIA

EUROPE

ARCTIC OCEAN

Bering Sea
St. Lawrence I.
Bering Strait
SEWARD PEN.
BROOKS RANGE
Point Barrow
QUEEN ELIZABETH ISLANDS
Ellesmere Island
Greenland (Kalaalit Nunaat)

Nunivak I.
ALASKA PEN.
ALASKA RANGE
Mt. McKinley
(6,684 ft.; 2,037 m)
ALEUTIAN ISLANDS
Beaufort Sea
Victoria Island
BOOTHIA PEN.
Baffin Bay

Kodiak I.
Gulf of Alaska
YUKON PLATEAU
Baffin Island
Baffin Island

Great Bear Lake
Southampton I.
Hudson Strait
Davis Strait

ALEXANDER ARCHIPELAGO
COAST MTS.
Great Slave Lake
Labrador Sea

QUEEN CHARLOTTE ISLANDS
Peace R.
CANADIAN SHIELD
LABRADOR

Vancouver I.
Athabasca R.
N. Saskatchewan R.
Hudson Bay
LAURENTIAN HIGHLANDS

PACIFIC OCEAN

ROCKY MOUNTAINS

Mt. Rainier
(14,410 ft.; 4,392 m)
CASCADE RANGE
Columbia R.
Lake Winnipeg
Newfoundland

Cape Mendocino
COAST RANGES
Snake R.
Missouri R.
Lake Superior
Prince Edward I.
Cape Breton I.

SIERRA NEVADA
Great Salt Lake
BLACK HILLS
GREAT PLAINS
Lake Michigan
Lake Huron

GREAT BASIN
Platte R.
CENTRAL LOWLANDS
Lake Erie
Cape Cod
Long I.

Point Conception
Mt. Whitney
(14,494 ft.; 4,481 m)
Mt. Elbert
(14,433 ft.; 4,399 m)
COLORADO PLATEAU
Arkansas R.
Ohio R.
APPALACHIAN MTS.

ATLANTIC OCEAN

Guadalupe I.
LOWER CALIFORNIA
OZARK PLATEAU
Tennessee R.
Mt. Mitchell
(6,684 ft.; 2,037 m)
Cape Hatteras

Eugenia Point
Red R.
Mississippi R.
COASTAL PLAIN
Bermuda I.

SIERRA MADRE OCCIDENTAL
Rio Grande
Cape Canaveral
FLORIDA PEN.

False Cape
Gulf of California
SIERRA MADRE ORIENTAL
Gulf of Mexico
FLORIDA KEYS
BAHAMAS

WEST INDIES
VIRGIN IS.

YUCATÁN PEN.
Cuba
GREATER ANTILLES
Puerto Rico
Barbuda
Antigua
LESSER ANTILLES

CAYMAN ISLANDS
Hispaniola
LEEWARD ISLANDS
St. Kitts and Nevis
Guadaloupe
Dominica

Jamaica
Martinique
St. Lucia
WINDWARD ISLANDS
Barbados

Citlaltepetl
(18,696 ft.; 5,700 m)
Caribbean Sea
St. Vincent
Grenada

CENTRAL AMERICA
Aruba
Curaçao
Bonaire
Tobago
Trinidad

ISTHMUS OF PANAMA

SOUTH AMERICA

NORTH AMERICA PHYSICAL

Elevation

Feet	Meters
Over 13,001	Over 4,001
6,501–13,000	2,001–4,000
3,001–6,500	1,001–2,000
1,501–3,000	501–1,000
701–1,500	201–500
0–700	0–200
Below sea level	Below sea level

▲ Mountain peak

0   300   600 miles
0   300   600 kilometers

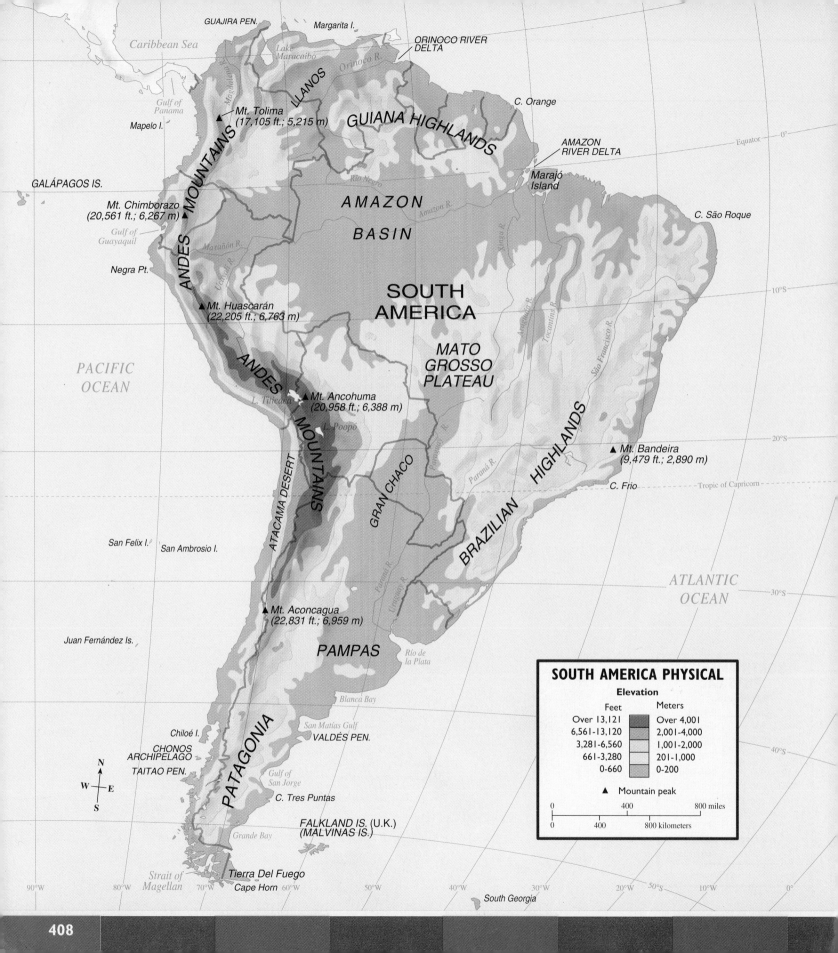

GUAJIRA PEN.
Margarita I.
Caribbean Sea
Lake Maracaibo
ORINOCO RIVER DELTA
Orinoco R.
LLANOS
Magdalena R.
GUIANA HIGHLANDS
C. Orange
AMAZON RIVER DELTA
Gulf of Panama
▲ Mt. Tolima
(17,105 ft.; 5,215 m)
Mapelo I.
GALÁPAGOS IS.
Río Negro
Marajó Island
Equator — 0°

AMAZON
Amazon R.
C. São Roque

Mt. Chimborazo
(20,561 ft.; 6,267 m) ▲
BASIN
Gulf of Guayaquil
Marañón R.
Negra Pt.
Ucayali R.

ANDES MOUNTAINS

SOUTH
AMERICA
Negro R.
Xingu R.
Madeira R.
Tocantins R.
10°S

▲ Mt. Huascarán
(22,205 ft.; 6,763 m)

São Francisco R.

MATO
GROSSO
PLATEAU

PACIFIC
OCEAN

ANDES MOUNTAINS
L. Titicaca
▲▲ Mt. Ancohuma
(20,958 ft.; 6,388 m)
L. Poopó

▲ Mt. Bandeira
(9,479 ft.; 2,890 m)
20°S

BRAZILIAN HIGHLANDS

ATACAMA DESERT
GRAN CHACO
Paraná R.
C. Frio — Tropic of Capricorn

San Felix I.
San Ambrosio I.

ATLANTIC
OCEAN
30°S

▲ Mt. Aconcagua
(22,831 ft.; 6,959 m)
Paraná R.
Uruguay R.

Juan Fernández Is.

PAMPAS
Río de la Plata

Blanca Bay

Chiloé I.
San Matías Gulf
VALDÉS PEN.

CHONOS
ARCHIPELAGO
TAITAO PEN.
40°S

N
W — E
S

PATAGONIA
Gulf of San Jorge
C. Tres Puntas

FALKLAND IS. (U.K.)
(MALVINAS IS.)

Grande Bay

Strait of Magellan
Tierra Del Fuego
Cape Horn

South Georgia
50°S

SOUTH AMERICA PHYSICAL
Elevation

Feet	Meters
Over 13,121	Over 4,001
6,561–13,120	2,001–4,000
3,281–6,560	1,001–2,000
661–3,280	201–1,000
0–660	0–200

▲ Mountain peak

0   400   800 miles
0   400   800 kilometers

90°W   80°W   70°W   60°W   50°W   40°W   30°W   20°W   10°W   0°

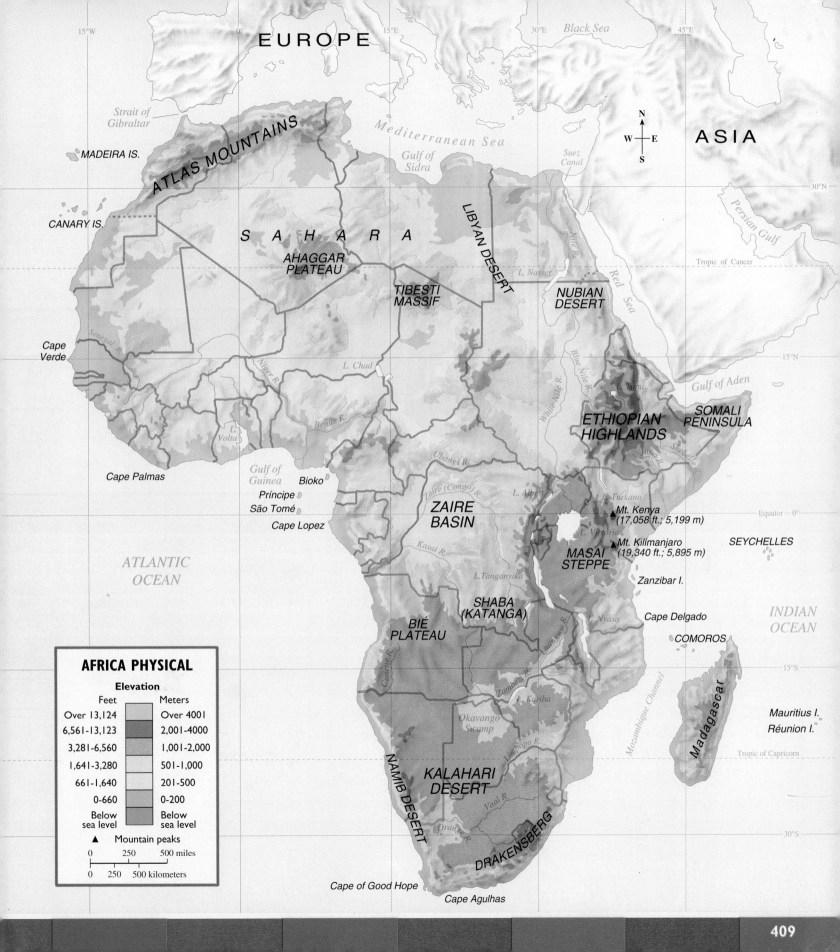

EUROPE

ASIA

Strait of Gibraltar

MADEIRA IS.

ATLAS MOUNTAINS

CANARY IS.

S A H A R A

AHAGGAR PLATEAU

TIBESTI MASSIF

LIBYAN DESERT

NUBIAN DESERT

Mediterranean Sea

Gulf of Sidra

Suez Canal

Persian Gulf

Black Sea

Tropic of Cancer

Red Sea

L. Nasser

Nile R.

Cape Verde

Senegal R.

Niger R.

L. Chad

Benue R.

Blue Nile R.

White Nile R.

L. Tana

Gulf of Aden

ETHIOPIAN HIGHLANDS

SOMALI PENINSULA

Cape Palmas

Gulf of Guinea

Bioko

Príncipe

São Tomé

Cape Lopez

ZAIRE BASIN

Zaire (Congo) R.

Ubangi R.

L. Albert

L. Victoria

Turkana

Mt. Kenya (17,058 ft.; 5,199 m)

Mt. Kilimanjaro (19,340 ft.; 5,895 m)

SEYCHELLES

Equator — 0°

MASAI STEPPE

Kasai R.

Zanzibar I.

ATLANTIC OCEAN

SHABA (KATANGA)

BIÉ PLATEAU

L. Tanganyika

Nyasa

Cape Delgado

INDIAN OCEAN

COMOROS

Cunene R.

Zambezi R.

Kariba

Okavango Swamp

Madagascar

Mauritius I.

Réunion I.

Tropic of Capricorn

NAMIB DESERT

KALAHARI DESERT

Limpopo R.

Vaal R.

Orange R.

DRAKENSBERG

Mozambique Channel

Cape of Good Hope

Cape Agulhas

AFRICA PHYSICAL

Elevation

Feet	Meters
Over 13,124	Over 4001
6,561–13,123	2,001–4000
3,281–6,560	1,001–2,000
1,641–3,280	501–1,000
661–1,640	201–500
0–660	0–200
Below sea level	Below sea level

▲ Mountain peaks

0   250   500 miles

0   250   500 kilometers

ATLANTIC
OCEAN

Ireland
BRITISH ISLES
Great Britain

SVALBARD

ARCTIC
OCEAN

NORTH
LAND

MADEIRA IS.

*Strait of
Gibraltar*

IBERIAN
PENINSULA

BALEARIC IS.

PYRENEES

ALPS

Corsica

Sardinia

*Tyrrhenian
Sea*

Sicily

Malta

*Ionian
Sea*

BALKAN
PENINSULA

*North
Sea*

Baltic Sea

SCANDINAVIAN
PENINSULA
LAPLAND

KOLA
PEN.

*Barents
Sea*

*Novaya
Zemlya*

*Kara
Sea*

YAMAL
PEN.

TAYMYR
PEN.

CENTRAL
SIBERIAN
PLATEAU

CARPATHIAN MTS.

NORTH EUROPEAN PLAIN

URAL MOUNTAINS

WEST
SIBERIAN
PLAIN

SIBERIA

Adriatic Sea

Aegean Sea

ANATOLIAN
PLATEAU

Black Sea

CAUCASUS
MOUNTAINS

Caspian Sea

KIRGIZ
STEPPE

*Aral
Sea*

KAZAK
UPLANDS

ALTAI MTS.

L. Balqash

Crete

Mediterranean Sea

Cyprus

*Suez
Canal*

SINAI
PENINSULA

SYRIAN
DESERT

Tropic of Cancer

ZAGROS MTS.

ELBURZ MTS.

PLATEAU
OF
IRAN

TURAN LOWLAND

TIAN SHAN

TARIM
BASIN

AFRICA

ARABIAN
PENINSULA

Persian Gulf

HINDU KUSH

PAMIRS

KUNLUN SHAN

TIBETAN PLATEAU

Red Sea

RUB AL' KHALI
DESERT

Gulf of Oman

GREAT
INDIAN
DESERT

HIMALAYAS

Mt. Everest ▲
(29,028 ft.
8,848 m)

Salween R.

GANGES PLAIN

Gulf of Aden

*Arabian
Sea*

DECCAN
PLATEAU

Godavari

WESTERN GHATS

EASTERN GHATS

*Bay of
Bengal*

Equator

LAKSHADWEEP

MALDIVE IS.

*Sri
Lanka*

ANDAMAN
IS.

NICOBAR
IS.

N
W   E
S

INDIAN
OCEAN

EURASIA PHYSICAL

Elevation

Feet		Meters
Over 13,120		Over 4,000
6,561–13,120		2,001–4,000
3,281–6,560		1,001–2,000
1,641–3,280		501–1,000
661–1,640		201–500
0–660		0–200
Below sea level		Below sea level

0   500   1,000 miles
0   500   1,000 kilometers

NEW SIBERIAN ISLANDS

East Siberian Sea

Laptev Sea

Bering Sea

CHERSKI RANGE

VERKHOYANSK RANGE

KOLYMA RANGE

CENTRAL RANGE

KAMCHATKA PENINSULA

SIBERIA

L. Baikal

Sea of Okhotsk

Sakhalin

KURIL ISLANDS

Hokkaido

GREATER KHINGAN RANGE

MANCHURIAN PLAIN

Sea of Japan

Honshu

MONGOLIAN PLATEAU

Great Wall

KOREAN PEN.

Mt. Fuji
(12,389 ft.; 3,776 m)

GOBI

Shikoku

JAPANESE ARCHIPELAGO

Kyushu

NAN SHAN

Yellow Sea

Korea Strait

MARSHALL IS.

NORTH CHINA PLAIN

RYUKYU IS.

East China Sea

Okinawa

PACIFIC OCEAN

GILBERT IS.

BOHEA HILLS

Taiwan

MARIANA IS.

Guam

Yangtze (West) R.

Luzon Strait

Philippine Sea

Hainan

Luzon

CAROLINE IS.

South China Sea

Samar

PHILIPPINE ISLANDS

PALAU IS.

SOLOMON IS.

New Ireland

Mindoro

Panay

INDOCHINA PENINSULA

Palawan

Negros

Mindanao

ADMIRALTY IS.

New Britain

VANUATU (NEW HEBRIDES)

Halmahera

Celebes Sea

MOLUCCAS

New Guinea

MAOKE MTS.

New Caledonia

MALAY PENINSULA

Ceram

ARU IS.

Coral Sea

Strait of Malacca

Celebes

Buru

Java Sea

Arafura Sea

Borneo

EAST INDIES

Sumatra

Bangka

GREATER SUNDA ISLANDS

Sumbawa

Lombok

Flores

Timor

MENTAWAI IS.

Java

Bali

Sumba

LESSER SUNDA ISLANDS

Gulf of Thailand

AUSTRALIA

411

Some words in this book may be new to you or difficult to pronounce. Those words have been spelled phonetically in parentheses. The syllable that receives stress in a word is shown in small capital letters.

For example: Chicago (shuh KAH goh)

Most phonetic spellings are easy to read. In the following Pronunciation Key, you can see how letters are used to show different sounds.

PRONUNCIATION KEY

a	after	(AF tur)	oh	flow	(floh)	ch	chicken	(CHIHK un)
ah	father	(FAH thhur)	oi	boy	(boi)	g	game	(gaym)
ai	care	(kair)	oo	rule	(rool)	ing	coming	(KUM ing)
aw	dog	(dawg)	or	horse	(hors)	j	job	(jahb)
ay	paper	(PAY pur)	ou	cow	(kou)	k	came	(kaym)
						ng	long	(lawng)
e	letter	(LET ur)	yoo	few	(fyoo)	s	city	(SIHT ee)
ee	eat	(eet)	u	taken	(TAYK un)	sh	ship	(shihp)
				matter	(MAT ur)	th	thin	(thihn)
ih	trip	(trihp)	uh	ago	(uh GOH)	thh	feather	(FETHH ur)
eye	idea	(eye DEE uh)				y	yard	(yahrd)
y	hide	(hyd)				z	size	(syz)
ye	lie	(lye)				zh	division	(duh VIHZH un)

A

adobe (uh DOH bee) A mixture of straw and clay shaped into blocks and sun-dried to use as bricks. p. 219.

agriculture (AG rih kul chur) The science and business of growing crops and raising livestock. p. 154.

altitude (AL tuh tood) Height above sea level. p. 272.

American Revolution (uh MER ih-kun rev uh LOO shun) The war between Great Britain and its 13 colonies from 1775 to 1783. p. 40.

ancestor (AN ses tur) A person or group of people from whom someone is descended. p. 53.

apprentice (uh PREN tihs) A person learning a trade or craft from a master craftsperson. p. 184.

aqueduct (AK wuh dukt) A structure of pipes or an artificial channel used to transport water. p. 249.

B

barge (bahrj) A flat-bottomed boat used on inland waters to transport goods. p. 39.

barter (BAHR tur) To pay for goods or services with other goods instead of with money. p. 184.

basin (BAYS un) A bowl-shaped area of land almost entirely surrounded by mountains. p. 261.

bay (bay) A part of a lake or an ocean that extends into the shoreline. p. 80.

boulder (BOHL dur) A large rock rounded or worn by the action of water or weather. p. 94.

boundary (BOUN duh ree) A line that separates one place from another. p. 14.

brand (brand) To burn an identification mark on the hide of an animal with a hot iron. p. 228.

broadcasting (BRAWD kast ing) Making something public by means of radio or television. p. 118.

C

canal (kuh NAL) A waterway dug across land and used for boats and ships to travel through. p. 104.

canyon (KAN yun) A deep valley with high, steep sides. p. 36.

cargo plane (KAHR goh playn) A plane that transports only freight. p. 207.

cavern (KAV urn) A large cave. p. 243.

chaparral (chap uh RAL) A thick growth of shrubs or thorny bushes. p. 229.

climate (KLY mut) The kind of weather a place has over a long period of time. p. 10.

coast (kohst) The land along the edge of an ocean or a sea. p. 12.

colony (KAHL uh nee) A territory settled by people from a distant land but under the control of that land. p. 40.

commonwealth (KAHM un welth) A political unit similar to a state. p. 16.

commute (kuh MYOOT) To travel back and forth on a regular basis. p. 69.

Conestoga wagon (kahn us TOH guh WAG un) A covered wagon drawn by horses or oxen. p. 182.

Confederate States of America (kun-FED ur iht stayts uv uh MER ih kuh) The nation formed by the Southern states that withdrew from the Union. p. 145.

Constitution of the United States (kahn stuh TOO shun uv thhuh yoo-NYT ihd stayts) The document that contains the basic laws of the United States. p. 41.

continent (KAHN tuh nunt) One of the seven large land areas on Earth. p. 7.

Continental Divide (kahn tuh NEN-tul duh VYD) The highest points of land that separate rivers and streams flowing eastward from those flowing westward. p. 286.

cottage industry (KAHT ihj IHN dus-tree) The production, for sale, of goods at home, usually on a small scale. p. 183.

county (KOUNT ee) A political division of a state. p. 288.

cove (kohv) A small sheltered body of water. p. 62.

crude oil (krood oil) The oil that comes directly from the ground, before it is refined. p. 224.

currency (KUR un see) The money in use for buying and selling goods. p. 77.

current (KUR unt) A stream that flows in the ocean. p. 12.

D ━━━━━━━━━━━━━━

dam (dam) A wall or barrier preventing the flow of water. p. 248.

democracy (dih MAHK ruh see) A form of government in which the people elect representatives to make the laws and run the country. p. 120.

descendant (dee SEN dunt) A person born of a certain family or group. p. 161.

desert (DEZ urt) A place with very little rainfall and few plants. p. 30.

distribution (dihs trih BYOO shun) The process of getting goods to stores and markets. p. 160.

document (DAHK yoo munt) A written or printed statement that gives proof and information. p. 18.

drover (DROHV ur) A person who drives cattle or sheep. p. 209.

Dutch (duch) Of or relating to the Netherlands, its people, or its language. p. 68.

E ━━━━━━━━━━━━━━

earthquake (URTH kwayk) A shaking and trembling of the earth's surface. p. 316.

economical (ek uh NAHM ih kul) Thrifty; not wasting anything. p. 20.

economist (ih KAHN uh mist) A person who studies the ways people use goods and services. p. 251.

economy (ih KAHN uh mee) The production and distribution of goods and services. p. 56.

elevated train (el uh VAYT ihd trayn) A train that rides above ground on a bridgelike structure. p. 205.

elevation (el uh VAY shun) The height of something, often in relation to sea level. p. 55.

engineer (en juh NIHR) A person who is trained to plan and build structures such as roads, canals, bridges, and buildings. p. 124.

environment (en VYE run munt) The surroundings in which a person, animal, or plant lives. p. 133.

erode (ee ROHD) To wear away the earth's surface by wind, running water, ice, or waves. p. 217.

export (eks PORT) To send goods to another country for sale or use. p. 121.

extinct (ek STINGKT) Having no more living members; having died out. p. 63.

F ━━━━━━━━━━━━━━

federal (FED ur ul) Having to do with the national government of the United States. p. 120.

feedlot (FEED laht) Large fenced-in pen in which cattle are fed. p. 198.

fiesta (fee ES tuh) A holiday or celebration. p. 251.

financial (fih NAN shul) Having to do with money. p. 335.

folded mountain (FOHL dihd MOUNT un) A mountain formed when rock layers are squeezed together. p. 261.

foothill (FOOT hihl) A low hill at the base of a mountain or mountain range. p. 37.

foreign (FAWR ihn) Outside a person's own country. p. 77.

fort (fort) A strong building or enclosed area that can be defended against an enemy. p. 92.

freeway (FREE way) An express highway with limited entrances and exits; it has no tolls. p. 316.

freight (frayt) Goods transported by train, ship, truck, or other vehicle. p. 105.

G

gallery (GAL ur ee) A room where paintings and statues are shown. p. 125.

geography (jee AHG ruh fee) The study of Earth and how people use it. p. 33.

geologist (jee AHL uh jihst) A scientist who studies the rocks that make up Earth. p. 224.

ghost town (gohst toun) The remains of a settlement that people have abandoned. p. 271.

governor (GUV ur nur) The top elected official of a state or other political unit. p. 43.

grain elevator (grayn EL uh vayt ur) A large building where grain is stored before it is shipped. p. 190.

graze (grayz) To feed on growing grasses. p. 82.

Great Lakes Plain (grayt layks playn) Low land that stretches along Lake Erie and Lake Ontario. p. 91.

growing season (GROH ing SEE zun) The length of time between the last frost in spring and the first frost of fall. p. 138.

H

headquarters (HED kwort urz) A center of operations or business. p. 69.

heritage (HER ih tihj) What is handed down from past generations, such as beliefs and customs. p. 35.

high-tech industry (hye tek IHN-dus tree) Manufacturing that uses the latest engineering methods. p. 136.

hydroelectricity (hye droh ee lek-TRIHS ih tee) Electricity produced by the power of rapidly moving water. p. 248.

I

import (ihm PORT) To bring in goods from another country for sale or use. p. 121.

industry (IHN dus tree) The making and selling of a product or service. p. 35.

insurance (ihn SHOOR uns) Protection against loss or damage. p. 201

international (ihn tur NASH uh nul) Involving two or more countries. p. 76.

interstate highway (IHN tur stayt hy-way) A major road that goes from one state to another. p. 327.

invention (ihn VEN shun) Something that is created for the first time. p. 19.

iron ore (EYE urn or) Rock or earth containing iron. p. 186.

irrigate (IHR uh gayt) To supply land with water through ditches or sprinklers. p. 146.

J

jet stream (jet streem) A high-speed wind that moves around the earth at high altitudes. p. 313.

L

landform (LAND form) A feature of the earth's surface created by nature. p. 8.

lava (LAH vuh) Hot liquid rock at or close to Earth's surface. p. 304.

law (law) A rule made by the government for all the people in a town, state, or country. p. 14.

livestock (LYV stahk) Animals such as cattle or sheep that are raised for home use or to be sold. p. 184.

lock (lahk) An enclosed area, with a gate on each end, used for raising and lowering ships, allowing them to go from one water level to another. p. 189.

logger (LAWG ur) A person who cuts trees for lumber. p. 293.

logging (LAWG ing) Cutting down trees and taking the logs to a sawmill. p. 306.

M

mammal (MAM ul) An animal that is warmblooded and has a backbone. p. 62.

manufacture (man yoo FAK chur) To make or process something by using machinery. p. 57.

marina (muh REE nuh) A docking area where supplies are available for small boats. p. 109.

marsh (mahrsh) An area of soft, wet land. p. 154.

mass-produced (mas proh DOOST) Made in large quantities, usually by machinery. p. 106.

meatpacking (MEET pak ing) The process of preparing meat for people to eat. p. 198.

meat processing (meet PRAH ses-ing) The steps by which meat is separated into its usable parts, packaged, and distributed. p. 208.

mesa (MAY suh) A wide flat-topped hill or mountain with steep sides that rises from a plain. p. 218.

meteorologist (meet ee ur AHL uh-jihst) A person who studies changes in the atmosphere. p. 312.

metropolitan area (meh troh PAHL ih-tun ER ee uh) A large city with its surrounding suburbs, towns, and other communities. p. 287.

mill (mihl) Place where grains are ground into flour. p. 199.

mint (mihnt) A place where the government makes coins. p. 274.

N ▄▄▄▄▄▄▄▄▄▄▄▄▄▄▄▄▄▄

national park system (NASH uh nul pahrk SIHS tum) The group of parks, set aside by the government, that have importance to the nation. p. 243.

Native American (NAY tihv uh MER-ih kun) A member of the first group of people who settled and lived in North America. p. 53.

natural gas (NACH ur ul gas) A flammable gas found with oil deposits. p. 246.

natural resource (NACH ur ul REE-sors) Something that is provided by nature and is useful to people. p. 9.

nectar (NEK tur) A sweet juice found in flowers. p. 333.

nuclear energy (NOO klee ur EN ur-jee) Energy that is released when the structure of atoms is changed. p. 220

O ▄▄▄▄▄▄▄▄▄▄▄▄▄▄▄▄▄▄

obelisk (AHB uh lihsk) A tall stone pillar that has a pyramid-shaped top. p. 125.

open-pit mining (OH pun piht MYN-ing) Method of mining in which the soil is stripped from the surface of the earth. p. 291.

orange grove (OR ihnj grohv) A field of orange trees planted in straight rows. p. 154.

orchard (OR churd) A field of fruit trees planted in straight rows. p. 175.

ore carrier (or KAR ee ur) A large ship built for carrying ore. p. 187.

overfish (oh vur FIHSH) To fish so as to use up the supply of fish in certain waters. p. 65.

overlook (OH vur look) A place to view scenery. p. 235.

overwinter area (oh vur WIHN tur-ER ee uh) A warm area where monarchs live in the winter. p. 333.

P ▄▄▄▄▄▄▄▄▄▄▄▄▄▄▄▄▄▄

Pacific Rim (puh SIHF ihk rihm) Some countries surrounding the Pacific Ocean that are strong trade partners. p. 334.

panhandle (PAN han dul) A narrow strip of land extending from a larger land area. p. 218.

petrified (PE trih fyd) Having turned to stone. p. 243.

petrochemical (pe troh KEM ih kul) A chemical that comes from oil. p. 225.

plain (playn) A wide area of flat or gently rolling land that is often treeless. p. 31.

plantation (plan TAY shun) A large estate or farm where one main crop is grown. p. 134.

plateau (pla TOH) A large level area that is raised above the surrounding land. p. 260.

pollutant (puh LOOT unt) Something that makes something else impure, as a harmful chemical that gets into the air. p. 318.

pollution (puh LOO shun) Something that makes the air, soil, or water dirty or harmful. p. 64.

population (pahp yoo LAY shun) The number of people in a given area. p. 16.

population density (pahp yoo-LAY shun DEN suh tee) The average number of people per unit of an area, such as a square mile, in a country or state. p. 301.

port (port) A place on a river, lake, or ocean where ships can safely unload and load supplies. p. 63.

prairie (PRER ee) Flat or rolling land. p. 35.

precipitation (pree sihp uh TAY shun) The falling of moisture in the form of rain, sleet, hail, or snow. p. 29.

preserve (pree ZURV) A place where fish and wild animals are protected. p. 277.

process (PRAH ses) To make something step by step. p. 199.

prospector (PRAHS pek tur) A person who explores or searches for valuable minerals. p. 271.

province (PRAHV ihns) A division of Canada similar to a state in the United States. p. 292.

pueblo (PWEB loh) A large adobe structure in the Southwest built for housing a number of families. p. 219.

Q ▄▄▄▄▄▄▄▄▄▄▄▄▄▄▄▄▄▄

quarry (KWOR ee) A place from which minerals are cut, dug, or blasted. p. 291.

quill (kwihl) The stem of a feather, sharpened for writing. p. 67.

R

rain forest (rayn FOR ihst) A tropical forest with a thick growth of trees and a heavy rainfall. p. 9.

rain shadow (rayn SHAD oh) A region of reduced rainfall on the side of a mountain that is facing away from the wind. p. 285.

ranch (ranch) A large farm with grazing land for raising horses, cattle, or sheep. p. 228.

raw material (raw muh TIHR ee ul) A substance that has not been treated, processed, or prepared. p. 82.

refine (ree FYN) To make into a pure matter. p. 186.

refinery (ree FYN ur ee) A building with machines that change a natural resource to make it pure or to make different products from it. p. 224.

region (REE jun) An area of land whose parts have one or more common characteristics. p. 28.

research (REE surch) A careful study or investigation to find facts about a subject. p. 93.

reservoir (REZ ur vwahr) A place where water is collected. p. 248.

S

service (SUR vihs) A system of providing something needed by the public. p. 20.

service industry (SUR vihs IHN dus-tree) Business that has to do with work that helps people. p. 201.

sheriff (SHER ihf) The chief law officer of a county. p. 288.

smog (smahg) The combination of smoke and fog in the air. p. 319.

soot (soot) Black powder that is formed when certain things burn. p. 246.

source of a river (sors uv uh RIHV-ur) The place where a river begins. p. 203.

stampede (stam PEED) A sudden rush of a herd of frightened animals, such as cattle or horses. p. 230.

suburb (SUB urb) An area with homes next to or near a city. p. 68.

swamp (swahmp) An area in which water and wet, soft land mix together. p. 163.

T

tallow (TAL oh) The fat from cattle and sheep. p. 67.

tariff (TAR ihf) A tax on goods that come into or go out of a country. p. 251.

tax (taks) Money that people must pay to support the government. p. 43.

technology (tek NAHL uh jee) The scientific methods and ideas used in industry, agriculture, and trade. p. 162.

temperature (TEM pur uh chur) The degree of hotness or coldness. p. 29.

territory (TER uh tor ee) Land ruled by a nation or state. p. 16.

textile (TEKS tyl) Having to do with weaving fabrics; fabric made by weaving. p. 135.

theme park (theem pahrk) An amusement park in which all the attractions have a central theme. p. 162.

timber (TIHM bur) Trees, when they are considered a source of lumber. p. 263.

toll (tohl) A fee paid for the right to do or use something. p. 104.

tourism (TOOR ihz um) Promoting tourist travel and taking care of tourists. p. 82.

trade (trayd) The exchange of one product or service for another product or service. p. 116.

tributary (TRIHB yoo ter ee) A stream or river that flows into a larger stream or river or into a lake. p. 174.

U

Union (YOON yun) The Northern states during the Civil War. p. 145.

university (yoon uh VUR suh tee) A school of the highest level. p. 80.

urban planner (UR bun PLAN ur) A person whose job is to plan the development of a community. p. 108.

V

vaquero (vah KER oh) A Spanish word for "cowboy." p. 229.

volcano (vahl KAY noh) An opening in the earth out of which steam and melted rock may pour. p. 262.

W

water vapor (WAW tur VAY pur) Water in the atmosphere. p. 284.

wood pulp (wood pulp) A mixture of ground wood and chemicals used to make paper. p. 307.

INDEX

Page numbers in italics indicate illustrations.

418

ACKNOWLEDGMENTS

Grateful acknowledgment is made to the following publishers, authors, and agents for their permission to reprint copyrighted material. Every effort has been made to locate all copyright proprietors; any errors or omissions in copyright notice are inadvertent and will be corrected in future printings as they are discovered.

from *Bound for Oregon* by Jean Van Leeuwen. Text copyright ©1994 by Jean Van Leeuwen. Cover illustration copyright ©1994 by James Watling. Used by permission of Dial Books for Young Readers, a division of Penguin Books USA Inc.

"The First Thanksgiving" by Barbara Juster Esbensen from *A New England Scrapbook: A Journey Through Poetry, Prose, and Pictures* by Loretta Krupinski. Text copyright ©1993 by Barbara Juster Esbensen. Illustrations copyright ©1994 by Loretta Krupinski. Reprinted by permission of HarperCollins Publishers, Inc., and of Barbara Juster Esbensen.

from *The Floating House* by Scott Russell Sanders. Text copyright ©1995 by Scott Russell Sanders. Cover illustration copyright ©1995 by Helen Cogancherry. Reprinted with the permission of Atheneum Books for Young Readers, an imprint of Simon & Schuster.

from *George Washington's Socks* by Elvira Woodruff. Copyright ©1991 by Elvira Woodruff. Reprinted by permission of Scholastic Inc.

from *The Iron Dragon Never Sleeps* by Stephen Krensky. Text copyright ©1994 by Stephen Krensky. Cover illustration copyright ©1994 by John Fulweiler. Used by permission of Bantam Doubleday Dell Books For Young Readers, a division of Bantam Doubleday Dell Publishing Group Inc., New York, New York, U.S.A.

from *Justin and the Best Biscuits in the World* by Mildred Pitts Walter. Text copyright ©1986 by Mildred Pitts Walter. Cover illustration copyright ©1991 by Paul Tankersley. Reprinted by permission of Random House, Inc.

from "Letter to Grade 5-B, Larchmont, NY" by E.B. White from *Letters from E.B. White,* collected and edited by Dorothy Lobrano Guth. Copyright ©1976 by E.B. White. Reprinted by permission of HarperCollins Publishers, Inc.

from *The Trail on Which They Wept: The Story of a Cherokee Girl* by Dorothy and Thomas Hoobler. Text copyright ©1992 by Carey-Greenberg Associates. Illustrations copyright ©1992 by S.S. Burrus. Used by permission of Silver Burdett Press, Simon & Schuster Elementary Group.

Special thanks are given to the following: Sharon Alden, Fairbanks, AK; Linda and Claude Beaulieu and Michelle Beaulieu, Madawaska, ME; Philip Budlong, Mystic Seaport Museum, Mystic, CT; Liz Clancy, Denver Museum of Natural History, Denver, CO; Tom Elsen, American Popcorn Company, Sioux City, IA; Meg Haley, Old Sturbridge Village, Sturbridge, MA; Elizabeth Holmes, Buffalo Bill Historical Center, Cody, WY; Alexandra Howden, Zionsville, IN; Charles Lyons, Jr., Camden, NJ; Peter S. O'Connell, Old Sturbridge Village, Sturbridge, MA; June Saetre, Conner Prairie, Fishers, IN; Rebecca Huffstutler, The Witte Museum, San Antonio, TX.

CREDITS

Front Cover *Design, Art Direction, and Production* Design Five, NYC; *Photo* Dana Sigall. *Details* John Cancalosi/DRK Photo; Imagery; Lynn Gerig/Tom Stack & Associates; Eric Sanford/Tom Stack & Associates; Harold Sund; Comstock; Tom Bean/DRK Photo; Annie Griffiths/DRK Photo; Telegraph Colour Library/FPG International.

Maps Mapping Specialists Limited, *except 342–397:* Ortelius Design.

All photographs by Silver Burdett Ginn (SBG) unless otherwise noted.

Photographs M2: The Stockhouse, Inc. 1: *bkgd.* Tom Stack & Associates; *inset* Zig Lesczczynski/Animals Animals. 6: Frank Siteman/Stock Boston. 7: *t.* NASA/GSFC/Tom Stack & Associates. 10: Robert Fried/Stock Boston. 11: Brian Parker/Tom Stack & Associates.

15: *b.* Joe Colon. 16: Mitchell P. Warner/In-Depth Photography. 16–17: Jay Freis/The Image Bank. 17: Trevor Wood/The Image Bank. 19: *t.* © Lawrence Migdale/Photo Researchers, Inc.; *m.l.* HMS Images/The Image Bank; *m.r.* Myrleen Ferguson Cate/PhotoEdit. 20: *t.* Tom Pantages; *b.* Charles Weckler/The Image Bank. 21: *b.* Christopher Liu/ChinaStock. 26: Bob Daemmrich/Stock Boston. 28–29: Patrick Bennett for SBG. 30: *t.* Zig Lesczczynski/Animals Animals; *b.* Imagery. 31: Imagery. 32: *details* Ken Cole/Animals Animals; Ken Cole/Animals Animals; Marty Stouffer/Animals Animals; Miriam Agron/Animals Animals; Zig Lesczczynski/Animals Animals; David J. Sams/Stock Boston; B.G. Murray, Jr./Animals Animals; Roy Toft/Tom Stack & Associates. 33: Karen Preuss/The Image Works. 36: *t.* E.R. Degginger/Earth Scenes; *b.* © Tim Davis/Photo Researchers, Inc. 37: Stephen Saks/The Picture Cube. 46–47: *t.r.* Mark Segal/Tony Stone Images; *b.l.* Superstock; *b.r.* J. Greenberg/Southern Stock. 50: Division of Rare and Manuscript Collections, Carl A. Kroch Library, Cornell University, Ithaca, NY. 51: *b.l.* Old Sturbridge Village; *b.r.* Culver Pictures. 53: © TIG Productions/Courtesy, Pathway Productions. 54: Plimoth Plantation, Inc./Photo by Gary Andrashko. 55: The Bettmann Archive. 59: Schomburg Center for Research in Black Culture/New York Public Library. 60–61: *bkgd.* Plimouth Plantation, Inc. 62: *t.* © Mystic Seaport Museum. 63: Peabody Museum, Salem, MA. 64: Superstock. 66: *t.* Thomas Neill/Old Sturbridge Village. 67: *t.* Henry E. Peach/Old Sturbridge Village; *m.* Thomas Neill/Old Sturbridge Village; *b.* Bruce Fenton/Old Sturbridge Village. 69: *t.* The Hartford Ballet; *m.* Superstock; *b.* Connecticut Department of Economic Development. 71: David Young Wolff/Tony Stone Images. 74: Kjell Sandved/Uniphoto Picture Agency. 77: *m.,b.* Nancy Grimes for SBG. 78: *t.l.* Robert Laberge/Allsport; *b.l.* Jerry Wachter/Focus On Sports. 79: Ray Pfortner/Peter Arnold. 86: *inset* Ken Karp for SBG. 86–87: *bkgd.* Joseph Sohm/Tony Stone Images. 89: *t.* Michael Newman/PhotoEdit; *b.* Ken Lax for SBG. 93: David Lorenz Winston. 94: Jon Ortner/Tony Stone Images. 95: *l.* Harold L. Peterson Collection; *r.* Superstock. 98–101: *bkgd.* Art Wolfe/Tony Stone Images. 102: *t.l.,t.r.* The Granger Collection, New York; *b.l.* U.S. Department of Transportation, Federal Highway Administration; *b.r.* The Granger Collection, New York. 103: *t.* Keystone View Co./FPG International; *b.l.* Archive Photos; *b.r.* David Simson/Stock Boston. 104: Archive Photos. 105: *t.* Vince Streano/The Stock Market; *b.* Joseph Sohm/Stock Boston. 106: *t.l.* Barrie Rokeach/The Image Bank; *t.r.* Archive Photos; *m.t.* Archive Photos; *m.b.* Henry M. Holden/Archive Photos; *b.* Bob Abraham/The Stock Market. 109: Robert Brenner/PhotoEdit. 111: Dorey Sparre/Abbe Boon Productions for SBG. 112: *inset* Richard Hutchings. 112–113: *bkgd.* The Stock Market. 115: *t.* Andrea Brizzi/The Stock Market; *b.* SBG/Courtesy, Academy of Natural Sciences, Philadelphia, PA. 118: Richard Hutchings for SBG. 119: *b.l.* Henryk T. Kaiser/The Picture Cube; *b.m.* Mark Richards/PhotoEdit; *b.r.* Tony Freeman/PhotoEdit. 120: Superstock. 122: *t.* Courtesy, National Park Service, U.S. Department of the Interior; *b.* Courtesy, The Ellis Island Immigration Museum. 123: © David M. Grossman/Photo Researchers, Inc. 124–125: *bkgd.* Jim Schwabel/Panoramic Stock Images. 128–129: *bkgd.* Peter Beck/Uniphoto Picture Agency. 130: Richard Hutchings for SBG. 133: Department of Anthropology/Denver Museum of Natural History. 134–135: The Metropolitan Museum of Art, Gift of Edgar William and Bernice Chrysler Garbisch, 1963. (63.201.3). 135: *t.* The Bettmann Archive; *b.* The Granger Collection, New York. 136: *l.* Superstock; *r.* Rob Huntley/Lighstream/Museum of Textile History. 136–137: Kunio Owaki/The Stock Market. 139: *t.,b.l.* Lin Caufield Photographers/Algood Food Company; *b.r.* Tuskegee University Archives. 144–145: *bkgd.* William Blake/Picturesque. 146: J. Greenberg/Southern Stock. 149: Dorey A. Sparre for SBG. 156–157: Arie de Zanger for SBG. 158: *l.* Gary J. Benson/Comstock; *r.* Alex S. MacLean/Landslides. 159: *b.* Henry Horenstein/Stock Boston. 160–161: T.J. Florian/Southern Stock. 161: Letto/Stills/Retna. 162: The Bettmann Archive. 163: Comstock. 166–167: *bkgd.* Tom Stack & Associates; *details* The Delta Queen Steamboat Company; Peter Gregg/Imagery; © Rod Planck/Photo Researchers, Inc.; © William McKinney/Photo Researchers, Inc. 168–169: *bkgd.* Comstock. 173: Pete Saloutos/The Stock Market.175: *t.* Superstock; *b.* Andrew Sacks. 176: Aaron Haupt/Stock Boston. 177: *t.* Kunio Owaki/The Stock Market; *b.* Superstock. 180–181: *bkgd.* D. Cavagnaro/Peter Arnold. 184–185: Courtesy, Connor Prairie. 187: Dawson Jones/Stock Boston. 189: Han Blohm/Masterfile. 190: *t.l.* Tom

Algire/Tom Stack & Associates; *t.r.* Aaron Haupt/Stock Boston; *m.* Superstock; *b.* Leonard Gordon/Root Resources. 191: Greg Ryan & Sally Beyer/Positive Reflections. 194–195: *bkgd.* Don & Pat Valenti/Tony Stone Images. 196: Runk/Schoenberger/Grant Heilman Photography. 199: Andrew Sacks. 200: *bkgd.* Courtesy, Jolly Time Pop Corn; *insets* G.R. Lindblade & Company for SBG. 203: Alex S. MacLean/Landslides. 204: Martin A. Levick. 205: Steve Leonard. 206: *t.* Cameramann International; *b.* SBG/Courtesy, The Scheskowsky Family Collection. 207: Cameramann International. 209: Australian Picture Library/J. Carnemolla/Westlight. 211: Bob Daemmrich Photography. 212: *inset* Grant Huntington for SBG. 212–213: *bkgd.* Don Stevenson/Adstock Photos; Craig Wells/Adstock Photos. 215: The Granger Collection, New York. 217: *l.* Tom Bean/The Stock Market; *r.* John Cancalosi/Peter Arnold. 218: Mark Gamba/The Stock Market. 219: *t.* C/B Productions/The Stock Market; *b. The Last Night of December* by Peter Ray James, 34"x28"/Courtesy, The Turquoise Turtle, Sedona, AZ/Jerry Jacka Photography. 220: Don Stevenson/Adstock Photos. 221: *l.* Carter Smith/Sygma Photo News; *r.* NASA. 222: © Charles D. Winters/Photo Researchers, Inc. 223: The Texas Energy Museum. 224: *t.* Franklin D. Bodin/Stock Boston; *m.* The Image Bank; *t.r.* Russell Munson/The Stock Market; *b.l.* Comstock *b.r.* Russell Munson/The Stock Market. 228: Painting by William Henry David Koerner/Buffalo Bill Historical Center, Cody, WY. 229: *l.,t.m.* Buffalo Bill Historical Center, Cody, WY; *t.r.* Buffalo Bill Historical Center, Cody, WY/Gift of Irving H. "Larry" Larom; *b.m.* The Witte Museum; *b.r.* Courtesy, Panhandle-Plains Historical Museum, Canyon, TX. 231: Robert Frerck/Odyssey Productions. 232–233 *bkgd.* Ron Klein/Panoramic Stock Images. 242: Robert Frerck/Odyssey Productions. 243: © Jim Steinberg/Photo Researchers, Inc. 244: *Walk In Beauty* by Sam English. 246: John Zoiner. 248: *t.* Ann Duncan/Tom Stack & Associates; *b.* Brian Parker/Tom Stack & Associates. 248–249: Grant Heilman Photography. 249: © Calvin Larsen/Photo Researchers, Inc. 251: Bob Daemmrich Photography. 253: *t.* Shelley Boyd/PhotoEdit; *b.* Jerry Jacka. 254–255: *bkgd.* Tom Stack & Associates; *t.l.* E.R. Degginger/Color-Pic, Inc.; *t.m.* Imagery; *t.r.* Michio Hoshino/Minden Pictures. 256: *inset* Dorey Sparre/Abbe Boon Productions for SBG. 256–257: *bkgd.* Stan Olinski/The Stock Market. 261: J.R. Stafford/The Stock Market. 262: *t.* Arthur C. Smith III/Grant Heilman Photography; *m.* Leonard Lee Rue III/Stock Boston; *b.* C. Allan Morgan/Peter Arnold. 263: Grant Heilman Photography. 264: *l.* Eric Sanford/Tom Stack & Associates; *r.* Royce Bair/Uniphoto Picture Agency. 265: Thomas D. Mangelesen/Peter Arnold. 268–269: *bkgd.* The Granger Collection, New York. 272–273: Nathan Bilow/Allsport. 273: *l.* Brian Parker/Tom Stack & Associates; *r.* Denver Museum of Natural History. 274: Culver Pictures. 276–277: *bkgd.* David J. Cross/Peter Arnold. 279: David R. Frazier Photolibrary. 280: *inset* Dorey Sparre/Abbe Boon Productions for SBG. 280–281: *bkgd.* Tom Martin/The Stock Market . 282: *l.* David R. Frazier Photolibrary; *r.* Tom Tracy/The Stock Market . 285: © Jim Steinberg/Photo Researchers, Inc. 286: Earth Satellite Corporation (EarthSat). 288: *l.* Bob Daemmrich/Stock Boston; *r.* Lou Jones/The Image Bank. 289: Lawrence Midgdale/Stock Boston. 290: The Witte Museum. 291: Mark O. Burnett/Stock Boston. 293: Sherman Hines/Masterfile. 295: David R. Frazier Photolibrary. 296: *inset* Dorey Sparre/Abbe Boon Productions for SBG. 296–297: *bkgd.* Milton Rand/Tom Stack & Associates. 300: *l.* Norbert Wu/Peter Arnold; *r.* Paul Conklin/Uniphoto Picture Agency. 303: *t.* © Michael Giannechini/Photo Researchers, Inc.; *m.* John Shaw/Tom Stack & Associates; *b.* Uniphoto Picture Agency. 304: *t.* © Francois Gohier/Photo Researchers, Inc.; *b.* Greg Vaughn/Tom Stack & Associates. 305: *l.* The Oregonian; *r.* Rose Howerter/The Oregonian. 306: M&C Photography/Peter Arnold. 307: *t.* Runk/Schoenberger/Grant Heilman Photography; *b.* © Laima Druskis/Photo Researchers, Inc. 310–311: *bkgd.* Scotts Bluff National Monument/National Park Service. 312: Geoffrey Orth for SBG. 314: © Porterfield-Chickering/Photo Researchers, Inc. 315: Steve Terrill Photography. 316: Kim Heacox/Peter Arnold. 317: Mark E. Gibson/The Stock Market. 321: David Young-Wolff/PhotoEdit. 322: *inset* Dorey Sparre/Abbe Boon Productions for SBG. 322–323: *bkgd.* Thierry Cariou/The Stock Market. 324: David R. Frazier Photolibrary. 328: John Elk III/Stock Boston. 329: Thomas Kitchin/Tom Stack & Associates. 331: B. Nation/Sygma Photo News. 332: David Ulmer/Stock Boston. 335: *l.* Uniphoto Picture Agency; *r.* C/B Productions/The Stock Market.

336: Gary Conner/PhotoEdit. 339: © Russell D. Curtis/Photo Researchers, Inc. 340–341: Photo data gathered by Hank Brandli/Mosaic photographed by Trent Chase 342: *l.* The Bettmann Archive; *r.* Michael Melford/The Image Bank. 343: *t.* Phil Degginger/Color-Pic, Inc.; *b.* Johnny Johnson/Tony Stone Images. 344: *b.* Robert A. Ross/Color-Pic, Inc. 345: *t.* Grant Heilman Photography; *b.* Superstock. 346: *t.* Comstock; *b.* E.R. Degginger/Color-Pic, Inc. 347: *b.* Bob Thomason/Tony Stone Images. 348: *b.* Superstock. 349: *t.* E.R. Degginger/Color-Pic, Inc.; *b.* Michael Nelson/FPG International. 350: *l.* Inga Spence/Tom Stack & Associates; *r.* D. Holden Bailey/Tom Stack & Associates. 351: *t.* Robert & Linda Mitchell/Mitchell Photography; *b.* Michael Schneps/The Image Bank. 352: *t.* Phil Degginger/Color-Pic, Inc.; *b.* Superstock. 353: *r.* Comstock. 354: *t.* Donald Graham/Leo de Wys; *b.* Culver Pictures. 355: *b.* Don & Pat Valenti/Tony Stone Images. 356: *t.* © H. Reinhard/Okapia/Photo Researchers, Inc. 357: *l.* E.R. Degginger/Color-Pic, Inc.; *r.* Arthur C. Smith III/Grant Heilman Photography. 358: *l.* Superstock; *r.* Culver Pictures. 359: E.R. Degginger/Color-Pic, Inc. 360: *t.* E.R. Degginger/Color-Pic, Inc.; *b.* Bill Bachmann/PhotoEdit. 361: *t.* Andrew Holbrooke/The Stock Market; *b.* © Horst Pfingsttag/Okapia/Photo Researchers, Inc. 362: *r.* Kunio Owaki/The Stock Market. 363: *b.* E.R. Degginger/Color-Pic, Inc. 364: *t.* Kennan Ward/The Stock Market; *b.* © Holt Studios/Photo Researchers, Inc. 365: *t.* Runk/Schoenberger/Grant Heilman Photography; *b.* Lance Nelson/The Stock Market. 366: *t.* The Bettmann Archive; *b.* Grant Heilman Photography. 367: *t.* Steve Vidler/Leo de Wys; *b.* © Tim Davis/Photo Researchers, Inc. 368: *b.* Arie de Zanger for SBG. 369: *t.* Peter & Stef Lambretti/Tony Stone Images; *b.* E.R. Degginger/Color-Pic, Inc. 370: *l.* Superstock; *r.* E.R. Degginger/Color-Pic, Inc. 371: *t.* Phil Degginger/Color-Pic, Inc.; *b.* Michael Furman/The Stock Market . 372: *b.* Chris Minerva/FPG International. 373: *t.* Henryk Kaiser/Leo de Wys; *b.* The Bettmann Archive. 374: *t.* Comstock; *b.* Peggy & Ronald Barnett/The Stock Market. 375: *l.* © Vaughan Fleming/Science Photo Library/Photo Researchers, Inc.; *r.* © BBH Fotografie/Okapia/Photo Researchers, Inc. 376: *t.* FPG International. 377: *l.* Jim Strawser/Grant Heilman Photography; *r.* Benn Mitchell/The Image Bank. 378: *t.* Superstock; *b.* Bill Ivy/Tony Stone Images. 379: *r.* E.R. Degginger/Color-Pic, Inc. 380: *b.* E.R. Degginger/Color-Pic, Inc. 381: *b.* Superstock. 382: *r.* Paul Damien/Tony Stone Images. 383: *t.* Toby Rankin/The Image Bank; *b.* E.R. Degginger/Color-Pic, Inc. 384: *b.* Phil Degginger/Color-Pic, Inc. 385: *l.* E.R. Degginger/Color-Pic, Inc.; *r.* The Stock Market. 386: *r.* E.R. Degginger/Color-Pic, Inc. 387: *l.* SBG/Colonial Williamsburg Foundation; *r.* © Photo Researchers, Inc. 388: *t.* Superstock; *b.* E.R. Degginger/Color-Pic, Inc. 389: *b.* Daniel J. Cox/Tony Stone Images. 390: *t.* Comstock; *b.* © Michael P. Gadomski/Photo Researchers, Inc. 391: *t.* © Renee Lynn/Photo Researchers, Inc.; *b.* © Jim Weiner/Photo Researchers, Inc. 392: *t.* The Granger Collection, New York. 393: *t.* © Suzanne & Joseph Collins/Photo Researchers, Inc.; *b.* Murray Alcosser/The Image Bank. 395: *t.* Ken Stranon/The Stock Market; *b.* Howard Ross/Leo de Wys.

Illustrations M1–M19: Mike Lester/MKR Design. 6: Robert Roper. 8–9: Bill Morse. 10: Olivia McElroy. 38–39: Albert Lorenz Studio. 43: Jennifer Bolten. 53: John Suh. 54: Wendy Edelson. 56: Chris Van Dusen. 56–57: Robert Roper. 58–59: Jim McGinness. 62: Skip Baker. 64: Laszlo Kubinyi. 68–69: Robert LoGrippo. 81: Roz Schanzer. 94–95: Robert Roper. 95: Wendy Edelson. 96–97: John Edens. 116–117: Robert Roper. 121: Skip Baker. 124–125: Skip Baker. 136–137: Robert Roper. 138–139: Eliot Bergman. 139: Rebecca Merrilees. 140–141: Gary Davis. 146: Patrick O'Brien. 160: Alan Neider. 173: Sarah Jane English. 176: Virginia Kylberg. 176–177: Robert Roper. 178–179: Joe Boddy. 182–183: Chet Jezierski. 198: Tom Pansini. 201: Anthony Cericola. 203: Martucci Studio. 205: Robert Roper. 220–221: Robert Roper. 226–227: Rob MacDougall. 230: Bruce W. Kirby. 246: Martucci Studio,T/Maker Co. 261: Bob Swanson. 264–265: Robert Roper. 266–267: Pat Porter. 285: Robert Frank. 286: Drew-Brook-Cormack Assoc. 304–305: Robert Roper. 308–309: Bradley Clark. 318–319: Shelton Leong. 330–331: Stephen Bauer. 332–333: Bill Morse. 336–337: Andrew Shiff.